Knowledge Capture in Financial Regulation

Eva Becker

Knowledge Capture in Financial Regulation

Data-, Information- and Knowledge-Asymmetries in the US Financial Crisis

Springer VS

Eva Becker
München, Deutschland

Zugl. Dissertation, Universität Friedrichshafen 2014

ISBN 978-3-658-13665-9 ISBN 978-3-658-13666-6 (eBook)
DOI 10.1007/978-3-658-13666-6

Library of Congress Control Number: 2016937382

Springer VS

Printed on acid-free paper

This Springer VS imprint is published by Springer Nature
The registered company is Springer Fachmedien Wiesbaden GmbH

"Politics works in episodes, in short stories each finishing with a collectively binding decision, a symbolic gesture of conclusion. The political system is thus free to turn to new topics or to await feedback from old ones. But what happens with the risks?" (Luhmann 2008, 165)

Abstract

In 2007, the world economy was hit by a financial crisis of systemic nature and global reach. Confronted with the failure of (potentially) *systemically important financial institutions* (SIFIs), governments were forced to make a binary choice: To either rescue these institutions or let them go down, weighing up *moral hazard* and *too-big-to-fail expectations* on the one hand, and the risk of a market breakdown on the other. Financial regulation had apparently not kept pace with the fast-evolving, highly complex financial system. It is therefore widely agreed that the crisis was rooted in *economic as well as governmental failure.*

A growing dependency by policymakers and regulators on private expertise, especially in the area of financial governance, has been an issue of academic debate for some time now. However, the severity of *data-, information- and knowledge-related problems in financial regulation* became only evident in 2007 and 2008: Then, policymakers and regulators worldwide complained about insufficient data, information and expertise to assess the situation adequately, while they were at the same time forced to make far-reaching decisions, including bailouts and extensive financial guarantees. In view of an increased reliance by policymakers and regulators on data, information and knowledge provided by the financial industry, members of the European Parliament warned in their "Call for a Finance Watch" that the absence of *financial counter-expertise* presents a danger to democracy.

The author therefore assesses the US financial crisis as a *crisis of regulatory data, information and knowledge.* The US policy responses to the crisis, particularly the establishment of the Office of Financial Research (OFR), acknowledge and address the identified data, information and knowledge gaps. Yet, their role and nature remains undertheorized to this date. Based on semi-structured interviews with experts conducted by the author – complemented by speeches, testimonies and interviews from the US Financial Crisis Inquiry Commission – this study seeks to add definitional clarity to the debate. It is argued that data-, information- and knowledge-asymmetries represent *different sets of problems* in financial regulation. Moreover, it is shown that the US policy responses to the crisis are characterized by a narrow focus on data and information, while they fail to address a growing knowledge gap between regulators and their regulatees. Drawing on Capture Theory and recent reformulations thereof, we develop *knowledge capture* as a theoretic framework to assess financial regulation under conditions of 21st century complexity.

Content

List of Figures

List of Tables

1 Introduction

This book is yet another contribution to the large and constantly growing body of literature dealing with the financial crisis of 2007ff. – and at first sight, it looks like everything has been said and written about "the worst financial meltdown since the Great Depression" (Financial Crisis Inquiry Commission 2011, 3).[1] However, a closer look reveals that despite the endless number of research papers and government reports, experts still cannot agree on the exact causes of the crisis. More importantly, among the various contributing factors identified and discussed, some remain vague and require further research. The question whether systemic risk is merely an economic (Schwarcz 2008) or rather a political phenomenon (Levitin 2011) is exemplary in this regard.

Many believed that the music would stop one day, but only few broke off the dance to place lucrative bets on the breakdown instead (Nakamoto and Wighton 2007).[2] The crisis came as a surprise to most – Warren E. Buffet termed it an "economic Pearl Harbor" (Buffett 2010) – yet some saw it coming. Unfortunately,

---

1 When we speak of the financial crisis of 2007ff. – also labeled the Second Great Contraction (Reinhart and Rogoff 2009) and the Great Recession (Woolley and Ziegler 2012) – we refer to the financial crisis that had its roots in the US mortgage market, spread over to financial institutions engaged in the market for mortgage backed securities (MBSs) and collateralized debt obligations (CDOs), and ultimately infected the entire global financial system. It remains an open question whether the financial crisis is already over or not: Some state it is, some say it is not. The Fed's decision not to raise the federal funds rate as long as US unemployment remains above 6.5 percent indicates that at least the crisis policies are not yet over. Instead of taking a final stance on the matter, we want to refer to a very interesting interview with William Porter, Head of European Credit Strategy at Credit Suisse; he argues that "the crisis is not observable at all. But that does not mean it's gone away. It's gone underground" (Porter 2013).

2 In an interview with the Financial Times, Charles Prince, then CEO of Citigroup, described how "[w]hen the music stops in terms of liquidity, things will be complicated. But as long as the music is playing, we have got to get up and dance. We are still dancing" (Prince as quoted in Nakamoto and Wighton 2007). In his interview with the FCIC, Prince complains that his statement, and a similar statement he made at a dinner with Treasury Secretary Henry Paulson, are quoted quite often, but mostly taken out of the context: Prince was referring to the banks' lending business, more specifically the loans made to private equity firms. As he emphasizes, the quote has "had nothing to do with the mortgage business, it had nothing to do with what turned out to be CDOs. That was not part of my thinking or on the radar screen at all" (Prince 2010, 123).

the latter and much smaller group did not include many, if any, regulators.[3] In hindsight, the ignorance of public officials towards the mechanisms and channels through which the crisis would propagate during 2007 and 2008 is difficult to believe. In March 2007, Federal Reserve President Ben Bernanke testified before Congress that "the impact on the broader economy and financial markets of the problems in the subprime market seems likely to be contained" (Bernanke 2007b), and Treasury Secretary Henry Paulson made a similar statement (Faber 2010). It however turned out that the problems in the subprime markets were not contained. It appears that during the crisis months, government officials were essentially flying blind (Mendelowitz and Liechty 2010, 3). Hence, the crisis not only shed new light on a decade of deregulation and financial innovation, it also revealed that *policymakers and regulators were facing severe gaps with regard to financial market data, information, and knowledge* (see for example Black 2012; Financial Stability Board and International Monetary Fund 2009; Flood et al. 2010).

German sociologist Wolfgang Streeck has asked what social scientists can contribute to enhance our understanding of this "economic and political crisis of global dimensions" (Streeck 2011, 1). The financial crisis of 2007ff. represents the starting point for this book, but we do not want to add yet another analysis of the complex interplay between financial institutions, rating agencies, mortgage originators and regulators that finally mounted in the financial crisis. Our contribution focuses on a phenomenon that could be observed before and throughout the crisis, that has received little scholarly attention so far and that remains undertheorized to this date: Against the background of increased financial system complexity, we examine the *role and nature of data-, information-, and knowledge-related problems in financial supervision and regulation.*[4] As we show, certain

3 There are of course exceptions – the people who issued warnings were just not influential or convincing enough. As we will see throughout this book, former chairperson of the CFTC Brooksley Born provides an example here.

4 When we speak of financial regulation, we mean "the set of rules and standards that govern financial institutions" which aims at providing financial stability and protecting customers and takes "different forms, ranging from information requirements to strict measures such as capital requirements" (High Level Group on Financial Supervision in the EU 2009, 13). In line with the group chaired by Jacques de Larosière, we distinguish regulation from financial supervision, which covers "the process designed to oversee financial institutions in order to ensure that rules and standards are properly applied" (ibid.). We also agree with the de Larosière Report that regulation and supervision are not only closely intertwined, but also interdependent: Regulation cannot work if supervision is not effective and vice versa. Many of the US federal agencies have regulatory *and* supervisory responsibilities: The CFTC, which is responsible for the US commodity futures and option markets, had finalized 43 of the rules it was required to write by Dodd-Frank as of November 2013 (Davis Polk & Wardwell LLP 2013). But the CFTC is not only involved in rulemaking; it also oversees the futures markets, looking for abusive trading practices and fraud. Besides the CFTC, independent federal agencies relevant to our work are the Board of Governors of the Federal Reserve System, the Securities and Exchange Commission (SEC) and the Consumer Financial Protection Bureau (CFPB). Just like the CFTC and the Fed as well, they have important regulatory and supervisory mandates.

aspects of these problems have been known and discussed in academia for decades. The establishment of the Office of Financial Research (OFR) in Washington in 2010 in response to the crisis does nevertheless present a turning point. With the Dodd-Frank Act (DFA)[5], the US government not only acknowledged the existence of such problems, but also set out to solve them. Among the various US policy responses to the crisis, the OFR is therefore the most important one for the analysis at hand.[6]

The crisis triggered financial reform on both sides of the Atlantic. However, while stress tests and living wills, new resolution mechanisms and systemic risk oversight councils have been introduced in the US and elsewhere, the OFR presents a unique policy response to the crisis. Differences in reform reflect the fact that, while the financial crisis was an epidemic event of global reach, it started as a mortgage crisis in the United States, evolved into a sovereign debt crisis in the European Union and lingers on as a social and political crisis in the most severely affected national economies, such as Greece and Spain. The global crisis revealed that regulators had put too much emphasis on microprudential regulation and bank-internal risk models, that financial institutions were overleveraged and that their risk management was not effective. But the US crisis was also perceived as *a crisis of inadequate data and information and more importantly, of missing expertise.* We therefore focus our analysis on the US crisis, but refer to the European case wherever a comparative perspective proves to be helpful. Comparing Europe and the United States, the second distinctive feature of the US debate is a lively discussion about *legislative and executive capture as a cause for the crisis.* As we will see, information and knowledge deficiencies and the capture diagnosis are closely intertwined.

"Politics presents itself as a *system of societal control*", and according to Luhmann, it tends to "action rather than inaction" (Luhmann 2008, 173, emphasis added). When the crisis erupted, the US government responded case-by-case, and it appeared for some time as if Treasury had lost oversight and control of the financial system – up to the point when US Secretary of the Treasury Hank Paulson demanded a *bazooka* (The Economist 2008) to fight back the crisis and asked Congress to support the 700 billion US dollar Troubled Asset Relief Program

5 The complete title is Dodd-Frank Wall Street Reform and Consumer Act (111th Congress, Public Law 111-203, H.R. 4173.).

6 When we write about the US policy responses to the crisis, we refer to the Dodd-Frank Wall Street Reform and Consumer Protection Act (referred to as Dodd-Frank or DFA throughout this book) that was signed into law by President Obama in July 2010, but also to the bodies and measures established by Dodd-Frank: The Financial Stability Oversight Council (FSOC), the Office of Financial Research (OFR) and the Consumer Financial Protection Bureau (CFPB), to new requirements such as the Fed stress tests and living wills, but also to new authorities, such as the FDIC's Orderly Liquidation Authority (OLA).

(TARP).[7] *Regulation by deal* (Davidoff and Zaring 2009) was followed by system-wide short term policy responses, until Congress finally agreed on the Dodd-Frank Act, the most far-reaching regulatory overhaul in US financial regulation since the Great Depression (Obama 2009). Whether it constitutes *symbolic politics* (Edelman 1970) or substantial policy change is a question that will follow us throughout this book.

When looking at the US policy responses to the crisis, we have to be aware of the fact that some of the underlying causes and mechanisms of the crisis can eventually be resolved, while others cannot be overcome and will therefore persist. The majority of *structural issues*, for instance the remuneration practices for top executives, the quality of residential mortgage loans (originate-to-sell model) and the business model of rating agencies (issuer-pays model), either have been or could be altered by regulators. The same applies to many *regulatory issues*, such as pro-cyclical capital regulation. Yet, the *systemic features* of today's global and complex financial system remain: The interconnectedness of financial institutions via derivatives contracts; the complexity of certain large and global institutions, consisting of more than thousand legal subsidiaries each; the emergent properties resulting from a large number of autonomous, non-linear actors; the reciprocal behavior of its members; the interdependency of the interbank market and the real economy, to name just a few.[8] The nation states' ability to govern the financial system is therefore necessarily limited.

The financial system evolves at a pace that constantly increases regulators' non-knowledge of the financial system. As we will see, the question whether regulators have learned that lesson is crucial. The (over)confidence of the central actors – including policymakers, regulators and financial institutions alike –that *this time was*

7 According to Abolafia, "[a]mong the first framing moves in a crisis setting is an effort to define the degree of disruption". In case of the US financial crisis, Henry Paulson – who was convinced of the severity of the crisis – became what Abolafia terms a *reframer*: "Reframers advocating changed practices must be able to convince their constituency that the shock requires strong action" (Abolafia 2005, 212).

8 Following Dodd-Frank, the term *financial institutions* covers bank-holding companies (BHCs), financial market utilities (FMUs) and nonbank financial companies (NBFCs). BHCs are, according to the Bank Holding Company Act of 1956 (Public Law 85-511, 85th Congress, H.R. 6227), companies which directly or indirectly own or hold a minimum of 25 percent of two or more banks, but do not necessarily engage in banking themselves (see Sec. 2 of the Bank Holding Company Act for a more detailed definition). JPMorgan Chase & Co (JPMorgan), The Goldman Sachs Group, Inc. (Goldman), and Deutsche Bank AG (Deutsche Bank) fell under this definition as of November 2013 (Board of Governors of the Federal Reserve System 2013c). Financial market utilities are defined as systems or entities "for transferring, clearing, and settling payments, securities, and other financial transactions among financial institutions or between financial institutions and the system" (Board of Governors of the Federal Reserve System 2013b). Examples for FMUs are the Chicago Mercantile Exchange, Inc. or the National Securities Clearing Corporation. NBFCs provide banking services, but do not hold banking licenses; they are accordingly not allowed to take deposits. In 2013, two NBFCs were designated as systemically important by the FSOC: The insurance company American International Group, Inc. (AIG) and the financial services and leasing company General Electric Capital Corporation, Inc. (GECC).

different (Reinhart and Rogoff 2009), that they had outsmarted the market, and that they were able to control the system was certainly the most dangerous fallacy of the pre-crisis years (Willke and Willke 2012). The US government finds itself in the paradox situation that it must address the existing data, information and knowledge gaps, while it will ultimately be unable to close them. The resulting uncertainty might prove to be the biggest challenge to policymakers and regulators. It requires regulators to not only enhance their data and information collection abilities, but also to introduce "mechanisms for cognitive challenge" (Black 2012, 41) that enhance their learning capacities.

1.1 Eliminating Hobson's Choice, Or: A Binary Model of Systemic Risk

In 2008, the collapse of a number of systemically important financial institutions (SIFIs) – first The Bear Stearns Companies, Inc., then Lehman Brothers Holdings Inc. and then, among others, American International Group, Inc. (AIG), Federal National Mortgage Association (FNMA, commonly known as Fannie Mae) and Federal Home Loan Mortgage Corporation (FHLMC, known as Freddie Mac) – each confronted the US government with the *Hobson's choice* to either bail the SIFI out or let it go into disorderly bankruptcy at the risk that its failure triggers a systemic financial crisis (Tarullo 2010a; see also Wilmarth 2013, 1320; Goldstein and Véron 2011). The reference to Hobson implies that what looked like a binary choice at first sight turned out to be, at the latest after the Lehman bankruptcy, not really any choice at all: The US and European governments felt that in order to save the economy there was no alternative to rescuing their respective SIFIs, and so they did: The US government not only supported its failing financial institutions directly through bailouts, but also engaged in extensive deal-making to stabilize the system through mergers and acquisitions (see Blankfein 2010; Davidoff and Zaring 2009).[9] Against this background, we developed a simple binary model of systemic risk (see figure 1) that illustrates the *too big to fail* (TBTF) phenomenon from a governmental perspective. In theory, governments confronted with the failure of a financial institution have the choice to either bail it out or not bail it out. When an institution is bailed out (B), there are two basic options: The rescued institution was a SIFI (B.2), or it was not a SIFI (B.1). The interesting point is that once the institution is saved, we cannot find out what was the case. The failure of an

9 *Systemically important financial institutions* (SIFIs, or G-SIFIs for global SIFIs) are companies that are believed to trigger financial crises when they collapse, either because of their size or their interconnectedness or other factors that we will discuss in detail in chapter two. When SIFIs are perceived by the market as being systemically important, they are labeled as being *too big to fail* (TBTF); since 2010, Dodd-Frank requires the FSOC to officially designate the respective institutions as TBTF, thereby explicitly attributing systemic importance to certain market participants.

institution (A) again implies two possible futures: That the institution was a SIFI and its collapse triggers a systemic crisis (A.2); or that it was not a SIFI and its collapse does not trigger a systemic crisis (A.1).

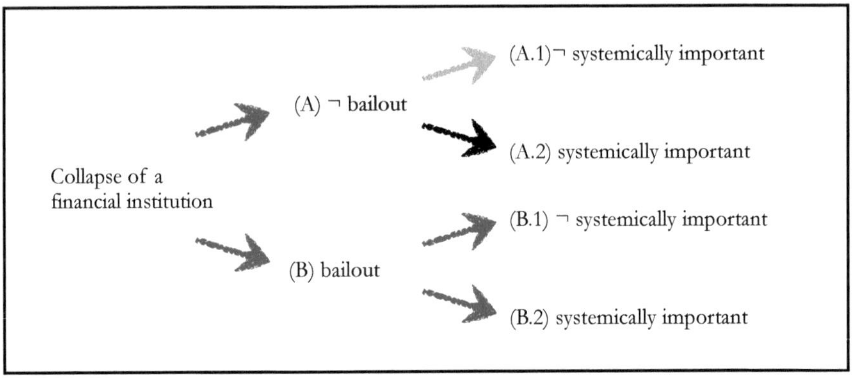

Figure 1: Binary model of systemic risk.

As the colored arrows indicate, each option comes at a different price: A.1 neither imposes costs on taxpayers (meaning *financial costs*), nor on governments (*political costs*), nor on other financial institutions and shareholders (*financial costs*). A.2 represents the Lehman case: For reasons to be discussed in greater detail in chapter three, the US government decided not to rescue the investment bank – a decision that was costly as it not only required governments to rescue the global financial system, but also resulted in a steep recession in the US and Europe. The political costs of the crisis, as well as their long-term impact on democratic governance, remain to be seen. A.2 puts the costs of a bailout (B) into perspective: They are high, but significantly lower than the costs of a full-fledged financial crisis. Interestingly, the costs for taxpayers and governments remain the same in both bailout cases, independent of the systemic relevance of the institution at hand. As we saw during the financial crisis of 2007ff., other financial institutions usually gain from a bailout.[10] The financial crisis reminded policymakers and market participants alike that the failure of a too big to fail institution is by far the worst option among the given four. Therein, it reinforced the implicit government subsidy for SIFIs – a phenomenon that will be discussed at-length in chapter three. Even though the

10 Other financial institutions gain from bailouts both directly and indirectly: When AIG was rescued by the US government, Goldman Sachs alone received more than 14 billion dollar from the rescue fund, based on outstanding contracts with the insurance company (Financial Crisis Inquiry Commission 2011, 377). As other financial institutions and the overall economy, it also benefited from an increased financial stability. Several institutions did also profit from government-backed mergers.

commitments made by the US government during the crisis were much higher than the actual payments, the fiscal costs of the crisis were immense.[11] The price for the Lehman Brothers collapse – including not only the bankruptcy fees that will exceed two billion US dollars (O'Toole 2013), but also the costs of the events directly triggered by the bank's failure – remains an issue of debate.

Looking at the key events throughout 2008, the pivotal question is whether the US government, when Bear Stearns and Lehman, AIG, Fannie Mae and Freddie Mac were effectively insolvent, really had the *choice to intervene or not to intervene* (Luhmann 2008, 173). The crisis showed that, confronted with a failing SIFI, governments are literally being taken hostage by their financial institutions. Have the US government and the Fed become *prisoners of the markets* (Yellen 2013b)? While the receiving side – the SIFI – is characterized by its global structure and reach, the giving side – the government and its central bank – is characterized by its national structure and reach, constraining the policy options of the nation states: Due to the size, interconnectedness and complexity of the institutions at stake, their scope of action is obviously limited. Some of the problems experienced throughout 2008 were of a structural nature: How could a national agency like the FDIC wind down a global institution like Lehman Brothers without a viable cross-border resolution authority or the respective agreements with other nation states? Other factors followed a political logic, and they are often overseen. Two central and exemplary questions for the team around Treasury secretary Paulson were how the public and the media would react to bank bailouts by a republican government and whether the government had the support of Congress for its rescue program TARP.[12]

The question whether governments have become prisoners of their markets persisted well throughout the reform period after 2008: Policymakers in the EU and the US expressed their concerns that tougher financial regulation could hamper the economic recovery. Interestingly, these concerns are all but new: A century ago, Wilson described how the US government had become the *foster-child* of special interests, as it was warned "at every move: 'don't do that; you will interfere with our

11 The costs of the financial crisis in the US are not (yet) agreed upon. A recent Federal Reserve Bank of Dallas research paper asked how much worse society is off compared to an estimation of the normal developments absent a crisis. It estimated an output loss of six to 14 trillion US dollar (Luttrell, Atkinson and Rosenblum 2013). The direct costs of the bailouts are yet another issue. As long as the money lent is not fully returned, and the US government owns bonds of the companies it rescued – the FDIC sold its last Citigroup bonds in September 2013, at a total profit of more than 13 billion US dollar (Henry 2013) – the total bailout costs will remain in the dark.

12 In his interview with the FCIC, former Treasury employee Neel Kashkari describes how the team around Henry Paulson held back its so called *break the glass plan*, the emergency action plan that would later become TARP, until it could be very certain that Congress would accept it. According to Kashkari, Treasury feared that if it would not pass, the plan itself might, in a self-fulfilling matter, reinforce the crisis it was designed to mitigate (Kashkari 2010).

prosperity'" (Wilson 1913). It appears that systemically important financial institutions have authority over nation states in two ways: Firstly, they pose a systemic threat to the financial system when failing. Secondly, the financial sectors of many western economies have become too important in terms of GDP and growth to get into their way with extensive regulation.[13] Lindblom has illustrated this point more generally when describing the dilemma nation states are facing: "Either the demands are met, or the corporation goes elsewhere" (Lindblom 1977, 180).

This book begins with a decision – the remarkable decision of the US Congress to establish an Office of Financial Research in order to address the data and information gaps experienced during the crisis. Starting from there, we describe and define data-, information-, and knowledge-related problems in US financial regulation. We show that the US government addresses these types of issues to different degrees, but largely underestimates the risks resulting from unknown unknowns. The term *waterbed effect* describes the phenomenon that when regulators cap prices, charges or payments in certain areas or market segments, an overall re-balancing of prices, charges or payments occurs in the market and ultimately leads to a price, charge or payment increase in another area or segment. Remuneration practices provide a good example here: A cap on fixed income leads to an increase in bank bonuses, and bank bonus caps induce increases in fixed income. A similar waterbed effect can be observed in financial regulation: When policymakers and regulators focus on one problem – e.g. to conduct micro-prudential oversight (pre-crisis), or to close data gaps (post-crisis) – they lose sight of other problems – in this case, to tackle macroprudential problems, or problems of knowledge that are difficult to overcome.

Going back to the model, the situation of the US government has changed since the crisis, at least on paper. Our simple binary model of systemic risk illustrates the policy options of the US government back in 2008, but it does not account for the changes induced by the Dodd-Frank Act in 2010. Once fully implemented, Dodd-Frank has the potential to alter the situation and the model accordingly. As we will discuss in greater detail in chapter four, the DFA limits the Fed's ability to act as a lender of last resort and provide direct support to single financial institutions. As a complementary measure, Dodd-Frank strengthens the FDIC's ability to resolve global, complex financial institutions. A future decision not to bail out a SIFI

---

13 The ratio of total financial sector assets to GDP has grown massively. In the UK, the ratio of deposit money banks' assets to GDP in percent has increased from 110 percent in 1991 to 192 percent in 2011, in Spain from 102 percent in 1991 to 232 percent in 2011. The increase was much more moderate in others countries, e.g. in Switzerland (163 to 181) and the US (61 to 62). However, we have to take a closer look at the growth of assets in other parts of the financial sector, e.g. at nonbank financial sector assets. Here, the ratio of assets to GDP has grown from 89 percent in 1991 to 297 in 2011 in the US (all data rounded and taken from the Worldbank's World Data Bank as of February 17, 2014, available on http://databank.worldbank.org/data/).

should, under the Orderly Liquidation Authority (OLA) of the FDIC, not result in a disorderly bankruptcy that triggers a financial crisis. While the OLA should improve the *crisis management of the US government*, other provisions tend to *prevent SIFIs from collapsing in the first place*: The Financial Stability Oversight Council (FSOC) designates systemically important institutions, leading to increased supervision by the Federal Reserve Bank. Higher prudential requirements and central clearing, stress tests and living wills should reduce the possibility of failure, too. The OFR, with a staff of 200 to 300, aims at collecting and aggregating data and gathers financial market information; besides, it ought to build up own financial expertise. As a result, government officials should – to use an expression coined by Mendelowitz and Liechty – never again be flying blind throughout a crisis (Mendelowitz and Liechty 2010, 3). Two aspects are important in this respect. First, the fact that the financial crisis was perceived as a *crisis of financial market data and information in the US* (Flood et al. 2010), much more than this was the case in the European Union. Second, and closely related, the EU financial crisis soon evolved into a full-fledged crisis of sovereign debt, redirecting the focus of reform to the nation states and their respective crises, as well as at the regulatory and supervisory architecture of the European Union. We will look at both reform agendas more closely in chapter four, and see how they differ and overlap.

Looking at the financial crisis as a crisis of data, information and knowledge redirects the analytical focus from mortgage lending and leverage, from macroeconomic imbalances and flawed incentive schemes, to the complexity of financial products, financial institutions and the system as such. It enables us to ask whether regulators actually understood the system they supervised and policed and if the set of struggling SIFIs had in fact become not only too big to fail, but also *too complex to manage*. To what degree did data, information and knowledge asymmetries between regulators on the one hand and regulatees on the other play a role in the recent financial crisis?[14] Were regulators constrained by their *bounded rationality* (Simon 1955), or were they, as one of our interview partners put it, "just chicken" and dared not to have a closer look at certain business practices? Whenever policymakers increased the transparency of a business or market, certain operations and trades apparently moved into some other, darker corner of the market, while at the same time, regulators failed to address the resulting unknowns.[15] While some argue that US regulators only need better data and information to regain control over the financial sector – a position that we term the *sufficiency argument*

14 The term *regulatee* refers to the supervised or regulated entity – meaning the financial institution affected by a rule or regulation.

15 In his interview with the FCIC, Gary Cohn from Goldman Sachs describes the mechanism by which dark markets evolve wherever transparency is increased. He adds that while transparent markets are officially regulated by the government, nontransparent markets such as the OTC market are regulated by the markets themselves (Cohn 2010).

throughout this book – others warn that building up the respective expertise is even more demanding, if not impossible. Yet, our analysis in chapter two of the systems characteristics of the 21st century financial system indicates that ultimately, systemic crises are *natural accidents* (Perrow 1981) and can accordingly not be prevented.

1.2 The Argument in Brief

Former US Secretary of Defense Donald Rumsfeld is well known for his unique speaking style. Referring to the potential existence of weapons of mass destruction in Iraq in 2002, Rumsfeld famously said:

> Reports that say that something hasn't happened are always interesting to me, because as we know, there are known knowns; there are things we know we know. We also know there are known unknowns; that is to say we know there are some things we do not know. But there are also unknown unknowns – the ones we don't know we don't know. And if one looks throughout the history of our country and other free countries, it is the latter category that tend to be the difficult ones. (Rumsfeld 2002)

There obviously is a certain humor and, as we now know, irony to this quote. However, the basic distinction that Rumsfeld draws between the differing phenomena of *known knowns*, *known unknowns* and *unknown unknowns* is correct and very well applicable to the situation faced by financial regulators: The things these regulators did not know – including the degree of interconnectedness and complexity of the financial system, as well as the risks posed by 21st century systemic risk – did in fact turn out to be the difficult ones. Rumsfeld's statement is the first of several quotes that we want to cite to explain our argument in brief. The second quote goes back to Brooksley Born, who was the head of the US Commodity Futures Trading Commission (CFTC) between 1996 and 1999. In 1998, Born attempted to examine and eventually regulate derivatives in the over-the-counter-market (OTC) market – a group of financial products that would later be called "financial weapons of mass destruction" by Buffett (2002, 6; see also Buffett 2010, for the extended argument) and that certainly was a centerpiece of the financial crisis. Born later explained that:

> I had had enormous concerns about the over-the-counter derivatives market, including credit default swaps, for a number of years. The market was totally opaque; we now call it the dark market. *So nobody really knew what was going on in the market.* (Born 2009)

Her efforts to examine what has been well termed *the other* and the *strange land* (Tett 2010) were strongly opposed not only by the financial industry, but also by other federal financial regulators and by Congress. In 2000, Congress passed the Commodity Futures Modernization Act (CFMA) to once and for all restrain the CFTC from regulating OTC derivatives. As a result, regulators' non-knowledge of what is now called the *shadow banking system* persisted and grew further. Born is a central figure in the narrative of the financial crisis: She saw the risks arising from unknown unknowns; in addition, she was one of the few regulators who actually identified them and, by addressing them, turned them into known unknowns. The case of Brooksley Born also shows that in the decades leading up to the financial crisis, regulators such as the CFTC did not have access to the relevant data and information to examine what was going on in certain fast evolving, highly innovative sectors of the financial market. Looking back, the former chief executive and chairman of Citigroup Sandy Weill asks whether regulators could have done better – admitting that he thinks "the answer is yes. But I think they were terribly handicapped by a lack of information. And by the direction that people wanted to go at that point in time" (Weill 2010).

Unfortunately, the problem was not limited to financial data and information, it also related to regulators' general knowledge and ability to understand the market. Former Fed president Alan Greenspan, who had always been an advocate of unregulated derivatives markets, provides us with a third central statement. After the risks had materialized, he admitted:

> I've got some fairly heavy background in mathematics […]. But some of the complexities of some of the instruments that were going into CDOs bewilders me. […] And I figured out that if I didn't understand it and I had access to a couple hundred PhDs, how the rest of the world is going to understand it sort of bewildered me. (Greenspan as quoted in Sorkin 2010, 90)

As these quotes show, the US financial crisis has not only been a crisis of bank liquidity and capital, of derivatives and mark-to-market accounting, of evaporating trust and herd behavior, but it has also been a crisis of *financial market data, information and knowledge.*[16] The crisis revealed that basic data and information, e.g. concerning the counterparties or subsidiaries of a financial institution, were either not available or not accessible for financial regulators. Besides, both regulators and policymakers do apparently "face a structural, widening epistemic gap between what they are able to know and what they need to know" (Weber

16 Unfortunately, neither experts nor policymakers do usually differentiate between problems related to inadequate data, information and knowledge. As we argue and explain over the course of this book, distinguishing between these three phenomena is not only important, but also a prerequisite to addressing them.

2012, 644f.). As Arthur Levitt, former chairman of the SEC, describes in his FCIC interview:

> There is regulatory capture without any question. [...] I think the 4000 people that worked for me were really patriots. These guys were all overworked and underpaid and terribly, terribly loyal. Yet, they lacked the skills to compete with the array of power represented by the business community, and their lobbyists and their lawyers and their staffs. That really reached a crescendo after the development of electronic markets that my Commission was responsible for [...]. Getting there and trying to arbitrate the battles between the various exchanges, and dealing with technologies, that in particular created the greatest void in terms of our ability to regulate an industry which was light years ahead of us in terms of technology. And I think that really went on in an accelerated pace after I left. (Levitt 2010)

The complexity of the financial market on the one hand and the limited processing capabilities of policymakers and regulators on the other result not only in a growing knowledge asymmetry between regulators and regulatees, but also in an *increased importance of private expertise in financial regulation.* Private sector lobby groups, "men who know so much about the matters they are talking of that you cannot put your knowledge into competition with theirs" (Wilson 1913, ch. VII) convince and overwhelm policymakers and regulators with technical details. While this development has been observed for decades and in different policy fields, the particular characteristic of the financial sector is a lack of private, non-profit expertise. The problem loomed large during the financial crisis and became explicit when Members of the European Parliament published their Call for a Finance Watch:

> the asymmetry between the power of this lobbying activity and the lack of counter-expertise poses a danger to democracy [...]. As European elected officials in charge of financial and banking regulations, we therefore call on civil society [...] *to organize to create one (or more) non-governmental organization(s) capable of developing a counter-expertise on activities carried out on financial markets* by the major operators [...] and to convey effectively this analysis to the media. As elected officials from different political families we may differ on the measures to be taken. But we are all together in wanting to create greater awareness in the public opinion on this risk for the quality of democracy. (Finance Watch 2010, emphasis added)

To address data, information and knowledge asymmetries between financial regulators and regulatees, the US government established the Office of Financial Research. While the post-crisis reform efforts in the US and the EU do partly overlap, the OFR presents a unique policy response to the crisis, based on the assumption that the crisis demonstrated "the inadequacies of the information infrastructure supporting the US financial system" (Flood et al. 2010, 1).

The financial crisis did not only lead to the creation of new regulatory bodies, it also triggered a lively debate in the US concerning the degree of *capture of policymakers and regulators by the financial industry*. As we argue towards the end of this book, a closer look on data, information and knowledge asymmetries in financial regulation sheds new light on the phenomenon: Research that is discussed in chapters five and six indicates that neo-liberal policies and (de)regulations were not so much pursued to deliberately serve industry interests, but rather because policymakers and regulators, defeated by financial market complexity, faced severe difficulties in formulating and advocating the public interest when it came to financial governance. The financial crisis of 2007ff. invites us to rethink *the agency relationship between policymakers and regulators on the one hand, and regulatees on the other*. Drawing on Capture Theory as proposed by George Stigler (Stigler 1971) and his fellow Chicago economists, as well as on recent capture research that was triggered by the US financial crisis (Kwak 2013; Weber 2012; Barkow 2013), and based on numerous interviews with industry and policymaking experts, we offer the *knowledge capture* concept as a new theoretical framework for financial regulation under conditions of 21st century complexity.

1.3 Literature Overview and Current State of Research

Providing an up-to-date overview of research related to this book is a challenging task for two reasons: First, while central issues – especially TBTF, systemic risk and macroprudential oversight – have been a subject of debate for several decades now, the financial crisis has led to a renewed and continuing academic interest in these topics. The number of potentially relevant publications is accordingly vast, and what is worse, it is constantly growing. Second, the situation is changing constantly. The moment we finished our analysis, new publications and reports came out and provided potentially important information. Especially the new US institutions remain work in progress, while Dodd-Frank implementation is far from being completed. Third, we build our argument on contributions from the disciplines of economics, political science, law and sociology. We are well aware that, as in every interdisciplinary research project, we risk falling short on each of them. Yet, to develop an adequate theoretical framework for the study of data-, information- and knowledge-related problems in financial regulation, we had to draw on contributions from different disciplines. Unfortunately, the general problem with overviews is that they tend to be more important the more difficult they are to provide. This section therefore presents a short introduction into the current state of research related to this book. Because of space constraints, we only briefly discuss the most important contributions and recommend the respective chapters for further information.

In hindsight, factors contributing to the crisis can be distinguished into *regulatory causes*, such as the housing policy of the US government, and *private sector dynamics*, such as the growing demand for OTC derivatives. Unfortunately, only few academics look at a third category of contributing factors, the *specific system characteristics* that differentiate the systemic crisis of 2007ff. from other financial crises (see Willke, Becker, and Rostásy 2013, and ch. two of this book). In this context, network analysis (see for example Vitali, Glattfelder, and Battiston 2011) and agent-based modeling (see for example Thurner 2011) are promising and growing fields of research.[17] Systemic risk research was, at least until the recent financial crisis, mostly confined to the finance and economics disciplines (see for example Davis 1995; De Bandt and Hartmann 2000; Kaufman 1996; Bisias et al. 2012, provide an overview of current research on systemic risk measures). The deregulation paradigm of the 1980s and 1990s, which was based on a strong belief in free markets and self-regulation, has prevented governance scholars and policymakers alike from examining systemic risk. The situation has changed fundamentally since 2008: Contributions by law scholars have enhanced our understanding of systemic risk and the financial crisis (see for example Levitin 2011; Anabtawi and Schwarcz 2011; Schwarcz 2008; Wilmarth 2002). We can also find a growing number of interesting publications in political science and sociology (see for example McCarty, Poole, and Rosenthal 2013; Mosley and Singer 2009, for an overview over current research questions in the field of International Political Economy; Lounsbury and Hirsch 2010).[18] In chapter two, to provide a systems theory perspective on systemic risk, we mainly draw on publications by Helbing (2010), Palmer and Maher (2010) and Willke et al. (2013). Important and closely related is the issue of financial system complexity. In chapter three, we differentiate between three levels of complexity: The complexity of financial products (*micro-level complexity*), the complexity of too big to fail, or too complex to manage financial institutions (*meso-level complexity*), and the systems level (*macro-level complexity*) (Haldane and Madouros 2012; Stiglitz 2009b; Gai, Haldane, and Kapadia 2011; Haldane 2010; Hu 2012; Weber 2012; Gai 2013; Gai and Kapadia 2010). As we show, recent research indicates that complexity has increased on all three levels. Both the US and the EU financial reforms discussed in chapter four are not yet fully implemented. To assess these moving targets, we go back to the initial

17 Taleb doubts that agent-based models "work outside of research papers" (Taleb 2012b, 2).
18 We do not want to imply that the sociology discipline has not contributed to financial market literature in the past – the opposite is the case. Examining the social embeddedness of financial markets, sociologists have elaborated the role and behavior of the individuals that *make markets* (see for example Abolafia 1996; Knorr-Cetina and Preda 2005, therein especially MacKenzie 2005 and Fenton-O'Creevy et al. 2005).

government documents (including laws, reports, press releases, and speeches) and the accompanying media coverage. We make a few exceptions, however: Sorkin, based on interviews with government and market insiders, provides a detailed account of the crisis events and the respective governmental decisions (Sorkin 2010).[19] Davidoff and Zaring provide a detailed legal analysis of the government bailouts in 2008 (Davidoff and Zaring 2009). Wallach discusses the US policy responses against the background of the rule of law (Wallach 2010). And Acharya et al., in their book on Dodd-Frank, provide one of the early analyses of the regulatory overhaul in the US (Acharya, Cooley, et al. 2010b; see also Acharya et al. 2011). The situation in the EU is somehow different: While Dodd-Frank has been signed into law in 2010 and is gradually being implemented ever since, the European crisis has triggered an ongoing debate about the EU regulatory and supervisory structure and a future European Banking Union, a fact that is reflected in the numerous scientific contributions on the EU developments (see for example Pisani-Ferry and Sapir 2010; Fonteyne et al. 2010; Schoenmaker 2011; Ferran 2011; Ferran and Kern 2011). At the global level, the transformation of the Financial Stability Forum (FSF) to the Financial Stability Board (FSB) was also closely monitored by the academic community (Helleiner 2010a, 2010b; Griffith-Jones, Helleiner, and Woods 2010, especially: Momani 2010).

Turning towards the focus of this book, the role of data-, information- and knowledge-related problems in financial regulation has not received much scholarly attention so far. To begin with, "the literature often draws little distinction between information and knowledge. Expertise is treated as the obtainment of missing data" (McCarty 2013, 102). While financial policymakers and regulators describe insufficient data and missing expertise, they too do not often differentiate between problems related to data, as opposed to information, as opposed to knowledge. The distinction we draw in chapter five is mainly based on classic contributions by Zeleny (1987), Ackoff (1989) and Davenport and Prusak (1998), and aims to add definitional clarity to this rather vague set of problems.

To distinguish between the types of information asymmetries according to the actors involved, we employ and refine a four-category framework brought forward by Willke and Becker (2013). Interestingly, information and knowledge are corner stones of financial theory (Preda 2001, 16) – the respective literature on information and knowledge related problems is in fact vast (see Svetlova and van Elst 2012, for a current overview) – but financial theory focuses on asymmetries between market participants, and mostly leaves out regulator-regulatee relationships. As Preda complains, "information is mostly blackboxed, or seen as being mirrored by

19 The Financial Crisis Inquiry Commission referred to Sorkin's *Too Big to Fail (2010)* as well as to Lewis' *The Big Short (2011)* in numerous of its interviews (see for example Blankfein 2010; Das 2010). These contributions are not scientific analyses of the crisis, but they include many relevant insights and basic facts and accordingly provide a good starting point to assess the crisis.

securities' prices. A key task would be to open up this concept and push it to its ultimate consequences" (Preda 2001, 16). We draw on agency theory to grasp the relationship between regulators and regulatees, and the changes induced by increased information asymmetries (Mitnick 1984 and 1992; Moe 1984; Eisenhardt 1989; Shapiro 2005).

When we speak of knowledge, we refer to individual as well as organizational knowledge (see Castro et al. 2007, 48ff., for an overview of literature on both types). In our definition of knowledge we follow German sociologist Nico Stehr who understands knowledge as the *capacity to act*, or to *start something going* (Stehr 2007, 143; Ackoff 1989). Distinct from data and information, knowledge is closely tied to experience and practice (Becker and Willke 2013), and it is rooted in and confirmed by *communities of practice* (Willke 2002). It can be embodied in organizational rules and structures, but it requires human judgments and experiences to create knowledge. Boisot and Canals conclude that "there is no such thing as common knowledge and there is common information only to a limited extent. Only data can ever be completely common between agents" (Boisot and Canals 2004, 63).

In chapter six, we further develop our understanding of the role of information and knowledge asymmetries in financial regulation, based on Wagner's *Administrative Law, Filter Failure, and Information Capture* (Wagner 2010). Wagner draws on a number of studies dealing with information-related problems in environmental regulation to ultimately rework Stigler's Capture Theory (Stigler 1971). Even more central to this book is Weber's text on *Structural Regulation as Antidote to Complexity Capture* (Weber 2012). Looking at what regulators know and what they need to know to fulfill their mandates, Weber identifies "a structural, widening epistemic gap" that he traces back to increased financial system complexity (ibid., 644f.). Starting from there, he develops a new perspective of capture. Together with recent contributions from Etzioni (2009), Kwak (2013), McCarty (2013) and Barkow (2013), these two publications form a new and growing strand of capture research that takes into account current developments in political governance and regulation, particularly with regard to financial governance. To these concepts of cultural and cognitive, of information and complexity capture, this book adds a first investigation into *knowledge capture in 21st century financial regulation*. It aims to explain why industry interests could become increasingly dominant in financial regulation and how they contributed to the financial crisis.

1.4 Research Approach

In his Nobel lecture of 1974, Friedrich von Hayek warns that unlike "in the physical sciences, in economics and other disciplines that deal with essentially complex phenomena, the aspects of the events to be accounted for about which we can get quantitative data are necessarily limited and may not include the important ones" (Hayek 1974). Studies examining the causes of the financial crisis are multifaceted and numerous. The fact that the crisis is primarily approached in numeric terms – from the size of the rescue programs, to the increase of unemployment rates, bank leverage ratios, and sovereign debt in relation to GDP – conveys the impression that comprehensive studies must put quantitative research center-stage. How else could we deal with numbers, except with numbers? And how else could regulators counter the industry's arguments, except with data? The mandate of the Office of Financial Research, with its focus on data and information, clearly underlines this point. Yet, the financial crisis of 2007ff. was also perceived as a crisis of financial data: It decreased the credibility of the sophisticated calculations and models that had supposedly increased the safety of the system. The complex interplay of derivatives contracts, mark-to-market accounting, collateral agreements and counterparty behavior was apparently too complex to be modeled adequately (Buffett 2010). Interesting in this regard is also MacKenzie's case study of the LTCM collapse. Based on interviews with key participants, he describes how the hedge fund's sophisticated arbitrage activities were based as much in quantitative as in cultural knowledge, in an "understanding of matters like who held which bonds and why" (MacKenzie 2005, 77; see also Fenton-O'Creevy et al. 2005; Abolafia 1996). We therefore argue that, while quantitative analyses of the crisis are as important as they are legitimate, they alone are not sufficient. As the explanatory power of quantitative research is clearly limited, what is needed – not as an alternative, but as a complement – is an interdisciplinary and qualitative discussion of the causes and effects of the crisis. Von Hayek's argument, made long before the current crisis, encouraged us to approach the crisis in qualitative terms.

As the following figure illustrates, our approach combines a comprehensive literature review with a content-based, structured analysis of interviews, speeches, congressional testimonies, press releases and presentations. In addition, we base our analysis on laws and regulations, as well as on accompanying media coverage (figure 2).[20]

20 Much of our resources – especially the interviews, but also some testimonies, media articles and speeches – were not numbered. Several direct quotes do therefore not include a page number.

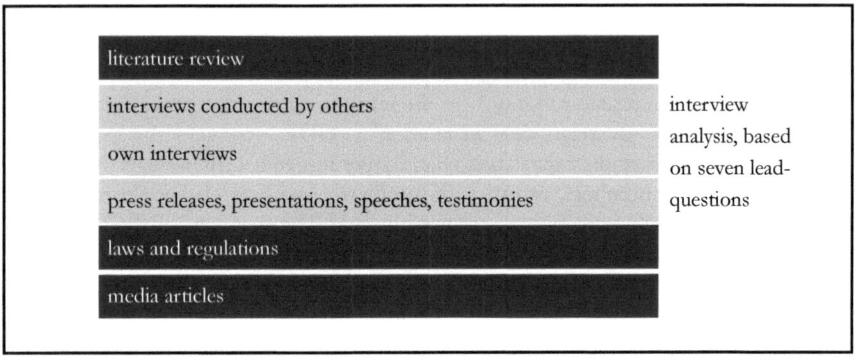

Figure 2: Research approach.

The existing interview material on the financial crisis is immense. We base our analysis on three types of interviews, adding up to more than 60 partly-transcribed interviews in total: The interviews conducted by the US Financial Crisis Inquiry Commission (FCIC), interviews undertaken by journalists, and last but not least our own interviews.[21] The FCIC alone has recorded more than 300 interviews with financial market experts that are now accessible via the FCIC's website.[22] Most FCIC interviews follow a similar logic, starting with a brief introduction of the commission's mandate, followed by an introduction by the interview partner, and then getting to the core question of what caused the financial crisis in the US and how the mortgage business and complex derivatives contributed to the crisis. In comparison, interviews conducted by journalists cover a much broader set of issues. This second set of interviews, available on the YouTube channels and web archives of broadcasting stations and government institutions, is, contrary to the FCIC interviews and our own interviews, non-standardized; yet it contains important information. The third group consists of a smaller number of interviews conducted by the author herself. In order to complement the publicly available material, these interviews explicitly examine data-, information- and knowledge-related problems in financial regulation. They are based upon a standardized field manual, and were fully recorded and transliterated whenever our interview partners agreed. To further increase our data-base, we included press releases, speeches, testimonies and

21 We conducted ten interviews between November 2012 and August 2013; unfortunately, we did not get the permission to record all of them, resulting in seven transcripts in total.

22 To sample the FCIC interviews, we took every third out of the 356 published interview files on the FCIC website. In addition, we selected the interviews that we expected to be relevant for our research, adding up to 163 FCIC interviews in total. Following our research questions, we partly transliterated 46 of these 163 recordings. They can be found in the appendix to this book.

presentations by central actors – policymakers, regulators and market insiders – into our research.[23]

The content-based interview analysis was structured by seven guiding research questions, not to be mistaken for hypotheses:

(1) Is systemic risk a rather economic or political phenomenon?
(2) Is financial governance exacerbated by an incongruence between nation states and global finance?
(3) Did data, information and knowledge asymmetries between regulators and regulatees contribute to the financial crisis?
(4) Do the US policy responses to the crisis represent a real policy change?
(5) Has the too big to fail phenomenon been resolved?
(6) Did the crisis happen due to regulatory capture?
(7) Has the financial system become too complex to regulate?

The research questions were not treated as hypotheses for good reasons. Based on a critical rationalist viewpoint, we do not believe that we are able to verify these phenomena (Popper 1994). At the same time, we agree with Hayek that, when investigating complex phenomena, Popper's approach has its limitations (Hayek 2007 [1967]). Going through the interviews and documents, we tried to find counterevidence as well as evidence, both contributing to the theoretical framework developed over the course of this book. During our research, we kept in mind that interview partners who did not mention data-, information-, or knowledge-related problems, might be counted as counterevidence, too. When confronted with an open question about the causes for the crisis, only very few experts did in fact name inadequate data and expertise. Therefore, despite the large number of interviews and other documents contributing to this book, our conclusion rests more on theoretical plausibility and deduction than on empirical data.

In addition to the material that found its way into the content-based analysis, we also base our understanding of the financial crisis of 2007ff. on a number of governmental reports: There are the reports and studies published by EU (Gerlach 2009; European Systemic Risk Board 2012, 2013a; European Central Bank 2010; High Level Group on Financial Supervision in the EU 2009), UK (Financial Services Authority 2009) and US institutions (Financial Stability Oversight Council 2011a, 2012a; Office of Financial Research 2012a; Financial Crisis Inquiry

23 We decided not to include media articles in our content analysis, yet they provided important information on government actions – such as the Flash Crash of 2010 and the SEC's attempts to investigate it – and therefore allowed us to construct several smaller case studies during the research process (Walton 1992). These in turn helped us to develop and corroborate our understanding of the phenomena at hand. Here, we mainly relied on articles from the New York Times, from the Washington Post, The Economist, and the Financial Times.

Commission 2011). In addition, the series of Global Financial Stability Reports by the IMF (2009, 2008), the reports published by the Group of Thirty (Group of Thirty 1997, 2009; Clark and Large 2011), and a set of international reports (International Monetary Fund, Bank for International Settlements, and Financial Stability Board 2009; Financial Stability Board 2011b) are of central importance. Among the contributions by governmental organizations, a joint report by the FSB and the IMF hints at the fact that information gaps did play a role in the crisis (Financial Stability Board and International Monetary Fund 2009).

As our field of research is wide, we also want to say a few words on what this book is not. First, the global financial crisis sets the stage for this study. It not only revealed a number of problems in financial governance, it also triggered policy responses from nation states and transnational governmental organizations alike. Yet, our focus lies on the US policy responses to the crisis (see figure 3). While we refer to the EU and to global financial reform for the benefits of comparative analysis in two subsections, our analysis of the transnational (EU) and international (Basel Committee and FSB) reform agendas is bound to be limited. These days, European financial reform in particular is a fast moving target, and we gladly leave it to others to reconstruct and analyze the reform process. Second, Dodd-Frank exceeds 900 pages. It requires countless regulations and interpretations from the US financial agencies. Again, we had to restrict ourselves – this time to the parts of the reform that, in a broader sense, relate to the focus of this book: Data-, information- and knowledge-related problems in financial regulation. Again, we touch upon other aspects of reform, but the picture we provide must be incomplete.

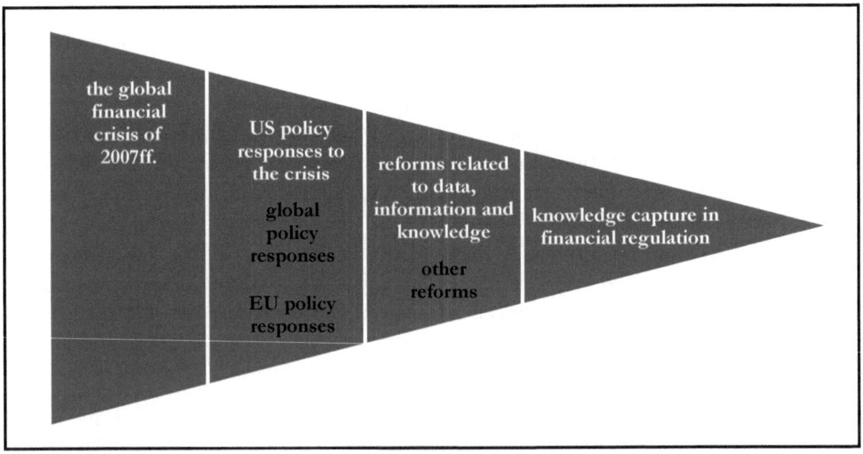

Figure 3: Focus and context of this book.

Based on our analysis of the crisis and the US policy responses, we develop a theoretical framework for the analysis of data-, information- and knowledge-related problems that we term *knowledge capture.* As the figure indicates, it is not applicable to financial governance per se. In our analysis, we mostly left out financial policymaking and focused on the regulatory agencies responsible for financial supervision and regulation instead. The reason lies in US politics: When President Obama signed Dodd-Frank into law in 2010, he in effect delegated the formulation of numerous rules, regulations, studies and reports to the federal financial agencies. As Coglianese argues, "especially when statutory language leaves major policy issues unresolved, administrative rules can hold greater significance than even the most important acts of Congress" (Coglianese 1994, 2).[24] As we will see throughout the course of this book, this is also the case with Dodd-Frank: The agencies decide on the technical details and definitions. To provide an example, Dodd-Frank required the CFTC and the Securities and Exchange Commission (SEC) to jointly define the terms *swap* (regulated by the CFTC) and *security-based swap* (regulated by the SEC). The rules and interpretations finished and published on nearly 600 pages in 2012 triggered the commencement of many Dodd-Frank measures, including reporting standards and capital requirements (Commodity Futures Trading Commission and Securities and Exchange Commission 2012). It was therefore the SEC and the CFTC that had to dive deep into the technical details of the derivatives business and, more importantly, to decide which specific products were to be excluded from all Dodd-Frank regulation applying to derivatives and which were to be included. Compared to Congress, the regulatory agencies therefore rely much more on financial data, information and expertise; vice versa, *gaps of information and expertise at the agencies provide access points for experts, i.e. industry interest groups.*[25] For industry interest groups, the US administrative agencies have therefore become an important lobbying addressee. The number of empirical contributions examining industry and private interest group influence on the executive agencies and on US Congress is vast (Kamieniecki 2006, even though he focuses on environmental policy and rulemaking, provides an excellent overview over research). While it is not the purpose of this book to prove the dominance of either group, the distinction between legislative and executive capture should be kept in mind when reading chapters five and six (Baumgartner and Leech 1998).

24 Croley goes so far to say that, because of the volume and the importance of agency decisions, "modern government *is* administrative government" (Croley 2008, 14). He also gives a detailed account of agency decision-making in the US, and emphasizes that agencies do not produce regulations in the strict sense, but instead write rules and orders (see ibid., ch. 5 for more information).

25 We also have to keep in mind that other capture strategies – e.g. attempts to influence government officials with campaign contributions – cannot be pursued to influence agency rulemaking because they are illegal.

We want to close with some general points: It is often argued that, to analyze change, one has to start with the (former) status quo. Even though we agree in principle, we refrain from analyzing the pre-crisis regulatory landscape in the US: For one because of space constraints, but more importantly because others have done a very good job in comparing the pre- and post-crisis situation (see for example Woolley and Ziegler 2012). Nor will we provide a detailed overview over US financial supervision and regulation: Jickling and Murphy provide an excellent report on the old and new responsibilities and authorities of the respective agencies (Jickling and Murphy 2010).

2 Narratives of the Global Financial Crisis

"I think one of the things this country really, really needs, and still doesn't have, is a narrative of what happened and why. What you're seeing in the country now I think is inchoate anger. They're just mad. They don't really know what they're mad about or who they're mad on, except bankers, and apparently incompetent politicians. But it is an inchoate anger because the story is just not well understood." (Blinder 2010)

The final report of the *National Commission on the Causes of the Financial and Economic Crisis in the United States* (Financial Crisis Inquiry Commission, or FCIC) was published in January 2011. Based on several hundred public hearings and interviews and millions of pages of emails and other documents, the commission staff examined, with particular emphasis on the role of complex derivatives and the US mortgage market, the causes of the financial crisis. It also explored why certain financial institutions had failed or might have failed without government support. The quote from US economist Alan Blinder at the beginning of this chapter was taken from an FCIC interview, and the FCIC report does in fact present a central narrative of the US financial crisis. Interestingly, four out of ten FCIC commissioners dissented from the report.[26] While three of these four could agree on a second narrative, one commissioner – Peter J. Wallison – published his own report, totaling three narratives of the financial crisis from the FCIC alone (Financial Crisis Inquiry Commission 2011). Another three years later, academics, finance professionals, regulators and policymakers still cannot agree on the exact roots and causes of the crisis. As one might expect, some crisis narratives pushed the window for new regulation wide open, while others blocked it up completely, suggesting that regulation had caused the crisis and emphasizing that markets should regulate themselves. As Blinder's statement indicates, given the public anger over bank bailouts and rescue programs, it might have been best – at least from a political rationale – to blame any group for causing the crisis. However, public finger-pointing at either the rating agencies or the investment banks, or even

---

26 Phil Angelides, Brooksley Born, Byron Georgiou, Bob Graham, Heather H. Murren, John W. Thompson signed the report; it was not supported by Keith Hennessey, Douglas Holtz-Eakin, Bill Thomas, Peter J. Wallison.

financial regulators, was neither feasible nor possible: The financial crisis of 2007ff. was just too complex to allow a simple explanation. Apparently, the 21st century financial system that broke down in 2008 had had many architects, including mega-banks and gigantic insurance companies, but also national financial regulators and global policymaking elites. When the risks materialized during 2007 and 2008, the causes were so intertwined that *responsibilities were difficult to assign* (Admati and Hellwig 2013, 199).

The OCC's Martin Pfinsgraff has identified four schools of thought, each putting another narrative of the crisis center-stage. As stated by the first school, the crisis was caused by the bad behavior of banks and mortgage originators; it can accordingly be traced back to remuneration and lending practices. School number two emphasizes the role of the US government, more specifically the government-sponsored enterprises (GSEs) Fannie Mae and Freddie Mac. According to this second narrative, the GSEs not only promoted private homeownership, but actively "subsidized and encouraged lax lending practices" (Pfinsgraff 2012, 2), ultimately creating the mortgage bubble.[27] School number three focuses on the rating agencies, i.e. the Nationally Recognized Statistical Rating Organizations (NRSROs), blaming them for understating the risks associated with certain derivatives products. School number four redirects our focus to the role of US regulators, as they did not anticipate and prevent the crisis: According to this line of argument, each respective agency "either lacked appropriate authority, was incompetent, or both" (ibid.). As these four schools of thought focus on the behavior of the actors involved – implying that the crisis would not have happened if they had only behaved differently – we want to term all explanations that fall into Pfinsgraff's categories *behavioral narratives* of the crisis, contrasting them to the *systemic narratives* of the crisis.[28] As we will see, this distinction is crucial: Not only do most reform debates shift from one side of the continuum (behavioral) to the other (systemic), gradually objectivizing over time (Mayntz 2010b, 11f.). More importantly, these types of narratives have fundamentally different implications for reform. Defining frames, or setting *schemata of interpretation* in Goffman's sense (Goffmann 1974, ch. 2; Soros 2010), determines the future policy options of governments; therein, the "period of

27 In a speech in 1994, President Clinton summoned the close relationship between private homeownership and the American Dream: "Today I want to talk with you about the dream of homeownership and the larger American dream of which it is a part and what we can do together to keep the economic renewal that began 21 months ago going. […] I think we all agree that more Americans should own their own homes, for reasons that are economic and tangible and reasons that are emotional and intangible but go to the heart of what it means to harbor, to nourish, to expand the American dream" (Clinton, 1994).

28 Soros adds a third narrative, stating that the crisis can neither be explained with behavioral nor with systemic factors, but with interpretations, dogmas or paradigms: "[I]t's the ideas or theories that guided the people […], it's the theories adopted by both the regulators and the market participants that proved to be false. It is the Efficient Market Hypothesis and the Rational Expectations Theory" (Soros 2010).

collective questioning" following a shock or crisis provides an opportunity for policy entrepreneurs to push through their interpretation of the events (Abolafia 2005, 212).[29]

Wallison's dissent from the FCIC report provides a good example here, because it identifies the housing policy of the US government as it was carried out by the GSEs as the major cause of the crisis (Wallison 2013). According to Wallison's narrative, US policy responses to the crisis are essentially misguided as they address, as he emphasizes, non-existent problems as interconnectedness, while the major problems – the GSEs – are not resolved (Interview with Peter J. Wallison, December 04, 2012, Washington; see also Scott 2012). In a different behavioral narrative, Taylor traces the crisis back to US monetary policy, blaming the Fed's low interest rate (Taylor 2009). As a third behavioral example, Lo suggests that greed and, once the risk materialized, unbridled fear caused the financial crisis (Lo 2011, 2). And fourth, Cohan identifies Wall Street incentive structures as a main cause for the crisis (Cohan 2010). Official government reports refrain from assigning single responsibility. The de Larosière Report, one of the most influential[30] crisis reports, argues that the crisis "results from the *complex interaction* of market failures, global financial and monetary imbalances, inappropriate regulation, weak supervision and poor macro-prudential oversight" (High Level Group on Financial Supervision in the EU 2009, 13, emphasis added). The UK's Turner Review emphasizes the role of self-reinforcing system characteristics, among them financial sector growth, increased complexity, and a "misplaced reliance on sophisticated maths" (Financial Services Authority 2009, 22). The authors describe how the characteristics of the *new global financial system*, together with macroeconomic imbalances, helped to "create an unsustainable credit boom and asset price inflation" (ibid., 28). The FCIC ascribes responsibility to regulators and supervisors, as well as to corporate governance and risk management ("a key cause"); to excessive borrowing and risk-taking, to a lack of transparency, to the government ("ill prepared for the crisis"), to mortgage-lending standards, to OTC derivatives, and rating agencies ("cogs in the wheel of financial destruction") (Financial Crisis Inquiry Commission 2011, xvff.). In these reports, human misconduct is clearly identified as a major cause of the crisis. Systemic narratives, in contrast, go without dramatis personae. Palmer and Maher argue, as we discuss in greater detail in section 2.2, that the crisis was a *Normal Accident* in Charles Perrow's sense: A "result of complexity and tight coupling" and as such the "product of system characteristics that lead to unintended interactions among multiple failures at the part, component, and/or subsystem levels" (Palmer and Maher 2010, 219; Perrow 1981). To understand the

29 As Blyth argues, financial ideas provide *legitimatory frameworks* for policymaking (Blyth 2003).

30 The report recommended the establishment of the European Supervisory Authorities (ESAs) and the European Systemic Risk Board (ESRB), as well as the restructuring of the Financial Stability Forum (FSF) to the Financial Stability Board. All four recommendations have been implemented.

financial crisis of 2007ff., we accordingly have to look at the *specific characteristics of the 21st century financial system*, and how they changed over time. For obvious reasons, greed and fear do not classify as specific characteristics of the post-Bretton Woods financial system. If the recent financial crisis was indeed a systemic crisis, and we have to be careful to clearly distinguish systemic from system-wide here, our analysis has to go beyond behavioral narratives – with far-reaching implications for future financial reform.

What caused the financial crisis? and *Why did the risks materialize in 2007 and 2008?* are two closely related, yet crucially different questions that ought to be discussed in this context. While the first refers to the structural weaknesses that facilitate a financial crisis, the second relates to the trigger that sets into motion a chain reaction that culminates in a system-wide crisis. According to the systemic narratives of the crisis, the breakdown was *triggered* by Lehman's collapse, but it was not *caused* by the investment banks' risky business or high bonuses. Analyzing the events of 2008, Bernanke defined triggers as "the particular events or factors that touched off the crisis" and structural weaknesses as the vulnerabilities "in the financial system and in regulation and supervision that propagated and amplified the initial shocks" (Bernanke 2010c, 1). As the Lehman collapse demonstrated, a systemic crisis is most likely triggered by the *paradox yet possible failure of a too big to fail institution*, but "threats to financial stability involve many institutions simultaneously and typically affect the system as a whole" (Bisias et al. 2012, 16). Triggers are random: Given a certain set of structural weaknesses, other endogenous or even exogenous events could set off the exact same developments.[31] As we show on the following pages, traders' typing errors and trading algorithms do also qualify as triggers, as they could potentially set off a chain reaction that leads to a financial breakdown. Policymakers obviously cannot eliminate all triggers, which is why we should best focus on the structural weaknesses of the system (see Perrow 2007). As we will see in section 2.1, the crisis has given rise to a debate about *micro- and macroprudential supervision and regulation*. Microprudential supervision and regulation focus on the safety and soundness of institutions that might, once they fail, trigger a systemic crisis. Macroprudential supervision and regulation ensure the stability of the system as a whole. While the microprudential reform agenda is challenging to implement but relatively clear in terms of means and ends, designing an effective macroprudential framework remains a difficult task. The Bank of Italy has recently warned that "in spite of the progress made, our understanding of MAP [macroprudential policy, EB] tools and their impact on the financial system and the

31 In 2008, the bankruptcy of Lehman Brothers provided the trigger. If it had not been Lehman Brothers, other endogenous events – the breakdown of a hedge fund or a money market fund – might have led to the exact same chain reaction, not to mention the wide variety of possible exogenous shocks to the financial system that did not play a role in 2008, but will in the future, such as terrorist attacks or natural disasters.

real economy remains very incomplete" (Panetta 2013, 1). In the following sections, we look at the crisis as a turning point, both in terms of broader economic beliefs and regulatory paradigms: Not only could we, as a result of the global financial and economic crisis, observe a paradigm shift from deregulation to reregulation from 2008 onwards, but also has the reform debate put macroprudential supervision and regulation back on the policymaking agenda. This brings us to the issue of systemic risk, which is at the heart of the macroprudential reform debate. As we will see, the debate is not only shaped by behavioral and systemic narratives of the crisis: Different understandings of systemic risk compete to explain what happened in 2008. More specifically, we seek to juxtapose economic and political concepts of systemic risk to ultimately provide a comprehensive, politico-economic approach (see Willke, Becker and Rostásy 2013).

2.1 From 1980 to 2010: Dominant Beliefs and Paradigm Shifts

Two terms that constantly reoccur in the crisis debate are *groupthink* and *herding behavior*. When it became apparent in September 2008 that the US government would not rescue Lehman, trust evaporated, banks stopped to lend to each other, markets froze, and mark-to-market accounting became essentially impossible for certain securities.[32] Heterogeneous investors became a homogeneous crowd.[33] But groupthink and herding behavior did also play a major and, in the context of this book, even more important role in *financial governance*. When Stiglitz provocatively wrote that market fundamentalism was "for a quarter of century the prevailing religion of the West" (Stiglitz 2009a, 346), he referred to groupthink in the academic, economic and, most importantly, *political system*. Many crisis narratives start in the 1980s and explain the crisis with a neo-liberal zeitgeist, a laissez-fair belief that less financial regulation was good for the economy and for society (see for example Campbell 2010; Mayntz 2010b; Vanoli 2010).[34] The British Academy,

32 An interesting strand of research examines the role of heterogeneous beliefs in financial markets. Based on Harrison and Kreps, it can be argued that investors buy stocks because they believe that other investors will overestimate their value in the future (Harrison and Kreps 1978, 323; see also Xiong 2013, for an overview on the link between bubbles, crises and heterogeneous beliefs).

33 Research indicates that investor behavior is in fact not as heterogeneous as one might think. MacKenzie , in his analysis of the LTCM collapse in 1998, argues that market participants copy the (assumed) trading strategy of successful funds – a fact that exacerbates problems in the market once a major institution struggles (MacKenzie 2005).

34 The report of the FCIC criticizes that "[t]he sentries were not at their posts, in no small part due to the widely accepted faith in the self-correcting nature of the markets and the ability of financial institutions to effectively police themselves. More than 30 years of deregulation and reliance on self-regulation by financial institutions, championed by former Federal Reserve chairman Alan Greenspan and others, supported by successive administrations and Congresses, and actively pushed by the

in a letter to the British queen, described how "politicians of all types were charmed by the market" (British Academy 2009, 2; see also Reed 2010).[35] A deep-rooted belief that government was the problem, not the solution (Reagan 1981), had led to a remarkable decade of financial deregulation (Perrow 2010, 315), or at least reregulation (Campbell 2010) – a trend that might well have continued if the crisis would not have put an abrupt end to it.[36] Former chairperson of the Federal Deposit Insurance Corporation (FDIC or the Corporation) Sheila Bair describes how European governments and fellow US regulators pushed for the implementation of the industry-friendly Basel II capital requirements in the US against the conviction of the FDIC (Bair 2012a) in the years prior to the crisis. As late as 2006, New York's Michael Bloomberg and Charles E. Schumer advocated, along the lines of the UK's Financial Services Authority (FSA, abolished in 2013), a more collaborative and solution-oriented, principles-based financial regulation. They argued that, competing with London, "New York cannot afford to lose its place as the global leader in financial services. We have to carefully redefine this balance of innovation and regulation. That is what we seek to do over the next several months" (Schumer and Bloomberg 2006). The underlying *clash of innovation and regulation* is a crucial point in the reform debate: The quote reflects "a broader contemporary social and political conversation that really sees innovation as ultimately beneficial, really important, not something that regulation should be getting in the way of" (Ford 2013; see also Siddique 2010). The IMF came to a similar conclusion:

> A strong belief by many policymakers in the efficiency of financial markets undercut a realistic appraisal of financial stability. Even as academic research increasingly began to question the efficient markets theory, policymakers tended to ignore the implications for systemic stability of financial market imperfections [...]. *Financial development and innovation were viewed as beneficial*, increasing access to credit and leading to an ever more efficient allocation of risks across the system. [...]. Regulation and supervision were

powerful financial industry at every turn, had stripped away key safeguards, which could have helped avoid catastrophe" (Financial Crisis Inquiry Commission 2011, xviii).

35 McCarty et al. speak of the *political bubble* that aided and amplified the market bubble (McCarty, Poole and Rosenthal 2013, 14).

36 Yet, some financial experts argue that the crisis was caused by overregulation (Interview with Peter J. Wallison, December 04, 2012, Washington). They do in fact have a point: The assumption that financial markets have been deregulated at large is certainly a strong oversimplification (Calomiris 2010). To start with, certain areas – such as traditional banking, including deposit taking and lending – were strongly regulated. The overall number of supervisors and regulators per bank in the US and the UK, as well as the extent and complexity of global rules and regulations, indeed indicates that the regulatory burden in certain areas has increased. Other market areas, such as the OTC derivatives market, were not regulated at all. This *dark market* (Born 2009) grew massively during the pre-crisis years. Light-touch regulation does accordingly not imply the absence of financial supervision and regulation; it rather alludes to policymakers' fundamental ignorance towards emerging risks in the financial system.

> increasingly light-touch and reliant on self-correcting market forces. (International Monetary Fund 2010, 7, emphasis added)

The global financial crisis marks a break with laissez-fair regulation, at least in its strong form. It challenged the common belief that financial innovation is per se beneficial (Blinder 2010). Deutsche Bank, under broad-based public scrutiny and interest, announced plans for a cultural turnaround (including changes in its remuneration practices and its capital base, see Deutsche Bank 2012a), and Joseph Stiglitz declared that the crisis would mean for market fundamentalism "what the fall of the Berlin Wall was to communism" (Stiglitz 2008). Yet, while many argue that the crisis "paved the way for a less market-friendly, more stability-oriented, approach" (Ferran 2012a, 14), we still cannot be sure whether the financial crisis will, in the long run, change global financial governance fundamentally: "what paradigm should replace the old is still unclear, although the contours of the new conventional wisdom are becoming clearer" (Black 2012, 4).[37] What we do know is that the crisis has brought macroprudential supervision and regulation back on the policymaking agenda.

Academics and policymakers agree that financial regulation and supervision in the pre-crisis decades had a dangerously *narrow microprudential focus* (see for example Hanson, Kashyap, and Stein 2011; The Warwick Commission 2009; High Level Group on Financial Supervision in the EU 2009). The assessment of financial risk was limited to the individual risk of financial institutions, rather than the institutions' collective risk (Acharya, Cooley, et al. 2010a), therefore completely ignoring the "systemic implications of common behaviour" (The Warwick Commission 2009, 12). The microprudential focus of financial regulation, which was particularly dominant in Basel I and II, can be traced back to two underlying beliefs: Firstly, that the financial system would be safe and sound if only each financial institution was safe and sound (Gai 2013, 2) – a belief that is, as we will argue in the proceeding section, naïve from a systems perspective. Secondly, that due to superior data, information and knowledge, the financial institutions themselves were best suited to evaluate the risks resulting from their books (Tarullo 2008), forming the basis of Basel II's internal ratings-based approach (IRB). As we will argue in greater detail in chapter five, it is certainly true that financial institutions have a *data, information, and knowledge lead over regulators*. However, this does not imply, as the crisis has convincingly demonstrated, that they are in fact the better risk managers. Ultimately, Basel II was never fully implemented in the US, as the crisis events revealed that it did not sufficiently address systemic risk and

37 The US Dodd-Frank Act that was signed into law in 2010 is still not fully implemented. As Coffee emphasizes, once a law is signed and the agencies take over from Congress to write the detailed rules, "the public's attention turns elsewhere and business interest groups reestablish their usual dominance over the technical process of policy implementation" (Coffee 2012, 310).

had to be revised (Acharya, Pedersen, et al. 2010; Bair 2012a). Exemplary for many, Bernanke called for a policy change, stating that regulators and supervisors should augment the "traditional microprudential, or firm-specific, methods of oversight with a more macroprudential, or systemwide, approach that should help us better anticipate and mitigate broader threats to financial stability" (Bernanke 2009b).

Reinhart and Rogoff argue convincingly that certain types of financial crises share a similar logic and reoccur regularly throughout the centuries (Reinhart and Rogoff 2009). The Dutch tulipmania of the 1630s (see Garber 1989) and the recent US housing bubble do in fact have some things in common. Yet, it is not only the crises that reoccur, but also the ensuing policy discourses. Even though Mayntz terms the post-crisis focus on macroprudential supervision the "most innovative change" (Mayntz 2012, 16) in financial governance, the concept has in fact been, just as the issue of systemic risk, a topic of debate in policymaking and academia for some time. As stated by Turner and Clement, it can be traced back to the Basel Committee discussions at the Bank for International Settlements (BIS) in 1979 (P. Turner 2010; Clement 2010):

> Prudential measures are primarily concerned with sound banking practice and the protection of depositors at the level of the individual bank. Much work has been done in this area – which could be described as the 'micro-prudential' aspect of banking supervision. [...] However, this micro-prudential aspect may need to be matched by prudential considerations with a wider perspective. This 'macro-prudential' approach considers problems that bear upon the market as a whole as distinct from an individual bank, and which may not be obvious at the micro-prudential level. (BIS Archives 7.18(15))

The macroprudential problems pointed out in the BIS paper – a fast growth of the overall market, the underestimation of tail-risk, and the banks' misperception of liquidity and funding risks – could be well observed in the crisis of 2007ff.. Twenty years later, the Group of Seven established the Financial Stability Forum (FSF) to integrate both perspectives and address systemic risk. A report to the BIS by Hans Tietmeyer, then President of the German central bank (*Deutsche Bundesbank*), identified the three major challenges of the time, all of which came back on the policymaking agenda during the crisis of 2007ff.:

> There are three aspects to this: firstly, overcoming the separate treatment of micro-prudential and macro-prudential issues; secondly, bringing together the major international institutions and key national authorities involved in financial sector stability [...]. [...] strengthened efforts are necessary to help identify incipient vulnerabilities in national and international financial systems and concerted procedures are needed for a better understanding of

> the sources of systemic risk and to formulate effective financial, regulatory and supervisory policies to mitigate them. (Tietmeyer 1999, 2f.)

The FSF did not live up to its expectations. In 2010 it was transformed into the Financial Stability Board (FSB) and received a new mandate and new resources to mitigate systemic risk and enhance macroprudential supervision (see chapter four of this book). Will this time be different? It appears that experts did in fact express their concerns during the 1980s and 1990s, but given the wide-spread neo-liberal beliefs of the time, the policy responses were rare and largely ineffective (Helleiner 2010a). As we argue in chapter five and six, data, information and knowledge asymmetries might have also played a major role. This time, the policy responses are far-reaching, at least on paper. Whether they really mark a turning point is, as we will see throughout this book, not yet clear: Dodd-Frank has been signed but not yet fully implemented – and the devil of financial reform lies in the complex and highly technical details. As Admati and Hellwig argue with regard to global risk weights for banks: "the financial crisis showed that Basel II was flawed. Basel III attempts to correct some of the flaws in Basel II, but it has not changed the overall approach" (Admati and Hellwig 2013, 183).

2.2 A Pre- and Post-Crisis Understanding of Systemic Risk

While the US Financial Stability Oversight Council is mandated to monitor and address systemic risk, the Office of Financial Research has the task of collecting the data required to fulfill this mandate. Some warn that the term systemic risk "is widely used, but [...] difficult to define and quantify" (International Monetary Fund 2009, 113), yet the OFR staff argues that to manage systemic risk, one has to be able to measure it (Bisias et al. 2012; see also Office of Financial Research 2013a). Bisias et al. provide a recent overview of systemic risk analytics. Even though they endeavor to measure systemic risk, the OFR researchers warn that "a single consensus measure of systemic risk may neither be possible nor desirable" as it "invites a blindsided surprise from some unforeseen or newly emerging crisis mechanism" (Bisias et al. 2012, 2). As we showed in the context of micro- and macroprudential supervision, a narrow focus on certain aspects of systemic risk, for instance on TBTF institutions, would in fact bear huge risks. The OFR is responsible for data and information collection on systemic risk in the US, and it is mandated to advise the federal agencies on related issues; the described dilemma is therefore not a theoretical one, but of a very practical nature. Beginning with the pre-crisis understanding of systemic risk, and turning to the financial crisis of 2007ff. that is widely perceived as *the systemic financial crisis*, the current chapter discusses economic and political perspectives on systemic risk to ultimately integrate both into a political-economic concept of systemic risk. Whether systemic risk can in fact be measured or not is, as we will see, a central question.

Even though systemic risk was not a widely discussed phenomenon in political science prior to the crisis, policymakers and regulators were well aware of systemic risk before 2008. In 2004, during his tenure as President of the New York Fed, Timothy Geithner stated:

> Although we have a rich history of banking crises in our past, and have watched other countries confront such crises more recently, it's been some time since we've experienced the prospect or the reality of a systemically significant bank failure in this country. It is important that knowledge among practitioners of this art of bank resolution does not fade with time and is not dulled by the comfort of the relative stability and financial resilience we have been fortunate enough to enjoy over the past decade and more. (Geithner 2004)

He identified six changes in the market structure with an implication for systemic risk: First, the increased importance of a small number of very large financial institutions – a development that has been reinforced by the mergers and acquisitions of the recent financial crisis. Second and third, Geithner named the increased importance of nonbank financial institutions (such as money market funds and hedge funds) and central clearing and settlement structures. Fourth, he referred to the growth of US government-sponsored enterprises that could be observed during the lead-up to the crisis, Fannie Mae and Freddie Mac. Fifth, Geithner mentioned a more complex risk and compliance management, and sixth, the overall increase of global financial integration. As he emphasized, these changes made the financial system *stronger and weaker* at the same time (ibid.). While the identified characteristics decrease the possibility of a severe crisis, they increase the severity of a crisis when it occurs – a phenomenon that is described as the *robust-yet-fragile tendency* of complex financial systems (Gai 2013, 10f.) and can also be observed in the context of high-risk technologies. Regulators did not take into account how these new and interlocking features had fundamentally changed the nature of the global financial system, and slowly transferred it from a loosely to a tightly coupled system (see Bookstaber 2007; International Organization of Securities Commissions 2011).[38] While economic actors can hardly be blamed for not anticipating and understanding these mechanisms, policymakers have to face

38 According to Willke and Willke, a tightly coupled financial system differs from a loosely coupled financial system in (1) the nature of the relations and interdependencies between the system components, the blurring boundaries between (2) nation states and national economic systems and (3) between formerly separated business models that leads to the re-emergence of financial conglomerates, (4) the influence of actors like rating agencies, and finally the increased homogeneity of (5) paradigms and economic assumptions, as well as (6) risk strategies (Willke and Willke 2012, 42).

the question of why they could not protect financial stability (*the Fed*) and social welfare (*the government*).

There are many more pre-crisis analyses of systemic risk, among them a report on *Global Institutions, National Supervision and Systemic Risk* from the Group of Thirty (1997), defining systemic risk as "the sudden, unanticipated event that would damage the financial system to such an extent that economic activity in the wider economy would suffer", and arguing that to "qualify as systemic, shocks must reverberate through and threaten the financial system, not just some small part of it" (ibid., 3). Here, a crisis is misleadingly labeled as *systemic* if it affects large parts of the financial system. In a European Central Bank working paper, De Bandt and Hartmann anticipated the events of 2008; focusing on the risk resulting from TBTF institutions, they defined systemic risk as the risk that a systemic event triggers an initial shock, leading to the failure of one or more institutions, "although they have been fundamentally solvent ex ante, or if the market(s) affected in later rounds also crash and would not have done so without the initial shock" (De Bandt and Hartmann 2000, 10). In view of these systemic risk assessments, it would be outright wrong to say that the relevant policymakers and supervisors were not aware of systemic risk. Against the background of the financial crises in Russia, East Asia and Brazil, they drew a picture that came quite close to what happened in 2007ff.. The issue even made it, as Tsingou puts it, "onto the front pages of newspapers" (Tsingou 2007). However, policymakers obviously underestimated the depth and breadth of a truly systemic financial crisis on the one hand and its impact on the political system on the other. Reinhart and Rogoff (2009) explain this underestimation of risks with a *this time is different* bias: Policymakers believed that financial innovation – mostly in the area of securitization – had made the financial system significantly safer. As Reinhart and Rogoff indicate, financial crises are typically preceded by a wrong sense of security, both within the market and at the side of policymakers and supervisors. This was certainly the case in the lead-up to the crisis of 2007ff.. Even more importantly, policymakers and regulators saw that fundamental changes were underway, but did not take into account how they increased systemic risk.

The financial crisis of 2007ff. led to a re-definition of systemic risk. Accounting for the depth and breadth of the recent crisis, the International Risk Governance Council (IRGC) determined that

> systemic risks typically span *more than one country* and *more than one sector* of the economy. They are *not under the control* of any one organization, but affect and must be addressed by many stakeholders at once. [...] Systemic risks may be relatively low in frequency, but they have broad ramifications for human health, safety and security, the environment, economic well-being and the fabric of societies. (International Risk Governance Council 2010, 9)

As claimed by the IRGC, systemic crises – in the area of finance, but also in other areas such as health or infrastructure – do not only affect the broader economy: They affect society as a whole. As such, systemic crises require political intervention. As we could well observe in 2008, in systemic financial crises governments enter the stage shortly after the financial drama unfolds to rescue the economy in a *deus ex machina* manner. They step in to avert that "the failure of a particular quantum of institutions will result in a socially unacceptable macroeconomic contraction" (Levitin 2011, 446). According to Levitin, a systemic crisis not only affects the whole system – as the Group of Thirty definition says – in fact, it is "the risk of socially unbearable macroeconomic consequences of micro-economic failures" (ibid.) that characterizes a systemic crisis. As Levitin's definition reflects, and as we will discuss in the following subsections, the financial crisis of 2007ff. forcefully demonstrated that there is a *political and societal aspect to systemic risk* (Willke, Becker, and Rostásy 2013).

2.2.1 A Systems Theory Perspective on Systemic Risk

Since the onset of the financial crisis, the number of scientific contributions dealing with systemic risk has skyrocketed. While there was only limited literature on systemic risk in political science up to 2008, finance and economics had started to deal increasingly with the subject in the 1990s (Greenspan 1995, 1). In finance research, *systematic* or *systemic risk* traditionally refers to undiversifiable risk, market risk or aggregated risk (Dichev 1998; Hansen 2013).[39] Against this background, it is clear why – when the financial crisis hit and quickly spread from the United States to Europe – some observers spoke of systematic risk and some of systemic risk, resulting in a "great deal of confusion about what types of risk are truly 'systemic'" (Schwarcz 2008, 196). While we gladly leave it to finance scholars to discuss adequate definitions of systematic risk, we argue that the debate about systemic risk should take into account basic findings from systems theory: Systemic risk encompasses more than *threatening the whole financial system*, or *system-wide*, meaning that "it involved the entire financial system in the Unites States, and in Europe, not so much in Asia, but in the United States" (Interview with Peter J. Wallison, December 04, 2012, Washington). As we argue, it instead refers to the risks that result from the normal, yet dangerous operational mode of a complex and tightly coupled system.

39 To name just a few papers: In 1972, Hamada discussed the effect of a firm's capital structure on the systematic risk of common stocks. Twelve years later, Mandelker and Rhee evaluated the impact of leverage on the systematic risk of common stock (1984); and in the late 1990s, Dichev (1998) asked in an article in the Journal of Finance whether the risk of bankruptcy was a systematic risk. Hansen defines systematic risks as "macroeconomic or aggregate risks that cannot be avoided through diversification" (Hansen 2013, 4).

To illustrate its basic dynamics, academics and policymakers have compared the financial crisis of 2007ff. to natural disasters, epidemics, and technical breakdowns. Haldane, for example, makes such a comparison between the crisis and the SARS epidemic in China in 2002 (Haldane 2009).[40] Palmer and Maher draw on Perrow's *Normal Accident Theory* to explain the crisis (Palmer and Maher 2010; Perrow, in his case study, examined an accident at the US nuclear power station Three Mile Island, see Perrow 1984).[41] What the breakdown at Three Mile Island, SARS and the financial crisis have in common is that they occurred in complex systems that exist in various contexts, including biologic, ecologic, social, engineered and geopolitical contexts (International Risk Governance Council 2010). As we will discuss in greater detail on the following pages, ecologic and economic systems have in common that they are "by nature unpredictable accumulations of effects, breachings of threshold values, suddenly occurring irreversibilities, and uncontrollable disasters" (Luhmann 2008, 186). Put simply, complex systems consist of parts interacting in a non-simple way and are characterized by the fact that their whole is more than the sum of their parts (Simon 1962, 468). Microprudential supervision, which focuses on the safety and soundness of individual banks, is therefore unable to draw a reliable picture of the state of a system.

Complex systems are constituted by a large number of autonomous, interacting actors and therefore difficult, if not impossible, to govern. While these interacting actors are mutually coupled and adaptive towards each other, their interactions are usually non-linear (Helbing 2010; Schwarcz 2009). *Non-linearity* in the context of complex systems means that simple cause-effect relationships do not exist (International Risk Governance Council 2010, 14). Complex systems can be distinguished from linear systems due to (1) their *higher number of interconnections*, (2) their *types of connections* (common mode relationships, branching relationships, and feedback loops), and (3) the degree to which these relationships and interactions are *comprehensible and predictable* by the people who operate them (Palmer and Maher 2010, 222f.; Senge 1996).[42] Palmer and Maher argue that, other than loosely coupled systems, tightly coupled systems such as the current financial system are characterized by a low degree of *resilience*: First, their performance standards tend to be high – meaning that if standards are not met, the system fails completely instead of performing at an inferior rate. Second,

40 SARS stands for Severe Acute Respiratory Syndrome.

41 Perrow himself argues that the financial crisis was not a natural accident but rooted, in line with the behavioral narratives at the beginning of this chapter, in human misconduct (Perrow 2010).

42 We can conclude that the financial system has evolved from a linear to a complex system as it became increasingly interconnected, and as securitization and financial integration changed the nature of financial connections within the system. Financial system complexity – including the complexity of products and financial institutions – will be discussed at-length in chapter three.

design requirements are rigid: "If unexpected contingencies arise, there is little opportunity to modify the system's design" (Palmer and Maher 2010, 226). Third, tightly coupled systems have a low degree of redundancy, meaning that the entire system fails if a part of it fails. And fourth, when a certain tipping point is reached, the system unwinds "quickly and inexorably" (ibid.), leaving operators with no opportunity to intervene (Bookstaber 2007). These characteristics of complex systems lead to what Eigen and Winkler term "irreversible 'once-and-for-all' decisions" (Eigen and Winkler 1981, 229). As already indicated, such complex systems are *robust yet fragile.*

The 21st century financial system is also characterized by its high degree of *reciprocity* – meaning that traders and investors base their decisions on their observations of other traders' and investors' observations (Knorr-Cetina and Bruegger 2002, 925ff.). In such an environment, "investors make their investment decisions by anticipating what other investors will do" (Schwarcz 2009, 234).The interactions between the system elements, and again this is especially the case in the financial system, "need not be direct or physical; they can involve sharing of information, or even be indirect" (OECD Global Science Forum 2009, 6). As we saw during 2008, financial institutions do not need to be directly linked via contracts to interact. Distrust and rumors proved to be sufficient to bring financial intermediation to a halt, and they exacerbated the self-reinforcing dynamics that are a central feature of all complex systems. *Emergence* is another important feature of complex systems (Willke, Becker, and Rostásy 2013, ch. 2.1.1). Emergent properties are novel patterns that cannot be explained by the characteristics of the system elements, but only by their interaction (OECD Global Science Forum 2009, 6). As a result of such properties, complex systems evolve in dynamic, probabilistic and non-predictable ways (Helbing 2010, 3; see also Hayek 2007 [1967]). Extreme events, termed fat-tail events or *Black Swans*, occur much more frequently in complex systems than a normal distribution would indicate (Taleb 2007). Systems thinking teaches us that breakdowns of complex systems, including the financial system, are in fact not only likely – instead, "the completely normal, regular operational mode of the system, as it is, can lead to the self-destruction of the system" (Willke, Becker, and Rostásy 2013, 15). While endogenous and exogenous events bear the potential to trigger systemic financial crises, one should be aware that – as the OFR emphasizes – "even absent external shocks, financial activity can generate threats to financial stability" (Office of Financial Research 2012a, 2). Systemic crises will accordingly happen again, and financial governance will not be able to prevent them. When Greenspan defined systemic risk as "some sort of significant financial system disruption", he added that "one observer might use the term 'market failure' to describe what another would deem to have been a market outcome that was natural" (Greenspan 1995, 7). Even though the argument was made in a different context, it holds true from a systems theory perspective. In complex systems, small changes might have a strong effect, while major changes might have no effects (Helbing 2010, 9). *Fat finger errors* provide a good example here. They are defined as "a typographical error supposedly caused by hitting the wrong key, or by making mistakes when inputting a quantity into a computer" (Financial Times 2013). The initial error might be small – adding an additional zero to a number – but the consequences can be enormous. A fat finger error at the Japanese brokering firm Mizuho Securities in 2005 triggered chaos at the Tokyo Stock Exchange, as an "unnamed and, presumably, shortly to be unemployed broker managed to sell shares worth £1.6bn in a local recruitment agency which, itself, carried only a market value of little more than £50m" (McCurry 2005). The trader had intended to sell one share at 610,000 yen, when he accidentally sold 610,000 shares at one yen a piece, loosing more than 200 million US dollars (Miller 2006). With the rise of automated and high-frequency trading, such fat finger errors have become a very serious problem. Supported by algorithms, traders have fewer opportunities to make mistakes – yet *the few mistakes they make have a much greater impact*. Automatic trades executed by computers at huge volumes and at very high speed add to the complexity of the trades; when a fat finger error occurs in this environment, it triggers erroneous trades that cascade through the system and trigger other erroneous trades until they are finally stopped.

But complex systems do not need external triggers to break down. A software-update at Knight Capital Group, which was one of the largest HFT companies in the US before it collapsed in 2012, triggered what is now known as the *Knightmare*: In August 2012, one of Knight's trading algorithms started to sell at low and buy at high prices both at large volume and high speed, effectively loosing the difference in price (Philips 2012). What had happened? As it is impossible to simulate complex systems, new algorithms cannot be tested under real conditions.[43] When operating in such systems, they may interact with other algorithms in ways that cannot be predicted. As the SEC found out, Knight Capital had forgotten to delete or deactivate an older algorithm from its trading software several years ago; then, one of the company's technicians failed to copy a new algorithm on one of the company's servers in 2012 (Securities and Exchange Commission 2013a). A few days later, Knight received orders that activated the older algorithm on the single server which lacked the new algorithm and that server began to execute false orders at high speed. Knight lost more than 450 million US dollars in 45 minutes, and was quickly sold before it could collapse. According to the SEC's Gregg Berman, high-frequency trading has blurred the distinction between fat finger errors and events caused by dysfunctional software. Addressing both, exchanges and brokers have installed what Berman terms "kill switches" – firewalls or automated trading stops

43 As Weber states, "no marriage of economics, computer science, and physics is anywhere close to being able to create a complete model of real financial markets" (Weber 2012, 691).

that reduce the damage resulting from trading errors (Berman 2013). Yet, they have not managed to prevent them completely.

What distinguishes the financial system from other complex systems is the impact of behavior that is specifically human – including fear and panic, reciprocity and information-driven shifts – making the system even harder to predict and more difficult to govern. Allan Mendelowitz, who is a member of the group of financial experts that has successfully lobbied Congress to establish the Office of Financial Research – CE-NIF – identifies major overlaps between weather forecasting on the one hand and financial market supervision on the other.[44] According to Mendelowitz, the unpredictability of the financial system roots in a lack of granulated financial data, just as it has been the case with weather forecasts in the past.

> When I was a child broadcast news and newspapers always included weather forecasts. However, everybody used to joke about how the forecasts were worthless because their predictions were rarely correct. Today, when you look at weather forecasting the situation has been transformed, you find incredibly good forecasts. Why do we now have such good forecasts? Over the past 50 years the science of weather forecasting has changed dramatically. Weather forecasters have created algorithmic models of weather patterns that surround the earth and these models are fed with a constant and massive stream of data from airborne sensors, satellite observations, and ground station monitoring equipment from all over the globe. (Interview with Allan Mendelowitz, December 03, 2012, Washington)[45]

Mendelowitz envisions a financial market where much more data are collected and aggregated by a central federal agency, and where these aggregated data provide regulators with a reliable *financial market forecast*. And there is a certain truth to his argument: Weather data have indeed become much more accurate and broad over the last decades, while financial market data were, at least up to and during the financial crisis, of low quality and reach.[46] However, even high-quality weather forecasts do not enable meteorologists to improve the weather, and it is highly unlikely that financial market data will enable policymakers and regulators to prevent systemic crises. Besides, economic systems are shaped by humans – while

44 CE-NIF stands for Committee to Establish the National Institute of Finance. The group of financial experts lobbied Senator Jack Reed to include the OFR in Dodd-Frank and was ultimately successful (Interview with Allan Mendelowitz, December 03, 2012, Washington).

45 Minor amendments were made by the interviewee to the quotes presented in the book. The original arguments being made were fully maintained.

46 In the 1960s, six percent of the forecasts in Germany deviated more than five degrees Celsius from the actual temperature. In the 1990s, this number had shrunk to 0.6 percent (Deutscher Wetterdienst 2009).

winds and clouds do not care about rumors, financial markets do. A financial crisis warning, contrary to a storm warning, might well emerge into a self-fulfilling prophecy. The OFR researchers are well aware of these problems: "In an ideal world", they argue, "systemic monitoring would work like the National Weather Service, providing sufficiently advance notice of hurricanes for authorities and participants to intervene by pre-positioning staff and resources, minimizing exposures, and planning for the impending event and immediate aftermath" – yet, they conclude that it "may be too much to hope for in the case of financial stability" (Bisias et al. 2012, 21).

2.2.2 A Politico-Economic Approach to Systemic Risk

According to a joint publication by the IMF, the BIS and the FSB, a systemic crisis is "(i) caused by an impairment of all or parts of the financial system; and (ii) has the potential to have serious negative consequences for the real economy" (International Monetary Fund, Bank for International Settlements, and Financial Stability Board 2009, 5f.). Like most definitions, these institutions describe systemic crises and systemic risk as financial and economic phenomena, and accordingly invite us to assess systemic risk in numeric terms. The OFR, which is at the forefront of systemic risk analytics, argues along similar lines. In a recently published paper, OFR researchers conclude that to identify and address systemic risk, supervisors and regulators need the respective data and models: "The starting point for all of these directives is the accurate and timely measurement of systemic risk. The truism that 'one cannot manage what one does not measure' is especially compelling for financial stability" (Bisias et al. 2012, 1). Gai, in a paper published after the OFR survey, classifies episodes as systemic crises where *more than five percent of the system default* (Gai 2013, 21), or where a minimum of *ten percent of the banking system engages in hoarding*, meaning that the banks stop their lending activities on the interbank market (ibid., 39).

Such quantitative approaches are convincing in their basic simplicity. In view of the binary model of systemic risk introduced in chapter one, the idea that a systemic crisis alarm goes off at the US Treasury when ten percent of the banking system engage in hording, or when a financial institution with a defined number of counterparties threatens to fail, and then – and only then – the government steps in to rescue the economy, is compelling. And yet two factors make this scenario highly unlikely. The first lies in the *difficulty of defining specific yet comprehensive indicators* of systemic risk. Anabtawi and Schwarcz define systemic risk as "the risk that a localized adverse shock, such as the collapse of a firm or market, will have repercussions that negatively impact the broader economy" (Anabtawi and Schwarcz 2011, 2). We then have to ask when to speak of a negative impact on the broader economy, and whether the trigger could be any firm or any market or if it must have a certain size.[47] Gai's model therefore includes a specific quantitative assumption to differentiate between non-systemic and systemic financial crises (Gai 2013). Yet, when we get to systemic risk measurements, systems thinking teaches us that in complex systems, minor changes might have huge effects, while major changes might have no or small effects, increasing the likelihood of both false-positive and false-negative alarms. Countless, non-linear financial actors interact in unpredictable ways and the system's emergent properties make it impossible to extrapolate future from past sources of systemic risk. Taleb accordingly argues that such risks – tail risks as he terms them – cannot be measured: "the rarer the event, the harder it is to compute its probability – yet the rarer the event, the larger the consequences" (Taleb 2012b, 2). The second, widely underestimated difficulty lies in the *nature of the decision*: When the US Treasury steps in to save a failing institution or sector, it *ultimately follows a political, not an economic rationale.* How else are we able to explain that the US government rescued the small investment bank Bear Stearns, but did not rescue the much bigger investment bank Lehman Brothers?[48] Besides, we have to keep in mind that the US government not only acted to lessen the severity of the financial crisis, but also accepted partial responsibility for contributing to systemic risk. Today, it is widely agreed that "there was market failure, but there was also government failure" (Stiglitz 2009b, 17; see also Barofsky 2013), both before and throughout the crisis. For obvious reasons, politics are difficult to include in systemic risk models. And yet, in their *Survey of Systemic Risk Analytics,* Bisias and his OFR colleagues provide an overview over 31 quantitative systemic risk measures (Bisias et al. 2012). However, even though they clearly see systemic risk as an economic phenomenon, the OFR researchers come to the conclusion that – given the complexity and dimensionality of the phenomenon, as well as the constant changes induced by what they term *political, institutional and cultural* factors – the OFR is "unlikely to ever develop a single measure of systemic risk; [...] multiple measures must be used to piece together a coherent, albeit incomplete, view of possible threats to financial stability" (ibid., 28).

The events of 2007 and 2008 do indeed indicate that political and societal arguments play a major role in government responses to a financial crisis. As their impact is not only difficult, but rather impossible to model, the explanatory power of merely economic definitions and models of systemic risk must be limited. Levitin therefore argues that

47 Looking at Rheinhart and Rogoff's (2009) comparative analysis of financial crises, one can conclude that their work is merely definitional: Global financial crises, especially as opposed to regional financial crises, are not given, but have to be defined as such. What appears to be objective is in fact ridden with prerequisites. Besides, systemic risk appears to be difficult to model in quantitative terms – Hansen provides an overview of the challenges to quantitative systemic risk modeling from an econometric viewpoint (Hansen 2013).

48 As we show in the following chapter, the US government provided a different explanation.

> systemic risk is not quantifiable in economic terms. In some circumstances, a 1% increase in the cost of capital or unemployment might be a sufficient macroeconomic impact to make an individual firm's failure pose a systemic risk; in other situations, the threshold might be a 10% increase. While systemic risk is about individual firms' failure having broader economic consequences, what makes such consequences systemic or not is ultimately *a valuation driven by social norms and political culture*. Systemic risk is ultimately *a political, rather than an economic, matter*. (Levitin 2011, 451, emphasis added; see also Clark and Large 2011, 41f.)

In view of the shortcomings of a merely economic framework, it is important to look at both approaches to systemic risk – the economic and the political – to finally integrate them into a comprehensive, politico-economic concept that takes into account not only the global nature of systemic risk, the political and economic developments contributing to it, but also its consequences for society.[49] Here, Levitin's argument is crucial, as it takes into account the role of the government in systemic financial crises, as well as its societal dimension. We cannot say whether Bear Stearns, AIG and the GSEs were truly systemic; but the US government decided that they were. Policymaking and regulation therefore did not only set the stage for the crisis; rather they are at the heart of systemic risk.

In an interview, President George W. Bush described his decision to support the AIG and GSEs' bailouts. He put the crucial events of September 2008 into the broader historical context that shaped the crisis perception of economic policymakers in the US and Europe (see Pauly 2009); his account also illustrates the political logic of systemic risk:

> I was in the Roosevelt Room and Chairman Bernanke and Secretary Paulson, after a month of every weekend where they're calling, saying, we got to do this for AIG, or this for Fannie and Freddie, came in and said, the financial markets are completely frozen and if we don't do something about it, it is conceivable we will see a depression greater than the Great Depression. So I analyzed that and *decided I didn't want to be the President during a depression greater than the Great Depression*, or the beginning of a

49 Interestingly, even scholars who admit that the crisis had its root in policymaking argue that systemic risk is, in its core, an economic phenomenon. In one of our interviews, Acharya argued exemplarily: "I would say in the end it's an economic phenomenon [...]. But it could be caused by political processes. So there have been historical crises that probably were not always deeply rooted in political failures or regulating failures. But there have been many crises also where it is the case that, you know, governments have asked financial sectors to do more, to try to stimulate housing at all costs. So, I would say very often political problems are sufficient to cause a systemic crisis. [...]. But it's not a necessary condition, I think it would easily get a financial crisis that is probably not rooted in any political failures" (Interview with Viral Acharya, November 28, 2012 New York).

> depression greater than the Great Depression. (Bush 2008, emphasis added)[50]

After the AIG and GSEs' rescues, the team of government officials around US Secretary of the Treasury Hank Paulson hoped that Congress would be willing to support the 700 billion US dollar Troubled Asset Relief Program (TARP). As we will discuss in greater detail in chapter four, the political mood that prevailed before Lehman collapsed had been quite different: Back then, against the background of the Bear Stearns rescue, the government felt it could not step in and rescue another investment bank, even though it must be assumed that it knew about the potential ramifications resulting from a Lehman bankruptcy (McDade 2010). In the binary model of systemic risk that we introduced at the beginning of this book, we distinguished between the political and economic costs of a systemic financial crisis. As we see now, another distinction has to be made between the economic and political arguments for and against a government intervention.

This brings us back to the question of whether governments actually have a choice to either rescue a failing SIFI or not, the latter implying that they are essentially highjacked by TBTF institutions. The analysis so far indicates that every systemic crisis is declared political at one point in time. The following quotes support this argument:

> It's hard for me to imagine any government in place [...] that would have been able to say: ok, there is this crisis happening, but it's not the business of politics. (Interview with Philip Wallach, December 04, 2012, Washington)

> Now, of course, when you have a systemic crisis inevitably you constantly need to backstop the system in some form or the other. Backstopping the system requires a fiscal coordinator for that. And so it inevitably becomes some political issue, becomes relevant at that point. (Interview with Viral Acharya, November 28, 2012, New York)

> I went home that night [after voting for the TARP rescue program, EB] and my wife told me she had never before seen me quite look that way, just in

50 In his interview with the FCIC, Taylor challenges this fear of a second Great Depression. He argues that there is no "credible story that we would have had a Great Depression without the interventions. I just don't see that at all. [...] One of the things I found most of concern in terms of public policy is [...] the kind of behind-closed-doors discussion about Great Depression [...] that, you know, the run up to the hill and saying that 'If you don't do this, it's going to be Armageddon and we'll have riots in the streets and whatever was said, I think without people knowing about it. I remember at that time various politicians, Senators asking me 'What do you think about this claim that there is Armageddon?' – and I said 'I don't know, no one said that to me, where are you getting that from?'" (Taylor 2010). This strengthens our argument that policymakers and regulators just did not know or understand what was happening, and in accordance with the model presented in chapter one, they felt they had to rescue most institutions.

> terms of how overwhelming and scary it was […]. Often when facing such a difficult moment, I will, just for myself, I won't usually share it, write down 'why vote for this', 'why not vote for this', and I remember at the top of it I wrote 'the best vote I've ever cast, and the worst vote I've ever cast'. You just knew you had to do it. (Brown 2013)

The described political logic of systemic risk is a largely underestimated factor. The US government was ultimately able to contain the crisis, but we have to keep in mind that some states with particularly large banking sectors in relation to GDP would not have weathered the financial crisis if they had not received the support of the IMF and the EU – among them Ireland and Iceland. Systemic financial crises challenge the sovereignty of the nation states, as they reveal a fundamental incongruence between global SIFIs on the one hand, and nationally limited policy options on the other. Confronted with systemic risks, nation states "fall prey to the fallacy of sovereignty", being "semi-sovereign at best" (Willke, Becker, and Rostásy 2013, 44; see also Streeck 2013, 20f.).

Based on Luhmann's argument that politics is "a self-referentially closed system, and whatever it declares to be political is thereby political" (Luhmann 2008, 160f.), we argue that the crisis became a political issue the moment the US government bailed out Bear Stearns. Conversely this means that a crisis might be defined as systemic for political reasons, but in fact be a minor financial or economic crisis. Looking at the bailouts that took place in other industries and countries over the last decades, one might very well ask whether those rescues addressed mere liquidity problems, or followed a political rationale.[51]

With regard to the role of the US government in causing the crisis, Robert Jenkins – member of the Financial Policy Committee of the Bank of England – made an interesting observation:

> I have not heard many bankers accept blame for the crisis but quite a few within the regulatory ranks have acknowledged their failings. But for avoidance of doubt, let me say it here and now: the regulatory establishment blew it! We messed up in two ways: first we misjudged the breadth and depth of the risks that many banks were running. Second, we misjudged bankers' ability to judge and manage those risks. […] How could we have been so dumb as to believe that bankers were so smart? Both groups belong to the human race and the human race is hubris hungry and error prone. (R. Jenkins 2012, 4f.)

We should keep his second argument in mind when we get to the issue of data, information, and knowledge asymmetries and the resulting policy implications. For

51 In October 2009, the German Financial Times reported that FC Schalke 04, a German football club, would be bailed out by its hometown Gelsenkirchen because it was systemically relevant for the region; Cyprus was deemed to be systemically relevant for the Euro zone. Many more examples could be found.

now, we stay with the question implicitly raised by Jenkins whether both regulators and regulatees should take responsibility for the crisis. Interestingly, the point is not whether Wall Street and the City of London had their part in causing the crisis – as we will see in chapter three, financial institutions deliberately increased financial complexity in order to circumvent regulation – it is whether one can blame financial institutions, or their employees, for not anticipating or mitigating the crisis.[52] The US government and the Federal Reserve Bank are in a fundamentally different position: They are responsible for *social welfare* and *financial stability* respectively, and evaluated against their mandates, they failed. As Andreas Lehnert of the Federal Reserve Board put it in one of our interviews, "an interesting and novel definition of a systemic crisis would be one that sort of puts in jeopardy the credibility of the existing regulatory regime" (Interview with Andreas Lehnert, December 05, 2012, Washington).

2.2.3 A Short Excursus on the LTCM Rescue of 1998

Even though the FSOC designates systemically important institutions, it is difficult to safely conclude or preclude the systemic relevance of a financial institution before its litmus test, which is its actual breakdown. As we will discuss in greater detail in chapter four, the Council has developed a set of criteria to determine the systemic relevance of a financial institution and designated a first set of nonbank financial companies and financial market utilities as systemically important. These institutions are assumed to present a threat to the stability of the US financial system when failing.

Apparently, bailed-out Bear Stearns was not the first US financial institution that was perceived by the government as being TBTF. In 1998, the nearing collapse of the hedge fund Long-Term Capital Management L.P. (LTCM) prompted the US government to act: The New York Fed arranged a private bailout, meaning a 3.5 billion dollar recapitalization, by a consortium of banks (Spiro 1998).[53] Their direct exposure to LTCM was smaller than their share in the bailout, but the participants feared that the fund's collapse would induce much higher costs. Put differently,

52 Financial institutions have been blamed for their wrongdoings, yet the number of prosecutions fell short of people's expectations (Rakoff 2014; Barrett 2013).

53 Davidoff and Zaring have convincingly argued that to respond to the crisis of 2007ff., the US government "has been doing deals – the sorts of deals that it usually leaves to the private sector" (Davidoff and Zaring 2009, 466), a fact that they explain with the investment banking background of central government officials, including Treasury Secretary Paulson. Interestingly, deal-making also played a major role in 1998, and the government officials involved – among them Robert Rubin as US Secretary of the Treasury – were also veteran dealmakers.

public officials and market experts[54] believed that an LTCM bankruptcy would trigger a systemic crisis:

> Had the failure of LTCM triggered the seizing up of markets, substantial damage could have been inflicted on many market participants, including some not directly involved with the firm, and could have potentially impaired the economies of many nations, including our own. (Greenspan 1998)

LTCM had heavily invested in interest rate derivatives. Its collapse was triggered by the Russian financial crisis: When Russia defaulted on its external debt, the liquidity of the highly leveraged hedge fund quickly evaporated.[55] The basic mechanisms that caused the crisis of 2007ff. – pro-cyclical capital requirements and counterparty collateral calls, both resulting in an asset price downward spiral, could be well observed in 1998. In addition, the fear of an LTCM collapse froze markets where LTCM was expected to hold larger positions (MacKenzie 2005, 75). As claimed by one participant of the bailout meeting at the New York Fed, the group of central and investment bankers discussed "systemic risk issues" (Spiro 1998). Rumors spread that Lehman Brothers was in effect bankrupt (MacKenzie 2005). The Fed believed that, had the consortium not rescued LTCM, "this could have had a widespread, adverse, systemic impact on the financial system" (Born 2009). As claimed by Brooksley Born, the LTCM case was in effect a "mini-2008": It revealed the contagion risk resulting from OTC derivatives. It demonstrated the fragility of highly-leveraged institutions (ibid.), and it showed that sophisticated diversification and securitization could not eliminate market risk.[56] LTCM was renowned not only for its outstanding success, but also for its illustrious board of directors: Robert C. Merton and Myron S. Scholes, who had received the Nobel Prize in Economic Sciences in 1997 for their method to determine the value of derivatives, were both on the board. Yet, LTCM could not outsmart the market. Some have argued that an LTCM collapse would have had a self-healing effect on the financial system as "it might have been better to have experienced a milder version of a downturn in 1998 than the more severe version of 10 years later" (Cowen 2008; see also Reinert and

54 Bear Stearns was the only member oft he group that did not participate. Whether it did not expect that an LTCM collapse would trigger a systemic crisis, or whether it simply chose to free ride, cannot be said in hindsight.

55 MacKenzie argues that, even though the crisis was triggered by the Russian default, it was caused by the fact that the success of LTCM had motivated other investors to imitate the hedge fund's portfolio, a behavior that ultimately resulted in a "superportfolio" of overlapping positions: "Sales by some holders of the superportfolio moved prices against others, leading to a cascade of self-reinforcing adverse price movements" (MacKenzie 2005, 65).

56 The LTCM collapse also let to the creation of the Financial Stability Forum, the predecessor of the FSB that was established in 2010 (Black 2012, 8; cf. Moschella 2012 – other than Black, Moschella traces the creation of the FSF back to the Asian Financial Crisis).

Reinert 2006). Some even suggest that the New York Fed, when it prevented the risks related to high leverage, short-term funding, OTC derivatives and mark-to-market accounting from materializing, paved the way for a much more devastating crisis in 2007ff. (Taleb 2012a). The Mexican and the Asian financial crisis had been contained. LTCM was rescued. The market was, after all, under control.

The CFTC's Brooksley Born, who had warned her fellow regulators about the threats posed by increasingly opaque financial markets, was reaffirmed by the LTCM crisis that policymakers and regulators just did not know enough about these markets. Yet, despite the LTCM collapse, US regulators and policymakers did not feel the need to address the systemic risks resulting from interconnectedness, contagion, and complexity:

> None of us, none of the regulators had known until Long-Term Capital Management phoned the Federal Reserve Bank of New York to say they were on the verge of collapse. Why? Because we didn't have any information about the market. [...] – *So LTCM happens, and for a brief period there is this eagerness to regulate... but it very quickly evaporates. Why?* – Because everything was all right. Because all the big banks did step in and solve the problem by taking over LTCM and incurring losses themselves. But they protected the fabric of the economy. And Congress was told by the over-the-counter derivatives dealers, by some of the other regulators, that this was an anomaly, this was not indicative of dangers in the market. And I think any consideration of regulation probably came and went within a few days, because it was less than a month later that Congress passed a statute saying that the CFTC could take no regulatory action in the over-the-counter derivatives market for the next six months. (Born 2009)

What we do not know is whether the US government would have bailed out the hedge fund absent a private solution. What we can assume is that the successful deal-making attempts by the Fed did supposably shape the government response to the financial crisis of 2007ff..

2.3 Entering the Stage of 21st Century Financial Folly

Financial crises come and go. They have many faces and, like cats, they have many lives (Bhagwati 1998, 10). Crises are usually preceded by a strong belief that this time is different (Reinhart and Rogoff 2009), that skilled people with sophisticated models can outsmart the system. Then, another crisis comes and reminds us of the fragility of the financial system, opening up a window of opportunity for financial reform. Reports are written and agencies installed. But the bad memories fade away quickly and reforms have to be pushed through before "collective amnesia about the causes and consequences of the financial crisis" (Barr 2013) takes over and the window closes again (Geithner 2011). Hubris, collapse, downturn and reform could all be well observed in the context of the financial crisis of 2007ff.. The ensuing question is: Was this just another financial crisis, or was the crisis different when compared to past crises? One of our interview partners captured the debate quite well when he described how "nobody wonders if there is a difference in size. I guess the question is: Is there a difference in kind?" (Interview with Philip Wallach, December 4, 2012, Washington).

In our interviews, market experts explained how mistakes made by regulators (Interview with Viral Acharya, November 28, 2012, New York), political ideology (Interview with Allan Mendelowitz, December 03, 2012, Washington), the US housing policy (Interview with Peter J. Wallison, December 04, 2012, Washington) and complex securitization (Interview with Rainer Stollhoff, August 14, 2013, Berlin) distinguished the recent crisis from past crises. As we argued in this chapter, the various crisis narratives are still competing for the *prerogative of interpretation*. Lehnert states that systemic crises happen periodically, the last one in the US being the Great Depression, but that no such crisis "had ever happened to the set of institutions and regulators that existed in 2007. So from their experience, it was totally outside" (Interview with Andreas Lehnert, December 05, 2012, Washington). While we assume that all of these factors did play a role, and that the recent crisis was in fact outside the experience of financial regulators, we want to argue that there was a fundamental difference in kind, which was the *systemic nature* of the crisis. Again, we have to be careful to distinguish systemic from system-wide.

In 1907, a century before the start of the current financial crisis, the US banking system had stood at the brink of collapse once before. Back then a group of bankers under the lead of financier J.P. Morgan rescued the US economy. One might conclude that financial crises do not necessarily have to be solved by governments, and this is certainly true. Comparing the 1907 and 2007 crises, one can identify a number of intriguing parallels. However, following Bruner's analysis, there are three important differences between the two: *higher complexity, faster speed and greater scale*. Systemic crises exceed the capacities of private actors:

> The complexity of markets today is magnitudes higher than a century ago. We have subprime loans that even the experts aren't sure how to value. We have trading positions [...] which the exposure is not clear. And we have the institutions themselves that are so complicated that it's hard to tell who among them is solvent and who is failing. (Bruner 2008; see also Markowitz 2010)

During the recent crisis, the US government stepped in as a lender of last resort. This time, no private player was in the position to stop the contagion. The financial crisis of 2007ff. demonstrated that "someone has to be in a position to bail out troubled banks that have the potential to destabilize entire markets" (Pauly 2009,

958). When a financial institution threatens to fail, and its government decides that the institution is systemically important – meaning that a default would have *socially unbearable consequences* – the government steps in and arranges a rescue. According to Levitin, systemic risk is a political phenomenon because it is ultimately about the *allocation of losses.* Whether the government acts as a *dealmaker*, as it was the case when LTCM collapsed in 1998, or as *lender of last resort*, depends on the nature of the systemic event, as well as on the willingness and ability of other private actors to support a fellow institution. What is central is that whenever the government decides to bail the failing institution out, it is the taxpayer who bears the losses.[57] Therefore, systemic risk has to ultimately be perceived in political and societal terms. As emphasized by Willke et al., "there is no systemic crisis as long as the political system does not perceive and define a given situation as *politically* unbearable because the social impact of the crisis cannot be accepted *politically*" (Willke, Becker, and Rostásy 2013, 94f.). With TBTF looming large, the *resolution of systemically important institutions* must be the starting point for a comprehensive concept of systemic risk, and we will further discuss it in the following chapter. As Lehnert emphasizes, there are two types of crises, and the financial crisis of 2007ff. clearly falls into the second category. The first group includes crises that are manageable because regulators have formally or informally planned for them; the second group comprises crises "that simply by the nature of the things that happen in the crisis call into question the legitimacy of the entire regulatory apparatus as it exists" (Interview with Andreas Lehnert, December 05, 2012, Washington). In 2008, the failure of a systemically important institution was an incident not formally planned for. In the US, the crisis clearly called into question the legitimacy of the US Office of Thrift Supervision (OTS). It had had disproportionate close ties to its regulatees and was abolished in 2011. Other bodies, among them the US Treasury via the FSOC and the OFR, were able to expand their mandates. The US government was ultimately able to contain the crisis, yet the European crisis lingers on, with uncertain consequences for political cohesion and legitimacy.

The major challenge is that the next crisis will most likely differ from the last one. Janet L. Yellen, in her interview with the FCIC, expressed her fear that regulators might not be able to prevent another global crisis.

> I am hopeful we can do a better job. I feel it's critically important to try to ramp up what we do. You know, the next financial crisis will be something completely different. And will we have the ability to spot it? And of course there is always an incentive for the dangerous activity to migrate into some new spot that is not where we're looking. This is really hard. I believe we are

57 Rheinhart and Rogoff show that the bailout itself is not that costly; it is the subsequent economic downturn that leads to massive increases in public debt (Rheinhart and Rogoff 2009).

> highly motivated to do a better job. Not to let anything like this happen again. (Yellen 2010)

The financial system evolves at rapid pace, and the risks it poses apparently evolve in tandem. Its continuing transformation to a global, complex, tightly coupled system did not go unnoticed. In 1995, Robert Merton described "revolutionary changes in the structure of the world's financial markets and institutions and in our understanding of how to use them to provide new investment opportunities and ways of managing risk" (Merton 1995, 462). A perceived need for better macroprudential supervision led to the establishment of the FSF. Brooksley Born, reassured by the collapse of LTCM, called for better data and information on the largely unknown OTC derivatives market (Born 2009). But the FSF was considered largely ineffective, and Born's warnings were incompatible with the common thinking of the time. Among the problems revealed by the crisis of 2007ff., the *common thinking among policymaking and market elites* is most central (Shiller 2010). In hindsight, it is difficult to believe that doubts were expressed but largely ignored (Tett 2010; D. Baker 2010). As Willke and Willke emphasize, the incomprehensibility of the financial system is "less dangerous when actors understand their inability to (fully) understand [...] complex systems. It is most dangerous when people, in particular professionals, disregard their ignorance and feel certain about the systems they are dealing with" (Willke and Willke 2012, 48f.).

What else can we learn? Distinguishing between the behavioral and the systemic narratives of the crisis, and focusing on the latter, is crucial. Regulators cannot possibly eliminate all triggers, and as long as the structural weaknesses of the system remain, we are continually on the verge of another systemic crisis. The crisis also demonstrated that policymakers and regulators provided the soil for systemic risks to grow "by allowing – even encouraging – the system to become more complex and tightly coupled" (Guillén and Suárez 2010, 267; see also Admati and Hellwig 2013).[58] As we will see in the following chapter, financial complexity increased at high speed and on various levels.

58 Willke et al. provide a long (but non-exhaustive) list of the government decisions that increased financial complexity, providing the ground for the crisis. It includes the decision by the US government to replace the Glass-Steagall Act with the Gramm-Leach-Bliley Act in 1999, to repeal the uptick-rule from 1938 which had forbidden certain types of short selling, the decision not to regulate the shadow banking system, including certain derivatives and for instance the money market fund industry, as well as the decision not to monitor and clear over-the-counter derivatives (Willke, Becker, and Rostásy 2013, ch. 4.2).

3 Multi-Level Complexity: The 21st Century Financial System

"Modern finance is complex, perhaps too complex. Regulation of modern finance is complex, almost certainly too complex. That configuration spells trouble."
(Haldane and Madouros 2012, 19)

It has been argued that complexity presents the "greatest financial-market challenge of the future" (Schwarcz 2009, 213). When Alan Greenspan admitted that 21st century markets had become too complex to understand – not only for lay people, but also for financial experts – he made one of the most intriguing statements with regard to the financial crisis:

> I've got some fairly heavy background in mathematics [...], [b]ut some of the complexities of some of the instruments that were going into CDOs bewilders me. [...] And I figured out that if I didn't understand it and I had access to a couple hundred PhDs, how the rest of the world is going to understand it sort of bewildered me. (Greenspan as quoted in Sorkin 2010, 90)

The FCIC interviews with GSE employees give the impression that people in central positions did not comprehend their business (see for example Bisenius 2010; Maheras 2010). In his interview with the FCIC, the renowned hedge-fund manager David Einhorn convincingly argues that the Lehman top management did not understand the trades on its books, and the risks they implied (Einhorn 2010). This brings us to yet another narrative of the financial crisis left out in the preceding chapter: The narrative of the US crisis as a crisis of regulatory data, information, and knowledge. Flood et al. describe how

> [t]he recent financial collapse has laid bare the inadequacies of the information infrastructure supporting the US financial system. Technical challenges around large-scale data systems interact with significant economic forces involving innovation, transparency, confidentiality, complexity, and organizational change, to create a [...] problem. (Flood et al. 2010, 1)

While it is widely agreed that complexity set the stage for the financial crisis, "the character of this complexity, its systemic properties, and whether it should be eliminated or built upon, remains far less clear" (Porter 2009, 5; see also Cetorelli, McAndrews, and Traina 2014). To start with, complexity is often confused with complicatedness – yet, as illustrated in chapter two, "complex markets are not only complicated; they are also characterized by uncertainty and unpredictability that call into question the continued viability of public regulatory control over market activities" (Weber 2012, 665). Besides, it is often overlooked that complexity has increased on different levels of finance: Financial complexity roots in the system characteristics of 21st century finance, but it also originates from too big to fail institutions, as well as from financial products that are overly complex (see Stiglitz 2009b, 15). In chapter three, we therefore provide a three-level-structure to examine financial complexity, looking at systemic complexity (*macro-level complexity*, section 3.1), at organizational complexity (*meso-level complexity*, section 3.2) and at the level of the financial product (*micro-level complexity*, section 3.3). As we will see, they are closely intertwined – yet, they require different policy responses, and should therefore be distinguished. Our framework does not take into account a forth type of complexity brought forward by Haldane and Madouros: With their seminal text *The Dog and the Frisbee*, the authors have fuelled the debate about *regulatory complexity* in the area of financial regulation (Haldane and Madouros 2012). It will accompany us throughout chapters three and four. Towards the end of the third chapter, we get to the question whether financial innovation has actually become a strategy by financial institutions to circumvent regulation and oversight (section 3.4). This brings us to the question of whether financial complexity should, in the words of Tony Porter, *be eliminated or built upon* (section 3.5).

The current policy debate goes into two directions: As we illustrate on the following pages, a growing number of business insiders, academics and policy-makers – among them Andrew Haldane from the Bank of England, former FDIC chair Sheila Bair, and Phil Angelides, Co-Chair of the FCIC – argue that the complexity of financial institutions should be reduced markedly, eventually by breaking up the biggest institutions (Bair 2012b; Haldane 2012; Angelides 2012). Others believe that establishing a size cap for financial institutions is either not necessary or not sufficient to prevent systemic crises (Krugman 2010; John Walsh, former Comptroller of the Currency, has argued that banks did not manipulate the Libor index because of their size but for other reasons, see Rehm 2012; Lawrence Summers and Timothy Geithner have also strongly opposed a size limit for banks, see Wilmarth 2013, 1425). Asked whether TBTF financial institutions should be broken up, former US Secretary of the Treasury Robert Rubin countered that:

> Too big to fail isn't a problem with the system. It is the system. You can't be a competitive global financial institution serving global corporations of scale without having a certain scale yourself. The bigger multinationals get, the bigger financial institutions will have to get. (Wilmarth 2013, 1426, quoting Robert Rubin as quoted in Rothkopf 2012, 266)

Is the growth of financial institutions an irreversible trend? As we will see, bank size is only one of several critical issues, among them interconnectedness and contagion. Returning to the systemic narrative once again, and looking at it "through the lens of complexity theory, the operational challenge to financial regulation emerges in full relief" (Weber 2012, 648).

3.1 Interconnectedness and Contagion: Complexity at the Systems Level

We already discussed the issue of financial system complexity when examining systemic risk in the second chapter. As we argued, the 21st century financial system is *complex as opposed to merely complicated* (Weber 2012): Non-linear, reciprocal actors interact in unpredictable ways; small changes can have huge effects, while large changes might have no effects; the system is robust yet fragile – exogenous triggers and system-internal developments can result in a breakdown of the entire system. Two aspects, interconnectedness and contagion, require further examination. They are often referred to as features of the financial system, even though strictly speaking only interconnectedness presents a feature, and contagion can be a consequence of interconnectedness as well as of financial product complexity (Schwarcz 2009). It is widely agreed that increased interconnectedness was a major contributing factor in the recent financial crisis (cf. interview with Peter J. Wallison, December 04, 2012, Washington; Scott 2012). In an interconnected financial system, contagion can occur either directly via contractual relationships between financial institutions – banks, insurances, hedge funds or clearing houses, for example – or indirectly, independent of the system's degree of interconnectedness. As we will see on the following pages, this distinction is crucial.

As Gai et al. argue, financial system complexity is, just as systemic risk, neither easy to quantify and measure nor easy to define; what can be said is that "it will be increased by *intra-financial system activity*" (Gai, Haldane, and Kapadia 2011, 17, emphasis added): Direct and indirect links between the nodes in the financial network form an "intricate web of claims and obligations" (Gai and Kapadia 2010, 2401), and each link adds to financial system complexity. As the following figure illustrates, some nodes are more central than others. Borrowing from epidemiology, Haldane and May have coined the term *super-spreader institutions* for the biggest nodes (Haldane and May 2011, 354).

From a network perspective, financial institutions are the nodes in the network, and the contracts between them – covering hedging, borrowing and clearing activities – represent the links in between. Direct contagion spreads through the financial network via counterparty exposure. As direct contagion has a factual basis in the underlying legal contracts, it is easier to predict than indirect contagion (even though, as we will see in section 3.3, certain financial products make it difficult for financial institutions to ascertain to which loans or bonds they are ultimately exposed). In view of the LTCM case discussed in chapter two, one can expect that the consortium of commercial and investment banks that ultimately rescued LTCM knew their direct exposure to the hedge fund; they obviously judged their indirect exposure to be much higher, and therefore agreed to rescue the hedge fund rather than let it fail. The Lehman case perfectly illustrates the difference between direct and indirect contagion. Scott, who believes that the role of interconnectedness in the financial crisis of 2007ff. is largely overestimated, finds evidence that "the direct impact of Lehman's collapse on these counterparties was not as problematic or destabilizing as many feared it would be. In fact, no major financial institution failed as a result of its direct exposure to Lehman Brothers" (Scott 2012, 2). But in September 2008, indirect contagion spread through the financial system via certain self-reinforcing mechanisms. Contrary to direct contagion, indirect contagion does not require direct contractual links in the network: The collapse of a major financial institution leads to distrust and fear. But it also has certain structural implications: Drops in asset prices lead to increased liquidity needs that result in further asset sales; together with fire sales, mark-to-market accounting forms a downward spiral; more and more institutions are required to write down the value of their assets, which again forces them to sell assets, leading to value losses in many different asset groups. Rumors about liquidity shortage and collateral calls start to spread, becoming self-fulfilling prophecies as more and more investors start to sell certain stocks short. The grown liquidity needs of each institution, in combination with a general uncertainty about counterparty solvency, lead to a freeze of the interbank market. In their interplay, these self-reinforcing mechanisms form a systemic crisis. *Liquidity hoarding* is one such mechanism. As Gai et al. show in their network simulation, "the decision by a single bank to hoard liquidity makes it harder for banks that were previously borrowing from it to meet their own liquidity condition without resorting to hoarding themselves" (Gai, Haldane, and Kapadia 2011, 11). To hoard capital and stop institutional lending makes sense from the perspective of a single institution; however, what Luhmann has argued for the field of politics is also very true for markets: "what may be rational when done by a few may no longer be rational when done by many" (Luhmann 2008, 156).

The issue of indirect contagion brings us to the behavioral aspects of financial crises. Indirect contagion can spread via highly formalized rules and regulations, such as minimal capital requirements for banks; but it can also occur in the form of rumor and fear, again leading to hoarding behavior. Direct contagion was contained in the US by arranging rescues and bailing out institutions: The interconnections persist, but liabilities are fulfilled. However, no private institution or government or financial regulator can stop a rumor from spreading, it can only interrupt the indirect contagion mechanism by stepping in and guaranteeing all liabilities, as was the case in Germany when chancellor Angela Merkel and then minister of finance Peer Steinbrück guaranteed German private savings in 2008 (Benoit and Wilson 2008; see Schultz 2008, for the original wording), or in the US when the US Treasury announced that it temporarily guaranteed Money Market Funds against losses in 2008 (Henriques 2008) – or it might install automated mechanisms – *kill switches*, such as automated trading stops, or *buffers*, such as capital requirements and countercyclical capital buffers. In systemic crises, trust and confidence evaporate. The de Larosière Report argues in fact that the Lehman failure led to a full-fledged *crisis of confidence*: After the US government let Lehman fail, financial institutions could neither trust their counterparties nor the US government anymore (High Level Group on Financial Supervision in the EU 2009, 12). Once the downturn had begun, it was difficult to stop.[59]

Willke and Willke suggest a range of reforms to enhance the resilience of complex financial systems, among them the wide-spread use of principles-based regulation and measures to transfer the financial system from a tightly- to a loosely-coupled system (Willke and Willke 2012). Some of the described self-reinforcing mechanisms, such as liquidity hoarding, are addressed with higher capital requirements or countercyclical capital rules under Basel III. Yet, the policy responses to the recent financial crisis addressing financial complexity mostly focused on institutional complexity, more specifically on increasing the data and information available on financial institutions, and on establishing a viable resolution mechanism for TBTF institutions. This brings us to the issue of too big to fail institutions – banks, funds, insurances, clearing houses that are highly interconnected nodes in the financial network, and that might actually be *too complex to manage*.

3.2 The Role and Nature of 21st Century Financial Institutions

Adapting to a *global business environment* and *changes in financial regulation*, but also as a result of *regulatory and tax arbitrage* (Goldstein and Véron 2011, 28), the global banking business has undergone significant changes over the last decades. In the 1990s, Greenspan stated that "until fairly recently, bank balance sheets were

59 Lehman's CEO Richard Fuld believed until the end that if the SEC could only ban the naked short-selling of its shares a collapse might be prevented (Fuld 2008; see also Sorkin 2010).

simple in structure – deposits, capital, loans, and reserves – […] However, the largest banks are now gradually moving away from their traditional role" (Greenspan 1995, 2). In the US, we can identify three major trends: The absolute number of banks has decreased while the relative size of US banks has increased, resulting in a *higher degree of concentration* in the banking system. Besides, the *complexity of these organizations, including their structure and business*, has grown (Dudley 2012). Last but not least, the so-called *shadow banking system* grew largely unnoticed prior to the crisis; it is a part of the financial system that comprises mostly unregulated institutions, services and products, such as money market funds and hedge funds, but also unstandardized OTC derivatives developed and sold by banks and nonbanks (Bernanke 2012). In the 1990s, Born pushed for better data and information on these *dark markets* (Born 2009), but was not successful. As less regulation means less supervision, it is difficult to get data and information on these institutions and services. Fortunately, the existing data on banks and the classic banking business help us to illustrate the described developments.

Between 1970 and 2012, the five largest US banks were able to triple their share of assets from 17 to 52 percent (Fisher and Rosenblum 2012). Haldane reports that the total share of assets of the three largest US banks grew fourfold, from ten to 40 percent between 1990 and 2007, while the share of the five largest global banks, compared to the 1000 largest banks worldwide, rose from around eight percent in 1998 to about 16 percent in 2009 (Haldane 2010, 9). The following chart summarizes data on FDIC-insured commercial banks. It illustrates how the total number of banks has gradually decreased, while the banks' overall size, measured in total assets, has massively increased.

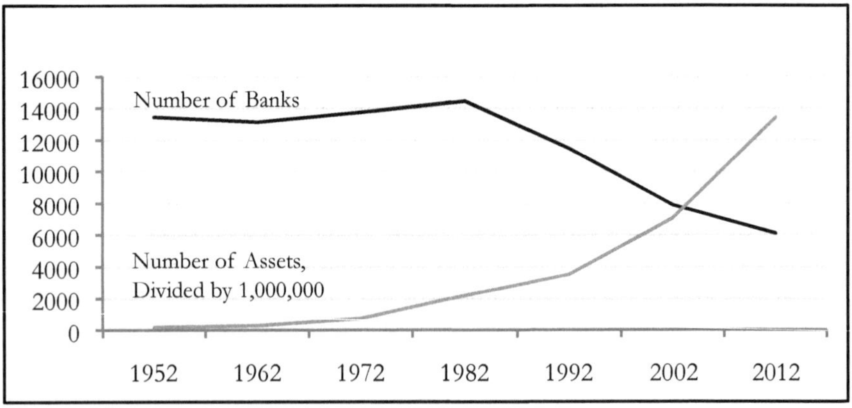

Figure 4: Number and size of FDIC-insured banks (figure based on the FDIC's historical statistics on banking).

While it is difficult to name all contributing factors – there are many, to be sure – it is widely agreed that changes in US regulation largely contributed to these trends (see Wilmarth 2002, for an in-depth analysis of changes in the US banking sector between 1975 and 2000). To name some of the landmark decisions in the US: In 1994, Congress allowed authorized bank-holding companies (BHCs) to buy interstate banks, as well as state and national banks to install interstate branches; as a result, large nationwide banks evolved, and the share of assets held by the largest banks more than doubled between 1990 and 2005 (Wilmarth 2013, 1360). After the repeal of the Glass-Steagall Act of 1933 in 1999, US financial institutions were allowed to engage in banking, securities and insurance. Formerly separate banks, securities firms and insurance companies merged into complex financial conglomerates, banks' balance sheets grew further and their overall business diversified. Size and complexity have therefore increased in tandem (Fisher and Rosenblum 2012). The structure of these global and highly diversified financial institutions differs considerably from other global corporations: According to IMF and Bank of England data, the largest and most complex financial institutions have 2.5 times more majority-owned subsidies than a comparable set of manufacturing firms (Herring 2009, 3). It is argued that, in their complexity and opaqueness, these institutions represent a source of systemic risk themselves (Herring and Carmassi 2012; Dudley 2012). Based on differences in the bank bond ratings issued by US rating agencies (Moody's, Standard & Poor's), Morgan is in fact able to show that banks are more opaque and therefore more difficult to assess than non-financial firms (Morgan 2002). Shortly after the enactment of Gramm-Leach-Bliley in 1999, Wilmarth warned that "the growing concentration of securities and derivatives activities within a small group of major financial institutions increases the likelihood that the failure of any big institution could create systemic risk and trigger a costly bailout by federal regulators" (Wilmarth 2002, 224). This brings us to two terms that were at the heart of the financial crisis, and that are central in the current policy debate: *Too big to fail* and *too complex to manage.*

3.2.1 Understanding the Too Big to Fail Phenomenon

Gai is able to show that concentration in the financial system increases systemic risk (Gai 2013). Four years before the Lehman collapse, Stern and Feldman argued that due to the increased concentration and complexity of bank operations, the long-known problem of TBTF banks had become much more severe (Stern and Feldman 2004, 2).[60] Since then, both concentration and complexity – measured in terms of bank subsidiaries (Herring and Carmassi 2012) and assets – have increased even further, especially during and after the crisis. The Dodd-Frank Act, which is

60 Lehman's CEO Richard (Dick) Fuld admits in his interview with the FCIC that he "never heard about too big to fail until after the fact" (Fuld 2010).

often described as the most radical overhaul of US financial regulation since the Great Depression, explicitly aims at ending TBTF. Three years later, policymakers and academics widely agree that TBTF lives on (see for example Warren 2013a; Baxter 2013; Bair 2013).

The term *too big to fail* is as prominent as it is misleading. As a matter of fact, TBTF financial firms are not too big to fail, but *too big to let them fail*. When they fail – and as the financial crisis has demonstrated, they do fail – they are bailed out by someone, and because of the sheer size of today's financial institutions, that someone is most likely the government, more specifically the taxpayer. Besides, TBTF is not only a matter of *bigness* or size (Cetorelli and Goldberg 2014). As we will illustrate on the following pages, the TBTF phenomenon is rooted in a variety of factors, such as the interconnectedness and substitutability of a firm or a service. The IMF has therefore suggested to replace the term TBTF with TITF – *too important to fail* (see for example Ötker-Robe et al. 2011; Lagarde 2013) – while others have brought forward alternate terms as *too interconnected to fail* (see for example Bernanke 2009a; Markose et al. 2010), *too complex to fail* (Herring and Carmassi 2012), *too big to manage* (Interview with Philip Wallach, December 04 2012, Washington) or *too complex to manage* (Fisher and Rosenblum 2012). We will nevertheless stay with the term TBTF, for two reasons: It is not only common among policymakers, scholars and journalists; it also illustrates – in spite of, or rather because of its shortcomings – how our understanding of the TBTF phenomenon has evolved since the onset of the crisis: What first appeared to be a matter of size soon turned out to be a far more complex phenomenon. We will first provide a definition of TBTF, then turn to the related phenomenon of moral hazard, and finally discuss how TBTF fits into the bigger picture of increased organizational complexity.

The TBTF phenomenon is at the core of systemic risk because systemic crises can be triggered by the collapse of a TBTF financial institution. Bernanke accordingly defines a TBTF institution as one "whose *size, complexity, interconnectedness, and critical functions* are such that, should the firm go unexpectedly into liquidation, the rest of the financial system and the economy would face severe adverse consequences" (Bernanke 2010c, 20, emphasis added).[61] In order to avoid these *severe adverse consequences*, governments either arrange a private rescue of the failing TBTF institution as it was the case with LTCM and a set of institutions during the recent financial crisis, or they step in and bail the institution out. As implied in Bernanke's definition, TBTF goes beyond size: The Dodd-Frank Act introduces a broad definition of TBTF based on the nature, scope, size, scale, concentration and interconnectedness of an institution or a mixture of

61 As we will see in the context of the Lehman case (section 4.1), the term *unexpectedly* is of central importance here.

these (Section 113 of DFA). As we will illustrate in chapter five, Dodd-Frank also extends the concept of TBTF beyond financial institutions on *financial market activities*. Under Dodd-Frank, certain products or even complete industries – such as the money market fund industry – might be designated as systemically important.

Few TBTF financial institutions do ever need government support, but the fact that they can rely on a rescue represents a competitive advantage. The TBTF phenomenon is therefore described as an implicit government guarantee and most likely results in *indirect government subsidies*. Unfortunately, these "are easier to describe than measure" (Haldane 2010, 4). Policymakers and academics do not yet agree on the exact amount of the subsidy, but the fact that it does exist is widely accepted (cf. Strongin et al. 2013).[62] A recent Bloomberg study estimates the annual US subsidy to be about 83 billion dollar in total (Bloomberg 2013b, 2013a; see also Ueda and di Mauro 2012; Yellen 2013b), Acharya et al. consider its total value to range around 20 billion dollar per year, amounting to 100 billion dollar in the crisis year 2009 (Acharya, Anginer, and Warburton 2013), while Baker and McArthur argue that the annual subsidy to the 18 biggest US bank holding companies amounts to 6.3 (*minimum*) or 34.1 billion (*maximum*) US dollar (Baker and McArthur 2009, 2). Recent studies indicate that TBTF institutions not only profit from lower funding costs but also from better ratings as the ratings incorporate the government guarantee:

> According to Moody's, official support in 2009 for the 50 largest banks translated on average into a three-notch upgrade of their rating (from A3 to Aa3), up from a two-notch upgrade in 2006 (from A1 to Aa2). In addition, as recently as December 2009, about one quarter of all bonds issued by banks with higher than average credit default swap (CDS) spreads featured some form of government guarantee. (Bank for International Settlements 2010, 79)

For decades, the government guarantee for TBTF institutions was rather implicit – as the Lehman case showed, the market could never be sure whether an institution would be rescued or not. In 1975, Mayer discussed the possibility that governments publish lists of banks they are willing to rescue, but decided that this was an unlikely scenario (Mayer 1975, 605). In 1984, the US government bailed out Continental Illinois Bank, which was at that point the nation's seventh-largest bank. In his

62 Contrary to what recent discussions about the government subsidy suggest, the phenomenon is several decades old. In his FCIC interview, hedge fund manager George Soros describes how he factored in the implicit government guarantee for systemically important industries or market sectors in the 80s: "I can recall an instance, going way back, when I had a very large position in British government bonds and I was very close to blowing up and I thought of actually, if it really came to that, that I would go to the Bank of England and ask them to protect the government bond market. So even I, and even before these whole things developed, this goes back to actually to early Thatcher days, this was in the early 80s. 79 or 80. So even I had this implicit guarantee in my mind" (Soros 2010).

subsequent testimony before Congress, the Comptroller of the Currency explained that Continental Illinois had been rescued because it was too big to fail. He hesitated to name other TBTF institutions, to finally admit that the eleven largest US banks might be systemically important, too. The day after, Tim Carrington published an article in the Wall Street Journal – *U.S. Won't Let 11 Biggest Banks in Nation Fall* – where he explicitly named these TBTF banks (Morgan and Stiroh 2005).[63] The list, even though it was only semi-official, made the implicit guarantee more explicit. The WSJ article had immediate positive effects on the stock returns of these eleven banks (O'Hara and Shaw 1990), it increased confidence in these same banks and accordingly resulted in better bond ratings (Morgan and Stiroh 2005). Then, the Federal Deposit Insurance Corporation Improvement Act (FDICA) enacted by Congress in 1991 authorized the FDIC to extend its protection to uninsured depositors if a large bank failed and it expected "serious adverse effects on economic conditions or financial stability" (Wilmarth 2002, 300). The act primarily aimed at restricting the FDIC's possibilities to rescue banks, but it also officially recognized the existence of TBTF (Hoenig 1999, 10), resulting in inadequate risk pricing especially with regard to the banks named in 1984 (Morgan and Stiroh 1999). Since the FSOC as well as the FSB and the Basel committee published their lists of systemically important financial institutions in 2012 and 2013, the government subsidy has become even more explicit. Firms like American International Group (AIG) or General Electric Capital Corporation (GECC) are now officially designated as systemically important financial institutions under Dodd-Frank. Their designation should reduce the risk of failure from the outset; in the case of failure, their status triggers a resolution mechanism explicitly designed for TBTF institutions. And yet, Dodd-Frank might ultimately have increased systemic risk. As we will argue in chapter five, the US government was not yet able to end TBTF. However, it established new measures to monitor and resolve TBTF institutions.

Backed by their governments, TBTF firms can take higher risks. Closely related, TBTF incentivizes excessive risk-taking by the institution's creditors (Bernanke 2007a) and lax oversight by the institution's shareholders. Going back to the late 1990s, these problems clearly contributed to the LTCM collapse: Not only was LTCM over-leveraged but its creditors did not evaluate how risky the hedge fund's strategy actually was.[64] TBTF is therefore closely related to the economic concept of *moral hazard*, meaning that these institutions, their creditors and their shareholders take higher risks because they do not have to bear the losses – as a result, private risks become public. In the absence of a TBTF tax or levy, it is in fact highly rational for financial institutions to seek systemic relevance: A financial institution's

63 Interestingly, Carrington's list differed from the set of national banks that the Comptroller had actually meant (O'Hara and Shaw 1990) – a fact that the market did not care for.

64 It is said that the fund's major creditors were completely surprised by LTCM's total leverage ratio.

"CEO worth his or her pay has understood [...] the impeccable institutional if not individual logic of becoming too-big-to-fail" (Pauly 2008, 80).

As the risk of TBTF institutions is not priced adequately, TBTF is a self-reinforcing mechanism: TBTF institutions have a competitive advantage that further extends their lead, which is why Mary Schapiro as chair of the SEC distinguished two different types of systemic risk:

> (1) the risk of sudden, near-term systemic seizures or cascading failures and (2) the longer-term risk that our system will *unintentionally favor large systemically important institutions* over smaller, more nimble competitors, reducing the system's ability to innovate and adapt to change. We must be very careful that our efforts to protect the system from near-term systemic seizures do not inadvertently result in a long-term systemic imbalance. (Schapiro 2009, emphasis added)

Whether one agrees with Schapiro's argument that there are two types of systemic risk or not, the point she makes is quite central: Because of their systemic importance, TBTF institutions grow naturally, increasing their systemic importance even further. In normal times, this process takes place gradually; during crises, mergers and acquisitions – arranged and sometimes funded by government – lead to major shifts in the TBTF landscape. TBTF is a self-reinforcing mechanism for a second reason: Each rescue of a TBTF institution increases market expectations for future bailouts. Ratings of UK banks support this argument (Haldane 2010, 4f.). As TBTF is closely tied to perception – Ben Bernanke admits that TBTF exists as long as the market believes it exists (Warren 2013a; see also Hoenig 1999, 10) – this is a very important point.

The Bear Stearns bailout raised expectations of future bailouts. As we will discuss in chapter four, the US government felt it had to disappoint these expectations for political (support of Congress and the electorate) and economic (restoring market discipline) reasons. The shock that was then triggered by the Lehman default reflected the strong bailout expectations within the market. The collapse of a TBTF institution is never a standalone event – instead, the government's options are constrained but past (non)bailout decisions and a bailout decision will have an impact on future expectations and subsidies.

> To many practical people the suggestion that a large bank be allowed to fail may seem to represent dogmatic adherence to standard economic doctrine, a victory of ideology over pragmatic common sense. [...] After all, the social costs of failure are immediate, while the advantages of permitting failure are indirect and removed into the future. But this pragmatic position should be rejected because it ignores externalities over time. *If we prop up a large bank because the direct costs of doing so outweigh the cost of allowing it to fail, then the next time a large bank is in danger of failing it is likely to be*

> *propped up too.* [...] When one includes the cost of moving down this slippery slope in the cost of saving a large bank, then the costs of allowing it to fail may seem small by comparison. (Mayer 1975, 609f.)

The mechanisms and phenomena examined in this section are well described by Goldstein and Véron, and they add a third, political aspect to our list of TBTF challenges: First, TBTF institutions exacerbate systemic risk; second, they distort competition; and third, the way that governments deal with TBTF institutions leads to a decrease of public trust in the system and therefore undermines accountability and responsibility (Goldstein and Véron 2011, 2f.; see also Stern and Feldman 2004, ch. three). The underlying question is *whether the public can trust a government that is open to blackmail by TBTF institutions.* The rescue of TBTF institutions, together with Greenspan's confession that he and his Fed staff were not able to understand certain financial products as quoted at the beginning of this chapter, could well be interpreted as total capitulation by the state to the complexity and overwhelming dominance of finance.

3.2.2 Too Complex to Manage, or: Jamie Dimon Wishes to See Everything

The crisis raised the question of whether certain financial institutions are not only too big too fail, but also *too complex to manage* (see for example Buffett 2010). The debate was fueled by JP Morgan's announcement in April 2012 of trading losses amounting to two billion dollar. A JP Morgan trader called the *London Whale,* and *Lord Voldemort* after Harry Potter's famous antagonist, had placed such outsized trades that other traders were able to identify them and bet against them.[65] Because of the size of the trades, JP Morgan had difficulties to unwind them and was unable to sell without deteriorating the prices in the market (Zuckerman and Patterson 2012). The losses would later add up to five billion dollars and might grow even further. At the time the trades were placed, the Office of the Comptroller of the Currency (OCC) that oversees JP Morgan's Chief Investment Office in London had around 70 supervisors placed inside the bank. However, the bets placed by the London Whale did not alarm the OCC examiners until late April, even though in mid-April 2012 the Chief Financial Officer of JP Morgan had said that "all of those positions are fully transparent to the regulators" (ibid.). When JP Morgan announced the losses, CEO Jamie Dimon called the incident a "complete tempest in a teapot" (Langley 2012). The reason simply might have been that Dimon did not know the trade.[66] Based on interviews with bank

65 The trader, Bruno Iksil, was based at JPMorgan's *Chief Investment Office* (CIO) in London.

66 Mendelowitz argues: "If you look, Jamie Dimon had a reputation for being the best of the financial CEOs. He had a trade that lost eight or nine billion dollars in one quarter. Why? Because nobody in the organization had a clue what was out there, because they lacked the data to collect within the firm to understand what the exposure is" (Interview with Allan Mendelowitz, December 03, 2012, Washington).

executives and Washington officials, the Wall Street Journal provided a detailed picture of the situation inside JP Morgan.

> On April 30, associates who were gathered in a conference room handed Mr. Dimon summaries and analyses of the losses. But there were no details about the trades themselves. 'I want to see the positions!' he barked, throwing down the papers, according to attendees. 'Now! I want to see everything!' When Mr. Dimon saw the numbers, these people say, he couldn't breathe. (Langley 2012)

The London Whale incident is interesting in many respects: First, it shows that the ability of on-site examiners to monitor and identify risks at complex financial institutions is quite limited; second, it demonstrates that even the most respected CEOs apparently cannot oversee all complex trades conducted by their institutions – no matter how big and potentially relevant they are; and third, it raises the question whether global systemically important financial institutions (G-SIFIs) are in fact too complex to manage. Following Hu it can be argued that information asymmetries within the organization – rooting either in internal principal-agent problems, in stove piping or siloing of information or in cognitive biases – make it impossible to provide a *true picture* of highly complex financial firms (Hu 2012, 1674f.; 2009, 3). We will revert to this point in chapter five on data, information and knowledge asymmetries.

An important side effect of the Libor scandal as well as of the London Whale incident was that current reform efforts were strengthened.[67] Just like the TBTF debate, the discussion on the London Whale incident culminated in the question whether the biggest, most complex institutions should be broken up.

3.2.3 A Short Note on Being Too Big to Jail

In February 2013, Attorney General of the United States Eric H. Holder, in his testimony before the Senate Judiciary Committee on Oversight of the U.S.

67 Asked about the impact of the London Whale trading losses at JPMorgan, Debbie Matz, chairperson of the US National Credit Union Administration, answered: "The only impact is really long-term. If Congress was leaning toward reducing the regulatory environment, this might give them pause. So it might provide consumers with a more regulated environment and more protections; I don't see a financial effect – at least immediately" (Matz 2012). The LIBOR scandal apparently had a similar effect: Greenberger describes how in May 2012, "there were bipartisan bills in the house [...] that were technical amendments that were undoing Dodd-Frank. And I felt, I felt, and obviously we were up against the wall, and that was two o'clock in the afternoon. At five o'clock, Jamie Dimon gave his press conference about the London Wale. And the world turned. It turned for like two months, but it did turn. This bill, a very dangerous bill, that had bipartisan support to make a technical amendment to repeal Dodd-Frank, they were having a mark-up session a week from that day, that was cancelled. And we never heard from it again. And we got breathing room. We got breathing room again with the LIBOR scandal. But again, this breathing room is a couple of months. And then we're back up against the wall" (Greenberger 2013).

Department of Justice (DoJ), admitted that some financial institutions in the US had become *too big to be prosecuted.* He expressed his concern stating that

> the size of some of these institutions becomes so large that it does become difficult for us to prosecute them, when we are hit with indications that if you do prosecute, if you do bring a criminal charge, it will have a negative impact on the national economy, perhaps even the world economy. And I think that is a function of the fact that some of these institutions have become too large. [...] I think it has an inhibiting influence, impact in our ability to bring resolutions that I think would be more appropriate. (Holder 2013)

Asked about his opinion on Holder's statement, former SEC chairman Arthur Levitt answers "that that's a very realistic statement that most politicians would stay away from"; he goes on that "there is no question but that these institutions are very unlikely to be the object of a criminal prosecution. They'll try other methods of punishing them [...] but I doubt that the institutions that are too big to fail are likely to be indicted for criminal activity" (Levitt 2013). Earlier developments indicate that the DoJ has indeed been careful not to prosecute systemically important financial institutions: In December 2012, the New York Times described how the department had "decided against indicting HSBC in a money-laundering case over concerns that criminal charges could jeopardize one of the world's largest banks and ultimately destabilize the global financial system" (Protess and Silver-Greenberg 2012).[68] Lanny Breuer, head of the department's criminal division, admitted that the *collateral damage* – meaning job losses but also an expected shock to the financial system – influenced the decision against a prosecution of HSBC (Braithwaite 2012; see also Weil 2012, on recent settlements between UBS and the DoJ; Barofsky 2013). After hearing these arguments the DoJ chose not to criminally charge HSBC. Knowledge asymmetries might also have played a role, as "law enforcement on Wall Street requires serious intellectual firepower" (Taibbi 2011).

HSBC was ultimately able to settle the case for 1.92 billion US dollar. The important question is: Is HSBC an isolated case, or was it exemplary? Wilmarth identifies a broader trend that started in the late nineties, criticizing the current lack of criminal enforcement actions against systemically important banks and their executives; he argues that the "too big to jail" doctrine has evolved over time:

> Criminal referrals by bank regulators to DOJ fell sharply soon after wave of bank and thrift failures ended in the early 1990s. Bank regulators made over 1,800 criminal referrals in 1995 but made only about 70 referrals per year between 2006 and 2010. OTS failed to make a single criminal referral between 2000 and 2010, despite the collapse of several of the largest

68 HSBC stands for Hongkong & Shanghai Banking Corporation Holdings plc.

> institutions it regulated, while OCC made only three referrals during the same period. [...] By late 2012, DOJ had prosecuted more than 2,000 real estate agents, mortgage brokers and borrowers for criminal fraud but had not indicted a single top financial executive or any of the big financial institutions that financed the housing bubble. (Wilmarth 2013, 1372f.)

Enforcement efforts against large financial institutions were apparently weaker than those against smaller firms: They resulted in administrative rather than court proceedings; within these proceedings the employees of large institutions received lower sanctions (Gadinis 2012, 679; his study examines cases from 1998, 2005, 2006 and 2007, and it only covers the SEC). Holder's testimony made explicit what public officials had indicated for some time: Based on their government guarantee, SIFIs and SIFI shareholders can take higher risks; the "exalted status" of these institutions leads to a "sense of immunity from the law" (Fisher 2013). As early as 2002, Wilmarth discussed enforcement actions against Bank of America and Citicorp under the headline of "too big to discipline adequately" (Wilmarth 2002). Based on both the testimony and the HSBC case, the question was now publicly raised whether certain financial institutions were not only TBTF but also too big to jail.

In this context, Sorkin has illustrated the important difference between *prosecuting financial firms* and *prosecuting individual employees*. He argues that bringing a criminal case against a financial firm most likely puts the company out of business, harming not only the responsible managers but in fact all employees, with potential side effects for business partners and subcontractors. According to Sorkin, Holder's statement is not so much problematic but demonstrates that the Justice Department should focus on the employees responsible for the crime (Sorkin 2013). Whether Sorkin is right or not is not subject of this book. The debate is nevertheless important: If some firms are too big to be prosecuted and others are not, we have to draw another distinction – with too big to jail financial institutions on one side and institutions threatened by future prosecution on the other, adding a third mechanism to the self-reinforcing logic of TBTF. The too big to jail debate confirms the impression that national governments are unable to discipline global, complex, systemically important financial institutions (Wilmarth 2002, 307).

3.2.4 Differentiating Between Systemic Risk and TBTF

TBTF and systemic risk are two closely related phenomena. However, even though the US policy responses to systemic risk focus on too big to fail institutions, TBTF and systemic risk are not identical and we should be careful not to reduce systemic risk to too big to fail. TBTF lies at the heart of systemic risk: The failure of a TBTF institution can trigger a downturn that sets off a systemic crisis. But the failure of a TBTF institution is not the only possible trigger for a systemic crisis. To start with, we have to distinguish between *endogenous and exogenous triggers*. The collapse of a TBTF firm, a fat finger error or an erroneous HFT algorithm are endogenous triggers for financial crises, meaning that they come from within the financial system. The list of potential exogenous triggers is long and includes events such as terrorist attacks and natural disasters. To provide an example, the FSOC met three times to discuss the impact of tropical storm Sandy on the US financial markets (Willke, Becker, and Rostásy 2013, 131). The difference from a political point of view is the moral hazard associated with TBTF: When a highly leveraged financial institution fails and triggers a systemic crisis, such as was the case with Lehman, society in effect pays the banks' bills. TBTF events might therefore, over the long run, bring into question the legitimacy of the governments and public bodies regulating and policing these financial institutions. While financial firms should internalize the risks they take, this cannot be said of exogenous triggers.

TBTF is ultimately about the allocation of losses (Levitin 2011) – George Soros terms it a "distributional problem" (Soros 2010) – and must therefore be far up on the policymaking agenda. Even so, Mendelowitz and Liechty have compellingly argued that a regulatory and supervisory focus on TBTF institutions is too narrow to address systemic risk:

> One prevailing line of thinking is that systemic risk can be managed by identifying a relatively small number of systemically important institutions and regulating them especially well. There are critical conceptual errors in this thinking. When it comes to systemic risk, the whole is greater than the sum of the parts. Even if there were no large, systemically important institutions, there would still be the risk of systemic failure. (Mendelowitz and Liechty 2010, 6)

The pre-crisis focus on microprudential supervision and regulation appears to persist, and it is apparently difficult to overcome. We cannot solve systemic risk without addressing TBTF. Yet, based on the assumption that systemic risk has its roots in the characteristics of a global, complex and tightly coupled financial system, it cannot be overcome by just resolving the TBTF phenomenon – the basic system characteristics remain the same, and downturns will be triggered by other events. Addressing TBTF is therefore necessary but not sufficient; reducing the relevance of a small set of nodes in the network does indeed reduce the fragility of the system, but not to nil. Even worse: It bears the risk of diverting policymakers away from other important issues (A. Turner 2010) and creates a dangerous, false sense of security that we will discuss in the following chapters of this book.

3.3 Complex Products – Financial Weapons of Mass-Destruction?

The financial crisis of 2007ff. shed new light on the risks resulting from complex derivatives trades, especially with regard to leverage as well as counterparty and tail risk. More accurately, these risks were known before the crisis (see for example Fenton-O'Creevy et al. 2005) but largely underestimated by policymakers. Derivatives contracts have a long history in finance, and they were traditionally used to hedge or mitigate risks. From the mid-1990s onwards, both scale and complexity of this type of security increased massively (Financial Services Authority 2009, 14).[69] Today, derivatives are tools for hedging *and* speculating, and they also allow greater leverage. Against this background, Levitin speaks of a financial Frankenstein: Securitization was well intentioned and it did work at the beginning but got out of control in the pre-crisis period (Levitin 2010a). When Alan Greenspan described the bewildering complexity of financial products, he referred to *collateralized debt obligations* (CDOs). While other securities, especially *asset-backed securities* (ABSs) and *credit default swaps* (CDSs), did also play a central role in the crisis, CDOs are especially complex.

Credit default swaps are used to hedge risks related to financial products, including CDOs. They can essentially be compared to insurances: If a house burns down and the owner has fire insurance, he or she will receive the guaranteed insurance sum. A CDS provides insurance against various eventualities, including bad weather (farmers), increasing grain prices (muesli producers) or defaulting CDOs (CDO owners). The crucial and controversial difference between conventional insurance and a CDS is that you would have to own the house to insure it against fire, but you would not have to hold the underlying asset to buy a credit default swap. Following the CDS logic, it is possible to buy fire insurance for the house of a neighbor, then hope that it will burn down. CDSs can accordingly be used for hedging as well as for speculating.

Put simply, *asset-backed securities* are securities backed by an asset: They derive their value from an underlying mortgage, credit card, student loan or car loan that provides a continuous cash flow from the borrower to the bank and from the bank to the buyer of an ABS. What distinguishes a *collateralized debt obligation* from an ABS is that each CDO pools a set of ABSs. Buyers of a CDO pay a certain amount of money to a so-called Special Purpose Vehicle (SPV). The SPV creates the CDO by using the funds to invest in a portfolio of ABSs (Alblescu 2010). Since the creation of the first CDO in 1987, different types of CDOs have been developed (Goodman, Lucas, and Fabozzi 2007). In order to diversify risks, CDOs were mostly multi-sectoral at the beginning: Based on diverse asset classes such as

69 Derivatives and securities are sometimes difficult to distinguish. Securities are commonly defined as tradable assets of any kind; they include derivative contracts, but also equity and debt securities. Derivatives comprise a variety of products, including futures, options and swaps.

student loans, car loans, mortgages etc., CDOs were assumed to be very safe investments. When certain ABS classes started to perform poorly in 2002, the CDO industry turned to the lucrative and supposedly safe housing market and started to focus on *mortgage-backed securities* or MBSs (Financial Crisis Inquiry Commission 2011, 130). In 2002, MBSs provided 35 percent of total CDO collateral; in 2004, this number had gone up to more than 50 percent (ibid.). The next important innovation in the area of structured finance was a CDO built of other CDOs, a so-called CDO squared, a process that further increased the complexity of securities.

The complexity of CDOs derives from their design: CDOs are structured into tranches, with each tranche bearing a different degree of default risk. Each investor can accordingly choose the preferred risk level. Incoming cash always flows from the top to the bottom of a CDO: "Senior CDO notes are paid before mezzanine and lower subordinated notes are paid, with any residual cash flow paid to an equity piece" (Duffie and Gârleanu 2001, 41). The lower the tranche, the higher the risk of default and the higher the interest rate. What makes CDOs so complex is the repackaging process that is illustrated in figure six: To create a CDO, the SPV takes the lower-rated tranches of a set of ABSs and repackages them into a CDO. To build squared CDOs, the lower-rated tranches of CDOs are again repackaged. The high degree of diversification – each CDO consists of a large number of small pieces of ABSs, or in the case of a CDO squared of a larger number of small pieces of CDOs – was supposed to make a CDO less risky. While the default of one mortgage underlying an MBS might be very likely, the chance that 500 out of the 1000 securities underlying a CDO would default was considered to be close to zero. Because of the additional diversification benefits achieved by repackaging the underlying securities, 80 percent of these CDOs were given triple-A ratings by the rating agencies (Financial Crisis Inquiry Commission 2011, 127).

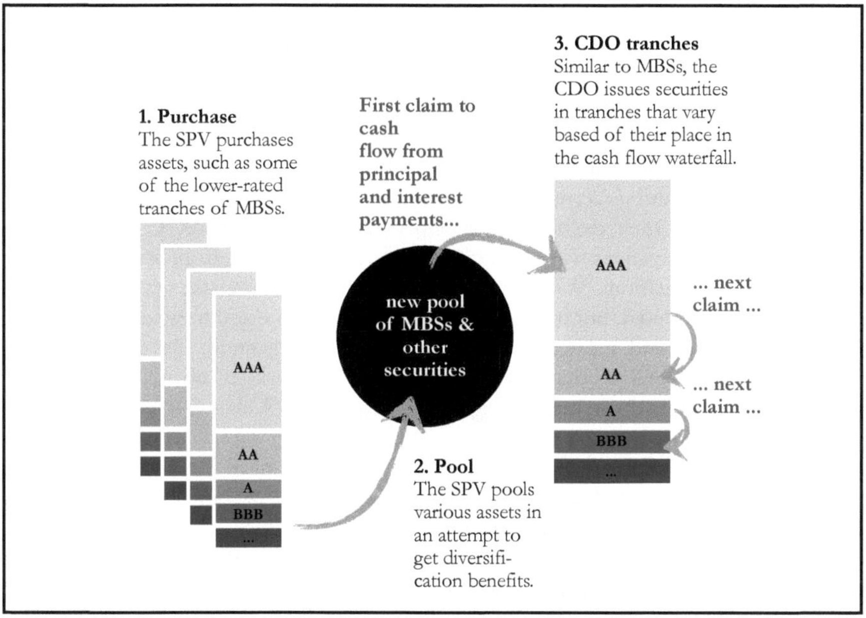

Figure 5: Collateralized Debt Obligations (figure based on Financial Crisis Inquiry Commission 2011, 128).

The housing boom in the US did not only coevolve with a growing CDO market, it also lead to an increased demand for credit default swaps to hedge the resulting risks. AIG alone sold protection against losses from mortgage-backed securities amounting to 79 billion US dollars (ibid., xxiv). The CDO and CDS market accordingly grew in tandem. Detailed analyses of the housing crisis and the role that MBSs and CDOs played in the mortgage drama can be found elsewhere and should not be duplicated here (see for example Demyanyk and Hemert 2011; Lewis 2011; Financial Crisis Inquiry Commission 2011; Fligstein and Goldstein 2010). Important for our analysis is the fact that certain sophisticated products, such as CDSs and CDOs, have increased the complexity of the financial system tremendously (Gai 2013, 9), essentially by raising the number of (opaque) interconnections in the financial system. The Turner Report argues that "the development of securitised credit has ended up producing the worst financial crisis for a century" (Financial Services Authority 2009). More specifically, Henry Hu, a law professor and former director of the SEC's division of risk, strategy and financial innovation, argues that the *informational problems*, more precisely the *informational asymmetries* related to ABSs, contributed to the financial crisis (Hu 2012, 1602). The complexity of the securities rendered a sufficient understanding impossible: "Even if all information about a complex structure is disclosed, complexity increases the amount of information that must be analyzed in order to value the investment with a degree of certainty" (Schwarcz 2009, 221).

Taken together, mortgage-backed securities, collateralized debt obligations and credit default swaps built a complex net of contractual relationships between borrowers, mortgage originators, securitization firms, investment banks, hedge funds, insurances and government sponsored enterprises. All three of them, in their interplay, revealed their destructive potential during 2007 and 2008. The fact that the majority of derivatives were sold over-the-counter and therefore less transparent worsened the situation: When the housing market collapsed, every financial institution was affected, but it was difficult to find out how and to what degree. The problem goes beyond mortgage-related derivatives. In general, the emergence of sophisticated financial products, which comprise "networks of claims in their own right", has heightened the overall degree of complexity (Weber 2012, 684; see also Haldane 2011, 13).

Paul Volcker famously said that the only useful financial innovation he could think of in the past 20 years was the automated teller machine (ATM) (Volcker 2009), and Mayntz speaks of *so-called "financial innovations"* (Mayntz 2010a, 179; 2013, 16). And yet, CDOs are a classic example for a financial innovation: They did not only possess new product characteristics but also reached a high degree of market penetration. The financial crisis then called into question the widespread belief that financial innovation is *per se* beneficial. Besides, it appeared that complexity was not a byproduct of financial innovation; instead, financial innovators seemed to deliberately add complexity to their products not only to deepen information asymmetries between sellers and buyers but also in order to circumvent financial regulation: "The 'new-product generation machines' of investment banks, hedge funds and other firms have been, and are likely to continue to be, better-staffed and stronger than the structures that oversee their operations. This suggests a further motivation for greater product complexity – to elude regulation" (Anabtawi and Schwarcz 2011, 29). As we will discuss in the following two sections, the same assumption basically applies to the complexity of financial institutions.

3.4 Innovators vs. Regulators: Science Running Amok

Financial innovation on the one hand and financial regulation on the other are linked to each other in at least two ways: First, *regulation shapes innovation* both positively and negatively. During the financial crisis, the argument that too much regulation would hinder financial innovation and growth and slow down the economic recovery in the US was one of the major arguments, if not the major argument, against Dodd-Frank. The concerns were not new: As already indicated in the second chapter of this book, the described clash of regulation and innovation has some tradition in the area of finance. Shortly before the crisis, Margaret Cole, Director of Enforcement at the UK's FSA, warned that "regulators must be very wary of the damaging effects they can have on creativity, innovation and competition" in the financial sector (Cole 2006). Back then, the belief that financial innovation was per se beneficial was *conventional wisdom*, at least in Washington (Wilmarth 2013, 1294), and the *Washington Consensus* made it "virtually impossible for regulators to articulate concerns or even to have concerns" (Ford 2013).

Secondly, from the perspective of politics and regulation, financial innovation can be perceived as a *strategy for regulatory arbitrage*.[70] As the preceding section on CDOs has illustrated, the more complex securities get the more difficult it is to understand them, to monitor and supervise their use, to assess their relevance and to finally regulate them. We want to argue that a certain degree of data, information and knowledge asymmetries between regulatees (lead) and their regulators (lack) is inherent to all regulator-regulatee-relationships, representing the regular asymmetries "between informed insiders and uniformed outsiders" (Tufano 2004, 12). However, asymmetries are always a question of degree, and the massive asymmetries that have become characteristic of the 21st century financial system are, to a large degree, of an artificial and strategic nature (Merton 1995).[71] Recent rules and regulations mirror the complexity (but not the speed – see High Level Group on Financial Supervision in the EU 2009) of financial products; at the same time, financial regulators build-up their troops: Between 1980 and 2011, the ratio of UK regulators to UK financial sector employees grew from one to 11,000 to one to 300 (Haldane and Madouros 2012, 9). Yet, it is highly unlikely that financial policy-making and regulation can keep up with financial innovation.

In view of the highly sophisticated products that were at the heart of the recent financial crisis, Hu speaks of *science running amok* in a *financial Jurassic Park:*

> In the face of relentless competition and capital market disintermediation, big financial institutions have hired financial scientists to develop new financial products. Typically operating in an international wholesale market

70 In his interview with the FCIC, securities expert Satyajit Das warns his interviewers that he "can develop as many sorts and forms of leverage as humanly possible to get around the rules" (Das 2010). David Jones from the Federal Reserve Board describes how easy it is to circumvent a leverage ratio: "[J]ust move it off-balance-sheet, the simplest thing in the world, that's what these guys can do in their sleep" (Jones 2010).

71 Whether financial innovation adds to social welfare and whether its net impact is good or bad is yet another (undecided) issue. Tufano provides an informative overview on the two positions and as he shows, both sides bring forward good arguments (Tufano 2004). Merton for example has argued that financial innovations reduce transaction costs and information asymmetries (Merton 1995, 463).

> open only to major corporate and sovereign entities – a loosely regulated paradise hidden from public view – these scientists push the frontier, relying on powerful computers and an array of esoteric models laden with incomprehensible Greek letters. (Hu 2009)

According to this narrative, financial innovators exploit their knowledge lead over regulators to circumvent, as Stiglitz puts it, "laws and regulations designed to ensure the efficiency, equity, and stability of the financial sector" (Stiglitz 2009b, 13; see also Partnoy 2010). In 1986, Kane described the interplay between regulation and innovation as a regulatory dialectic (figure seven), arguing that politics and industry mutually adjust to each other through regulation on the one side and innovation on the other (Kane 1986). Now it appears that financial institutions have adapted to their regulatory environment not only by adapting, but also by deliberately increasing complexity, thereby provoking complex regulation.

The Basel accords provide a good example here. Confronted with increased complexity both at the organizational and product level, the accords delegated the risk weighting of assets to the banks themselves. These in turn have developed "techniques for 'risk-weight optimization' that allow them to choose investments that are in fact riskier than the supervisors believe" (Admati and Hellwig 2013, 184). It is therefore argued that Basel II encouraged financial institutions to increase complexity (Haldane and Madouros 2012; Admati and Hellwig 2013). Dodd- Frank, once fully implemented, might increase complexity even further.[72] In this sense, financial regulators can be well compared to Goethe's famous *Zauberlehrling*: The sorcerer's apprentice brings a broomstick to life. When he realizes that he cannot control it, he splits the broomstick into two with an axe. To his horror, he is not able to stop the stick: Both pieces come to life and, when split again, reduplicate once more. In response to the recent financial crisis, policymakers aim to regulate certain complex products. To provide an example: In 2012, the SEC and the CFTC jointly defined on 600 pages which types of derivatives are to be considered as

72 If the argument provided here is true that financial institutions evade regulation though innovation, it should be possible to spot a growth in finance patenting over the last decades and especially high numbers after important policy decisions such as Dodd-Frank (once it is fully implemented). Unfortunately, there is little literature on the history and development of finance patenting. Lerner argues that the importance of financial innovation is widely accepted but that the empirics of financial innovation are hardly explored (Lerner 2009, 1). Two facts are of great importance here: First, there is no clear definition of a financial patent. Tufano defines financial innovations broadly as "the act of creating and then popularizing new financial instruments as well as new financial technologies, institutions and markets", but he admits that it is already difficult to distinguish between financial product and process innovations (Tufano 2004, 4f.). Second, finance patenting behavior in the US has been strongly influenced by court decisions such as the US Supreme Court decision in the State Street Bank and Trust v. Signature Financial Group case, each having a huge impact on the number of finance patents (Lerner 2009, see also Tufano 2004). Finance patenting might therefore not be an indicator for financial innovation, but a mere reflection of judicial milestones.

swaps under Dodd-Frank regulation (Brush 2012; see also Haldane and Madouros 2012). The only commissioner who did not approve the document, Bart Chilton, justified his opposition by expressing his fear that the definition would again allow the financial industry to circumvent it: "I'm a little concerned that if you go back to the financial crisis, complexity in financial products is really what got us. People didn't know what was what. [...]. I'm a little concerned that these good forwards, these forwards used for legitimate purposes, are going to morph, kind of chimerical" (Commodity Futures Trading Commission 2012). In April 2013, Bloomberg L.P. filed a complaint against the CFTC, arguing that the Commission's decision to announce different margin requirements for two different types of derivatives, namely swaps and futures, has created "an opportunity for arbitrage between financial swaps and interchangeable 'swap futures' contracts", thereby threatening "the viability of Swap Execution Facilities [...] that Congress [...] sought to foster in order to enhance transparency and further public interest" (Heider, Hoerova, and Holthausen 2009).

Complex products cause a second type of asymmetry: It is not only regulators that lag behind in terms of knowledge and information but also buyers such as private borrowers and investors. Henderson and Pearson describe how "financial institutions can exploit investors by creating precisely the securities or other financial instruments for which investors are willing to overpay" (Henderson and Pearson 2009, 1). With regard to private borrowers, the crisis revealed that certain mortgage contracts were systematically designed to be not or poorly understood.

> According to the Wall Street Journal, in the early 1980s, the typical credit card contract was a page long; by the early 2000s, that contract had grown to more than 30 pages of incomprehensible text. The additional terms were not designed to make life easier for the customer. Rather, they were designed in large part to add unexpected – and unreadable – terms that favor the card companies. (Warren 2007, 2; see also Warren 2010)

This observation led to the establishment of the Consumer Financial Protection Bureau, or CFPB, in the US; we will take a closer look at it in chapter four. The CFPB is supposed to spot and prosecute deceptive behavior and protect consumers. As we will show, the Bureau is surprisingly successful in achieving its goal. The question remains how regulators should deal not only with product complexity, but with financial complexity in general.

3.5 Can and Should Financial Complexity be Eliminated?

When he was asked by the FCIC about the causes of the crisis, Neel Kashkari answered:

> Right away complexity, that people did not fully appreciate, you know, mortgage backed securities and CDOs [...] that is clearly part of the problem. I mean, again, many things were just risk, people did not know they were actually there. And this goes back to my point that you cannot legislate wisdom. People did not understand how risky overnight funding was because it had never blown up before. (Kashkari 2010)[73]

Prior to the crisis, legislators and regulators seemed to give in to increased financial complexity, as they delegated central supervisory functions to the private sector: US regulation increasingly relied on ratings conducted by rating agencies, e.g. in the context of SEC registration requirements (Schwarcz 2002),[74] and the Basel accords adopted this practice by incorporating private ratings into its bank capital adequacy requirements (Jackson 2001).[75] In this regard, the crisis marked a turning point. It not only revealed how little regulators actually knew about the system they were bound to monitor and police; it also called into question the widespread belief that financial innovation was ultimately beneficial. The value added by complex products and financial conglomerates seemed to be small when compared to the rescue programs brought up to save the economy.

The crisis experience brought new and radical reform ideas onto the agenda. To reduce the dependence of regulators on industry expertise, Dodd-Frank requires US agencies to review their use of ratings (Sec. 939A of Dodd-Frank). In view of insufficient data, information and knowledge, the US government established the Office of Financial Research. Systemic risk watchdogs like the US FSOC were established in several countries. As we will see in the following chapter, the FSOC has wide-ranging authorities, including the breakup of financial institutions that threaten financial stability. Haldane and Madouros have called for a *simplified and streamlined regulatory framework* including a complexity tax (Haldane and Madouros 2012, 14). Senators Warren, McCain, Cantwell and King introduced what they termed a *21st Century Glass-Steagall Act* to once again separate commercial and investment banking (Warren 2013b). Looking at these developments, the question arises whether US financial regulation undergoes a paradigm shift from innovation-friendly to anti-complexity regulation. However, while the described changes might in fact turn out to be far-reaching, fears to hamper innovation and growth are still widespread. Once again, we are reminded of the basic incongruence

73 Kashkari was interim Assistant Secretary of the Treasury for Financial Stability in 2008 and 2009 and oversaw the Troubled Asset Relief Program (TARP).

74 More specifically by the Nationally Recognized Statistical Rating Organizations or NRSROs.

75 As emphasized by Haldane and Madouros, "[t]he length of the Basel rulebook, if anything, understates its complexity. The move to internal models, and from broad asset classes to individual loan exposures has resulted in a ballooning in the number of estimated risk weights. For a large, complex bank, this has meant a rise in the number of calculations required from single figures a generation ago to several million today" (Haldane and Madouros 2012, 7).

between national financial policymaking on the one hand and global finance on the other: In view of radical reforms, global financial conglomerates can simply threaten to move somewhere else. Confronted with Warren's plans to restore Glass-Steagall, JP Morgan's Jamie Dimon countered that his institution, because of its size, is able to

> bank Caterpillar in like 40 countries. We can do a $20 billion bridge loan overnight for a company that's about to do a major acquisition. Size lets us build a $500 million data center that speeds up transactions and invest billions of dollars in products like ATMs and apps that allow your iPhone to deposit checks. We move $2 trillion a day, and you can see it by account, by company. These aren't, like, little things. And they accrue to the customer. *That's what capitalism is.* (Pressler 2012, emphasis added)[76]

Other initiatives such as the establishment of central clearinghouses for OTC derivatives aim to reduce the complexity related to opaque financial products. Hu discusses how regulators could keep pace with the financial pipeline, e.g. by enhancing their supervisory capacities, but he concludes, "the extraordinary informational asymmetry between regulators and market participants can make this unrealistic. [...] financial institutions generally may develop an ABS without any governmental clearance" (Hu 2012). Against the background of the financial crisis of 2007ff., and in view of subsequent events such as the London Whale trading loss and the 2010 Flash Crash, it is in fact highly unlikely that regulators could supervise the financial innovation. The crucial point about dark markets is, after all, that they exist *because* they are dark (Cohn 2010).

As indicated at the beginning of this chapter, it appears that governments confronted with 21st century financial complexity have two basic options, *either to build upon or to eliminate it* (Porter 2009), both of which will accompany us throughout this book. Building upon financial complexity can mean delegating regulatory and supervisory functions to the market, thereby broadening the use of self-imposed industry standards and guidelines and increasing the overall reliance on self-regulation and quasi-private governance regimes. The question would then be how to "set adequate contextual conditions for firms to apply and profit from intelligent self-control" (Willke and Willke 2012, 175). Here, we should keep in mind that industry experts are boundedly rational agents and that, as Kashkari puts it, *wisdom cannot be legislated.*[77] The second option, *eliminating financial*

---

76 This overall development is surprising insofar as for many decades, and going back to the Sherman Antitrust Act of 1890, huge corporations in the US were viewed with suspicion: "Size, in the American lexicon, means power, and the bigness of business was perceived as both an economic and political threat to democracy" (Bell 1973, 6).

77 Problems resulting from bounded rationality will be discussed at-length in the fifth and sixth chapter of this book.

complexity or at least reducing it, would require initiatives on all three levels of complexity identified in this chapter, e.g. central clearing (products), ring-fencing (organizations) and financial transaction taxes (system).[78] Such measures should, as Helleiner emphasizes, "also help to constrain the ability of market participants to dominate regulatory debates through their expertise" (Helleiner 2010a, 16). With regard to the policy responses to the financial crisis, we have to add a third option: Few believe that regulators will ever be able to catch up with financial institutions, yet US policymakers have established the OFR to enhance their ability to collect data and information on financial products, organizations and the system as such. Research and data accumulation, which both aim at *reducing uncertainty and non-knowledge*, accordingly have to be added to the set of available policy options (see Knight 1964, 347). So what should be done to cope with financial market complexity? A basic and current problem that is evident both in Dodd-Frank and the Basel accords is that financial and regulatory complexity grow in tandem (Haldane and Madouros 2012).[79] This correlation can be observed in other legal areas, too: In 1992, Schuck observed a general tendency of the legal system to become more complex (Schuck 1992) and traced it back both to special interests – groups of people or organizations who profit from but do not bear the costs of legal complexity – as well as to an increasingly complex society in general. Orts basically described the same development in the area of environmental law, observing not only "cognitive limits to protecting the environment through detailed orders" but also an ever increasing number of new and revised laws that limit the systems' processing capacity until it "breaks down under its own weight" (Orts 1995, 1241).[80] As a first step in the right direction, legislators and regulators should accordingly reduce the complexity of their own laws, rules and regulations: "Because complexity generates uncertainty, [...] it requires a regulatory response grounded in simplicity, not complexity" (Haldane and Madouros 2012, 19). Fighting complexity with complexity is, from a systems theory perspective, contradictory (Senge 1996). If national governments cannot directly reduce organizational and product complexity because of their own constraints (both with regard to borders and regulators' processing capabilities), and if legislation cannot possibly keep pace with the markets (pertaining speed and complexity), what other options remain?

---

78 Knight discusses the possibility of "slowing up the march of progress" to decrease uncertainty about the future (Knight 1964, 347).

79 Financial regulation has cultivated its own specific dark areas, as the financial system has cultivated its dark markets: Complex rules and regulations require knowledge only possessed by highly rewarded experts, and only a small group of experts is actually able to understand the details and intricacies. One might argue that the only ones profiting from this development are law and accounting firms.

80 More specifically, Orts advocates a shift from traditional command-and-control regulation to reflexive regulation; the latter is, as he argues, less static and hence better suited to react to a fast evolving and complex environment and body of knowledge than traditional forms of regulation (Orts 1995, 1252ff.).

Complex systems increase the risks resulting from known and unknown unknowns. As we will show in chapter five, not addressing financial system complexity will accordingly lead us directly into the next crisis. As Weber argues, greater "resilience is only achievable through scaling back complexity" of the financial sector (Weber 2012, 710), while Willke and Willke call for a reform of the regulatory sector instead:

> The crisis brings forth all the known risks and weaknesses of a combination of tight coupling and complex interaction of the system's parts. Since 'normal accidents' [...] are basically inevitable accidents within the parameters of a given system, and since the financial system's volatility and instability are endemic, the point is not to avoid crises but *to improve the organizations' and regulators' capacity to cope with crises and to improve the architecture of global finance* so as to reduce the most vicious weaknesses of tight coupling. (Willke and Willke 2012, 43)

Policymakers have indeed responded to the financial crisis of 2007ff. with changes in the architecture of global finance. The US has also introduced comprehensive reforms at the national level. If and how these reforms address the challenges presented by complexity, opacity and non-knowledge is a question that should be kept in mind while reading the next chapter.

4 US Policy Responses to the Crisis

"The impossibility for the political system effectively to control other systems with an adequate grasp of consequences and limited risk is inversely proportional to the facility with which such decisions can [be] put into force and, however sporadically, actually implemented. The astonishing expansion of competence in the welfare state begets a gigantic and uncontrollable machinery for increasing risk." (Luhmann 2008, 145)

The continuous transformation of the sovereign nation state is a widely discussed topic in political science literature (see for example Sassen 1996; Willke 2006). Over the last quarter of the 20th century, globalization has challenged the traditional understanding of the nation state characterized by exclusive territory and power. The crisis then confirmed a basic incongruence between national financial policymaking on the one hand and global finance on the other (Willke, Becker, and Rostásy 2013). In 2008, when confronted with the collapse of globally interconnected TBTF institutions, the power of the nation states was mostly limited to bailouts; even worse, governments felt there was no alternative to rescuing failing institutions. Apparently,

> a gap had opened up between the economic and the political organization of the world. The economic world has been globalized. Its institutions have a global reach and have operated by maxims that assumed a self-regulating global market. The financial collapse exposed the mirage. It made evident the absence of global institutions to cushion the shock and to reverse the trend. (Kissinger 2009)

Today, a small but growing group of financial intermediaries operates on a truly global scale. The financial crisis of 2007ff. forcefully demonstrated the implications for financial governance: Systemic risk is a phenomenon of global reach while the actual power of the nation state to mitigate it is alarmingly limited. Post-crisis financial reform must be viewed against this background. Without doubt, the crisis opened a window of opportunity for fundamental policy change, but with regard to the ongoing reform efforts the question remains whether the policy responses to the crisis present a turning point in global financial governance or if they will turn out to be yet another example of merely *symbolic politics* (Edelman 1970).

Financial regulation evolves in response to crises (Begg 2009, 1108), and the recent crisis revealed that regulators were badly prepared to deal with TBTF financial institutions. The orderly resolution of cross-border banks has accordingly become a high-priority topic on the global reform agenda. As we argued in chapter two, Levitin's contribution to systemic risk research is outstanding as it not only emphasizes the importance of a resolution mechanism for TBTF firms, but also incorporates political accountability and legitimacy into the concept of systemic risk (Levitin 2011). As we will see throughout this chapter, the resolution mechanism for SIFIs is an integral part of the US Dodd-Frank reforms; whether the crisis will alter the understanding of sovereignty and legitimacy is yet another question – its impact might well be limited to establishing central bank stress tests, to strengthening peer reviews by the IMF, and to changing the bank-internal risk models set up by finance quants (Patterson 2010; Manzoor 2013). As we saw in chapter two and three, a systems theory perspective on the crisis has clear implications on policymaking and regulation. Against this background, we also have to ask how current reforms address financial complexity, and if they take into account changes in the system characteristics of the 21st century financial system. These questions should be kept in mind while reading this chapter on policy responses to the crisis.

In the following sections we distinguish three sets of US policy responses: (1) the *ad hoc, short-term* policy responses during the first crisis months, such as the rescue of Bear Stearns, (2) the *medium-term, system-wide* policy responses, such as the Troubled Asset Relief Program (TARP), and (3) the *long-term, system-wide* policy responses imposed by the Dodd-Frank Act. Our framework is based on a publication by Seabrooke and Tsingou (2010) who differentiate between case-by-case responses and what they term responses *in a systemic context*. As we will see, the US policy responses gradually moved from one side of this continuum to the other. Starting with the ad hoc policy responses in 2007 and 2008 (section 4.1), we approach the US policy responses chronologically. We then turn to the key medium-term response towards the end of 2008, TARP (section 4.2), and ultimately get to the long-term policy responses included in the Dodd-Frank Act of 2010 (section 4.3). Neither of these subsections claims to be exhaustive – Dodd-Frank alone exceeds 800 pages and deals with different aspects of financial regulation such as remuneration practices and advisers to hedge funds; here, we focus on Title I (termed *Financial Stability*, establishing inter alia the FSOC and the OFR), Title II (introducing the Orderly Liquidation Authority), and Title X (establishment of the Bureau of Consumer Financial Protection).[81] We also look at stress tests and living wills and discuss how Dodd-Frank addresses TBTF. To put the US policy

81 The sections on the FSOC and the OFR are, with regard to structure and content, based on chapter 5.3 of Willke, Becker and Rostásy (2013).

responses into the larger context of global financial reform, we then look at European (section 4.4) and global (section 4.5) reform efforts to address systemic risk. To provide a comparative analysis, special emphasis is placed on the European Systemic Risk Board (ESRB) and the Financial Stability Board.

	short-term (ad hoc)	**medium-term (system-wide)**	**long-term (system-wide)**
national reach	Rescue of Bear Stearns	TARP	**FSOC, OFR, CFPB**
transnational reach	Rescue of Dexia	Deposit Guarantee	ESRB
global reach	–	–	FSB

Table 1: Analytical context of the FSOC and OFR assessment.

As we will see throughout this chapter, reform efforts in the US and the EU do partly overlap, yet there are also crucial differences. The financial crisis of 2007ff., even though it is often referred to as *the global financial crisis*, did not expose an identical set of weaknesses and problems on both sides of the Atlantic. While the Lehman collapse led to a recession in the US, it became a full-fledged, continuing sovereign debt and economic crisis in several EU countries. Here, the crisis called into question the regulatory and supervisory architecture as such: Financial integration had apparently outpaced policy integration, which is why the European institutions now focus on transforming the Economic and Monetary Union (EMU) into a European Banking Union. The US faced a slightly different set of problems: Here, the crisis did also reveal institutional shortcomings, especially deficiencies in the cooperation between financial regulators, but the crisis did not trigger such fundamental changes in the overall regulatory architecture as it did in the European Union (the US Office of Thrift Supervision, or OTS, was abolished, while the FSOC, the OFR and the CFPB were established; yet, all the other regulators remained and essentially kept their mandates). As it turned out during 2008, the fate of Bear Stearns, AIG and the GSEs was closely tied to complex derivatives that had not even been on regulators' radar until the crisis. As a result, the US government was forced to rescue and guarantee institutions and entire markets without having access to the relevant data and information, essentially flying blind (Mendelowitz and Liechty 2010, 3). Therefore, the US crisis was, among other things, perceived as a crisis of regulatory data, information and knowledge. To address this problem, the US government established the Office of Financial Research, presenting a somehow unique policy response to the financial crisis. As we will see, the strong focus of US reform on consumer financial protection is also characteristic for the US policy responses.[82]

4.1 Stretching the Law: Case-by-Case Responses in the US

Of the many crisis months, September 2008 stands out due to the astonishing number of case-by-case government responses. But the US government had actually tried to stop contagion from the residential housing market to the financial sector several months earlier. In March 2008, it orchestrated a takeover of the struggling investment bank Bear Stearns by JPMorgan, a deal that was backed by a 30 billion dollar loan by the Federal Reserve against Bear Stearns' weak collateral (Sorkin 2010, 77f.).[83] Bear Stearns specialized on securities that were tied to subprime mortgages (Financial Crisis Inquiry Commission 2011; see Lewis 2011, for a detailed description on the initial subprime crisis) and among the five biggest Wall Street banks, it was most leveraged (Davidoff and Zaring 2009). As two of Bear Stearns' mortgage-related hedge funds had declared bankruptcy in July 2007, Bear Stearns as the holding company was the financial institution suspected to fail first.

The fear of a Bear Stearns collapse was apparently contagious: US officials worried that a Bear Stearns collapse would trigger a run on the other investment banks, setting in motion a downward spiral like the one that would later be triggered by the Lehman bankruptcy. When the JPMorgan/Bear Stearns deal became public, New York Times journalist Roger Lowenstein commented: "What is scary is the degree to which the Fed assimilated the alarmism on the Street: 'These guys are so afraid of an economic cycle,' a hedge-fund manager remarked. And without public airing or debate, it stretched the implicit federal safety net under Wall Street" (Lowenstein 2008). According to the FCIC, Bernanke would later justify the deal with a potential domino effect of a Bear Stearns collapse:

> Stearns, which is not that big a firm, our view on why it was important to save it – you may disagree – but our view was that because it was so essentially involved in this critical repo financing market, that its failure

82 The following sections describe the US policy responses to the crisis; we did not include all rescue programs and lending facilities, as we did not think that every aspect of government intervention was important in the context of this book.

83 In fact, the Fed and JPMorgan purchased 29.97 billion dollars of Bear Stearns assets, with a 1.15 billion dollar loan from JPMorgan and a 28.82 billion dollar loan from the New York Fed. JPMorgan agreed to take the first 1.15 billion dollar of losses, and the Fed bore the risk of any losses exceeding 1.15 billion dollar (Financial Crisis Inquiry Commission 2011, 290).

> would have brought down that market, which would have had implications for other firms. (Financial Crisis Inquiry Commission 2011, 291)

Timothy Geithner as president of the New York Fed and Treasury Secretary Hank Paulson basically made the same argument:

> Could you just imagine the mess we would have had? If Bear had gone there were hundreds, maybe thousands of counterparties that all would have grabbed their collateral, would have started trying to sell their collateral, drove down prices, create even bigger losses. There was huge fear about the investment banking model at that time. [...] you would have had Lehman going...almost immediately if Bear had gone, and just the whole process would have just started earlier. (Financial Crisis Inquiry Commission 2011, 291, quoting Paulson)

The Bear Stearns case was a signal in two ways: First, it showed that even the long-established Wall Street firms could fail. Second, it demonstrated that the Fed and the Treasury were willing to prevent a failure. Emphasizing the first point, Paulson would later argue that from the day of the Bear Stearns rescue on, other market participants had time to prepare for the insolvency of another investment bank, especially Lehman Brothers, as it was expected to be the next in line (Sorkin 2010, 288). In fact, the opposite happened, as the Bear Stearns rescue made the hitherto implicit government guarantee for TBTF institutions explicit.

At the end of March 2008, shortly after the Bear Stearns rescue, the Fed launched a 200 billion dollar program called *Term Securities Lending Facility* (TSLF) to directly address the problems in the US mortgage market and to "unfreeze the nation's panicky credit markets" (Grynbaum 2008). Via TSLF, investment banks and other primary dealers could get access to safe Treasury securities against risky mortgage-backed securities as collateral (Financial Crisis Inquiry Commission 2011, 286). For the first time since the Great Depression, the Fed used section 13(3) of the Federal Reserve Act of 1932, this time to legitimize both the Bear Stearns bailout and TSLF and arguing that it was facing the *unusual and exigent circumstances* required by the Act (ibid., 287). Section 13(3) had, as we will illustrate towards the end of this section, been designed as a *grey hole* or *legal door* to open during times of crisis. Basing the rescue of Bear Stearns on section 13(3) of the Federal Reserve Act was nevertheless a highly controversial move:

> A former Congress – one long gone, but intimately acquainted with the trials and tribulations of financial crises – had seen fit to provide executive branch officials with a particular tool to be used in difficult times, and in the face of a potential crisis they used it. The remarkable aspect of this action is that [...] Emergency was declared quietly, by a few unelected officials, who then

> declared themselves capable of wielding only-vaguely-constrained powers to meet the crisis. (Wallach 2010, 7)

But this was only the beginning.

In July 2008, the Office of Thrift Supervision closed the failing GSE IndyMac. Around that time it became public that the government discussed plans to save the remaining two housing giants, the GSEs Freddie Mac and Fannie Mae (Duhigg 2008). Paulson would later explain why a bailout was inevitable: "after the housing market dried up in the summer of 2007, the key to getting through the crisis was to limit the decline in housing, prevent foreclosures, and ensure continued mortgage funding, all of which required that the GSEs remain viable" (Financial Crisis Inquiry Commission 2011, 310). The two GSEs were not only large but also interconnected: They did business with virtually every Wall Street company. The Treasury Secretary was able to convince Congress to pass the *Housing and Economic Recovery Act* (HERA) at the end of July, which allowed Treasury to provide capital to the GSEs. On September 7, the two "kings of leverage" (ibid., xx) were then brought under conservatorship.[84] According to Congressional Budget Office projections, the total federal outlays for the GSEs could reach 389 billion dollars by 2019 (Congressional Budget Office 2010, 8). A fact that is central in the context of this book is that, as the FCIC reports, the Treasury Department did not understand the exposure and financial condition of Freddie Mac and Fannie Mae until August 2008 (Financial Crisis Inquiry Commission 2011, xxi), but had nevertheless made the decision to recue them.

The fact that Lehman ran out of money only one week later came as a huge surprise for the officials at the Treasury Department (Financial Crisis Inquiry Commission 2011, 321) and also for Lehman's top management Sorkin (2010). That Lehman could become insolvent had been known and discussed after the Bear Stearns collapse, but the Fed and the Treasury apparently underestimated the speed and severity of Lehman's downfall. First, the Treasury and the Fed unsuccessfully tried to arrange a solution similar to the LTCM rescue. After that, Bank of America and Barclays considered buying Lehman Brothers. When Bank of America finally decided against the deal and the British Financial Services Authority (FSA) did not give the required approval for a deal with Barclays (Sorkin 2010; Financial Crisis Inquiry Commission 2011), Lehman ran out of options. Then the government decided, contrary to what was expected by Lehman and the market, not to bail out the investment bank (Federal Deposit Insurance Corporation 2011, 11). From the vantage point of political science, one question deserves particular prominence: Why did the US government decide not to save Lehman Brothers? The FCIC description of the crucial weekend of September 13/14 goes as follows:

---

84 The structure and business of the GSEs had been controversial for some time (see Mankiw 2010), but September 2008 was not the point in time to wind them down.

> [A] consortium of banks would fail to agree on a rescue, two last-minute deals would fall through, and the government would decide not to rescue this investment bank – *for financial reasons, for political reasons, for practical reasons, for philosophical reasons*, and because, as Bernanke told the FCIC, if the government had lent money, 'the firm would fail, and not only would we be unsuccessful but we would have saddled the taxpayer with tens of billions of dollars of losses.' (Financial Crisis Inquiry Commission 2011, 325, emphasis added)

When we look at the four reasons brought forward by the FCIC – financial, political, practical, and philosophical – the importance of political reasons for the decision can hardly be overestimated.[85] Internal documents and interviews provide evidence that the government just did not have the political support for a government rescue of the investment bank only one week after the GSEs had been bailed out:

> We need to talk. … I just can't stomach us bailing out Lehman. … Will be horrible in the press don't u think (Treasury Chief of Staff Jim Wilkinson in an email as quoted in Financial Crisis Inquiry Commission 2011, 330).

> [Resolving Lehman] should be done in a way that requires minimal temporary support. … No more Maiden Lane LLCs and no equity position by [the] Fed. Moral hazard and reputation cost is too high. (New York Fed Senior Vice President Patricia Mosser as quoted in Financial Crisis Inquiry Commission 2011, 331)

> There was a criticism of bailing out Wall Street. It was a combination of *political unwillingness* to bail out Wall Street and a belief that there needed to be a *reinforcement of moral hazard*. There was never a discussion about the legal ability of the Fed to do this. […] There was never discussion to the best of my recollection that they couldn't [bail out Lehman]. It was only that they wouldn't. (Merrill Lynch CEO John Thain as quoted by the Financial Crisis Inquiry Commission 2011, 342, emphasis added)

Lehman filed for bankruptcy on September 15, 2008. Just like Paulson, Bernanke would later justify the decision to let Lehman fall by saying that "the troubles at Lehman had been well known for some time", and that investors had had the time to prepare for a Lehman bankruptcy (Financial Crisis Inquiry Commission 2011, 340). Going back to chapter two and looking at Bernanke's definition of TBTF institutions as firms "whose size, complexity, interconnectedness, and critical

85 In his interview with the FCIC, Taylor describes how the Penn Central Transportation Company, a railroad company that filed for bankruptcy in 1970, was not bailed out by the government because the law firm of then President Richard Nixon was somehow involved and he therefore had to recuse himself (Taylor 2010).

functions are such that, should the firm *go unexpectedly into liquidation*, the rest of the financial system and the economy would face severe adverse consequences" (Bernanke 2010c, 20, emphasis added) reflects this point. Interestingly, the Lehman collapse had been expected, but its non-bailout came as a huge surprise.

A second, legal argument brought forward was that the Fed was not allowed to provide liquidity to Lehman under section 13(3) because, contrary to Bear Stearns, Lehman could not provide sufficient collateral to secure the loan *to the satisfaction of the Federal Reserve Bank* (Federal Reserve Act, Section 13(3)). According to this narrative, the government had essentially no choice but to let Lehman fail (Financial Crisis Inquiry Commission 2011; Alvarez et al. 2010). However, it is convincingly argued that the "absence of any objective criteria in the statutory language for the sufficiency of collateral leaves the extent and value of the collateral within the discretion of the Reserve Bank" (Alvarez et al. 2009, 6; see also Taylor 2010) and that the value of Bear Stearns' collateral had also been disputable. Davidoff and Zaring, in their legal analysis of the US bailouts, argue that Paulson's explanation does not stand up to critical scrutiny and that the government "wanted to make a statement" (Davidoff and Zaring 2009, 493) when it let Lehman fail. In this respect, Lehman was trial and error: The government did make a statement, but did not dare make another one. Interestingly, two other important decisions were made that same day. The Federal Reserve Board decided to bail out another company by invoking section 13(3) of the Federal Reserve Act: AIG immediately received a 85 billion dollar loan to meet its obligations and would later receive another 49.1 billion dollars under TARP (Financial Crisis Inquiry Commission 2011, 349f.). Secondly, Bank of America took over Merrill Lynch.[86] What had started as a subprime mortgage crisis had now become a full-fledged financial crisis. To prevent a bank run, the Fed extended the lending programs that were already in place, allowing financial companies to borrow from their FDIC-insured depository affiliates (ibid., 354). After the Reserve Primary Fund *broke the buck* on September 16 because of its exposure to Lehman – meaning that its net asset value fell below the usual dollar – a run on the money market fund (MMF) industry started, and the government set up a new lending program for the MMF industry that was ultimately able to stop the run.

This first phase of government intervention can best be characterized as *adhocracy* (Wallach 2010) or *regulation by deal* (Davidoff and Zaring 2009). Wallach argues that, in view of both uncertainty and the inadequance of the existing policy tools, policymakers started to *stretch the law* (Wallach 2010, 6), taking unconventional and unprecedented action to address the crisis. How was that possible? As already indicated at the beginning of this section, administrative law

86 The remaining investment banks would either become bank holding companies (Goldman Sachs and Morgan Stanley) or be sold (Washington Mutual, Inc. to JPMorgan Chase; Wachovia to Wells Fargo & Company) during the following weeks.

contains *grey and black holes* that implicitly or explicitly allow the executive to deviate from the law in case of emergency "because legislators and executive officials will never agree to subject all executive action to thick legal standards, because the inevitability of changing circumstances and unforeseen circumstances means they could not do so even if they tried" (Vermeule 2009, 1133). Section 13(3) of the US Federal Reserve Act, which was used extensively during the financial crisis, provides a good example here. The basic argument, going back to John Locke, is that every government has the right and duty to take extra-legal actions if an extraordinary situation occurs. Whether the decision is legitimate or not is, as was the case with the recent crisis management, decided in retrospective: "Prerogative is nothing but the Power of doing publick good without a Rule" (Locke, as quoted by Fatovic 2004, 430). The controversial German jurist Carl Schmitt has argued that all liberal democracies have to stretch or break the law in case of major emergencies, because no legal rule can include all future developments (Vermeule 2009). As a result, "extraordinary moments in the political life of a nation invariably challenge the strength of its commitment to values that are considered unassailable and unexceptionable in normal circumstances" (Fatovic 2004, 429). Following the same logic that can be found in the context of output legitimacy, time proves whether a policy response is legitimate or not. We have to keep in mind that many of the ad hoc decisions that were taken in 2008 were diametrically opposed to the basic values of the Republican Party. The collapse of a systemically important financial institution obviously provides a prototype for an economic emergency situation: "In a bailout, there are no preset rules. Each bailout is a system unto itself. Bailouts might follow similar patterns, but this is because of expediency, not because of legal requirements" (Levitin 2011, 481). The US has a long history of exploiting grey and black holes during times of financial distress (Wallach 2010). Wallach identifies Franklin D. Roosevelt's declaration of wartime emergency powers for economic emergencies to end the Great Depression, as well as his use of the *Trading with the Enemy Act* of 1917 to induce a national banking holiday of four days (ibid., 4f.). With regard to the recent financial crisis, he however criticizes that the "emergency actions have shifted from extralegal actions accompanied by retroactive judgment to broad delegation of powers to crisis executives"(ibid., 3). Congress became only involved when the team around Treasury Secretary Hank Paulson needed a system-wide, medium-term policy response to stop the financial downward spiral.

4.2 TARP as a System-Wide, Medium-Term Policy Response

In mid-September of 2008, Bernanke and Paulson came to the conclusion that "the time had come for a systemic solution", and that "deciding the fate of each financial firm one at a time wasn't working" (Sorkin 2010, 421; Davidoff and Zaring 2009, 467). The law could not be stretched endlessly, and the downturn had not yet been stopped. In order to stop the case-by-case solutions, it was decided to ask Congress for a new authority to increase the Treasury's flexibility, to demonstrate that the government had the political will and the leverage it required to save the system and – last but not least – to regain control of the overall situation. Neel Kashkari, then Assistant Secretary of the Treasury, described the situation as follows:

> One thing that was constant about the crisis is that *we were always behind.* It was always morphing and manifesting itself in ways we didn't expect. [...] So we knew we'd get one shot at this authority and it was important that we provided ourselves maximum firepower and maximum flexibility. We specifically designed the authority to allow us basically to do whatever we needed to do. (Financial Crisis Inquiry Commission 2011, 359f., emphasis added)

Paulson had said that he needed a *bazooka* to stop the crisis (The Economist 2008; The Wall Street Journal 2008). Maximum firepower and maximum flexibility were ultimately achieved through the 700 billion dollar Troubled Asset Relief Program (TARP) that was approved by Congress and signed by President Bush in October 2008. Its original purpose was to buy or insure troubled assets from the banks, thereby creating a market (as well as a market price) for these assets and getting the bad assets out of the banks' books. [87] To provide help to both non-financial institutions and financial institutions, the Fed created yet another program, the Commercial Paper Funding Facility that allowed these firms to roll over their debt (Financial Crisis Inquiry Commission 2011, 373). However, as the overall situation got worse, the Treasury started to rethink TARP: It was neither clear how the government would decide which specific assets to buy and what price to pay, nor that the program could be set up fast enough. It was therefore decided to rather use the TARP authority, termed a blank check by George Soros (2010), to recapitalize the financial sector directly. Via the newly formed *Capital Purchase Program*, the Fed purchased shares of preferred stock and warrants from several hundred financial institutions in the US. The largest bank holding companies, investment banks, and clearing and settlement banks – Bank of America, BNY Mellon, Citigroup, Goldman Sachs, JPMorgan, Merrill Lynch, Morgan Stanley, State Street,

87 Troubled assets were defined as: "(A) residential or commercial mortgages and any securities, obligations, or other instruments that are based on or related to such mortgages, that in each case was originated or issued on or before March 14, 2008, the purchase of which the Secretary determines promotes financial market stability; and (B) any other financial instrument that the Secretary, after consultation with the Chairman of the Board of Governors of the Federal Reserve System, determines the purchase of which is necessary to promote financial market stability, but only upon transmittal of such determination, in writing, to the appropriate committees of Congress" (Congressional Budget Office 2009, 1).

and Wells Fargo – were essentially forced to participate in the program (see Sorkin 2010, 256ff. for a detailed description of the respective meeting between Bair, Bernanke, Geithner, Paulson and the banks' CEOs; see also Congressional Budget Office 2009). To further increase overall confidence in the markets, two new FDIC programs were launched the next day: The first guaranteed certain senior debt for some holding companies and all FDIC-insured companies; the second insured certain non-interest-bearing deposits for all FDIC-insured institutions (Financial Crisis Inquiry Commission 2011, 374).[88] In the meantime, the case-by-case government responses went on: In November, Citigroup received a lifeline from the government. In December, GM and Chrysler received approval for bailout funds (Guillén and Suárez 2010, 273) – a part of the TARP funds was invested in and lent to automobile manufacturers and auto finance companies via the *Automotive Industry Financing Program* (Financial Crisis Inquiry Commission 2011, 375).

4.3 The Regulatory Overhaul: Dodd-Frank as a System-Wide Policy Response

As early as 2004, Geithner argued that "it is important that the standards applied to the largest financial institutions at the core of our financial system are calibrated to reflect their systemic relevance" (Geithner 2004). A central lesson from the crisis was that regulation and supervision did not adequately reflect the systemic relevance of certain financial institutions, and that they needed to be revised. The Dodd-Frank Wall Street Reform and Consumer Protection Act (Dodd-Frank or DFA) was designed to increase macroprudential regulation and supervision (Bernanke 2010c, 15) and aimed at ending TBTF. While advocates of more government and regulation have argued that financial markets should be fundamentally restructured by the government, e.g. by reducing the size of SIFIs, and while advocates of less government and regulation have argued that the US government has caused the crisis and should stop to intervene, Dodd-Frank takes a position that is located somewhere in the middle: The law does not alter the basic market structure, but it provides regulators with better monitoring instruments and new authorities to control it (McCarty 2013, 99). In this section, we look at the new institutions established by Dodd-Frank, namely the FSOC, the OFR and the CFPB. Besides, we examine how the DFA addresses TBTF directly. The leading question of our analysis is how the modified regulatory and supervisory architecture addresses

88 Later on, several amendments were made to the initial TARP program. Dodd-Frank did for instance reduce the TARP funds to 475 billion US dollar (Sec. 1302).

financial system complexity and problems related to data, information and knowledge asymmetries.

President Obama signed Dodd-Frank into law in 2010. It is widely described as the most far-reaching re-regulation of finance in the United States since the Great Depression. As the preface says, it was enacted "[t]o promote the financial stability of the United States by improving accountability and transparency in the financial system, *to end 'too big to fail'*, to protect the American taxpayer by *ending bailouts*, to protect consumers from *abusive financial services practices*, and for other purposes" (preface to Dodd-Frank, emphasis added). The Dodd-Frank key reforms are:

- The establishment of two new organizations, the Financial Stability Oversight Council and the Office of Financial Research to understand, identify and address systemic risk.
- The establishment of a Consumer Financial Protection Bureau (CFPB).
- The introduction of certain measures to address the too big to fail problem, namely the Orderly Liquidation Authority that enables the FDIC to wind down big and complex institutions, and the requirement for systemically important financial institutions to submit orderly resolution plans, or *living wills*, on a regular basis, as well as of
- expanded powers for the Fed to supervise SIFIs, and a limitation of the Fed's and the government's powers to provide liquidity or bail out banking institutions.
- The establishment of the Volcker rule to limit proprietary trading.
- The introduction of derivatives regulations.

Dodd-Frank is not yet fully implemented and as already indicated, the implementation process shapes the law to a notable degree. However, observers agree that Dodd-Frank will change the way banking business is carried out, and that "it is going to alter the structure of financial markets in profound ways" (Acharya, Cooley, et al. 2010a, 1). Analyzing Dodd-Frank in detail would go beyond the scope of this book – the act alone has 848 pages, and as Dodd-Frank requires about 400 detailed rule-makings, the majority of which is work in progress, it might once completed amount to 30,000 pages of rulemaking in total (Haldane and Madouros 2012, 8). Our focus here lies on the establishment of new institutions – namely the CFPB, the FSOC and especially the OFR – as they are highly relevant in the context of data-, information- and knowledge-related problems. We will first have a look at the FSOC's mandate, structure and proceedings and then proceed with the OFR before we provide a brief analysis of the CFPB. The Volcker rule and the regulation of derivatives will not be discussed in this book – not only because they are less important in the context of data, information and knowledge asymmetries, but also because their reach and impact depends very much on the technical details set by the agencies (Coffee 2012).

4.3.1 The Financial Stability Oversight Council[89]

When it made the decision to establish a systemic risk oversight council, the US government had basically two options: To either adapt the UK/Japan model and merge the existing bodies into a single macroprudential entity, or to maintain the fragmented regulatory structure of the US financial system and introduce a new, additional macroprudential body. It chose the latter option and created the Financial Stability Oversight Council as a loose forum for coordination and co-operation between the existing federal financial regulators in the United States. Preserving the highly specialized knowledge of each regulator in its respective regulatory and supervisory area was a major argument for the US model: Shortly before Dodd-Frank came into force, Bernanke argued that to give "all macro prudential responsibilities to a single agency risks creating regulatory blind spots, as [...] the skills and experience needed to oversee the many parts of our complex financial system are distributed across a number of regulatory agencies" (Bernanke 2010b). The material is organized as follows: We will first describe the FSOC structure, its purpose and duties, as well as its accountability; we will then get to the Council's non-legal and legal authorities, putting special emphasize on the latter. Other systemic risk councils were established in France, Denmark and UK. As we will see, while all systemic risk councils seek influence, the FSOC holds actual power.

FSOC Structure

The FSOC was established with the enactment of Dodd-Frank. The "loose umbrella organization" (Cooley et al. 2010, 69) brings together ten voting members: The Treasury Secretary, who serves as chairman of the FSOC, the chairperson of the Fed Board of Governors, the Comptroller of the Currency, the director of the Bureau for Consumer Protection, the chairpersons of the Securities and Exchange Commission, the Federal Deposit Insurance Corporation, the Commodity Futures Trading Commission, and the National Credit Union Administration Board, the director of the Federal Housing Finance Agency and an independent member with insurance expertise who is appointed by the President (Sec. 111(b)). These member organizations build the direct organizational environment of the FSOC (see figure eight). The directors of the Office of Financial Research and of the Federal Insurance Office, a state insurance commissioner who must be selected by the state insurance commissioners, a state banking supervisor who must be selected by the state banking supervisors and a securities expert who must be selected by state

89 Chapters 4.3.1 and 4.3.2 of this book are based on the research and analysis of Willke et al. (2013, ch. 5.3.2 and ch. 5.3.3).

securities commissioners, have a supervisory role and build the group of nonvoting FSOC members (Sec. 111(b)). Some of the FSOC's voting and non-voting members are more central to the work of the FSOC than others: The Treasury Department hosts the FSOC; the OFR conducts research for the FSOC, and based on Sec. 118 of Dodd-Frank, it also funds the Council; and the Fed performs the supervision of SIFIs that results from the FSOC designations.

As the structure of the Council indicates, the FSOC has a strong mandate for coordination and collaboration, therein addressing two of the major US problems identified during the crisis (Willke, Becker, and Rostásy 2013). Federal regulators had not only failed to communicate with each other; they had also entered fierce competition for regulatory charters (Wilmarth 2013, 1390).[90] The Council's objective is to build strong relationships within the group of domestic supervisors and regulators, increasing cooperation and collaboration within the highly fragmented regulatory system of the US; moreover, it aims at strengthening cooperation with international and transnational bodies, thereby establishing a more global perspective in US financial supervision (Willke, Becker, and Rostásy 2013, 126). As the Government Accountability Office (GAO) emphasized in its first FSOC assessment, "FSOC's effectiveness in providing for a more comprehensive view of threats to U.S. financial stability hinges to a large extent on collaboration among its many members, almost all of whom have their own independent regulatory responsibilities" (Clowers 2013, 4). However, statements by government officials and insiders indicate that collaboration within the FSOC works well (Willke, Becker, and Rostásy 2013) – or, at least, better than it did before.

90 In this context, a statement made by New York's mayor Michael Bloomberg and Charles E. Schumer, Democratic senator from New York, is especially queer: The two criticized the US financial regulators for "often competing to be the toughest cop on the street" (Schumer and Bloomberg 2006).

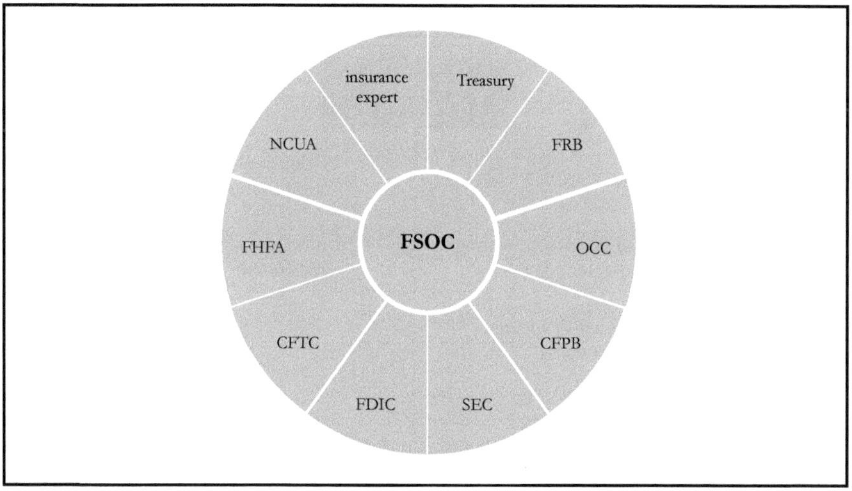

Figure 6: The organizational environment of the FSOC (Willke et al. 2013, 128).

As the following figure shows, the Council is organized in three committees and a number of sub-committees that roughly correspond with the key areas of the Dodd-Frank reform: A Deputies Committee, a group of Standing Functional Committees and a Systemic Risk Committee. The Systemic Risk Committee reflects the differentiation between micro- and macroprudential regulation that the crisis has brought back on the supervisory agenda, consisting of an Institutions and a Market Sub-Committee. Among the Standing Functional Committees, the Data Sub-Committee provides the organizational link to the OFR.

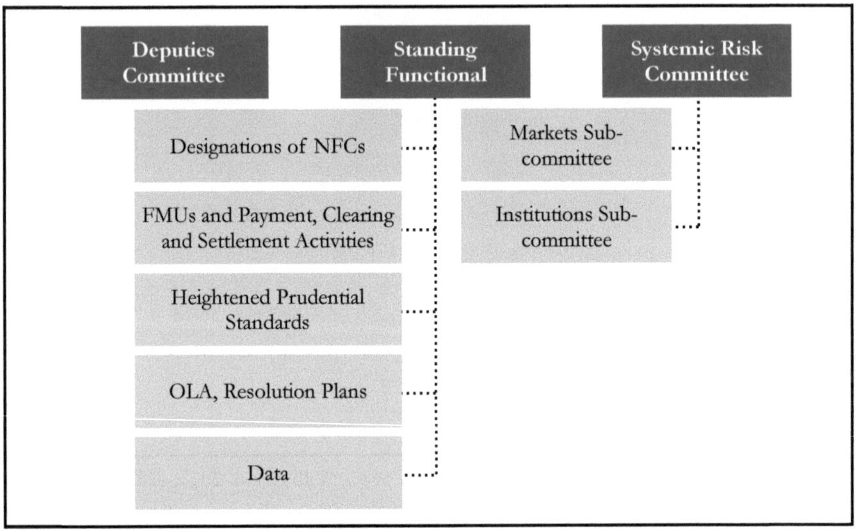

Figure 7: FSOC structure (Willke et al. 2013, 130).

It is difficult to find exact information on the size of the Council. The FSOC budget information for 2011 and 2012 projected 17 FSOC employees for 2011 and 24 employees for 2012, including administrative, legal, and policy staff (Financial Stability Oversight Council 2011b). A projected increase in labor costs indicates that the FSOC plans to substantially increase its workforce in 2013 (Financial Stability Oversight Council 2013b).f

FSOC Purpose and Duties

The purpose of the FSOC is outlined in section 112 of Dodd-Frank (emphasis added) as follows:

(A) to *identify risks to the financial stability of the United States* that could arise from the material financial distress or failure, or ongoing activities, of large, interconnected *bank holding companies or nonbank financial companies*, or that could arise outside the financial services marketplace;

(B) to promote market discipline, by *eliminating expectations* [...] that the Government will shield them from losses in the event of failure; and

(C) to respond to emerging threats to the stability of the United States financial system.

The duties of the FSOC as in section 112 of Dodd-Frank can be summarized as:

- to collect data and information from its members and from other agencies, as well as to direct the OFR to collect information, and to facilitate information sharing and coordination among its member agencies and with other agencies;
- to monitor the marketplace and identify potential threats to financial stability;
- to require supervision by the Fed Board of Governors for nonbank financial companies (NFCs) that may pose risks to US financial stability in the event of distress or failure;
- to make recommendations to the Fed Board of Governors concerning the establishment of heightened prudential standards for nonbank financial companies and large, interconnected bank holding companies (BHCs);
- to identify systemically important financial market utilities (FMUs) and payment, clearing and settlement activities;
- to monitor domestic and international financial regulatory proposals and developments;
- to advise Congress on issues regarding US financial stability;
- to recommend general supervisory priorities and principles to its member agencies;
- to identify gaps in financial regulation;
- to make recommendations to primary financial regulatory agencies;
- to review and, as appropriate, submit comments to the SEC and any standard-setting body with respect to existing or proposed accounting principles, standards, or procedures;
- to provide a forum for discussion and analysis of emerging market developments and financial regulatory issues, and the resolution of jurisdictional disputes;
- to annually report to and testify before Congress.

The FSOC duties and purposes are clearly not designed to handle ad hoc emergency situations like the ones observed during 2008; instead, the Council is set up to prevent systemic risk from building up in the first place.

Willke et al. draw a detailed picture of the FSOC agenda from 2010 to April 2013. They are able to show that during the first two and a half years after its establishment, the Council was strongly occupied with internal issues: The FSOC committee structure, the transparency policy of the Council, the confidentiality of Council information in general, the rules of the organization of the Council as well as the reports for Congress required by Dodd-Frank, but especially the annual reports and the annual budget were dominant issues (Willke, Becker, and Rostásy 2013). Besides these internal issues, the designation of NFCs and FMUs played a major role, followed directly by MMF reform (ibid.). This comes as no surprise: The designation power presents – as the following subchapters will show – the most important authority of the FSOC.

FSOC Accountability
The members of the Council are held accountable insofar as each of them, together with the Council's annual report, has to submit a signed statement to Congress, stating whether all reasonable steps to provide financial stability and mitigate systemic risk have been taken or not (Sec. 112(b)). The FSOC is also required by the Government Performance and Results Act (GPRA) of 1993 to produce strategic plans, annual performance plans and performance updates (Clowers 2013, 11). In its role as chairperson of the Council, the Treasury Secretary has to appear regularly before the House and the Senate to discuss the Council's efforts and the annual report (Sec. 112(c)). Through various mechanisms, Dodd-Frank attempts to hold the FSOC, as well as its individual members, accountable for their actions (or non-actions):

> if something happens in this coming year, either it's in this report, and we have something that's on the way right now to try to address it. Or [...] it's like a [...] rock from out of space that no one could see coming. That forces people to really pay attention to a systemic crisis, because the next time there is a financial crisis the first thing people will do is go back to the annual report and say: was this thing in the report? And if not, why not, and if so, what are we supposed to do about it? (Interview with Andreas Lehnert, December 05, 2012, Washington)

The American government scholar James M. Landis, who was the second person to hold the post of SEC chairman, has pointed out that to place "responsibility directly upon a specific group means that a finger can be publicly pointed at a particular man or men who are charged with the solution of a particular question" (Landis 1947 [1938], 28). When we look at the pre-crisis architecture of the US supervisory system, the FSOC constitutes a clear improvement with regard to macroprudential responsibility and accountability. The accountability mechanisms for the FSOC – are they weak or are they strong enough? – are nevertheless a controversial issue (Clowers 2013). The first two annual reports were approved unanimously by the FSOC voting members (Financial Stability Oversight Council 2012a, 2013a), but received criticism for having missed serious threats (Clowers 2013, 8). The first GAO assessment of the FSOC in 2012 revealed a set of weaknesses and challenges: The GAO acknowledged the Council's efforts to establish internal structures, committees and rules regarding the designation process. It however called for "more systematic approaches that are forward looking and help prioritize threats to the financial system" (ibid., 1). The FSOC should also improve its transparency, monitor the implementation of its recommendations, assess their impact, clarify certain responsibilities with the OFR, and further work on its collaboration efforts (Clowers 2013).

FSOC Legal Authorities

Via the OFR, the FSOC possesses wide-ranging authorities to collect data and information. We want to leave these authorities aside for a moment and discuss all OFR-related aspects of Dodd-Frank in the following chapter. What distinguishes the FSOC from other systemic risk councils is its power to designate nonbank financial companies and financial market utilities as systemically important. According to Sec. 117 of Dodd-Frank, certain financial institutions are automatically declared systemically important. All entities that were a *bank holding company* with total consolidated assets of 50 billion dollars or greater as of January 2010, that received financial assistance under TARP, and/or ceased to be a bank holding company after January 1 of 2010 are subject to enhanced prudential standards and supervision by the Fed. With regard to the many mergers and acquisitions during the crisis, section 117 also applies to the financial institutions that succeeded such entities. According to Dodd-Frank, "such entity shall be treated as a nonbank financial company supervised by the Board of Governors, as if the Council had made a determination under section 113 with respect to that entity" (Sec. 117(b)).

Sec. 113 of Dodd-Frank empowers the Council to also determine the supervision and regulation of certain *nonbank financial companies* by the Fed.[91] To designate such an institution as systemically important, the Council has to decide whether "material financial distress at the U.S. nonbank financial company" (the *First Determination Standard*) or its "nature, scope, size, scale, concentration, interconnectedness, or mix of the activities [...] could pose a threat to the financial stability of the United States" (the *Second Determination Standard*). According to Sec. 113(a), it has to consider in the designation process:

- the extent and nature of the NFC's leverage, of its off-balance-sheet exposures, and of its transactions and relationships with other significant financial companies;
- the importance of the NFC as a source of credit for different entities (households, businesses, communities, etc.) and as a source of liquidity for the United States financial system;
- the extent to which assets are managed rather than owned by the company, and the extent to which ownership of assets under management is diffuse;
- the nature, scope, size, scale, concentration, interconnectedness, and mix of the activities of the company;

91 According to Title I of Dodd-Frank, nonbank financial companies are domestic and foreign companies that are "predominantly engaged in financial activities", with certain exceptions, for example bank holding companies.

- the degree to which the NFC is already regulated;
- the amount and nature of the financial assets of the NFC, and of its liabilities, including the degree of reliance on short-term funding;
- any other risk-related factors that the Council deems appropriate.

Based on the guiding principles set by Dodd-Frank, the FSOC has developed a three-stage designation process for NFCs. It involves "both quantitative analysis and the Council's qualitative judgment" (U.S. Department of the Treasury 2012) and takes into account the potential impact of an NFC's failure (evaluation based on size, substitutability and interconnectedness) and its vulnerability (evaluation based on leverage, liquidity risk, maturity mismatch and the existing regulatory scrutiny) (ibid.). Stage one consists of several static quantitative thresholds to identify an initial set of NFCs for further evaluation. During stage two, the FSOC assesses – based on publicly available or voluntarily provided information – whether the NFCs identified pose a threat to the stability of the United States. Stage three gives the NFCs under consideration the opportunity to submit additional information.

Stage 1
First, the Council will apply *uniform quantitative thresholds* to identify those nonbank financial companies that will be subject to further evaluation. A nonbank will be further evaluated if it has at least 50 billion dollars in total consolidated assets, and if it meets any one of the following thresholds: 30 billion dollars in gross notional credit default swaps outstanding for which the nonbank financial company is the reference entity; 3.5 billion dollars in derivative liabilities; 20 billion dollars of total debt outstanding; 15 to 1 leverage ratio, as measured by total consolidated assets to total equity; or 10 percent ratio of short-term debt to total consolidated assets
Stage 2
The Council will analyze the nonbank financial companies identified in Stage 1 using a *broad range of information available* to the Council primarily through existing public and regulatory sources.
Stage 3
The Council will *contact each nonbank financial company* that the Council believes merits further review to collect information directly from the company that was not available in the prior stages. Each nonbank financial company that is reviewed in Stage 3 will be

notified that it is under consideration and be provided an *opportunity to submit written materials* related to the Council's consideration of the company for a proposed determination.

Table 2: Process for nonbank financial company designation (Willke, Becker and Rostásy 2013, 134).

Compared to the relatively vague categories given in Dodd-Frank, these three stages are much more formalized. And yet the FSOC acknowledges the limits of formalization, stating that

> the Council does not believe that a determination decision can be reduced to a formula. Each determination will be made based on a company-specific evaluation and an application of the standards and considerations set forth in section 113 of the Dodd-Frank Act, and taking into account qualitative and quantitative information that the Council deems relevant to a particular nonbank financial company. (Federal Register Vol. 77 2012, 21642)

As the second chapter of this book indicates, an over-formalization also bears the risk of focusing on the single institution, losing sight of the system as such.

In July 2013, the FSOC designated the first two NFCs as systemically important: AIG and a General Electric Capital Corporation, Inc. (GECC). Both designations had been expected by the media (Scism and Zibel 2012), and neither of the companies requested a Section 113(e) hearing before the Council to appeal against the designation (Financial Stability Oversight Council 2013c). In September 2013, the FSOC added Prudential Financial, Inc. to the list.

Based on Title VIII of Dodd-Frank (the *Payment, Clearing, and Settlement Supervision Act of 2010*), the designation power of the Council also applies to financial market utilities (FMUs) and certain payment, clearing and settlement activities. It is important to differentiate between the two, because the Council has decided to deal with them in separate rulemakings (Federal Register Vol. 76 July 27, 2011, 44763). While it has not yet decided on a process to identify and evaluate the relevant payment, clearing and settlement activities, it has already identified a first set of systemically important FMUs. Dodd-Frank defines an FMU as "any person that manages or operates a multilateral system for the purpose of transferring, clearing, or settling payments, securities, or other financial transactions among financial institutions or between financial institutions and the person" (Sec. 803(5)). Based on Section 804, the FSOC must designate FMUs and payment, clearing and settlement activities as systemically important, taking into account:

- the aggregate monetary value of transactions processed through or carried out by the FMU;

- the aggregate exposure by the FMU to its counterparties;
- the relationship, interdependencies, or other interactions with FMUs or payment, clearing, or settlement activities;
- the effect that the failure of or a disruption to the FMU would have;
- any other factors that the Council deems appropriate.

Roughly a year before the first NFC designations, the Council announced that it had identified eight systemically important FMUs. Compared to the two NFCs, these companies are much less known to the general public.[92] The FMU designation process consists of two steps:

- First, the Council evaluates whether the failure of or a disruption to the functioning of the FMU now or in the future could create or increase the risk of significant liquidity or credit problems spreading among financial institutions or markets. The first step is "largely data-driven" (Federal Register Vol. 76 July 27, 2011, 44764).
- Second, the Council decides whether the spread of such liquidity or credit problems among financial institutions or markets could threaten the stability of the financial system of the United States. In this second step, the FMU "will be subject to a more in-depth review, with a greater focus on qualitative factors, in addition to other institution and market specific considerations" (ibid., 44765).

Systemically important FMUs are subject to additional examinations and reporting requirements (ibid., 44764). The analytical framework of the first stage is laid out in the following table.

Consideration (A): Aggregate monetary value of transactions processed by an FMU
(A)(1): Number of transactions processed, cleared or settled by the FMU
(A)(2): Value of transactions processed, cleared or settled by the FMU
(A)(3): Value of other financial flows that may flow through an FMU
Consideration (B): Aggregate exposure of an FMU to its counterparties
(B)(1): Credit exposures to counterparties

92 As of July 2012, the FSOC designated the Clearing House Payments Company L.L.C. in its role as operator of the Clearing House Interbank Payments System, CLS Bank International, the Chicago Mercantile Exchange, Inc., the Depository Trust Company, the Fixed Income Clearing Corporation, ICE Clear Credit LLC, the National Securities Clearing Corporation and the Options Clearing Corporation as systemically important (Financial Stability Oversight Council 2012b).

(B)(2): Liquidity exposures to counterparties
Consideration (C): Relationship, interdependencies, or other interactions of an FMU with other FMUs or payment, clearing or settlement activities
Consideration (D): Effect that the failure of or disruption to an FMU would have on critical markets, financial institutions or the broader financial system
(D)(1): Role of an FMU in the market served
(D)(2): Availability of substitutes
Consideration (E): Any other factors that the Council deems appropriate

Table 3: Stage one of the FMU designation process (figure based on Federal Register Vol. 76 July 27, 2011).

As is the case with the NFC designation process, the FMUs are first evaluated in quantitative terms to sort out the smaller and less interconnected institutions (see table 3). The second stage then allows for qualitative factors, although it remains unclear what they are and how they are applied. The third element of the designation authority – the payment, clearing and settlement activities addressed in Title VIII – still remains to be formed. Its relevance became clear in the context of MMF reform during 2012, when the FSOC flexed its muscles for the first time: The collapse of Lehman Brothers had triggered a run on one of the biggest MMFs, the Reserve Primary Fund, in September 2008. As described in the preceding section, the Treasury stepped in and guaranteed the one dollar share price of MMFs to stop the panic (U.S. Department of the Treasury 2008). In view of the run, it became common sense among policymakers and regulators that the MMF industry required stronger regulation. A first set of new rules was introduced during 2010, requiring MMFs to hold a larger amount of liquid assets (Investment Company Act Rule 2a-7). The need for further MMF reform was then discussed at-length in the FSOC annual reports of 2012 and 2013 (Financial Stability Oversight Council 2012a, 2013a). During summer and fall of 2012 it turned out that the SEC could not agree on a more substantial reform: Mary Schapiro, then chairperson of the Commission, was unable to convince three of her five commissioners (three Democrats, two Republicans) of her proposal. After her defeat, Schapiro stated that "she would now support efforts by other regulators to force reform on the industry" (Popper 2012). Before Dodd-Frank, efforts to reform the MMF industry probably would have died at that point; however, one month after the SEC announced its decision to stop proceeding with MMF reform, Geithner in his role as chairman of the FSOC sent a public letter to the Council members, urging the group to "use its authority under section 120 of the Dodd-Frank Act to recommend that the SEC proceed with MMF reform" (Geithner 2012, 2). Geithner acknowledged that the SEC was, due to its expertise and authority, best suited to implement MMF reform; he however argued that the Council should "take active steps in the event that the SEC is unwilling to act in a timely and effective manner" (ibid., 3). Based on Dodd-Frank, the Council had two options: To either designate certain MMFs as systemically important NFCs under Title I of Dodd-Frank; or to apply its Title VIII authority to designate certain payment, clearing or settlement activities, meaning the MMF industry as a whole. While it is was yet clear at the time how the designation of a whole industry or sector would de-facto work, the FSOC was able to push forward a reform initiative that would otherwise have come to a halt.[93]

FSOC Non-Legal Authorities

The case of MMF reform brings us to the non-legal powers of the FSOC. In November 2012 – exercising its Sec. 120(a) authority "to provide for more stringent regulation of a financial activity by issuing recommendations to the primary financial regulatory agencies to apply new or heightened standards and safeguards" for the first time – the Council publicly proposed recommendations for MMF reform to the SEC (Financial Stability Oversight Council 2012c). The case of MMF reform shows exemplary that, even though the Council recommendations are not legally binding – meaning that the accountable agency, in this case the SEC, cannot be forced to implement an FSOC proposal – they nevertheless create a pressure for reform on the primary agency. The overall process as outlined for the Council in Sec. 120 – to first propose reform options, to then seek public comment, to ultimately recommend reform options to the primary agency and to report to Congress the status of implementation – keeps the issue up on the political agenda. Three months after the FSOC's proposed rulemaking, the presidents of the twelve US Federal Reserve Banks published a letter to the council, jointly supporting the efforts and the proposal (Rosengreen 2013). It took the SEC until June to finally suggest two reform alternatives (Securities and Exchange Commission 2013b). The proposed reforms do not go as far as the ones proposed the year before under Mary Schapiro's chairmanship at the SEC. However, they present a step forward, or at least a step into the right direction. With regard to the public comment period, it will still take some time until reforms are ultimately adopted.

The Section 120 authority illustrates the power of *framing, blaming and shaming* as is usually exercised by NGOs (Ahmed and Potter 2006). We argue that,

93 At this point it is important to note that the FSOC's designation authority is ultimately indirect: While the Council decides upon the designation, it cannot supervise the designated institution itself, but instead authorizes the Fed to do so (Kern and Lantz 2012). In this respect, Dodd-Frank expands the authority of the Federal Reserve Bank. But even though the Council has no direct supervisory authority over financial institutions, it "plays an important role in regulation, because firms that it designates as systemically important come under a consolidated supervisory regime that may be considerably more stringent than the standards that apply to non-systemic firms" (Jickling and Murphy 2010, 24). In addition, the FSOC must approve decisions by the Fed to shut down SIFIs posing a threat to financial stability (ibid.).

besides the legal powers of the Council, it is its ability to publicly blame and shame current policy (in)actions and developments that makes the FSOC a powerful new player in Washington. This non-legal power is certainly backed by the legal authority to designate. Interestingly, the Council used its recommendation authority in 2012, before it was even clear whether the Council could exercise Title I and VIII to designate MMF institutions or their activities, which is why the Council's actions where perceived as risky by the media: "Depending on how the SEC reacts to these recommendations, detractors are likely to conclude the FSOC's authority is either toothless or too harsh" (Lamson and Favretto 2013). Of equal importance is the Council's potential for bringing together the relevant regulatory agencies. As one of our interview partners argued, the FSOC provides not only a forum for coordination and cooperation between the agency heads; more importantly, it is the place where senior staff from the respective agencies get to know each other and informal networks evolve.

4.3.2 The Office of Financial Research

The Office was established in 2010 to address the problems related to insufficient data, information and knowledge that became evident during the financial crisis in the US (Flood et al. 2010). While systemic risk councils have been established in the US and elsewhere, the creation of the OFR presents a unique policy response to the crisis. Since the day Dodd-Frank was signed into law, the mandate and authority of the Office have been a subject of controversial debate in the media and the financial arena: According to our research, US financial regulators feared that the OFR would double their data collection efforts, while financial institutions threatened to leave the United States in order to protect their confidential information. Interestingly, the OFR has not yet received much attention from political scientists (cf. Willke, Becker, and Rostásy 2013). We will provide an overview over the mandate and structure of the OFR, and then discuss to the legal authorities of the Office. Whether the OFR can in fact mitigate systemic risk through data and information collection will be discussed in the last part of this section.

OFR Mandate and Structure

The Office of Financial Research was established within the Treasury Department (Sec. 152 of Dodd-Frank). Its purpose and duties are to fill data gaps (*data collection*), to standardize data types and formats (*data standardization*), to conduct applied and essential long-term research (*research*), to develop tools for risk measurement and monitoring (*risk monitoring*), to make these data available to the FSOC member agencies and to support their data collection efforts (see Sec. 153 for the original wording). Its mandate as well as its first publications indicate that the focus of the OFR lies in *data aggregation and analysis*. Yet, its duty to perform research (Sec. 153(a)) exceeds pure data collection and should result in learning processes and the buildup of OFR-specific expertise. In a conference paper of 2010, the OFR researchers further substantiated the overall task of the OFR: To assess *firm-wide as well as system-wide risk*, the Office should collect data that "can resolve the fundamental questions of who [...] is obligated to pay how much to whom, on which future dates, and under what contingencies" (Flood et al. 2010, 2). The OFR's dedication to establishing a global Legal Entity Identifier (LEI) system, which is in effect a system of barcodes that helps to identify all entities in market transactions, must be seen in this context (Reed 2014).[94] Dodd-Frank directed the OFR to build two centers: the *Data Center*, which focuses on data collection, and the *Research and Analysis Center*, which is required to "conduct, coordinate, and sponsor research to support and improve regulation of financial entities and markets", to "maintain expertise in such areas as may be necessary to support specific requests for advice and assistance from financial regulators" and to "conduct studies and provide advice on the impact of policies related to systemic risk" (Sec. 154(c)). The mandate and the structure of the OFR are accordingly twofold: To collect data on the one hand, and to acquire maintain expertise on the other.

94 Since its establishment, the OFR has hosted a few conferences and published several articles in its working paper series. Just as the OFR annual reports, these papers give us an idea of OFR agenda; they dealt with *data transparency and confidentiality* (Flood et al. 2013), *stress testing and stress scenario selection* (Bookstaber et al. 2013; Glasserman, Kang, and Kang 2013; Flood and Korenko 2013), *financial contagion* and hedge fund contagion (Glasserman and Young 2013; Akay, Senyuz, and Yoldas 2013), *contingent capital* instruments (Chen et al. 2013), *cyclical macroprudential policy* (Elliott, Feldberg, and Lehnert 2013), *agent-based modeling* (Bookstaber 2012), and *risk management and risk analytics* (Flannery et al. 2012; Bisias et al. 2012). This list does not include any articles that were published after August 2013.

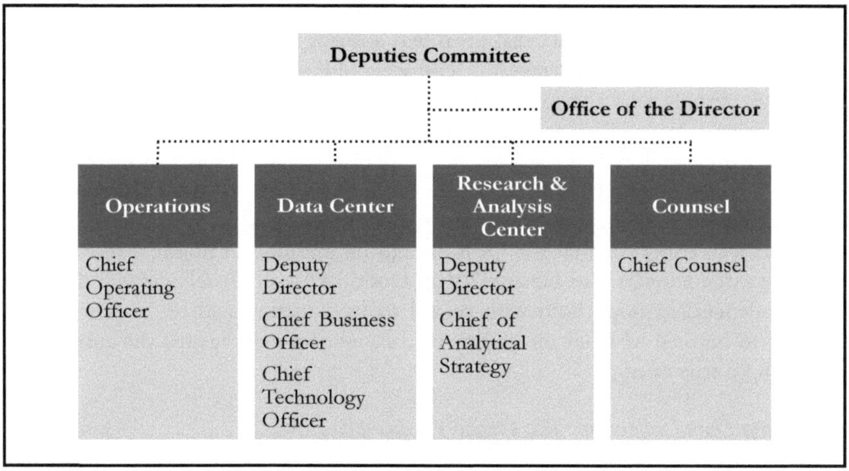

Figure 8: The internal structure of the OFR (Willke et al. 2013, 144).

While the FSOC heavily relies on the expertise and staff of its member agencies, the OFR requires its own *skilled workforce* to fulfill its mandate. According to its first Director Richard Berner, the OFR plans to employ 275 to 300 full time employees by 2014/2015, and had reached a staffing of 140 by March 2013 (Berner 2013b, 3). Sec. 152(i) of Dodd-Frank requires the Office to establish an academic and professional fellowship program for experts from the private and the public sector, transferring "new technologies and approaches" that help the OFR to fulfill its mandate (Office of Financial Research 2012b, 17). Fellows should not only conduct research at the OFR, but also train their colleagues based on their prior working experience. Interestingly, the Office acknowledges that it needs "access to fresh thinking and a diverse range of views" (ibid., 22). And yet its search for applicants to the OFR fellowship program is limited to academics with a background in "finance, econometrics, macroeconomics, applied sciences, financial data management, data security, and information technology" (Office of Financial Research 2012c).

A fact that deserves particular prominence especially in comparison to the established financial regulators is the Office's *high degree of independence*, both in terms of funding and structure. To fund itself, the OFR levies a tax on systemically important BHCs with total consolidated assets of 50 billion dollars and greater, as well as on all NFCs that are subject to enhanced supervision by the Fed Board of Governors (Sec. 155 of Dodd-Frank). As Congress has successfully slowed down Dodd-Frank implementation by either shortening agency budgets or overwhelming the limited agency staff with additional responsibilities, the independent funding of the OFR is of central importance.[95] The degree of independence from other regulators as well as from financial firms was a major subject of debate. Tarullo had feared that an independent research entity would, without the support of other regulators, simply lack the expertise to collect and analyze the relevant data and information: "Data collection and analysis are not done in a vacuum; an agency's duties will inevitably reflect the priorities, experience, and interests of the collecting entity" (Tarullo 2010b, 16). On the other hand, he argued that the OFR should not be required to find the lowest common denominator with the other regulators (ibid.). It was also clear that the OFR should be immune to political and industry pressure (Mendelowitz and Liechty 2010). Dodd-Frank ultimately created the OFR as an independent body both with regard to its structure and its funding, and it remains to be seen whether the arguments brought forward against the current set-up will hold true or not.

Enforcing Data Collection: The Office's Subpoena Power

To get access to financial data and information, the Office relies on the cooperation of its industry counterparties. One of the Office's major challenges is to differentiate between public and confidential data and to develop and guarantee an adequate and secure infrastructure to collect, process and work with these data (Flood et al. 2010, 4). Given the case that a financial institution possesses relevant data and is not willing to share them, the OFR has the authority to ultimately enforce its request: Dodd-Frank grants the OFR *subpoena power*. While the OFR seems to be a paper tiger that mainly conducts and finances systemic risk research at first sight, Sec. 153 of Dodd-Frank provides some teeth. Whether it will bare these teeth or even use them is not yet clear. One of our interview partners used the metaphor of a Rorschach inkblot test to describe the situation: What people see in the OFR tells much about their anxieties and everyone sees something else (Interview with Andreas Lehnert, December 05, 2012, Washington). Gorton warned that the Office "could have the greatest impact" (Gorton 2012, 47). The Bloomberg Business Magazine ascribed "unusually strong powers" to the OFR, calling it the "CIA of financial regulators" (Schmidt 2010). Fox News described the OFR as the "most powerful federal agency you've never heard of", as it "can compel just about any company in America to turn over to the federal government sensitive internal data, even proprietary information" (Rosen 2012). Skeel warned that the OFR "could become yet another channel of Treasury influence" (Skeel 2010, 11). The CE-NIF, the intellectual father of the Office, could observe only "limited authority" on the part of the OFR (Committee to Establish the National Institute of Finance 2012). As often, the truth lies somewhere in-between: As Lehnert argues, the financial industry was concerned about the OFR's wide-

95 According to its former chairman Gary Gensler, especially the CFTC is hampered in its efforts by significant underfunding (Eichler 2012; Gensler 2012; Systemic Risk Council 2012).

reaching statutory authority when the Dodd-Frank Act was first passed, but that in the subsequent two years, the OFR focused on research on systemic risk rather than broad use of its data gathering authority (Interview with Andreas Lehnert, December 05, 2012, Washington).

Interestingly, it was not only the financial industry that had concerns regarding the OFR: Other regulators feared that their mandate overlapped with the data collection efforts of the Office. Based on the Paperwork Reduction Act of 1980 that prohibits US agencies from collecting the same data twice, they were concerned that the OFR might seriously affect and constrain their work (ibid.). Again, the reality proved to be different. So far, the OFR has mainly focused on systemic risk research and its Legal Entity Identifier (LEI) initiative (Office of Financial Research 2013b). According to one of our interview partners, it does not replicate other agencies' data collection efforts, but rather relied on the data and information collected by the FSOC members, and it also received support by the Council members when working on its inaugural annual report for 2012 (Interview with an OCC representative, December 06, 2012, Washington).

4.3.3 The Consumer Financial Protection Bureau

Title X of Dodd-Frank, entitled *Consumer Financial Protection Act of 2010*, requires the establishment of the Consumer Financial Protection Bureau (CFPB or *the Bureau*) as an independent executive agency within the Federal Reserve System to "regulate the offering and provision of consumer financial products or services under the Federal consumer financial laws" (Sec. 1011(a)). Before the creation of the CFPB, seven federal agencies shared responsibility for US consumer financial protection, while not a single agency had a consumer protection focus; the majority of their authorities and duties was transferred to the new Bureau in 2011 (Kennedy, McCoy, and Bernstein 2012). The establishment of an authority focusing on consumer protection distinguishes the US from the EU policy responses to the crisis: In the EU, all three European Supervisory Authorities (ESAs) are tasked with enhancing consumer protection (Ferran 2012b).

As of April 2014, the CFPB was organized in six divisions: Operations; Consumer Education & Engagement; Supervision, Enforcement & Fair Lending; Research, Markets & Regulations; External Affairs; and Legal (Consumer Financial Protection Bureau 2014). The Bureau is mandated to educate and inform consumers of financial products, to collect and handle consumer complaints, to "identify risks to consumers and the proper functioning of such markets", as well as to implement and enforce federal consumer financial law (Sec. 1021(c)). In addition, it should identify and address "outdated, unnecessary, or unduly burdensome regulations" (Sec. 1012(b)). The CFPB's general powers comprise consumer education, rulemaking and enforcement. A fourth important pillar of the Bureau's work is to study and monitor consumer financial markets, including the collection of consumer complaints (Kennedy, McCoy, and Bernstein 2012, and Carpenter 2014, provide a detailed overview over the CFPB's mandate and authorities). Of the three basic functions of the CFPB – *educating, enforcing and studying* – the first and the third are of special importance in the context of data-, information- and knowledge-related problems. With regard to education, the Bureau argues that informed consumers are "the first line of defense against abusive practices" (Consumer Financial Protection Bureau 2014). It therefore aims to improve *financial literacy* in the United States (Consumer Financial Protection Bureau 2013).[96] Regarding the third function, studying, the CFPB collects and analyses information about consumers, service providers and the overall market.

The idea to establish a new agency for consumer protection was initially put forward by Elisabeth Warren (Campbell et al. 2011, 106; Obama 2013). Warren had already argued before the financial crisis that a Financial Product Safety Commission should be set up to protect consumers from dangerous financial products and unsound business practices:

> Just as the Consumer Product Safety Commission (CPSC) protects buyers of goods and supports a competitive market, we need the same for consumers of financial products – a new regulatory regime, and even a new regulatory body, to protect consumers who use credit cards, home mortgages, car loans, and a host of other products. (Warren 2007, 1)

With regard to its institutional structure, the Bureau is in a good position to actually fulfill its mandate: First, contrary to most independent agencies, it is neither controlled by the executive nor the legislative. Secondly, it has a solid funding through the Fed but is not controlled by the Fed (Woolley and Ziegler 2012). And thirdly, it is not led by the typical multimember board but by a single director. As Zywicki elaborates, "[f]ew bureaucratic agencies in American history, if any, have combined the vast power and lack of public accountability of the CFPB" (Zywicki 2013, 856). Interestingly, the independence of the Bureau extends to its employees. As Kennedy et al. emphasize, CFPB researchers are allowed "to conduct self-directed research and to publish in their own names where permitted by law, without Bureau approval of the policy content"; they are optimistic that such a setting "will promote honest investigation, independent thinking, and open discussion that will support evidence-based – rather than myopic or ideological – policymaking" (Kennedy, McCoy, and Bernstein 2012, 1155f.).

Partly due to its independence, the CFPB was one of the most controversial parts of Dodd-Frank: Since its establishment, Congress has considered bills

96 The underlying assumption that informed consumers make better choices will be discussed in chapter five – it feeds into the idea of the rational consumer that we contrast with Herbert Simon's concept of bounded rationality.

suggesting a complete breakup of the CFPB as well as bills suggesting changes to the funding and leadership structure of the CFPB (Carpenter 2014, 1). The CFPB's first director, Richard Cordray, was nominated in 2011 but it took two years for him to be confirmed by the Senate, as Republican senators blocked a vote in order to delay and weaken Dodd-Frank implementation (Depillis 2014). A major argument by its opponents was that changes were required "to ensure accountability and transparency at the bureau" (McConnell 2013). The overall attitude towards the CFPB changed markedly once it had taken up its work. In July 2013, Cordray was finally approved as director of the Bureau. The New York Times editorial board hailed the CFPB for being "so effective, even under fire" and predicted that, with Cordray as director, "the agency can build on its already notable accomplishments, including a crackdown on abusive credit card tactics that has refunded more than $400 million to six million customers" (The New York Times Editorial Board 2013). Even though establishment had been strongly opposed, the CFPB appears to have gained recognition among both sides of the political spectrum: "There is one provision that many proponents of financial reform point to as a clear success: the Consumer Financial Protection Bureau. Americans now have an independent consumer bureau to protect them from mortgage, credit-card and other lending abuses that ran rampant before and during the crisis" (Douglas 2013; see also Woolley and Ziegler 2012, 44). According to the Wall Street Journal, "the CFPB has made significant inroads with financial-industry officials who had initially opposed the regulator's creation", as it "has listened to industry concerns about several rules and been willing to make tweaks even after those rules were finalized" (Zibel 2013). Other observers credit the Bureau to be open to input from all sides, and put much emphasis on learning from other regulators, consumers and the financial industry (Kennedy, McCoy, and Bernstein 2012).

4.3.4 Stress Tests and Living Wills

At first sight, it does not seem to make much sense to discuss stress tests and living wills in one section. We decided to do so nonetheless, because the two measures share a certain psychological component. A securities analyst at Crédit Agricole made the remarkable statement that "living wills are simply an exercise to make some people feel better" (Mayo, cited by Silver-Greenberg and Schwartz 2012). Although both living wills and stress tests fulfill, as we will show, important functions beyond *making people feel better*, especially with regard to data, information and knowledge, they do in fact aim at restoring trust and reassuring financial institutions and investors that the market is stable and under control.

Bank Stress Tests

Designated NFCs and BHCs with total consolidated assets of 50 billion dollar or more are required by Sec. 165(i) of Dodd-Frank to participate in annual stress tests conducted by the Fed – the so called *bank stress tests* – that evaluate "whether such companies have the capital, on a total consolidated basis, necessary to absorb losses as a result of adverse economic conditions" (Sec. 165(i)(1)(A)). These companies also have to undergo semi-annual, company-run stress tests. Annual company-run stress tests are also mandatory for smaller BHCs and certain other financial institutions.[97] The stress scenarios simulate an economic downturn, including – among other factors – an increased unemployment rate and a drop in equity and housing prices to evaluate whether the current capital base of the biggest banks provides a sufficient buffer under adverse economic conditions.

According to Fed Governor Daniel Tarullo, recent bank stress tests showed a significant increase in the quality and quantity of US bank capital since the crisis (Board of Governors of the Federal Reserve System 2013c). The key objective of the tests, to demonstrate that the biggest financial institutions have enough capital to absorb substantial losses by lifting "the fog of uncertainty over bank balance sheets" (Geithner 2009a), has apparently been achieved. While it is widely agreed that the US stress tests were very effective in restoring trust (see for example Bookstaber et al. 2013), several questions remain. The first is whether it is too easy for the banks to pass the tests, and whether the scenarios run in the tests are sufficiently severe (Eavis and Protess 2013; Bair 2012a, ch. 15; Bair is especially critical towards the Citigroup stress tests).[98] The second relates to the stress tests' side effects: Former Fed employee Til Schuerman warns that the more important the Fed stress tests become, the harder the banks try to provide optimal results (Schuermann 2013). *Stress test arbitrage* is therefore likely to occur: According to Bookstaber et. al, the current US tress tests run only two sets of stress scenarios, and "if supervisors rely on a small and fixed set of scenarios, banks are likely to learn to anticipate the features of a scenario, [and] financial institutions will learn to shape their activities to exploit weaknesses in scenario design" (Bookstaber et al. 2013, 7). Stress tests are also expected to lead to an even greater homogeneity of the banks' risk models (Interview with Rainer Stollhoff, August 14, 2013, Berlin), and we have learned from the recent crisis as well as from the LTCM case that *homogeneity breeds fragility* (Haldane 2010, 12; Haldane and May 2011; Beale et al. 2011).[99] And last but not least, a dangerous side effect of the tests is an *either true*

97 This rule applies to BHCs with total consolidated assets between ten and 50 billion dollars, as well as to state member banks and savings and loan holding companies with total consolidated assets of more than ten billion dollars.

98 Yet, several banks have failed the Fed's stress tests, among them Citigroup (2011 and 2013). At Citigroup, the failed tests led to changes in the banks leadership – with Vikram Pandit being replaced by Michael L. Corbat in 2012 – and caps on its dividends (Corkery 2014).

99 We have to distinguish two different types of homogeneity. One the one hand, we have to ask whether financial regulation should be globally aligned in order to create a level playing field for finance. One the other hand the question arises whether finance itself is becoming increasingly homogeneous, and if this homogeneity increases systemic risk. With regard to regulatory homogeneity, Adair Turner as

or false sense of security among regulators as well as market participants, including the stress-tested banks (Borio, Drehmann, and Tsatsaronis 2012). Stress tests do indeed require underfunded banks to raise more capital, and yet the tests tend to focus on the symptoms (distrust) rather than fundamentally changing the underlying weaknesses (e.g. leverage, complexity, and short-term funding) (see Bair 2012a; see also Senge 1996). The stress tests aim to prove that the banks are safer – it must be clear, however, that the tests are based on a variety of quantitative assumptions and that these assumptions might be wrong. That the stress tests reflect the actual risks of the biggest US financial institutions is therefore highly questionable; even worse, the tests might increase the overall risk in the financial system through increased homogeneity on the side of the banks and a false sense of security on the side of the institutions' stakeholders and regulators.[100]

And yet, stress testing has been an important tool in banking for quite a while. The tests were for some time conducted by regulators externally, but typically by banks internally. In the 1990s, for instance, Congress required the OFHEO to adopt stress tests for the GSEs, and stress tests also played a role in the first major modification of the Basel capital framework (Bookstaber et al. 2013, 1). Since the financial crisis, stress tests have undergone a renaissance (Berner 2013a) and become a central measure for SIFI supervision. Up to March 2014, the OFR published three studies dealing with stress tests. According to their findings, the pre-crisis company-run stress tests "did not prepare financial institutions (or their regulators) for the 2008 financial crisis. Pre-crisis stress tests were not only limited in scope […] but also suffered from a failure of imagination" (Bookstaber et al. 2013, 1; see also Interview with Andreas Lehnert, December 05, 2012, Washington; Mankiw 2010; Black 2012). This is a major weakness in every stress scenario, and

---

the chairman of the FSA argued that "unless you can get a rigorous global agreement, there's a problem" (Gieve et al. 2009). The basic argument is that national systems of financial governance result in an *unlevel playing field*, and as capital knows no borders, it will move to where the conditions are best. We know this argument from one of our interviews: Hedge funds threatened to move to the Cayman Islands in case that the OFR would require them to reveal sensitive data (Interview with Andreas Lehnert, December 05, 2012, Washington). Opponents argue that homogenous rules and regulations would decrease the overall resilience of the financial system, hoping that an unlevel playing field would be more robust (The Warwick Commission 2009). The Basel accords and the standards set by the FSB are likely to increase the homogeneity of financial regulation. Besides, they are likely to push the strategies and business models of financial institutions into the same direction. As we know from recent adaptive behavior to Basel II, financial institutions adapt to a changing regulatory environment. Some of the recent policy measures accordingly bear the potential to increase the degree of homogeneity within the financial system. SIFIs are expected to align their portfolios with the (few) stress scenarios set by the central banks, foremost the Fed.

100 From the European case, we can also infer that stress tests do not provide a universal panacea for financial crises. The recent EU stress tests have proved to be rather ineffective, as we will see in the following section.

brings us back to the fundamental role of assumptions in all stress tests. The financial crisis is said to have changed stress testing substantially:

> Recognition of the shortcomings of pre-crisis risk management has engendered a more rigorous approach among bank supervisors. Today's stress testing in the U.S., which could be termed 'Version 2.0,' differs from the pre-crisis efforts in the level of supervisory engagement and in the key role that the testing now plays in the supervisory assessment of bank management's capital planning and risk management ability and the firm's capital adequacy. On a substantive level, Version 2.0 also differs from pre-crisis efforts in the level of detail of the data collections, the scale and granularity of the models (including the severity of stress scenarios), and the level of disclosure of results. (Bookstaber et al. 2013, 2)

The changes in stress testing reflect the recent shift from micro- to macroprudential supervision and regulation: Company-run tests before the crisis focused on the single institution. The tests conducted by supervisors today apparently present a first step in the direction of macroprudential measures, as the banks are subject to the same scenarios, and evaluated in comparison to each other. With regard to data-, information- and knowledge-related problems, the post-crisis stress tests are based on more and better data (Bookstaber et al. 2013). What is still underrepresented in the current tests are the systemic features, especially herding behavior, institutional interactions and interconnectedness among the banks, as well as between the banks and the real economy (ibid.).

Living Wills

The US deposit insurance authority FDIC has a good reputation for winding down banks and thrifts. But in 2008 it became quite clear how difficult it is to wind down global and complex banks, and how important it is for regulators to be able to wind down such institutions in an orderly way. Dodd-Frank provided the FDIC with new authorities to wind down systemically important financial institutions under the Orderly Liquidation Authority (OLA), but it also explicitly turned conventional bankruptcy into the "preferred resolution framework" (Wigand and Osterman 2013; see also Wigand 2013) for failing SIFIs. To address the related data, information and knowledge problems, Dodd-Frank introduces a new measure to prepare both regulators and banks for a potential collapse by collecting the relevant data and information for an orderly wind-down in advance. Based on Sec. 165 of Dodd-Frank, designated NFCs and BHCs have to submit *Resolution Plans* to the FSOC, the Federal Reserve and the FDIC, describing "the company's strategy for rapid and orderly resolution in the event of material financial distress or failure of the company" (Sec. 165). According to the FDIC, the so called *living wills* enable the institutions and their regulators "to understand and address the parts of the business that could create systemic consequences in a bankruptcy" (Wigand and Osterman 2013). To do so, a living will must provide:

- information regarding the manner and extent to which any insured *depository institution* affiliated with the company is adequately *protected from risks arising from the activities of any nonbank subsidiaries* of the company;
- full descriptions of the ownership structure, assets, liabilities, and contractual obligations of the company;
- identification of the *cross-guarantees* tied to different securities, identification of major *counterparties*, and a process for determining to whom the collateral of the company is pledged; and
- any other information that the Board of Governors and the Corporation jointly require by rule or order. (Sec. 165(d), emphasis added)

Living wills are, as they contain confidential data and information, divided into a detailed, confidential section and a much more general, public section. The latter is very much descriptive and mostly provides information about the activities, operations and subsidies of the banks. The public sections of the 2012 living wills did nevertheless provide some interesting facts: The living will of Deutsche Bank illustrates the bank's conception of a potential cross-border resolution; it describes how the bank's assets and liabilities would be transferred to a bridge bank by the *German Bundesanstalt für Finanzmarktstabilisierung* (FMSA), that would then enable the *Bundesanstalt für Finanzdienstleistungsaufsicht* (BaFin) to separate systemically important ("good") from not systemically important ("bad") parts of Deutsche Bank.[101] Interestingly, the bank assumes that US and German regulators would fully cooperate, "and the US regulators would not take actions that they may otherwise be entitled to take under applicable law but that would frustrate the implementation of the Transfer Order, such as the initiation of proceedings under the applicable U.S. resolution regimes" (Deutsche Bank 2012b, 28). Even though the US and the UK have been working on a cross-border resolution regime (Federal Deposit Insurance Corporation and Bank of England 2012), it is not yet clear if and how such a cooperation between the US and Germany would work in the case of a severe crisis, and there is no bilateral agreement yet. A lack of cross-border cooperation between nation states, as well as incompatible resolution regimes, are in fact perceived as a major obstacle to the orderly liquidation of SIFIs (Avgouleas, Goodhart, and Schoenmaker 2010). Only in February 2013 did the FDIC and the European Commission start a joint Working Group that meets regularly (Wigand

101 One interview partner argued that the German living wills basically reveal that banks assume that "Frankfurt pays" (Interview with Rainer Stollhoff, August 14, 2013, Berlin): "Aber das deutsche Bankentestament fand ich auch ganz spannend. Für mich stand da drin: Im Zweifelsfall zahlt immer Frankfurt."

2013). In their *Guidance for 2013 §165(d) Annual Resolution Plan Submissions by Domestic Covered Companies that Submitted Initial Resolution Plans in 2012*, the Fed and the FDIC identified global cooperation as a major obstacle for orderly and rapid resolutions as a

> risk that actions (or non-actions) of a Covered Company could incent host supervisors or resolution authorities or third parties to take actions (or abstain from actions) that could result in ring-fencing of assets or lead to other outcomes that could exacerbate financial instability in the United States and/or loss of franchise value, as well as uncertainty in the markets. (Federal Deposit Insurance Corporation and Board of Governors of the Federal Reserve System 2013, 5)

The processes and strategies for the wind-downs are outlined in the resolution plans; however, one has to ask whether the basic assumptions underlying living wills are realistic or not. According to Goldman Sachs (Goldman Sachs 2012, 3), the baseline assumptions as provided by the US supervisors for the 2012 living wills are:

- Sudden, idiosyncratic material financial distress at GS [Goldman Sachs] Group with no previous disruption to the markets.
- All Material Entities of GS Group have entered some form of bankruptcy.
- Markets are functioning normally.
- Other market participants are assumed to be in good financial condition.
- Funding markets are open for other market participants.
- No extraordinary government support.

Clearly, these assumptions deviate from the events that led to the financial crisis of 2007ff., calling the value of living wills for future crises into question. According to the living wills, to give just one example, banks assume that they would be able to sell certain business lines or subsidiaries easily. In the mergers and acquisitions of the crisis months, this was not the case: Back then, the government not only acted as a broker, it also subsidized several deals by agreeing to absorb losses above a certain threshold. In 2013, the FDIC and the Fed emphasized in their basic living will scenario that "markets are functioning and competitors are in a position to take on business", but also required the firms that assume asset sales to "take into account all issues surrounding its ability to sell in market conditions present in the applicable economic condition at the time of sale" (Federal Deposit Insurance Corporation and Board of Governors of the Federal Reserve System 2013, 8).

Some banks discussed the (limited) value of living wills in the public section of their 2012 plans. Deutsche Bank, Goldman Sachs and JP Morgan Chase, for example, argued that "resolution planning provides for a viable resolution approach and the mitigation of risks surrounding 'too big to fail' concerns" (Deutsche Bank

2012b, 4; see also Goldman Sachs 2012, 2; JPMorgan Chase 2012, 1). However, Goldman Sachs emphasized that "[t]he circumstances leading to the failure of a systemically important financial institution will likely be different than the specific assumptions listed above" (Goldman Sachs 2012, 31). And yet, Jeffrey M. Lacker, President of the Federal Reserve Bank of Richmond, argues that living wills are an important step towards ending too big to fail:

> The path toward a stable financial system requires that the unassisted failure of financial firms does not put the financial system at risk. The resolution planning process prescribed by Section 165(d) in Title I of the Dodd-Frank Act provides the road map for this journey. (Lacker 2013)

In accordance with his statement, Sandra Pianalto, President and CEO of the Federal Reserve Bank of Cleveland, pictures living wills as a pivotal tool for enhancing transparency, as transparency strengthens the belief in an effective resolution authority for systemically important banks:

> I think that successfully addressing the 'Too Big To Fail' problem requires the establishment of a credible resolution process, one that appears capable of safely managing the failure of systemically important financial institutions in times of distress. Achieving this credibility will, in turn, require a fair amount of informational and regulatory transparency. This is hard work, I know, but the gains from success are likely to be substantial. (Pianalto 2013)

The FDIC argues that, as an orderly wind-down of a SIFI requires extensive advance planning and a detailed resolution plan, living wills are conditional for its Orderly Liquidation Authority (Federal Deposit Insurance Corporation 2011, 10), which is described in detail in the following section.

Living wills are, like the majority of Dodd-Frank implementation, work in progress, and the overall process is of an iterative nature: Based on an extensive review of the inaugural living wills submitted in 2012, the Fed demanded additional information from the banks, for instance how liquidity constraints in a crisis would affect the bank's funding (Crittenden and Sparshott 2013), for the 2013 set.[102] By the end of 2013, about 125 banks have submitted living wills (Liberto 2013). As we

102 The Fed and the FDIC distinguish between three groups of financial companies: The first group of so-called "first-wave filers" includes all BHCs and foreign banking organizations with 250 billion dollars or more in non-bank assets. Bank of America Corporation, Barclays, Citigroup, Credit Suisse, Deutsche Bank, Goldman Sachs, Morgan Stanley and UBS submitted their first living wills in July 2012. Two more first wave filers, Bank of New York Mellon Corporation and State Street Corporation, submitted their plans in October 2012. The second group (second-wave filers) includes BNP Paribas, HSBC, RBS and Wells Fargo. The biggest group of third-wave filers includes approximately 115 firms, most of which ware foreign financial companies. The second and third group filed their initial plans in July and December 2013 (Wigand and Osterman 2013).

will discuss in greater detail at the end of this chapter, the resolution plans most certainly provide a *learning process* for both financial institutions and supervisors (Goldman Sachs 2012, 3): They require the banks to collect and provide certain data and information; and they show the FDIC and the Fed structural and organizational obstacles for an orderly resolution:

> If a plan is found to be deficient and adequate revisions are not made, the FDIC and the Federal Reserve may jointly impose more stringent capital, leverage, or liquidity requirements, or restrictions on growth, activities, or operations of the company, including its subsidiaries. Ultimately, the FDIC and the Federal Reserve, in consultation with the FSOC, can order the company to divest assets or operations to facilitate an orderly resolution under bankruptcy in the event of failure. (Wigand 2013)

It remains to be seen if living wills live up to the Fed's and the FDIC's expectations.

4.3.5 Ending TBTF: Orderly Liquidation and the Ban on Bailouts

While non-TBTF financial institutions can usually be wound down in an orderly process by their domestic resolution authority – which is the FDIC in the case of the US banks – the financial crisis revealed that the "failure of a large financial conglomerate can be a hugely complex affair" (Goldstein and Véron 2011, 28). The Lehman bankruptcy provides a good example. As the FCIC reports,

> the bankruptcy affected about 8,000 subsidiaries and affiliates with $600 billion in assets and liabilities, the firm's more than 100,000 creditors, and about 26,000 employees. Its failure triggered default clauses in derivatives contracts, allowing its counterparties to have the option of seizing its collateral and terminating the contracts. After the parent company filed, about 80 insolvency proceedings of its subsidiaries in 18 foreign countries followed. In the main bankruptcy proceeding, about 66,000 claims – exceeding $873 billion – have been filed against Lehman as of September 2010. (Financial Crisis Inquiry Commission 2011, 339f.)

While the stress tests were established to prevent the collapse of financial institutions in the first place, living wills are intended to prepare regulators and regulatees for a collapse should one actually occur. In addition, Dodd-Frank provides the FDIC with an Orderly Liquidation Authority (OLA) to wind down systemically important, complex, global institutions in an orderly, structured process. At the same time, it restricts the Fed's emergency lending authority. Both provisions were designed to end the TBTF problem.

The FDIC

Even though bankruptcy is the preferred resolution mechanism under Dodd-Frank, policymakers wanted to establish – in view of the Lehman bankruptcy – the OLA as a backstop for all cases where a bankruptcy would have severe effects on financial stability in the US. One might approve or disapprove the US government's decision to let Lehman fail, but it is widely agreed that the Lehman bankruptcy was a "disorderly, time-consuming, and expensive process" (Federal Deposit Insurance Corporation 2011, 3). After the Lehman experience, there was widespread consensus that the conventional bankruptcy processes are unworkable for SIFIs: "The corporate complexity of LCFIs is likely to defy efficient resolution in the event of bankruptcy" (Herring and Carmassi 2012, 221). Based on Title II of Dodd-Frank, the OLA therefore authorizes the FDIC to liquidate failing financial companies that pose a significant risk to US financial stability. It presents a new resolution authority especially for nonbanks. Against the background of the recent financial crisis, the OLA process addresses moral hazard directly: Dodd-Frank requires that, if a financial institution fails, creditors, shareholders and managers are held accountable:

> (1) creditors and shareholders will bear the losses of the financial company; (2) management responsible for the condition of the financial company will not be retained; and (3) the Corporation [meaning the FDIC] and other appropriate agencies will take all steps necessary and appropriate to assure that all parties, including management, directors, and third parties, having responsibility for the condition of the financial company bear losses consistent with their responsibility, including actions for damages, restitution, and recoupment of compensation and other gains not compatible with such responsibility. (Sec. 204(a))

In a conventional bankruptcy process, the FDIC would not be able to fund the covered SIFI in a timely manner or prepare the filing efficiently in advance (Bernstein et al. 2011, 14). Under its new authority, the FDIC pursues a *single-entry strategy*: First, the FDIC would be installed as the single receiver of the top-tier holding company and establish one or more bridge companies to which the assets and liabilities of the covered financial firm would be transferred to in order to "stabilize the key operations of the covered financial company by continuing valuable, systemically important operations" (Federal Deposit Insurance Corporation 2011). Secondly, it would assign losses to unsecured creditors and shareholders of the holding company, and thirdly transfer sound operating subsidiaries to a new solvent entity (Federal Deposit Insurance Corporation and Bank of England 2012, ii).

In 2011, the FDIC published an article entitled *The Orderly Liquidation of Lehman Brothers Holdings Inc. Under the Dodd-Frank Act*, where it illustrated how it would have dealt with the Lehman collapse if the OLA had already been in place in 2008 (Federal Deposit Insurance Corporation 2011). The paper, which has been described as naïve by some (see for example Lubben 2011, 2013), states:

> In the various accounts of the failure of Lehman it is noteworthy that senior management discounted the possibility of failure until the very last moment. There was apparently a belief, following the government's actions in respect of Bear Stearns, that the government, despite statements to the contrary, would step in and provide financial assistance and Lehman would be rescued. If Title II of the Dodd- Frank Act had been in effect, the outcome would have been considerably different. *Lehman's senior management would have understood clearly that the government would not and could not extend financial assistance outside of a resolution* because of the clear requirements in the Dodd-Frank Act that losses are to be borne by equity holders and unsecured creditors, and management and directors responsible for the condition of the failed financial company are not to be retained. (Federal Deposit Insurance Corporation 2011, 11f., emphasis added)

The OLA not only provides new authority to the FDIC; as the statement illustrates, it was established first and foremost to alter the behavior of struggling or failing SIFIs *before* the FDIC actually steps in and takes command. A second reason was to provide clarity and security and thus prevent a run on the bank. In the case of Lehman, the FDIC concludes that the bank would have accepted an early offer and found an acquirer before it was too late; the Commission would have evaluated the bids and, as required by Dodd-Frank, accepted the bid that maximized the value of Lehman's assets (Federal Deposit Insurance Corporation 2011).

Stephen J. Lubben asserts that "Dodd-Frank makes it harder to bail out a financial institution. But 'harder' does not mean 'impossible,' and that's just the kind of thing that can fuel a lot of terminal optimism by managers of companies in financial distress" (Lubben 2011). Many observers have expressed their doubts about the OLA's effectiveness, and whether it really would have changed the behavior of Lehman's senior management towards an early buy-out. It is also argued that despite the OLA, the FDIC could ultimately not solve cross-border resolution problems (see for example Bernstein et al. 2011, 27; Dudley 2012). And last but not least, the FDIC has not yet had any experience in winding down SIFIs, and the application of the OLA on the Lehman case represents only a thought experiment. To ultimately prove that it can deal with complex global financial conglomerates, the Commission would have to successfully liquidate a systemically important financial institution.

The evidence so far supports the believers and disbelievers in Dodd-Frank TBTF regulation. As already discussed in the third chapter of this book, recent studies show that TBTF institutions are still receiving substantial government subsidies. However, there are also signs for a shrinking subsidy. A fact that deserves particular prominence in this context is the downgrading by Moody's of Bank of America, Wells Fargo and Citigroup in September 2011. Shortly before the Fed announced that it had approved the final rule for resolution plans under Dodd-Frank in October 2011 (Board of Governors of the Federal Reserve System 2011), Moody's argued that

> under the rules recently finalized by the FDIC, the orderly liquidation authority included in Dodd-Frank demonstrates a clear intent to impose losses on bondholders in the event that a systemically important bank such as BAC [Bank of America, EB] was nearing failure. If fully implemented, the provisions of Dodd-Frank could further lower systemic risk by reducing interconnectedness among large institutions and could further strengthen regulators' abilities to resolve such firms. (Moody's 2011)

TBTF is clearly not yet over – but that does not imply that Dodd-Frank does not reduce it, at least to a certain degree. William C. Dudley of the New York Fed has characterized the US government's current approach to TBTF as "reducing the incentives for firms to operate with a large systemic footprint, reducing the likelihood of them failing, and lowering the cost to society when they do fail" (Dudley 2012). He himself asks the question of whether the better option would be "to take the more direct, but less nuanced approach advocated by some and simply break up the most systemically important firms into smaller or simpler pieces in the hope that what emerges is no longer systemic and too big to fail" (ibid.). We will get back to this point at the end of this chapter.

The Post-Dodd-Frank Federal Reserve Bank

The financial crisis not only showed how powerful the US Federal Reserve Bank actually is; it also demonstrated that it is very flexible. During and after the financial crisis of 2007ff., the role of the Fed has changed markedly: On the one hand, there are the legal, statutory changes induced by Dodd-Frank that we discuss on the following pages. According to Schoenholtz/Wachtel, Dodd-Frank triggers "the most important changes at the Fed since the Great Depression" (Schoenholtz and Wachtel 2010). On the other hand, there are the de-facto, behavioral changes that are – for instance – reflected in the Fed's balance sheet increase from 869 billion dollar in August 2007 to well over three trillion dollar in July 2013 (Board of Governors of the Federal Reserve System 2013a) and that included the stretching of the Federal Reserve Act in 2008 as described in this chapter. As we argue, the crisis has strengthened the Fed: During the negotiations of Dodd-Frank, it demanded greater power and new authorities to mitigate TBTF and systemic risk (Bair 2012a), and was granted them to some extent. However, Dodd-Frank has also limited the Fed's freedom of action in future crises.

First of all, Dodd-Frank adds a new responsibility to the traditional tasks of the central bank: Besides price stability and full employment, the post-Dodd-Frank Fed has a mandate for *enhancing financial stability and mitigating systemic risk* (Schoenholtz and Wachtel 2010). All BHCs with total consolidated assets of 50 billion dollars or more, as well as all NFCs, FMUs and all settlement and payment activities that are designated as systemically important by the FSOC, are subject to enhanced supervision by the Fed. In supervising these systemically important institutions, the Fed fulfills an important microprudential role within the new macroprudential supervisory architecture of the US. The Fed is also in charge of living wills and it has an important role in the OLA process. Moreover, it plays a central role in the work of the FSOC, which, especially in the first years after its establishment, relies heavily on the input of its members. In this regard, it's independent funding strengthens the Fed relative to the underfunded federal financial agencies, especially the SEC and the CFTC:

> As the parable goes, 'in the land of the blind, the man with one eye is king;' likewise, in the land of underfunded regulatory agencies, the independently funded agency is powerful. As a result of this independent funding the Fed has taken on an increasingly prominent role in the domestic regulatory environment. (Schnidman 2011, 89)

And yet, the reforms induced by the crisis have also weakened the Fed: Title XI of Dodd-Frank limits the Fed's possibility to provide emergency lending to collapsing SIFIs. Section 1101 states that "any emergency lending program or facility is for the purpose of providing liquidity to the financial system, and *not to aid a failing financial company*, and that the *security for emergency loans is sufficient* to protect taxpayers from losses and that any such program is terminated in a timely and orderly fashion" (Sec. 1101(a)(1)(B)(i), emphasis added). Dodd-Frank prohibits the Fed from rescuing individual financial institutions, and it requires sufficient collateral from institutions participating in future emergency lending programs – which is where the OLA comes into play, as it should enable the FDIC and the Fed to wind down such institutions and should also prevent the risk of failure from building up in the first place. Dodd-Frank aims at protecting taxpayers from losses, but it also wants to increase executive accountability both in the private and the public sector: In order to prohibit borrowing from the Fed by insolvent institutions, Dodd-Frank requests "a certification from the chief executive officer (or other authorized officer) of the borrower, at the time the borrower initially borrows under the program or facility [...] that the borrower is not insolvent" (Section 1101(a)(1)(B)(ii)). To increase Fed accountability, title XI authorizes the Comptroller General of the United States to audit the Fed Board of Governors, as well as any Federal Reserve Bank and any such credit facility or lending program (Sec. 1102(a)). In order to enhance transparency, section 1103 of Dodd-Frank requires the Fed Board to publish these GAO audits on its website after a certain period of time.

Dodd-Frank requires the Fed to establish the policies and procedures governing emergency lending as soon as practicable after the enactment of Title XI (Sec. 1101(a)), yet the detailed rules – defining what *sufficient* collateral or a *timely and orderly fashion* actually mean – still have to be written. It is argued that finalizing the rules on emergency lending would help to address the TBTF problem: "Depending on how strict the rules are, the banks might then realize that the Fed will not be a pushover in times of market stress" (Eavis 2013). As long as a smaller but still significant TBTF subsidy persists, it is highly questionable whether the market believes that the emergency-lending limit is effective. Just like the OLA, it will be ultimately tested by future systemic crises. The worst-case scenario would happen if the OLA did not work, but the Fed would be restricted in its lending possibilities: "If the new structures prove ineffective, the Dodd-Frank bill's elimination of emergency authority for some forms of Fed lending could make future crises even more devastating than the recent one" (Schoenholtz and Wachtel 2010). And in fact, it is often argued that the US crisis could be contained because of the resolute and joint response by the Fed and the Treasury. A similar response in the future will be explicitly prohibited by Dodd-Frank.

4.4 Putting the US into Context: A Short Look at EU Policy Responses

Not only did the financial crisis in the European Union endure much longer than it did in the US; EU policy responses to the crisis – beginning with the case-by-case, mostly national responses of 2008 and 2009, followed by such far-reaching reforms as the establishment of the European System of Financial Supervision (ESFS) in 2011, and ultimately leading to the establishment of a European Banking Union – took much longer. Goldstein and Véron identify four reasons why the European legislative response to the crisis was slow compared to US reform: First, when the crisis hit in 2008, the European Commission was awaiting its renewal.[103] Second, legislative proceedings as such are slower in the EU. Third, the EU had to fundamentally re-design its supervisory and regulatory architecture, leading to the establishment of the European Banking Authority (EBA), the European Securities and Markets Authority (ESMA), the European Insurance and Occupational Pensions Authority (EIOPA) and the European Systemic Risk Board (ESRB) as discussed in this section, while the US system of supervision and regulation basically

103 José Manuel Barroso was re-elected as president of the European Commission in 2009 and his Commission took office in 2010.

stayed the same.[104] And fourth, the EU was still fighting its banking crisis, while the US Fed had been able to restore the trust in the banking system with the stress tests of 2009 (Goldstein and Véron 2011, 11).

Comparing the US and the EU is fruitful for several reasons: First, the crisis revealed different weaknesses in both systems. Second, a comparative analysis sheds light on the strengths and weaknesses of the respective regulatory and supervisory systems. Third, the US and the EU differed in their policy responses to the crisis, and when compared, the respective reform initiatives are easier to assess and understand. Stress tests provide a good example. Such tests were conducted on both sides of the Atlantic, but the EU and US stress tests had largely different effects. Briefly summarized, the US stress tests were very effective in calming the markets and restoring trust and the EU stress tests were not.[105] The two macroprudential systemic risk supervisors – the ESRB in the EU, and the FSOC in the US – are another example: They resemble each other at first sight, but are – as we will see – in fact quite different, especially with regard to their authority and organizational set-up. Again, our focus lies on regulatory and supervisory problems related to data, information and knowledge.

The EU and the Economic and Monetary Union (EMU), together with their members, institutions and regulations form a complex interplay. Since the start of the EU financial crisis, these institutions and regulations have once more become a *moving target* as the EMU gradually evolves into a European Banking Union. The aim of this chapter is to enrich the US case study with a European perspective on the crisis. As current EU reform is not only a fast moving but also a very broad target – Wymerrsch speaks of a "new era" of financial regulation and supervision in the EU – we cannot delve deeply into the issue (Wymeersch 2012, 232). Therefore, instead of discussing the EU crisis and the reforms it triggered in great detail, we want to use the European case solely for the purpose of comparison, thus leaving out the aspects irrelevant for the US case (see Ferran 2012b, for a detailed analysis of the current EU reforms; Wymeersch 2012). We mostly focus on institutional change in the EU – what is the role of the new supervisory and regulatory bodies,

104 The Office of Thrift Supervision (OTS) was abolished by Dodd-Frank, while the other US financial agencies remained intact. As illustrated in the preceding section, new bodies were created and simply "added" to the existing structure.

105 According to Pisany-Ferry and Sapir, the EU supervisors wanted to conduct stress tests similar to the successful US tests, "but with so many limitations that it became almost meaningless." They identify three major problems: "First, the tests were conducted independently by national supervisors [...]. Second, in order not to interfere with the responsibility of national supervisors it was explicitly stated that the aim of the tests was not 'to identify individual banks that may need recapitalisation'. Third, results from a stress test based on a sample of 22 major European financial institutions was presented to the informal ECOFIN Council in early October 2009, but they only included aggregate information" (Pisani-Ferry and Sapir 2010, 360f.).

and how do they work? – to ultimately provide a comparative view on the US and EU institutions.

This chapter is organized as follows: We start with the European financial crisis and the weaknesses it revealed in the supervisory and regulatory architecture of the EU (4.4.1). The subsequent section discusses an argument that constantly recurred in the debate and that supports national instead of transnational supervision: The closer supervisory bodies are to financial institutions, the smaller the information asymmetries are between supervisors and financial institutions (4.4.2). Afterwards, we look at the new EU architecture, including the *European System of Financial Supervision* (ESFS) and its three European Supervisory Authorities – the *European Banking Authority* (EBA), the *European Securities and Markets Authority* (ESMA), and the *European Insurance and Occupational Pensions Authority* (EIOPA) (4.4.3) – as well as the newly established ESRB (4.4.4); we will also briefly discuss the altered role of the ECB (4.4.5). Again, it is important to bear in mind that the ESAs and the ESRB are moving targets. Broader political developments and major new regulations will change their role and mandate (Ferran 2012b), and first calls have already been made by the ESAs for broader mandates and extended powers (see for example Bernardino 2013).[106]

4.4.1 The EU Crisis, and the Weaknesses it Revealed

Today there is wide consensus that the European Union had no adequate crisis management infrastructure and that it was, in general terms, ill-prepared for a financial crisis (see for example High Level Group on Financial Supervision in the EU 2009, 12; European Commission 2009). In hindsight, it is quite clear that especially during the pre-crisis decade, European market integration evolved much faster than European policy integration (Pisani-Ferry and Sapir 2010, 341; see also Fonteyne et al. 2010). Even after the introduction of the Euro as the common currency, central measures for financial crisis management remained essentially national. The dominant principle of *home country control* that dates back to Basel I meant that "banks may operate through branches, they are supervised by the authorities of the countries where they are headquartered, and only the fiscal authorities of that country are responsible for bailing them out" (Pisani-Ferry and Sapir 2010, 344). In fact, major tools for mitigating systemic risk had remained national: The national treasuries not only had the authority to bail out financial

106 To give just one example, the EBA annual report 2012 stated that the establishment of the Single Supervisory Mechanism (SSM), while representing only a first step towards a European Banking Union, "won't go without an impact on the daily operations of the EBA", and change the EBA's voting modalities (European Banking Authority 2012a; see also P. Jenkins 2012). As we describe the new authorities for comparative reasons, we picture them as they were initially designed in 2010/2011, and we trace their activities during the first two to three years after their establishment. Wherever possible, we give a short outlook on how they might further evolve, taking account of the structural shortcomings of the current institutional architecture, as well as of the overall EU development.

institutions, the national central banks also acted as lenders of last resort, and deposit guarantee schemes were also organized nationally. The basic rationale behind the home country principle follows a simple logic: "If a country's authorities fail to properly regulate or supervise a bank, then that country has to deal with the banks' [sic!] problems, its possible failure, and any crisis management or resolution costs" (Fonteyne et al. 2010, 11) – put differently, he who pays the piper calls the tune. As a result, and to provide just two simple examples for the heterogeneity of the European financial system, insider trading sanctions ranged "from a few thousands of euros in one Member State to millions of euros or jail in another" (High Level Group on Financial Supervision in the EU 2009, 23), and deposit insurance differed considerably from country to country as well. The home country principle also hampered the resolution of systemically important, cross-border financial institutions, which turned out to be a major problem during the crisis.[107]

During the pre-crisis decade, the progress of financial integration increasingly confronted the EU with what Schoenmaker calls the *financial trilemma*: Financial stability, financial integration and national financial policies are incompatible objectives; while any two of the three can be combined, it is impossible to reach all three objectives at the same time, and as a result, one objective is weakened for the benefit of the others (Schoenmaker 2011, 1). Fonteyne et al. add two more dimensions. The tension between national political accountability and transnational financial stability as described in Schoenmaker's trilemma is complemented by "(ii) national fiscal authority versus transnational solvency and liquidity needs; and (iii) the accountability deficit versus host countries" (Fonteyne et al. 2010, 8). Up to the crisis, financial stability was compromised for the benefit of financial integration and national financial policies. When the crisis hit, varying deposit insurance schemes resulted in a flow of private savings so safe havens, destabilizing their home country banks. It also turned out that certain too big to fail banks were too big to save for their home countries, while there was no EU-wide rescue fund to bail them out.

The EU crisis is not yet over. What started as a US mortgage crisis evolved into a European banking and sovereign debt crisis, it then turned out to be a crisis of the architecture of EU financial regulation, and in view of the growing influence of right-wing parties in several EU countries including France, it might still emerge into a full-fledged *political and cultural crisis of the European Union*. This leaves

107 Two EU cases – Fortis and Dexia – demonstrated the need for a mechanism to liquidate such institutions in an orderly way. On the one hand, one could argue that the EU did not, contrary to the US, experience a single disorderly SIFI failure, and that Belgium, France and Luxembourg were even able to jointly save the Dexia group. On the other hand, the Benelux countries could not agree on a strategy to deal with Fortis, and one could conclude that a successful cross-border resolution largely depends on the circumstances and a good deal of luck.

the EU with two diametrically opposed options – *either less or more Europe* (Financial Services Authority 2009) – and as we argue, the new supervisory architecture that was implemented in 2011 indicates that the latter option is more likely.

4.4.2 Transnational vs. National Supervision: The Closer the Better Informed?

One recurring argument for *less Europe* is that the competent (national) authorities are closer to the respective financial institutions, having access to the relevant data and information and knowing these institutions better:

> *National supervisors know the banks well*, the political authorities have at their disposal a consistent legal framework and taxpayers' concerns can be dealt with in the democratic framework of an elected government. (High Level Group on Financial Supervision in the EU 2009, 33, emphasis added)

> Lack of knowledge or experience is another reason that might prompt a transfer 'downwards'. As a body based in Paris, ESMA cannot be expected to have the same in-depth understanding and appreciation of local conditions as competent authorities in Member States. The *importance of local knowledge* should not be underestimated. For one thing, national markets have grown and developed differently. (Schammo 2012, emphasis added)

> The European financial system is characterized by a high degree of heterogeneity. [...] Therefore, national supervisors have an advantage: They know better about regional specifics and the respective regulations. They have an *informational advantage*, leading to a more effective banking supervision. (Neyer and Vieten 2013, 11, translated by the author, emphasis added)[108]

> The main argument for rejecting a reform of supervisory arrangements was that since most banks were mostly national, there was an *informational advantage* in keeping supervision at a national level. However, when merger and acquisitions led to the emergence of pan-European banks, supervisory arrangements did not keep pace. (Pisani-Ferry and Sapir 2010, 346, emphasis added)

Many more reports and articles could be quoted here – and interestingly, we know these arguments from the US context: When policymakers had to decide to either

108 The original text says: "Das Finanzsystem in Europa zeichnet sich durch eine hohe Heterogenität aus. [...] Aufgrund dieser Heterogenität stellen nationale Aufseher einen Vorteil dar; sie erlangen in einem höheren Maße Kenntnis von den regionalen Besonderheiten und den entsprechenden Vorschriften. Sie haben somit einen Informationsvorteil, was sich vorteilhaft auf die Effektivität der Bankenaufsicht auswirkt."

keep their fragmented supervisory structure and create the FSOC as a coordinative forum for the existing regulators (the so-called US model), or to head towards a less fragmented architecture and establish a single supervisor (the so-called UK or Japan model), *being closer* to the supervised entities and – as a consequence – *being better informed*, was a major argument for the US model. By establishing the FSOC in its current form and structure, the US government chose the first, quasi-subsidiary option; the specialized knowledge in different areas of the financial markets that each agency possesses, and that embodies their respective working experience, was central to the decision. As Tarullo has argued: "Regulators with supervisory responsibilities for particular financial firms and markets are more likely to understand the relevance of particular forms of standardized data for risk management and supervisory oversight" (Tarullo 2010b, 10).

The debate in the European Union took a different turn: In view of their highly integrated financial market, European policymakers ultimately favored and supported the more homogenous, European supervisory structure of the ESFS. However, the new structure does to a certain degree account for the presented arguments: New supervisors have been established at the European level, but all three European Supervisory Authorities (ESAs) rely on their national counterparts, as the day-to-day supervision and the data collection authority remains with the competent national authorities.[109] It was argued that "for many fields of supervision direct contact with the supervised entities is necessary, or will require thorough knowledge of the local markets. Here, local supervision will remain the best solution, provided the latter is efficiently coordinated by the European authority" (Wymeersch 2012, 317).[110] And yet the fact that the ESAs do not have their *own access to data and information* concerning financial institutions in the member countries is often perceived as problematic:

> Access to information and the use of such information for monitoring, analyzing trends and preventing systemic risk, needs to improve. Financial stability data are collected from the 30 biggest cross-border insurance groups [...]. EIOPA, however, does not receive the data on an identifiable individual group level that would be necessary for performing EIOPA's tasks. Furthermore, EIOPA does not have direct access to any national supervisory data, although data are submitted to EIOPA upon request [...]. EIOPA should be granted the power to request supervisory data for any institution on a timely basis. (International Monetary Fund 2013a, 23, emphasis added)

109 Black speaks of the centripetal and centrifugal pressures that act on European Reform simultaneously (Black 2012, 8).

110 In this context, it is important to keep in mind that the national banks are – compared to the transnational banks – the much bigger group in the EU (International Monetary Fund 2013a, 7). Yet the transnational financial institutions are the problematic, i.e. systemically important, institutions.

The IMF points out another aspect of the problem: While the new system for financial supervision already embodies major data and information asymmetries, a lack of expertise at the side of the ESAs might become at least as problematic. Assessing the work of the EIOPA so far, the IMF argues that the authority has no adequate funding or budget flexibility to build up the expertise that it needs, especially during the early phase of its work (International Monetary Fund 2013b, 18).

4.4.3 The New European System of Financial Supervision

In both the EU and the US, the financial crisis revealed a lack of coordination and cooperation between the different supervisory and regulatory bodies – in the US between the respective federal agencies, in the EU between the national bodies on the one hand and the EU bodies on the other. Therefore, following the recommendations of the de Larosière Report (High Level Group on Financial Supervision in the EU 2009), the EU established the *European System of Financial Supervision* (ESFS). It brings together the European and national authorities and aims to ensure a "stable and single Union financial market for financial services" by "linking national supervisors within a strong Union network" (European Parliament and Council of Ministers 2010b). Within the ESFS structure, the three newly established, independent and supranational European Supervisory Authorities (ESAs) are required to closely cooperate with the respective national authorities. The ESAs emanate from the former EU Level-3 Committees, reflecting the traditional macro-sectors of financial supervision (Quaglia 2008, 441): In 2011, the Committee of European Banking Supervisors (CEBS) was transformed into the *European Banking Authority* (EBA), the *European Securities and Markets Authority* (ESMA) continues the work of the Committee of European Securities Regulators (CESR), and the *European Insurance and Occupational Pensions Authority* (EIOPA) replaced the Committee of European Insurance and Occupational Pensions Supervisors (CEIOPS). Compared to their predecessors, the ESAs have "significantly strengthened governance systems, powers, and operational autonomy" (Fonteyne et al. 2010, 83), and yet the home country principle persists in certain areas: The national supervisors remain responsible for the day-to-day supervision of financial firms (Schammo 2012, 773). Moreover, when compared to the respective US agencies (especially the SEC and the CFTC), the ESAs' powers are limited both with regard to rulemaking and enforcement, and supervision (Wymeersch 2012, 237).

Within the overall architecture of the ESFS, the ESRB is responsible for macroprudential supervision while the ESAs, together with their national counterparties, aim at microprudential supervision (see figure 8).

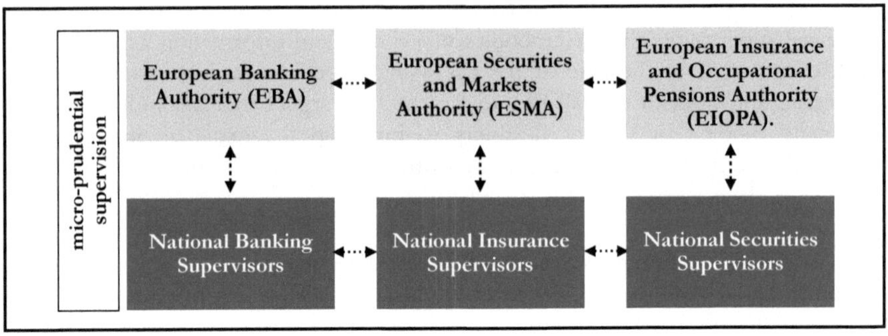

Figure 9: EU microprudential supervision (figure based on High Level Group on Financial Supervision in the EU 2009).

The set-up of the EFSF, and especially the role of the ESAs, might be well described as *two steps forward, one step back*: Though ESAs possess wide-ranging intervention powers, they have only limited day-to-day supervisory powers (as we will see later on, the ESMA is an exception here). While they are allowed to set standards, they lack the authority to ultimately enforce them. And even though their mandate requires them to collect and analyze certain data and information, the ESAs rely on the national authorities' will to cooperate, since they are the only authorities with direct access to the respective data and information. We will revisit these obstacles when we look at each ESA on the following pages.

The three ESAs resemble each other: They are all governed by a Board of Supervisors (BoS) that brings together the relevant national authorities from each Member State (voting members) and also incorporates representatives of the European Commission, the ERSB and the other two ESAs (non-voting members).[111] All ESAs are mandated to (1) improve the functioning of the internal market, (2) secure a sound, effective and consistent level of regulation and supervision, (3) ensure the orderly functioning of financial markets, (4) strengthen supervisory coordination internationally, (5) prevent regulatory arbitrage and promote an equal playing field, (6) ensure that risks are appropriately regulated and supervised, and (7) enhance customer protection; in accordance with their microprudential role, they should also pay attention to systemic risk that is posed by financial institutions (see Articles 1(5) of European Parliament and Council of Ministers 2010b, 2010d, 2010c). All ESAs are Union bodies with legal personality,

111 The BoS is the main decision-making body of the ESAs. Each BoS has a subgroup, the management board, which ensures that "the Authority carries out its mission and performs the tasks assigned to it" (European Banking Authority 2013). The management board is responsible for annual work programs, annual reports, budget and staff.

and all three of them can make legally binding and non-binding decisions (Wymeersch 2012, describes the powers of the ESAs in great detail).

European Banking Authority

The London-based EBA took over many of its responsibilities from its predecessor, the Committee of European Banking Supervisors (CEBS). It describes its overall objectives as maintaining "financial stability in the EU and to safeguard the integrity, efficiency and orderly functioning of the banking sector", and its main tasks as contributing, "through the adoption of binding Technical Standards (BTS) and Guidelines, to the creation of the European Single Rulebook in banking" (European Banking Authority 2013). In consultation with the ESRB, the EBA develops and conducts the *European banking stress tests* (European Parliament and Council of Ministers 2010b, Article 21), and is also required to contribute to the development of *recovery and resolution plans* (ibid., Article 25). In addition, it has a *wide range of data and information related tasks*, such as to collect data concerning consumer trends and to report on these trends, or to develop industry-training standards. Its area of expertise covers "banking, payments and e-money regulation as well as [...] corporate governance, auditing and financial reporting" (European Banking Authority 2012a). To fulfill its mandate, the EBA can make use of a number of *non-regulatory and regulatory documents*, among them regular and ad hoc reports, such as the EBA's annual reports, but also Guidelines, Recommendations and drafts of Binding Technical Standards. The latter have to be adopted by the European Commission, representing an indirect legal power for the EBA.

As it could be also well observed in the context of the OFR, during the first two years after its creation, the EBA focused on building up its organizational capacities and resources, for instance in the area of internal rules and procedures, IT and human resources (European Banking Authority 2011, 2012a). Its staff is expected to increase to 123 during 2013 (including temporary and contractual agents, but also assigned national experts) (International Monetary Fund 2013a, 10). In its regulatory work, it focused on Basel III implementation (*capital buffers, liquidity, remuneration and leverage ratios*) and prevention and resolution tools, heading towards a single rule book for the EU banking system (European Banking Authority 2011, 2012b). In its oversight work, risk assessment tools such as public stress tests and non-public risk dashboards, as well as increased cooperation between home and host countries, took center stage (European Banking Authority 2011). Regarding consumer protection, the EBA's emphasis lay on developing a strategy and priorities (ibid.) and on finalizing its first guidelines (European Banking Authority 2012b, 7).

According to an early assessment by the IMF, the EBA's achievements during its first two years were significant, even though certain constraints hampered and slowed down its efforts:

> In spite of *limited resources*, the achievements of the European Banking Authority (EBA) in its first two years of existence are significant, but the pace and prioritization of its activities have been *dictated by the crisis*. Efforts directly related to the crisis [...] may have diverted scarce resources and management attention from other aspects of its mandate related to enhancing convergence and quality of supervision in the European Union (EU). However, in its short existence, the EBA has been very active in its regulatory mandate, and 23 draft technical standards have been produced, the large majority of them related to capital. (International Monetary Fund 2013a, 4, emphasis added)

The IMF report criticizes the EBA's "cumbersome decision making processes" (ibid.), and its lack of direct access to relevant data: As already mentioned, the EBA relies on the national supervisory authorities (NSAs) to collect data from financial institutions, and it is not authorized to control the data it receives from the NSAs itself (ibid., 9f). According to the Financial Times, the stress tests conducted by this new European authority "have been met with open hostility by some national regulators, particularly in Spain, Italy and Germany" (Jenkins and Masters 2013). A fourth crucial point is the EBA's budget: The Authority is funded by the European Commission and the NSAs, meaning that the EBA's staffing policy is subject to EU budget rules, leading to an inadequate and inflexible financial situation (International Monetary Fund 2013a, 10f.) And last but not least, the EBA has only very few binding powers and lacks enforcement authority (ibid., 18f.; see also Neyer and Vieten 2013).

The European Securities and Markets Authority

The European Securities and Markets Authority (ESMA) is located in Paris. With regard to credit rating agencies (CRAs), EU policymakers followed the de Larosière Report recommendation and mandated the ESMA to register and supervise rating agencies (High Level Group on Financial Supervision in the EU 2009, 20). As the other ESAs, the ESMA is required to contribute to a single European rule book via its regulatory work (i.e. by developing guidelines), to support supervisory convergence (i.e. by investigating law breaches), to contribute to financial stability and crisis management (i.e. by supporting the ESRB), and to strengthen investor protection (i.e. by issuing warnings) (International Monetary Fund 2013c, 7f.; European Securities and Markets Authority 2012, 5). Generally speaking, the ESMA continues the work of its predecessor, the Committee of European Securities Regulators (CESR). However, while the CESR had a staff of about 50 employees in 2010, the ESMA intends to ultimately increase its staff to 120, again including temporary agents, contract agents and national experts (Schammo 2012, 783).[112] Its organizational growth reflects the expanded mandate and authority of the ESMA.

Interestingly, the ESMA's financing differs from the other ESAs as it is partly funded by the rating agencies it supervises (International Monetary Fund 2013c, 11). Due to its budget, it has a higher degree of independence than the other two ESAs (see Masciandaroa, Nietob, and Quintync 2011), and we can conclude from the US and the EU cases that an independent funding is of central importance. The ESMA's enforcement authority is a second distinctive characteristic: ESMA is not only authorized to withdraw a rating agency's license, it can also: "(i) temporarily prohibit the CRA from issuing ratings with effect in the EU, (ii) suspend the use for regulatory purposes of ratings with effect in the EU, (iii) require a CRA to bring the infringement to an end, (iv) issue notices, and (v) impose fines" (International Monetary Fund 2013c, 17; see European Securities and Markets Authority, 2012 and European Securities and Markets Authority 2011, for more information). In emergency situations, it has certain additional powers, e.g. temporary bans on certain short-selling activities.

The ESMA has not yet used its enforcement authority, but it has started to investigate the rating agencies' activities, for instance in the field of bank evaluation, where it criticized the rating agencies' outdated information, nontransparent procedures and insufficient warnings (Masters 2013b, 2013a).

A first IMF assessment of the ESMA's work was rather positive, stating that it

> has performed well during its first two years of operation, especially in connection with the single rulebook and credit rating agency (CRA) supervision. A significant number of technical standards, advice to the European Commission (EC), and opinions were developed. ESMA has also been able to build its expertise in connection with Credit Rating Agencies (CRAs) and has worked on the development of a risk framework to anchor its supervisory program. (International Monetary Fund 2013c, 4)

According to the IMF report, the work of the ESMA was hampered by a lack of resources (both in terms of money and time) and a lack of granular data. A third problem was that, due to its operational structure and its reliance on support by the NCAs, decisions were sometimes dominated by domestic interests (International Monetary Fund 2013c).

European Insurance and Occupational Pensions Authority

The European Insurance and Occupational Pensions Authority (EIOPA) is located in Frankfurt. Its mandate is "to support the stability of the financial system, ensure the transparency of markets and financial products and protect policyholders,

112 The IMF expects the ESMA to increase its staff to 160 in 2013 (International Monetary Fund 2013b, 13).

pension scheme members and beneficiaries. […] to monitor and identify trends, potential risks and vulnerabilities at the micro-prudential level, across borders and across sectors" (European Insurance and Occupational Pensions Authority 2012, 15). To be able to fulfill its mandate, EIOPA increased its staff from 57 in 2011 to 87 in 2012 and it was expected to further grow to 114 in 2013 (International Monetary Fund 2013b, 17). During its first two years, EIOPA has focused on one of its key responsibilities, the drafting of the Solvency II insurance standards. EIOPA's work, especially with regard to Solvency II implementation, is described as "intense and relevant" (International Monetary Fund 2013a, 30; see Gray 2013, for the current public debate on Solvency II).

However, EIOPA has been slowed down by several obstacles: Its funding structure, its inadequate access to information, and its limited powers – most of which apparently are recurring issues and represent a problem for all three ESAs. EIOPA's lack of financial and structural independence from the national authorities is well described by the IMF:

> The legal status of EIOPA is of an independent advisory body accountable to the European Parliament and the Council of the EU. However, the *financing structure could hinder effective independence*. National authorities contribute 60 percent of the budget, and the national authorities are the voting Supervisory Board members. Thus, BoS Members may be confronted with conflicts of interest while agreeing on the implementation of EIOPA's tasks and powers that impact their own powers and responsibilities as national supervisors. (International Monetary Fund 2013a, 18, emphasis added)

In May 2013, the head of EIOPA argued that the authority needed *independent funding and a direct access to data* to be more effective (Bernardino 2013, 2). EIOPA's powers are in fact quite limited. It can, for instance, issue warnings concerning certain insurance products or activities, given the fact that they pose a threat to the stability of the EU financial system. However, it cannot permanently restrict or prohibit these products or activities without permission by the Commission (International Monetary Fund 2013a).

4.4.4 The European Systemic Risk Board

The European Systemic Risk Board (ESRB or *the Board*) was established in 2011 at the ECB in Frankfurt as the European macroprudential supervisor within the newly created ESFS structure (European Parliament and Council of Ministers 2010a, Article 3(1)). In its role as a systemic risk watchdog, the Board can clearly be compared to the US FSOC. The mandates of the FSOC and the ESRB do partly overlap, yet there are crucial differences, especially with regard to the bodies' authorities. The Board's overall tasks as outlined more briefly in Article 2 are:

(a) to collect and analyze all the relevant and necessary information,
(b) to identify and prioritize systemic risks;
(c) to issue (public) warnings regarding those risks,
(d) to issue (public) recommendations for action in response to those risks,
(e) to inform the European Council about those risks,
(f) to monitor the follow-up to its warnings and recommendations,
(g) to cooperate closely with all the other parties to the ESFS and to provide the ESAs with the information they need to perform their tasks and to develop indicators for systemic risk identification and measurement together with the ESAs,
(h) to participate in the Joint Committee that brings together the ESFS members,
(i) to coordinate its actions with those of international financial organizations (such as, for instance, the FSB),
(j) to carry out other related tasks (European Parliament and Council of Ministers 2010a).

The ESRB focuses on *systemic risk oversight*, as the crisis revealed a lack of macroprudential oversight in the EU. Data and information related issues were perceived as a more pressing problem in the US, but they nevertheless found their way into the ESRB's mandate, too. National supervisors apparently did not share enough information with the ECB (Pisani-Ferry and Sapir 2010), and as a consequence, inadequate information became a problem during the financial crisis. Besides its focus on systemic risk, the ESRB is therefore required to collect and analyze relevant data and information, performing the tasks of both the FSOC and the OFR to some extent, while an entity comparable to the OFR has not been established in the EU. Besides *data and information collection*, the ESRB has an important (public) *warning function*. In addition, similar to the FSOC, it aims at increasing *EU-internal* (US-internal, respectively), as well as *global cooperation*.

While the FSOC is authorized to designate systemically important financial institutions and markets and might ultimately break up institutions posing a threat to the financial stability of the United States, the Board has neither legally binding powers nor a separate legal personality. Besides, it does not look at specific financial institutions, but monitors systemic risk and financial stability more generally (Kern and Lantz 2012, 4). However, just like the ESAs, it "forms an integral part of a structure within which hard enforcement powers are available and it will be empowered to act in ways that could trigger the exercise of those powers" (Ferran and Kern 2011, 4). Even though it is weaker than the FSOC, the soft-law body ESRB is – as Ferran and Kern emphasize – embedded in hard law structures, and might in fact prove to be highly effective:

> The practical impact of its 'advice' could be very strong indeed. What the ESRB has to say on matters that could be highly sensitive and politically-charged will have the potential to affect the Union as a whole, Member States, the European Supervisory Authorities, national supervisory authorities, and even the Commission. Indeed, if its pronouncements were not to be taken seriously, the new European framework for macro-prudential oversight would be fundamentally flawed. (ibid., 24)

In fact, Jean-Claude Trichet has argued that the ESRB would use its "moral authority" to overcome a lack of formal enforcement powers (Wilson 2011), and that it therefore "must speak convincingly and build up credibility over time" (Trichet 2011).

Information about the ESRB's internal structure is provided elsewhere in great detail and high quality and should not be repeated here (see for example European Parliament and Council of Ministers 2010a; European Systemic Risk Board 2013a; Ferran and Kern 2011). What is much more interesting in the context of this book is how closely the ESRB is related to the ECB, especially when compared to the FSOC: Following the de Larosière Report recommendation that the ESRB "should be set up under the auspices and with the logistical support of the ECB" (High Level Group on Financial Supervision in the EU 2009), the ESRB is located at and supported by the ECB in its analytical and preparatory work (Fonteyne et al. 2010, 83). It is chaired by the President of the ECB, and its first Vice-Chair is elected by and from the ECB's General Council (European Parliament and Council of Ministers 2010a, Article 5). The Board is also funded by the ECB. The ESRB is accordingly closely intertwined with its central bank, while the FSOC is hosted by the Treasury, chaired by the Treasury Secretary, and – via the OFR – funded through levies on financial institutions. All ESRB decisions are made by the General Board, composed of 37 voting members and 28 non-voting members (Ferran and Kern 2011, 21). The ECB, the national central banks, the Commission, the three ESAs, and the specialized committees of the ESRB are all represented in the General Board (Article 6) – a fact that adds value, but at the same time represents a serious challenge (European Systemic Risk Board 2013b, 6). Compared to the FSOC, which consists of ten voting and five non-voting members, the ESRB's decision-making body is much bigger. However, while size is an issue, the bigger problem might be the *strong representation of central banks' interests*, giving "insufficient weight to the fiscal element of financial stability" and leading to "over-representation of central banks at the expense of the insurance and securities sectors" (Ferran and Kern 2011, 22). Considering our argument that systemic risk must be perceived in economic and political terms, the central bank dominance on the ESRB's General Board evokes questions of political legitimacy, too.

In view of certain operational issues, as well as of the overall development towards a European Banking Union, the ESRB is – like the ESAs – likely to change:

> On the overall macro-micro interaction I believe that the ESRB is proving to be a useful platform. Nevertheless, the Governance of the ESRB should be improved in order to increase efficiency, maybe with a stronger role for the Steering Committee. It would also be important to reinforce the truly cross-sectoral nature of the ESRB and develop better access to information to improve the analysis and understanding of interconnectedness. (Bernardino 2013)

Current plans on a European Banking Union would alter the role of the ESRB. Against this backdrop, the ESRB reviewed its mission and organization as required by EU regulation in 2013 (Trichet 2011). It suggested "not to introduce fundamental amendments to the legislation establishing the ESRB", but to "make the ESRB mandate more specific so as to focus it on medium-long term threats to financial stability and on cross-financial sector vulnerabilities, also to delineate its mandate more precisely from that of other bodies" (Draghi 2013). Interesting from a comparative point of view is that the report recommended to "[i]nvestigate the option of upgrading the ESRB Annual Report to bring it in line with the more substantive Financial Stability Oversight Council (FSOC) Annual Report" (European Systemic Risk Board 2013b, 3). In this context, the FSOC serves as a role model – a fact that is quite delicate, given the GAO criticism of the Council's annual reports, as well as the much higher analytical quality of the OFR annual reports.

4.4.5 The European Central Bank

The financial crisis has not only led to the establishment of several new institutions in the EU – namely the ESRB and the three ESAs – but it has also fundamentally altered the role of the ECB. Since 2008, the ECB has expanded its influence and area of competence, a development that is often viewed critically, first and foremost with regard to the ECB's political legitimacy. Begg emphasizes that "[o]ne of the most vexed questions for the EU is how the European Central Bank's role should evolve" (Begg 2009). When the crisis hit in 2008, and it quickly turned out that the EU was weakly designed for crisis management, the ECB took the lead by providing liquidity to the frozen interbank market: Hodson and Quaglia argue that the ECB was "more decisive than EU finance ministers in responding to the global financial crisis", cutting not only its interest rate to a historical low but also using such unconventional measures as extending the maximum maturity of refinancing operations, accepting a wider range of assets as collateral from banks borrowing from the Eurosystem, and providing liquidity in foreign currencies, mostly US dollars (Hodson and Quaglia 2009; Trichet 2010). As a result, the ECB's balance sheet has grown dramatically. It is widely agreed that the Central Bank "was among the first to react swiftly" (High Level Group on Financial Supervision in the EU 2009, 12) – or, in the words of former ECB president Jean-Claude Trichet, reacted "bold and fast" (Trichet 2010). Then, in the middle of the crisis, Trichet argued that European reform should strengthen the role of the ECB when he made the following noteworthy statement:

> Macro-prudential supervision of the financial system by central banks needs to be strengthened. [...] The ECB and the Eurosystem have the *technical capacity* to assume a stronger role in macro-prudential supervision. Indeed, it would be a natural extension of the mandate already assigned to us by the Treaty, namely to contribute to financial stability. [...] The EU has the opportunity for an important institutional change. [...]. The ECB/Eurosystem stands ready to accept any additional responsibilities that the Member States may wish to assign to us, in accordance with the Treaty. (Trichet 2009, emphasis added)

It is often argued that central banks are in the best position for systemic risk supervision, because of their clear "macro-economic orientation" as well as their "concrete knowledge of financial markets" (Bank for International Settlements 2009, 6). While the central banks' independence from political pressure is another major argument, it can also be used as an argument against extended central bank responsibilities: Precisely because they are independent, central banks lack political legitimacy. Yet, two key observations from the financial crisis are that central banks in the US and the EU played a central role in mitigating systemic risk, and that the central banks tried to expand their role in macroprudential regulation and supervision (International Monetary Fund 2010; see Nier 2009, for a detailed discussion of central bank models with regard to macroprudential regulation). As changes in central banks are often triggered by crises, it comes as no surprise that the ECB responded to the crisis by demanding greater responsibilities (Bank for International Settlements 2009). It was also no surprise that the majority of national authorities and national central banks opposed the ECB's attempt, as the following written statement by Alistair Darling shows:

> It has always been clear that the financial services industry is global. Whatever we do in the EU must be consistent with this [...]. As part of this we need to be clear about what is and should be dealt with supra-nationally and what needs to be dealt with on a national basis. [...] Supervisory authority needs to be aligned with fiscal responsibility and this will be a very significant factor in limiting the extent to which national supervisors can devolve responsibility for the supervision of firms to a centralised body. (Darling 2009, 1f.)

Central banks have good reasons to increase the effectiveness of macroprudential supervision and regulation, minimizing the likelihood that they have to provide emergency liquidity to financial institutions (International Monetary Fund 2010, 17f.). At the same time, it is widely agreed that the most important central bank objective is financial and price stability, and that it is crucial that the central banks keep their monetary policy independence to fulfill this role (Weidmann 2013), that "any pressures to entrench the expanded policy role that central banks took on during the crisis and that are normally outside of their mandate should thus be resisted" (International Monetary Fund 2010, 25). In this context, Pauly rightly distinguishes between the technical and operational independence on the one hand, and the actual political independence of a central bank on the other (Pauly 2010, 17). It is widely agreed that the *politicization of central banks* that took place around the globe during the crisis bears massive risks. Taking diverse arguments into account, the EU established a systemic risk oversight board that is institutionally separate from the ECB, but also located at and supported by the ECB. It is viable to say that altogether, the ECB has further expanded its influence on financial supervision via the ESRB.

4.5 Changes in Global Financial Governance: The Establishment of the FSB

At the global level, a key reform in financial supervision and regulation triggered by the financial crisis was the transformation of the Financial Stability Forum into the Financial Stability Board by the Group of Twenty in 2009 (Helleiner 2010a). Although a broader analysis of all global policy responses, covering changes at other international institutions such as the IMF and especially the BCBS, would be quite informative, we want to focus on the FSB – due to space constraints, but primarily because it is the most valuable point of reference for the FSOC. In its basic structure, the FSB resembles the FSOC: It is designed as a loose network for cooperation and coordination, bringing together the international financial standard setting bodies (ISSBs) with other international organizations, as well as the national financial authorities, including finance ministers, central bank representatives and securities regulators.[113] By establishing the FSB, the Group of Twenty followed the

113 The type and number of country representatives on the FSB depend on its membership status. Some countries send three representatives (e.g. the US is represented by the Fed Board of Governors, the Treasury and the SEC; Germany by its central bank (Deutsche Bundesbank), its Ministry of Finance and the BaFin; and the UK by Her Majesty's Treasury, the Bank of England and the FSA); others send two, and other countries only one representative (FSB 2009, Annex A). The international bodies on the FSB are the BCBS, the Committee on the Global Financial System (CGFS), the Committee on Payment and Settlement Systems (CPSS), International Association of Insurance Supervisors (IAIS), the International Accounting Standards Board (IASB) and the International Organization of Securities Commissions (IOSCO).

recommendation of the de Larosière report "that a reformed FSF would [...] be in the best position for coordinating the work of the various international standard setters in achieving international regulatory consistency" (High Level Group on Financial Supervision in the EU 2009, 60).

International coordination is, as the crisis demonstrated, desperately needed, especially in the area of global SIFI resolution that is not covered by the Basel accords (Financial Stability Board 2013, 2011a). But will the FSB be able to solve the problems resulting from an incongruence between national financial policies and global financial institutions? In the year of its establishment, then Treasury Secretary Timothy Geithner famously called the FSB a *fourth pillar* of economic governance, complementing the global triumvirate of IMF, World Bank and WTO (Geithner 2009b), a statement that has been challenged ever since (see Griffith-Jones, Helleiner, and Woods 2010). As Helleiner illustrates, three aspects are important in this respect, and we will discuss each of them briefly. First, the FSB has extended the group of FSF member states, implying a greater reach and legitimacy of its initiatives. However, access to the FSB is still limited both in geographical terms and with regard to NGO participation. Second, to increase overall compliance by the member countries with international standards, the Board is equipped with four new mechanisms – yet, the FSB has, just as the FSF, no legal enforcement powers. And third, the FSB has a new, explicit mandate for macroprudential supervision and systemic risk oversight, complementing the newly established set of systemic risk oversight organizations, namely the FSOC and the ESRB (Helleiner 2010a).

It is widely agreed that the FSB's predecessor did not live up to the expectations of its founders, and that its independent impact on the international standard setting bodies was very limited, if not absent (Helleiner 2010b, 2010a; Donnelly 2012, 264). The FSF's work was hindered by its ambiguous and vague mandate and role, as well as its limited powers (A. Baker 2010a). Contrary to the FSB, it did not even have a full-time secretariat at the BIS in Basel (Moschella 2012, 392). We therefore start our brief analysis with the *mandate* of the FSB, as its importance cannot be overestimated. We will afterwards proceed with the FSB's *operational structure and authorities.*

According to its mandate (Financial Stability Board 2009, 2012), the FSB aims at:

- assessing vulnerabilities affecting the financial system and identifying and overseeing actions to address them;
- promoting coordination between authorities responsible for financial stability;
- monitoring and advising on market developments and their implications, as well as on best practice in meeting regulatory standards;

- undertaking joint strategic reviews of and coordinate the policy development work of the international standard setting bodies;
- supporting the establishment of supervisory colleges;
- managing contingency planning for cross-border crisis management;
- collaborating with the IMF to conduct early warnings;
- promoting FSB members' implementation of agreed commitments, standards and policy recommendations; and
- undertaking any other tasks agreed by its Members within the framework of its charter.

The FSB was established to increase global financial stability by setting standards, monitoring and issuing warnings, and through collecting and sharing relevant information. Regarding its structure, the FSB shares with the FSOC its strong coordinative role – both being *loose umbrella organizations* or *networks* (see Griffith-Jones, Helleiner, and Woods 2010, 7; Helleiner 2010a, 3; Willke, Becker, and Rostásy 2013) – and its mandate for systemic risk oversight. The FSB is located at the Bank for International Settlements in Basel; it is officially accountable to the G20 leaders, but it also informally reports to the IMF's International Monetary and Financial Committee (IMFC) (Helleiner 2010a, 7). An important point, especially in the context of this book, is the FSB's "knowledge generation function" (A. Baker 2010a, 20).

FSB Structure and Membership

While the FSF was a G7, somewhat exclusive initiative, the FSB has extended its group of members to the G20 countries and also to a greater set of international financial institutions. The Board is now in a better position to fulfill its mandate, which exceeds the coordination and monitoring of finance in the G7 countries and comprises global financial supervision and policymaking. It nearly presents the complete set of regulators of the 50 largest banks worldwide and close to 80 percent of world savings (Weber and Staiger 2014, 87). Yet, in view of its global mandate, one might ask whether its membership is still far too narrow (Helleiner 2010b). Some commenters hope that "the new members in the club will add legitimacy to the process" (Momani 2010, 36), especially as the FSB did revise its charter in 2012, thus further enhancing access to its consultation process for non-member countries (Financial Stability Board 2012). Regarding its membership, but also its internal structure, the FSB is still a tiny organization – at least when compared to the other international, highly formalized organizations, such as the BIS or the IMF. Besides a chairman and a steering committee, the FSB has a small secretariat of eight to 16 economists (Pauly 2010, 16; Donnelly 2012, 266), a changing number of working groups, standing committees, regional consultative groups, and a plenary that consists of the FSB members. The plenary is the main decision-making body of the

Board, operating on reaching consensus (Financial Stability Board 2009, Articles 6, 7 and 11; 2012). Regarding the FSB's composition, Helleiner speaks of an "odd mix of central bankers, finance ministry officials and supervisory and regulatory authorities from a relatively narrow group of countries alongside officials from international financial institutions and standard-setting bodies" (Helleiner 2010a, 3). Gadinis adds that, as 18 out of seventy Plenary members are political appointees, the FSB has a "deeply political character" (Gadinis 2013, 159).

New Compliance Mechanisms

Helleiner highlights the importance of the four compliance mechanisms introduced with the establishment of the FSB. First, all FSB members undergo mandatory peer reviews that base upon the Financial Sector Assessment Program (FSAP) reports of the IMF and the World Bank. The FSB charter requires them to publish the results (Financial Stability Board 2009, Article 5(d)). Looking at the record of conducted and published FSAP modules for G20 countries – in the past, central countries chose either not to participate, or not to publish the results – this clearly presents a major change for many FSB member countries (Walter 2010; Momani 2010). Second, all FSB members agreed to implement a set of key international financial standards and to also implement all new standards created by the FSB (Financial Stability Board 2009, Article 5(c); Group of Twenty 2009).[114] Third, all members are subject to mandatory theme- and country-based peer reviews. And fourth, the FSB members are required to actively encourage compliance with international prudential standards among all countries (Helleiner 2010b, 29). While certain challenges and ambiguities remain – how will non-compliance be penalized, and is the FSB staff able to effectively perform the peer review process? – it is widely agreed that these four mechanisms represent a major progress towards the FSF.

With regard to macroprudential supervision, three developments are noteworthy: First, the FSB now conducts reviews of the international bodies' policy development work; second, these same international bodies now have to report on

114 The 12 key standards for sound financial systems date back to 1999 and include the IMF's Code of Good Practices on Transparency in Monetary and Financial Policies, the IMF's Code of Good Practices on Fiscal Transparency and the IMF's Special Data Dissemination Standard in the area of *Macroeconomic Policy and Data Transparency*; the BCBS's Core Principles for Effective Banking Supervision, the IOSCO's Objectives and Principles of Securities Regulation and the IAIS's Insurance Core Principles set the standards for *Financial Regulation and Supervision*; *Institutional and Market Infrastructure* are regulated through the Core Principles for Effective Deposit Insurance Systems (BCBS/ International Association of Deposit Insurers, IADI), Insolvency and Creditor Rights (World Bank), the Principles of Corporate Governance (OECD), the International Financial Reporting Standards (International Accounting Standards Board, IASB), the International Standards on Auditing (International Auditing and Assurance Standards Board, IAASB), the Principles for Financial Market Infrastructures (CPSS/IOSCO) and the Recommendations on Combating Money Laundering and the Financing of Terrorism & Proliferation (Financial Action Task Force, FATF) (Financial Stability Board 2014).

their work to the FSB; and third, the FSB is authorized to develop its own standards to address macroprudential issues (Helleiner 2010a, 13). A fourth point has to be added: The commitment of the FSB's institutional environment to systemic risk supervision and regulation, especially of the BIS and the IMF, will certainly push the work of the FSB towards a stronger macroprudential mandate. The Board supervises global SIFIs directly through supervisory colleges, allowing the FSB "to directly impact regulatory supervision alongside the national regulators who are ultimately responsible for them" (Donnelly 2012, 272).

Transparency and Accountability of the FSB

In 2011/2012, the G20 leaders decided to revise the FSB's charter in order to "strengthen the FSB's capacity, resources and governance, including its establishment on an enduring organisation footing, strengthening its coordination role vis-à-vis other standard-setting bodies on policy development and implementation monitoring, and reconstitution of the FSB's Steering Committee" (Financial Stability Board 2012). The changes in the FSB's mandate increase the accountability and transparency of the FSB, but they also include amendments concerning decision-making and governance. According to Article 3 of the original mandate, the FSB had to "consult widely amongst its Members and with other stakeholders including private sector and non-member authorities" (Financial Stability Board 2009). The revised mandate requires the FSB to agree on a "structured mechanism on FSB policy proposals", and to "engage in dialogue with market participants *and other stakeholders*, including through round-tables, hearings and other appropriate events" (Financial Stability Board 2012, point 7, emphasis added). NGOs and academics had criticized the FSB's mandate as it provided "no available venues for civil society to engage in discussions with the leadership of the FSB" (Transparency International 2009).

To increase its transparency, the FSB now also wants to communicate more openly on its appointment processes and the positions it offers (Financial Stability Board 2012, point 9) and publish "detailed press releases following Plenary meetings and separate press statements on important policy decisions, as and when taken" (ibid., point 10). It has also announced plans to modernize its website (ibid.). The new charter includes an Article that explicitly demands greater accountability and transparency: Article 4 now requires the FSB to "discharge its accountability, beyond its members, through publication of reports and, in particular, through periodical reporting of progress in its work to the [...] Group of Twenty" (Financial Stability Board 2012).[115]

115 In the short report preceding the new charter, the FSB also advocated giving the Board a new legal form by transforming it into an association under Swiss law (Financial Stability Board 2012). Whether or not it will realize this plan remains to be seen.

Even though the FSB has, compared to the FSF, "made significant progress in achieving actual implementation of its recommendations" (Weber and Staiger 2014, 90), it remains a soft-law body and lacks authority to enforce its standards. It accordingly is an open question whether the FSB will be more successful in achieving global financial stability than its successor. As Willke et al. argue, the FSB "is supposed to operate *without clear competences*, *without sanctions* or enforcement mechanisms, with very *limited resources* and with a *complicated decision-making procedure*, which only works if consensus is achieved" (Willke, Becker, and Rostásy 2013, 110; Moschella 2012; Bair 2012a). Especially the required consensus between the FSB's members is likely to present a hurdle for substantial reform (Weber and Staiger 2014, 88).

4.6 Financial Reform Revisited: Where Do We Stand Today?

Kane describes financial regulation as a game within a game: "The principal game is the production and delivery of financial services. The subgame involves regulator-regulatee-customer jostling for position or dominance" (Kane 1986, 189). After the turbulent crisis months of 2008, and with Dodd-Frank signed into law in 2010, it appeared as if financial regulators (and customers) had strengthened their position vis-à-vis financial institutions. Yet, when we ask ourselves today whether US policymakers and regulators are on par with the financial system that they oversee and police, it is difficult to provide a clear answer. Does Dodd-Frank alter financial governance fundamentally, or will it only relieve the symptoms while the underlying disease lingers on? Davidoff and Zaring have, in their legal analysis of US policy responses to the crisis, succinctly described the typical course of such policy initiatives:

> The response often begins with the scramble of governments to keep up with fast-paced and deleterious market events, leading to an initial, ad hoc phase in government action, where emergencies are responded to with emergency-style rules and emergency-style process. In sufficiently serious crises, the next phase may be a legislative one – beginning with outraged congressional hearings and then new legislative authority. At about this time, implementation of the criminal investigations hit their stride, leading to the ex post punishment – often quite severe punishment – of a few symbols of the crisis, such as high-ranking CEOs and some unfortunate exemplars of excess. Finally, there is reform; *either reform forgone in favor of blue-ribbon commissions and minor regulatory reorganization, or reform embraced by new legislation and a restructuring of the financial regulatory system.* (Davidoff and Zaring 2009, 532, emphasis added)

Do the FSOC, the OFR and the CFPB represent a *minor regulatory reorganization*? – put differently, was the crisis severe enough to "stimulate policy innovation" (Pauly 2008, 80)? On the one hand, one could argue that substantial progress has been achieved with the introduction of stress tests and living wills through Dodd-Frank, the establishment of the FSOC, the ESRB and the FSB as systemic risk watchdogs, the adoption of higher capital and liquidity requirements via Basel III, and the establishment of a new US resolution authority, accompanied by transnational agreements for cross-border resolution. In one of our interviews, Acharya argued exemplarily that "I think this is a real change. I think it has certainly the potential to make real change. I think FSOC is already working" (Interview with Viral Acharya, November 28, 2012, New York). On the other hand, it might be the case that Dodd-Frank and the related promises – that "the American people will never again be asked to foot the bill for Wall Street's mistakes" (Obama 2010) – represents ineffective[116] or merely *symbolic politics* (Edelman 1970):

> The decision itself is regarded in the day-to-day business of politics as proof of success. One has been able to formulate it and push it through. One can mention it in reports on the past legislative period, and it is by no means unrealistic to assume that it has a modifying effect of circumstances. The question is only what effects? (Luhmann 2008, 164)

Streeck, for instance, argues that recent financial reform has "failed in almost all respects" (Streeck 2011, 19). The following illustration (figure 10) goes one step further, suggesting that policymakers believe and appear to have tamed the crisis, while the beast is in fact hiding underneath; the illustrator warns us that the next crisis will definitely come, and that it will be much worse than the one we have just experienced.

116 In his FCIC interview, Calomiris terms the Dodd-Frank Act "the worst piece of legislation in American history. It is not a serious piece of legislation, it is again not really addressing the key problems, and even worse, it is creating a lot of regulatory costs that are unrelated to the crisis" (Calomiris 2010). Barr makes a more balanced statement when saying that Dodd-Frank makes the system "safer, but not safe" (Barr 2013).

Figure 10: The next crisis (Roca 2014).

In view of the FSOC mandate, the OLA, living wills and the changes in the Fed's authority, it becomes clear that the post-crisis reform efforts in the US have a strong focus on TBTF. The reason is obvious: As illustrated in the second chapter of this book, TBTF lies at the heart of systemic risk – if not resolved, it might have severe consequences on the political legitimacy of the democratic governments that are forced to step in and rescue failing institutions and it therefore must be addressed. Yet, there is a certain danger that the risks resulting from financial complexity, regulatory uncertainty and non-knowledge are underestimated or even missed. As Stiglitz warns, "recent discussions have focused on ensuring that 'systemically significant institutions' are well regulated. However, what we have seen is a systemic failure, and such systemic failures can also arise from the correlated behavior of a large number of institutions, none of which is itself systemically significant" (Stiglitz 2009b, 17).[117]

In the third chapter of this book, we distinguished between different levels of financial complexity. When we look at the reform efforts in the US, it becomes clear that policymakers did not try to fundamentally reduce systemic, organizational and product complexity, e.g. by slowing down the development of new products, but rather attempted to keep pace with the developments through increased transparency and better data and information (living wills, stress tests, FSOC,

117 As the interview analysis conducted for this book shows, it is highly questionable whether Dodd-Frank sufficiently addresses TBTF.

OFR).[118] In his much-cited speech on *The Dog and the Frisbee*, Haldane warned that we should be careful not to address increased financial complexity with increasingly complex regulation (Haldane and Madouros 2012), yet Dodd-Frank and the related regulations do exactly that.

To address the complexity of financial institutions, and the risks posed by their disorderly failure, policymakers and academics advocate a size cap, or even a break-up of SIFIs. Sheila Bair however argues that TBTF is not about size but about complexity and that reforms "should focus on simplifying the megabanks so that they can easily be resolved" (Bair 2012a, 328). And yet, the biggest institutions have, through government supported mergers and acquisitions, grown further during the financial crisis. As a result, the global too big to fail and too complex to manage institutions have become even bigger. Hopes remain that living wills and the work of the OFR increase regulators' and regulatees' understanding of the risks resulting from complexity. The former Comptroller of the Currency John G. Walsh admits that the living wills might not make financial institutions smaller, but he hopes that "they will get smarter" (Walsh as quoted by Rehm 2012). The question is: Smarter in what respect? Will financial institutions be able to outsmart livings wills and stress tests? Or will these measures truly enable financial institutions and regulators to deal with financial complexity? Recent scandals suggest that regulators are again, or still, running behind their regulatees. In fact, it appears that finance has become so complex that regulators "lack the capacity to detect systemic risk and fraud" – even worse, regulators and policymakers "may be so extremely dependent on the industry for information, expertise, and talent that they are not able to exercise independent regulatory authority" (McCarty 2013, 100). As we will see in chapter five, data and information asymmetries are inherent to all markets and also to financial regulation. Yet, the severity of regulators and policymakers' knowledge gaps presents a recent phenomenon and massive problem.

Against this background, we should be aware of the side effects of the US reform efforts. Taleb, for instance, warns us of the Office of Financial Research, as

> this measure, if I read it well, aims at the creation of an omniscient Soviet-style central risk manager. It makes us fall into the naive illusion of risk management that got us here – the same illusion has led in the past to the blind accumulation of Black Swan risks. Black Swans are these large, consequential, but unpredicted deviations in the eyes of a given observer – the observer does not see them coming, but, my some mental mechanism, thinks that he predicted them. Simply, there are limitations to our ability to measure the risks of extreme events and throwing government money on it will carry negative side effects. (Taleb 2012b, 1)

118 If the FDIC and the Fed believe that an institution is too complex to be wind down, they might require it to restructure its business; yet, Sheila Bair herself admits that it is highly unlikely, if not legally impossible, that these regulators demand the break-up of a SIFI (Bair 2012).

We have argued that the financial crises of the 1990s, once they had been successfully contained, increased policymakers' and regulators' confidence: The system appeared to be under control and regulation and oversight were accordingly loosened in order to boost financial innovation and growth. The crisis brought an end or at least a pause to this development, but the reforms – especially the FSOC and the OFR – might yet again result in overconfidence and a wrong sense of controllability: "Risk measurement and prediction – any prediction – has side effects of increasing risk-taking, even by those who know that they are not reliable" (ibid., 3; see also Tuckman as quoted in Tankersley 2013).[119] Luhmann warns us that the possibility of governments to control finance is quite limited, and that the "expansion of competence in the welfare state begets a gigantic and uncontrollable machinery for increasing risk" (Luhmann 2008, 145).

Before we get to the problems related to data, information and knowledge, we have emphasize one optimistic point: With regard to the incongruence between national policymaking and global finance, one thing that policymakers have learned through *learning by doing* during the financial crisis of 2007ff. was ad hoc cooperation. Even though one could observe "episodes of nationalist panic as turbulence cascaded through the system" (Pauly 2009, 961) – Chancellor Merkel's unilateral promise that all German deposits are guaranteed by the German government in 2008 provides a good example here – cooperation behind the scenes increased:

> At the level of newspaper headlines, it appeared that economic nationalism had trumped all whenever finance ministers and national legislatures felt compelled to act. But behind the scenes, networks of state officials – from finance ministries to central banks to financial supervisors – expanded their collaborative, if hardly harmonious, work. (ibid., 971)

The FSOC is explicitly required to increase international cooperation, but we find other indicators beyond the mandates of systemic risk supervisors: The FDIC and the Bank of England have published a joint paper on resolving global SIFIs (Federal Deposit Insurance Corporation and Bank of England 2012). The EU, despite its weak crisis management structures, did not experience a single disorderly failure of a cross-border bank. Belgium, France and Luxembourg were able to jointly save the Dexia group (while the Benelux countries could not agree on a strategy to deal with Fortis), and governments also cooperated to provide foreign currency swap markets with US dollars (Draghi 2009).

---

119 Greenspan makes the analogous argument that "if you examine an organization incompletely, they tend to put a sign in their window that they were examined by the Fed. […] Partial supervision is dangerous because it creates a good housekeeping stamp with negative feedback" (Greenspan 2010, 4f.).

5 Knowledge Asymmetries in Regulation

"[T]he chief practical significance of knowledge is control." (Knight 1964, 239)

Suspicions that financial supervision and regulation are hampered by severe data, information and knowledge asymmetries between financial institutions on the one hand and financial regulators on the other are far from new. However, the financial crisis of 2007ff. did not only reveal the actual degree of financial system complexity, but also that policymakers and regulators, as well as financial institutions, did in fact lack the data, information and knowledge to fully assess the situation:

> The financial crisis made clear that the *understanding of the financial system* was deficient in many respects. [...] Likewise, the crisis revealed significant *deficiencies in the data available* to monitor the financial system. Financial data collected were too aggregated, too limited in scope, too out of date, or otherwise incomplete. (Office of Financial Research 2012a, III, emphasis added)

Based on that experience, the US government established the Financial Stability Oversight Council, the Consumer Financial Protection Bureau and, more importantly, the Office of Financial Research. As we saw in the preceding chapter, systemic oversight councils have been installed elsewhere, while the establishment of the OFR presents a unique policy response to the crisis. With the establishment of the OFR, the US government acknowledged the existence of data-, information- and knowledge-related problems in financial regulation and institutionalized efforts to address them. In accordance with its mandate, the Office focuses on data and information collection, yet it is also required by Dodd-Frank to build up knowledge concerning systemic risk: Section 153(3) entrusts the OFR with performing research and Section 153(4) requires the Office to develop tools to monitor and measure risks. Interestingly, Dodd-Frank neither provides a definition of data, information and knowledge, nor a description of the data-, information- and knowledge-related problems that hamper financial supervision and regulation. In chapter five, we want to fill that gap and develop an analytical framework for the distinction of data-, information- and knowledge-related problems in financial regulation.

One cannot discuss the role and nature of data, information and knowledge asymmetries in financial regulation without asking two basic questions. First, to what extent does regulation require knowledge about the industry? Landis argued in 1938 that "the art of regulating an industry requires *knowledge of the details* of its operation, ability to shift requirements as the condition of the industry may dictate, the pursuit of energetic measures upon the appearance of an emergency, and the power through enforcement to realize conclusions as to policy" (Landis 1947 [1938], 23f., emphasis added). What does this mean for financial regulation? The first question will be discussed under the heading of *knowledge-based regulation*. Secondly, several decades after Herbert Simon has dissolved the myth of rational choice and replaced it with the concept of *bounded rationality* (Simon 1997 [1947]), one has to ask whether a regulator provided with the relevant data and information is generally in the position to make the right decisions. The second question refers to what we label the *rational regulator*.

The material is organized as follows: In section 5.1, we draw mainly on Zeleny (1987), Ackoff (1989), Davenport and Prusak (1998), and Frické (2009) to provide a working definition of data, information and knowledge. Starting from there, section 5.2 seeks to describe and categorize data, information and knowledge asymmetries in financial regulation, based on statements and speeches by policymakers and regulators, on interviews with selected experts, as well as on academic literature from various fields of research. In section 5.3, we contrast the establishment of the OFR with Herbert Simon's concept of bounded rationality. Afterwards, we briefly discuss the privatization of legitimacy in financial regulation in section 5.4. We argue that the decision of the US government to establish the Office of Financial Research revealed a counterfactual belief in knowledge-based regulation: Certain measures aim at reducing financial complexity, but US regulators do first and foremost try to catch up with financial market institutions. They not only increase their data and information collecting efforts, but also try to build-up the relevant expertise. Against this background, section 5.5 discusses whether the art of regulation requires detailed knowledge (*knowledge-based regulation*) or not.

5.1 A Working Definition of Data, Information and Knowledge

In academia, it is widely agreed that data, information and knowledge are of a different nature. Having said that, it is astonishing that most policymakers and regulators do not distinguish between the problems related to data, information and knowledge that occurred during the crisis. The joint FSB/IMF report on *The Financial Crisis and Information Gaps* (Financial Stability Board and International Monetary Fund 2009, 2011) is exemplary in this regard: Instead of differentiating between data and information, the IMF staff uses both terms interchangeably. Testimonies, statements and interviews with officials reveal that supervisory and regulatory problems related to data, information and knowledge asymmetries are neither defined nor fully understood. However, all three problems appear to exist and seem to be quite pressing: Tarullo argues that the crisis "painfully demonstrated that regulators, financial institutions, and investors lacked *ready access to data*" (Tarullo 2010b, 9, emphasis added), while Ben Bernanke describes how "*supervisory expertise and information* have repeatedly proved invaluable" (Bernanke 2009c, emphasis added) during the crisis. At the beginning of this chapter, we therefore want to provide a working definition of data, information and knowledge, before we proceed to discuss their role in financial regulation. Following Frické (2009) and Shannon (1993), we believe that there is a broad variety of useful definitions of all three terms. We therefore do not want to give yet another universally valid definition, but instead develop a comprehensive understanding that allows us to discuss the role and relevance of data, information and knowledge in the context of the financial crisis.

Data, information and knowledge are not the same, yet they are closely related: Information builds on data and knowledge builds on information. The data-information-knowledge schema is used in management and organizational theory, computer science, knowledge management and library science, and it has become what Frické calls the "common currency of information science" (Frické 2009, 132). Together with wisdom, it forms the so-called DIKW pyramid (for *data-information-knowledge-wisdom*). It is often argued that the DIKW schema can be traced back to T. S. Eliot's play *The Rock* (Aven 2012; see also Rowley 2007), but as Eliot clearly had no scientific interest in data, information and knowledge, we can ignore his description in good conscience.

Based on Zeleny's *Management Support Systems: Towards Integrated Knowledge Management* from 1987, and Ackoff's *From Data to Wisdom* from 1989, data can be defined as the basic elements (Zeleny 1987) or symbols (Ackoff 1989) that information and knowledge are built upon. Data can be understood as observed differences about the state of the world surrounding us (Becker and Willke 2013) that can be collected by humans as well as machines. While it is sometimes argued that data are by definition true (Frické 2009), we hold the view that true or false are not categories that can be applied to data – first and foremost because data come into being through observation (Willke 2007, 123). Also, the search for a negative counterpart for data as pursued by Bernstein quickly comes to an end: The other side of data is neither "want of data" nor "missing data" (Bernstein 2009, 70); it is just no data or the absence of data, and following Watzlawick, even no data provide information (Watzlawick, Beavin, and Jackson 1969). Data then are the "essential raw material for the creation of information" (Davenport and Prusak 1998, 3). While information is still "partial and atomized" (Zeleny 1987, 59), it is also understood as being a richer, processed form of data: For its recipient, information has a meaning or value (Rowley 2007; Willke 2002).

To explain the crucial difference between data and information, Boisot and Canals employ cryptography where secret information is buried in data to encrypt it, and to re-extract information from these data one has to know the key to decrypt the data (Boisot and Canals 2004). To provide a simple example: The words *part eht ni si esuom eht* present pure data. The key, *read the sentence backwards!*, reveals the information that *the mouse is in the trap*. In line with Boisot and Canals, Ackoff argues that data "are of no value until they are processed into a useable [...] form" (Ackoff 1989, 3). Information accordingly contains a message (Davenport and Prusak 1998). What is central is that the same set of data might contain different information or messages for different recipients. As we have argued in the cryptography example, people knowing the key have access to information hidden in data. Yet, when receiving the message that the mouse is in the trap, most recipients would neither understand why they received the message nor what to make of it. For criminals who are involved in a kidnapping, these data may contain other information than they do for lay people. Based on that observation, one can state that people extract the meaning of data according to their knowledge. Keeping in mind Weick's concept of *organizational sensemaking*, we want to go one step further and argue in line with Boisot/Canals that the processing step from data to information represents, in the constructivist sense, an interpretation of the given set of data (Boisot and Canals 2004, 55).[120]

Knowledge, then, is the next processing step in the DIKW-hierarchy. It means knowing how a system works or being in the position to control a system (Ackoff 1989). Contrary to the fragmented character of data and information, knowledge has a network-like, organized, holistic nature; it enables humans to "make distinctions, choices and decisions" (Zeleny 1987, 63). All knowledge is closely tied to experience and practice (Becker and Willke 2013). Securities expert Satyajit Das estimates the number of experts "who would pass a fairly rigorous test on how derivatives work" and how they interact with the financial system at 2000 professionals worldwide; he argues that the *industrialization of finance* over the past two decades has led to an *extreme fragmentation of financial knowledge* (Das 2010a). The more specialized and dispersed experience and knowledge are, the greater are the challenges resulting from uncertainty: "Specialized knowledge is the proprietary realm and resource of 'communities of practice', creating non-knowledge and risk as an inevitable correlate of knowledge" (Willke and Willke 2012, 69). Even though knowledge can be embodied in organizational rules and structures, it requires human capabilities, such as human judgments and

120 Blyth argues that, as market participants interpret data and information based on their (diverging) knowledge and understanding of the market, increased transparency, meaning more and better data and information, would not necessarily increase financial market stability; he terms such problems *common knowledge problems* (Blyth 2003).

experiences, to create knowledge.[121] Boisot and Canals conclude that "*there is no such thing as common knowledge and there is common information only to a limited extent. Only data can ever be completely common between agents*" (Boisot and Canals 2004, 63).

The core elements of the basic data-information-knowledge schema are often supplemented by categories that provide one or more processing steps – such as *wisdom* (Zeleny 1987) or *understanding and wisdom* (Ackoff 1989) – where data, information and knowledge are organized in hierarchical order, and where, as in the DIKW hierarchy, each phenomenon "includes the categories that fall below it" (ibid., 3). According to Ackoff, this simple structure reflects the nature of the human mind, consisting of forty percent data, "thirty percent information, twenty percent knowledge, ten percent understanding, and virtually no wisdom" (ibid.). While we are well aware of the shortcomings of this concept, we want to leave it to others to provide good arguments against it (Frické 2009): As mentioned at the beginning of this section, we need a definition of data, information and knowledge that proves to be useful for our analysis of related problems in financial regulation. As we will see, existing data, information and knowledge asymmetries in financial regulation invite us to approach them in hierarchical order, too.

5.2 Knowledge Related Problems in Financial Regulation

In March 2008, *This American Life* journalist Ira Glass aired a radio show about the financial crisis; therein, Satyajit Das – a risk consultant who was also interviewed by the FCIC in 2010 – gave an interesting description of the relationship between financial firms and regulators. As he describes many aspects of the problem, we quote him at-length:

> Over the last few years, I have had quite a lot to do with central banks. [...] They're very intelligent people and very well meaning. But the problem is they've relied heavily on the banks to tell them what's going on. And there is obviously a conflict of interest. And they have never quite got the full

121 We will later get to the revolving door principle – people especially in the US moving back and forth from the private to the public sector throughout their careers. As one of the FCIC interviews illustrates, and as our definition of knowledge would indicate, the revolving door results in learning by doing: "I'm a huge fan of the revolving door. [...] I think I learned more, I learned a lot at the OCC in five years, I thought I knew reasonable matters as a banking lawyer, I earned a huge amount actually having to do with the OCC. Having said that, my two years at Bankers Trust were revolutionary in terms of my understanding how these mechanisms really work. And it would be enormously valuable for any examiner to actually, in mid-career, get inside and see how they actually function. And trying to get that back and forth is really valuable, including my coming in from the private sector as a lawyer. The Europeans don't do that. [...] I think that is not good" (Ludwig 2010).

> picture. And often when I explain to them something quite minor, like how the CDS market works, their response is: 'oh, I thought it was only for hedging. I didn't realize it was just purely speculative.' So there is this information gap which is now having to be filled at very short notice, which is obviously extremely problematic. [...] We don't even understand the actual quantum of the problem. – *You mean how big the problem is?* – Correct. To give you some perspective, less than 18 months ago, Ben Bernanke gave testimony to the effect that he thought the losses from subprime would be 50 billion US dollar, and the problems were contained. And he's not an unintelligent man. – *Right. In fact, he's an expert on the Great Depression.* – Exactly. So the fact that he could get it so wrong, that perhaps the people who think they understand and think they know perhaps know less than we think they know. (Das 2008)

More generally, the IMF stated that the supervision and regulation of new instruments and techniques, for instance of CDOs, did not keep pace with the market (International Monetary Fund 2008, xii). In chapter 5.2, we want to elaborate on a better understanding of these phenomena. Based on our working definition from chapter 5.1, we examine if and how these problems are described in testimonies, articles, media interviews, FCIC interviews and our own interviews on the financial crisis.

5.2.1 Data-Related Problems: Information Buried in Excel-Spreadsheets

Compared to information and knowledge, data are a minor issue in the economics and political science literature in general. Besides, the majority of policymakers and supervisors just did not see data as an important issue prior to the crisis (Interview with Andreas Lehnert, December 05, 2012, Washington). Then the crisis revealed that neither regulators nor the financial institutions themselves possessed the data regarded to be essential to understand and mitigate systemic risk. Data, defined as the raw material information are based upon, were either not available or not accessible. Especially *data accessibility* seemed to be a major problem. During the financial crisis, when the remaining big investment banks changed their charters to become bank holding companies and get access to the Fed discount window, the data submitted by these banks allowed revealing insights:

> At the height of the 2008 financial crisis one of the big investment banks – in order to change its charter - had to supply all its exposure data to the New York Federal Reserve Bank for analysis. [...], and on the date the data was due this investment bank gave the New York Fed its data in the form of about 14,000 Excel spreadsheets. A cynic might say that the data was provided in this highly fractured and difficult to access form in order to bury the New York Fed in data [...]. However, the reality is that the data was supplied this way because that was how the investment bank kept its data. Every trader had one or more Excel spreadsheets on his/her computer, and

> the investment bank supplied the data to the New York Fed from the traders' individual computers that were spread throughout the organization. [...] If you have an investment bank dumping 14,000 Excel spreadsheets on a regulator [...], it is unlikely that the management of the investment bank had adequate insight into the risk on its balance sheet. (Interview with Allan Mendelowitz, December 03, 2012, Washington)

Mendelowitz speaks of balance sheet data. However, the nature of unavailable and non-accessible data, as well as of the underlying data gaps, is not clearly defined and rather difficult to determine (see for example Engle 2010). The DFA, with its clear focus on TBTF institutions, distinguishes between two specific types of relevant data, and it can be assumed that Mendelowitz refers to both:

- *Financial Transaction Data*, meaning "the structure and legal description of a financial contract, with sufficient detail to describe the rights and obligations between counterparties", as well as
- *Position Data*, meaning "data on financial assets or liabilities held on the balance sheet of a financial company, where positions are created or changed by the execution of a financial transaction", including "information that identifies counterparties, the valuation by the financial company of the position" (Dodd-Frank Act, Sec. 151).

Dodd-Frank accordingly puts strong emphasis on interconnectedness and leverage. We would add a third type of data, *organizational data*, covering data about the institution's structure and legal entities and the nature of its internal connections as they are disclosed by financial institutions in their living wills. As Dodd-Frank demands, the data provided should allow an *independent valuation* of the situation and soundness of a financial institution by supervisors and regulators (ibid.).

The data needs defined by Dodd-Frank correspond with Tarullo's diagnosis that during the crisis, neither financial institutions nor policymakers and regulators had access to data that would have allowed them "to fully assess the value of complex securities, understand counterparty risks or identify concentrations of exposures" (Tarullo 2010b, 9). What was missing as well were data on the "degree and location of leverage in the financial system" (ibid., 6), just as "detailed and comprehensive data on the structure of financial networks" (Yellen 2013a). The collapse of the investment bank Lehman Brothers provides a good example in this context: According to the FSOC, resolving the bank "was hobbled by the snarled nature of insufficient, conflicting, and inconsistent data" (Financial Stability Oversight Council 2012a, 138). When Lehman failed, regulators could neither evaluate the value of Lehman's assets, nor the number and nature of the bank's contractual relationships, nor the number and structure of Lehman's legal subsidiaries. Referring to our binary model of systemic risk as introduced in chapter one, it was difficult to decide in September of 2008 whether Lehman Brothers was in fact a systemically important financial institution or not. In chapter two, we argued that the US government lacked the political will or majority to rescue Lehman; could it have proven Lehman's systemic relevance based on sufficient data, it might have convinced Congress to support a bailout of the investment bank.[122]

It later turned out that at the time of its collapse, Lehman had about 3000 legal entities. According to the examiner in the Chapter 11 proceedings of Lehman, the "available universe of Lehman email and other electronically stored documents is estimated at three petabytes of data – roughly the equivalent of 350 billion pages" (Valukas 2010, 30). The number of Lehman's open derivatives contracts was almost one million (Haldane 2010, 18f.). Herring and Carmassi provide a detailed account of Lehman's data storage chaos:

> Lehman also centralized its information technology so that data for different products and different subsidiaries were co-mingled. This was an efficient way of running the business as a going concern, but presents an enormous challenge in global bankruptcy proceedings. LB stored data in 26,666 servers, 20,000 of which contained accumulated emails, files, voicemail messages, instant messages, and recorded calls. [...]. Moreover, LB used approximately 2,700 proprietary, third-party, and off-the-shelf programs, each of which interacted with or created transactions data. The bankruptcy administrators must preserve, extract, store, and analyze data relevant to the entities they are dealing with. (Herring and Carmassi 2012, 225)

Today, these problems are well described and known – but back in September 2008, "government officials were flying blind" (Mendelowitz and Liechty 2010, 3). It is important to keep in mind that the Lehman bankruptcy was the biggest bankruptcy in US history (Mamudi 2008), yet it provides a realistic picture of the data gaps at systemically important financial institutions. Compared to the remaining SIFIs Lehman was a rather small investment bank.[123] Five years after the Lehman collapse the comparatively minor Senate investigation into the trading loss at JP Morgan's Chief Investment Office (CIO) was based on 90,000 documents, more than 200 recorded phone calls and instant messaging texts and 25 interviews with bank and regulatory personnel (United States Senate 2013, 2) – giving us a rough idea of the enormous amount of data that is processed inside TBTF financial institutions. The question is: What were the US policy responses to address these regulatory data gaps?

122 What is also central in the context of data-related problems is that not only supervisors and regulators lacked the respective data; based on Sorkin (2010), we can conclude that the bank's top management was in fact in a similar position.

123 According to Herring and Carmassi, eight large complex financial institutions (LCFIs) have more than 1,000 subsidiaries; the biggest, Citigroup, has nearly 2,500 majority-owned subsidiaries – minority interests and off-balance sheet vehicles excluded (Herring and Carmassi 2012, 200).

The institutional response was the establishment of the Office of Financial Research in 2010 as described in chapter four. The Office has the duty to *collect and maintain data*, to *provide data* to the FSOC and its member agencies, and to *standardize the types and formats* of the data that it collects and reports (Dodd-Frank Act, Sec. 153). A key part of its mission is to fill the gaps in existing data and analysis. According to a testimony before the Senate, in 2013 the OFR had already

> completed an initial inventory of purchased and collected data among FSOC member agencies and an inventory of internally developed data is underway. To improve the quality and scope of data available to policymakers, the OFR has established data-sharing agreements with a number of FSOC member agencies and continues to work on new ones as needed. (Miller 2013, 4)

The goal now is to "have the capacity to follow developments in all segments of the financial system, including parts of the financial sector for which data are scarce or that have developed more recently" (Bernanke 2010a) and to expand the overall "commitment to the collection and analysis of financial data" (Bernanke 2010b). In fact, one can observe in supervision and regulation "an increasingly strenuous insistence on the sole efficacy of data", as was diagnosed by Veblen in 1898 for the economics discipline more generally (Veblen 1898).

Both the establishment of the OFR and the post-crisis comments from Fed and government officials reveal the basic belief that (a) data can be sufficiently gathered and (b) be maintained and aggregated in a useful way – or, as was said in one Senate testimony: "In summary, the data and technology exist today to equip financial regulators with the tools necessary to monitor systemic risk. The only thing lacking is government action to make it happen" (Horne 2010, 4; see also Engle 2010). The fear that the government might be buried in data – or bury itself in data – is apparently not widespread. Putting the risk of data overload aside, two other obstacles do obviously remain: First, data on financial contracts and movements are as *global as the system itself*. Every effort to collect and analyze financial data must take into account the international dimension of financial data and the US must accordingly cooperate with regulators from other nations (Tarullo 2010b, 11). Tarullo describes current efforts to draw a standardized, global financial data map:

> There are already steps underway internationally to widen and deepen the array of financial data available to systemic risk regulators, filling gaps in the global network map. As in weather forecasting, this would help improve estimates of the initial conditions of the financial system. And as in weather forecasting, it is important these data are captured in a common financial language to enable genuinely global maps to be drawn. (Haldane and Nelson 2012, 18)

The report on *The Financial Crisis and Information Gaps*, which was jointly published by the FSB and the IMF in 2009, is quite clear on the point that data gaps have to be addressed by domestic *and* international financial bodies. It argues that the crisis was "not the result of a lack of proper economic and financial statistics" (Financial Stability Board and International Monetary Fund 2009, 9), but that "it exposed a significant lack of information as well as data gaps on key financial sector vulnerabilities relevant for financial stability analysis" (ibid.).

This brings us to the second and more important obstacle: Keeping in mind our definition of data, information and knowledge, it is obvious that *data collection is just the starting point*, while one must ultimately aim at building up the relevant expertise. Several problems arise – to begin with, transforming data to information to knowledge requires capable staff. However, as mentioned in chapter four, several regulatory agencies are massively underfunded, and the CFTC's Gary Gensler has complained that now that "data has started to be reported [...], we need the staff and technology to access, review and analyze the data" (Gensler 2013, 22). When questioned in a Senate hearing on the regulatory tools that are needed to monitor systemic risk, Horne stressed the need for *surgical data collection solutions*, arguing that the "transformation of this data into actionable information is neither easy nor inexpensive" (Horne 2010, 3).

While it is widely agreed, in view of the Lehman collapse and JP Morgan's CIO scandal, that more and better data are needed, policymakers and regulators disagree upon the value of these data. From the viewpoint of the DIK(W)-hierarchy, data are necessary, but not sufficient:

> Now, if they [the regulators] don't have adequate levels of aggregate data I think they could face certain amounts of handicap, [...] in what they could do. Even though they might have the right intentions and the right knowledge on what they need to do. So, I would say data are necessary for a good regulatory job, but they are not sufficient, because, as you said, *you could have all the data in the world but if you have the wrong paradigm, you are just going to fail.* (Interview with Viral Acharya, November 28, 2012, New York)

Yet another interview partner made the opposite argument, saying that if you have the data, you can manipulate it in ways to give you the knowledge – but without the data you cannot gain the knowledge (Interview with Allan Mendelowitz, December 03, 2012, Washington). Based on these observations, we want to distinguish two basic schools of thought and further elaborate on them in the following chapters. School number one believes that in order to mitigate systemic risk, regulators and supervisors need extensive and aggregated data: "With better data and better analytical tools, [...] we could measure, monitor and ultimately lessen systemic risk" (Engle 2010). They compare financial supervision with weather forecasting, where better data have led to much more precise predictions (data and information are accordingly sufficient for effective financial regulation, which is why we label this line of argument the *sufficiency argument*). School number two, then, places the emphasis on knowledge and expertise. Here, data are really just the starting point, while the second and much more important step is the build-up of one's own, independent knowledge (knowledge is accordingly required for effective financial regulation; this school of thought is closely related to the argument presented at the beginning of this chapter, stating that all regulation must be *knowledge-based*). We will get back to both schools towards the end of this chapter.

5.2.2 A Four-Category-Framework of Information Asymmetries

Information asymmetries are inherent to every market, and the reason is as simple as it is logic: Concerning origin, quality and value, a vendor at a market in Berlin or Beirut has more information about the tomatoes he sells than his clients. He might decide to declare them *organic tomatoes* and the people who buy them will have virtually no chance of finding out whether he is lying or not. Such information asymmetries are not only inherent to business-to-customer relationships, but can also be found in business-to-business relationships. Their basic logic applies to financial markets, too – with one important difference: While the vendor's client can demand to try the tomatoes and therefore easily verify at least a part of the vendor's assertions, financial products often have a degree of complexity that makes it impossible for customers to do so.[124] Information asymmetries in general and information asymmetries in financial markets in particular do accordingly receive much attention in economics literature. Starting with Hayek (1945), the list of potentially relevant publications, especially from economics and political economy literature, is in fact endless. Sociology adds yet another perspective to the problem.[125]

In the section, we draw on a small number of economic theories that are concerned with information asymmetries – the *Efficient Market Hypothesis* in the tradition of Eugene Fama, Joseph Stiglitz' antithetic approach to information

124 However, the example does also show that information asymmetries are neither bad per se, nor can they be fully eliminated. As Willke and Willke argue convincingly, information asymmetries are a question of degree: "The crucial point [...] is not information asymmetry but degree, quality and perceived consequences of ubiquitous information asymmetries. This raises a different and more political kind of question: What kinds of information imperfections/asymmetries should be left to market participants to deal with at their own risk and where should the line be drawn that triggers political intervention in order to create a more level playing field for market participants?" (Willke and Willke 2012, 89).

125 As Knorr-Cetina emphasizes, traders operate in an environment that is focused on and determined by information: "What discloses itself to participants in the mass of materials on their financial screens is not the presence of objects but the presence of information. What we are really dealing in, traders say, is information" (Knorr-Cetina 2005, 42).

asymmetries and finally *agency theory* – to further develop and enhance the four-category-framework of information asymmetries brought forward by Becker and Willke (2013).[126] It distinguishes between (a) information asymmetries between regulatees and regulators, (b) asymmetries between financial institutions and consumers, (c) inter-organizational information asymmetries and (d) internal information gaps; in this book, we focus on the first category. For regulator-regulatee relationships, we identify a set of problems identified in agency theory that are discussed in greater detail throughout the following section: First, the *agency problem* – principal and agent have differing goals; second, we can observe severe *information asymmetries* between regulator and regulatee; third, both parties can be principal *and* agent; and fourth, agency relationships vary due to their degree of *programmability*, meaning the degree to which appropriate behavior can be defined in advance.

A Brief Introduction Into the Efficient Market Hypothesis, and its Opponents

Information asymmetries are central to the *Efficient Market Hypothesis* (EMH) that goes back to the work of Eugene Fama. It applies to asset pricing, arguing that security prices in efficient markets do "at any time 'fully reflect' all available information" (Fama 1970, 383; see also Fama 1964). The underlying question here is whether investors are able to exploit market inefficiencies or if these inefficiencies actually even exist. The EMH concludes that if they do not exist, it is because stock prices fully incorporate all available information. A simple and often told story illustrates the point: A finance professor and a student find a 100 dollar bill on the street. When the student sets to pick it up, the professor tells him not to bother, saying: "If this was really a 100 dollar bill, it would not be there" (Malkiel 2003, 60).

Fama's publications set off a wave of research and debate and the EMH became a paradigm beyond economics and finance research. Then, in the 1980s, several papers argued that the EMH could not explain or even account for de-facto market volatility (see Shiller 2003; Shiller 1989, for a literature overview; see Hirshleifer and Riley 1979, for an early critique of the EMH in its weak and strong forms; and Fox 2009, for an overview of empirical evidence against the EMH; see also Machlup 1984, 110ff.; Fenton-O'Creevy et al. 2005). With the rise of behavioral economics in the 1990s, the EMH has become even more controversial, and Robert Shiller – himself being one of the most famous critiques of the EMH – argues that the theory had passed its height of dominance, at least in academics, in the 1980s

126 The interesting point about the framework brought forward by Becker and Willke is that it is actor-centered. According to the definition of data, information and knowledge brought forward in the current chapter, the information extracted from data ultimately depends on the knowledge of the recipient, a fact that an actor-centered approach can account for. In addition, the framework factors in that the financial crisis revealed "a glaring lack of relevant information on all sides" (Willke and Willke 2012, 91).

(Shiller 2003).[127] In the political arena, the EMH endured much longer. To what degree economic theories shape financial policies remains an open question; that they do find their way into politics can be taken for granted, and the EMH provides a good example here.[128] In 1977, Saari criticized the SEC for paying scant attention to the EMH in its securities regulation efforts, arguing that "the SEC should no longer ignore the overwhelming evidence of securities market efficiency in formulating its regulatory policy" (Saari 1977, 1056f.) and essentially claiming that the SEC's mandatory disclosure process, which aims at providing information to investors, is meaningless: Useful information, he concluded, reaches the market by other means (Saari 1977). In 1989, Frank H. Easterbrook – Chicago law professor and judge of the United States Court of Appeals – stated in an opinion of court that the SEC "believes that markets correctly value the securities of well-followed firms, so that new sales may rely on information that has been digested and expressed in the security's price" (Wielgos v. Commonwealth Edison Company, 892 F. 2d 509, 7th Cir. 1989). Many more examples can be found, and they suggest that in the 1980s, the EMH had well diffused into US Congress, agencies and courts, even though it was already challenged in academia at the time (Langevoort 1992; Weber 2012).[129]

Information is also center-stage in the works of Joseph Stiglitz, who undermined the traditional neoclassical economic model when assuming that, if the market fully reflected all information, "there would be no incentive for anyone to expend money to collect information" (Stiglitz 2001, 485). His argument is based on the observation that information is in fact a commodity: It not only has a price, but can also be purchased (Eisenhardt 1989, 64). Based on the commonplace assumption that information asymmetries are inherent to all interactions between humans – which is why it can be sold and bought – one can conclude that they must be reflected in financial interactions as well. In line with our example of the organic tomatoes sold at a market in Berlin, Stiglitz argues that due to the very nature of markets, *information must be imperfect and asymmetric*. Stiglitz' approach to information asymmetries is directly opposed to the EMH, where the inability of investors to exploit information asymmetries and to outpace the market is regarded as evidence for the absence of these same asymmetries: "Markets are

127 Ironically, both Fama and Shiller, together with Lars Peter Hansen, won the Nobel Price in Economics in 2013 "for their empirical analysis of asset prices" (The Royal Swedish Academy of Sciences, 2013).

128 This point relates to the question to what extent economics shape the economy – a phenomenon described as the performativity of economics. An edited book by MacKenzie, Muniesa and Siu (2007) provides a very good introduction into the current state of research and theory.

129 See also the U.S. Supreme Court decision on *Basic, Inc. v. Levinson* from 1988, where it was argued: "Recent empirical studies have tended to confirm Congress' premise that the market price of shares traded on well developed markets reflects all publicly available information, and, hence, any material misrepresentations" (Basic Inc. v. Levinson, 485 U.S. 224, 247, 6th Cir. 1988).

plagued by problems of information asymmetries, and there are incentives for market participants both to *exploit and to increase these information asymmetries*" (Stiglitz 2009b, 11, emphasis added). Going one step further, Stiglitz criticizes that economic modeling in the 20th century has assumed that information is perfect, even though "everyone recognized that information was in fact imperfect" (Stiglitz 2002, 461). Referring to the exploitation of uninformed or uneducated borrowers by sophisticated lenders as took place in the US during the years preceding the recent financial crisis, Stiglitz argues that regulations are imposed "to prevent such exploitation and to pursue a number of other social goals" (Stiglitz 2009b, 12).

Together with George Akerlof and Michael Spence, Stiglitz is considered the father of informational economics.[130] Stiglitz himself describes his agenda within the political economy of information as follows:

> There are asymmetries of information between those governing and those governed, and just as participants in markets strive to overcome asymmetries of information, we need to look for ways by which the asymmetries of information in political processes can be limited and their consequences mitigated. (Stiglitz 2002, 461)

While the EMH calls our attention to the existence or non-existence of information asymmetries within markets, Stiglitz adds a second and third type of information asymmetries: First, he names asymmetries between the governed and the governing. Second, he describes the informational disadvantage of the *regulator relative to the regulated* (Stiglitz 2009b, 13). We will put these three categories aside for the moment, and revert to them at the end of this chapter to further develop the four-category-framework of information asymmetries suggested by Becker and Willke (2013).

A More Extensive Introduction to Agency Theory

We are certain that there are, besides the approaches by Fama and Stiglitz, many more economic theories worth considering in the context of information asymmetries. We however want to limit ourselves on a third and last approach, which is agency theory.[131] Put broadly, agency theory "deals with relations in society where one party acts for another" (Mitnick 1984, 2). Distinct from the approaches by Fama and Stiglitz, agency theory is not confined to economics: It roots in law

130 Just like Fama and Shiller, these three men have been received the Nobel Prize in Economics, in this case for "their analyses of markets with asymmetric information" (The Royal Swedish Academy of Sciences 2001).

131 Fama has not only developed the EMH; in his article *Agency Problems and the Theory of the Firm*, he also deploys agency theory to analyze the separation of security ownership (shareholders) and control (managers) as it is often found in large corporations. Stiglitz described agency problems in his early works, too. In his examination of *Incentives and Risk Sharing in Sharecropping* of 1974, he analyzed the relationship of landlords (principals) and their workers (agents) in developing countries (Stiglitz 1974).

and is employed in political science as well. It is nevertheless fair to say that the economics formulation of agency theory is much more popular and diverse than its usage in other disciplines (Shapiro 2005; see also Mitnick 1992, who distinguishes between three cohorts of agency theory: the theory of the firm, or *positive approach*; the risk and information or *decision theoretic approach*; and the sociological or organizational, *social sciences approach*). In economic agency theory, the principal delegates work to an agent – e.g. the manager to his employee or the shareholder to her manager. The principal-agent model, which has been well described as the "analytic expression of the agency relationship" (Moe 1984, 756) and "economic theory of agency" (Shapiro 2005, 271), approaches the relationship between an agent (e.g. a corporate manager, or employee) and a principal (e.g. the shareholders of the corporation, or the employee's superior) in mostly quantitative terms. In political science, agency theory is used to describe the relationship between voter (principal) and politician (agent), between politician (principal) and bureaucrat (agent), or between regulator (principal, and agent) and regulatee (principal, and agent). Against the background of systemic risk and TBTF banks, Streeck has recently declared the international financial markets as the *new principals* of democratic states (Streeck 2011, 21).[132] Both the economic and the political strands of agency theory have in common that principal and agent pursue their own interests, which is why both principal and agent are typically characterized by diverging agendas and priorities. There are however important differences: While economic principals delegate work to their agents, the term *delegation* is sometimes misleading in political science. Regulators do not usually delegate their work to the entities they regulate (self-regulation presents an exemption here), but rather govern or interfere. Secondly, while agency theory puts the *contractual relationship* between principal and agent center stage, no such contract exists between regulator and regulatee, at least not explicitly.[133] The following illustration takes account of these differences: Here, the principal delegates or governs, while the agent decides, acts, or represents; the relationship is not necessarily a contractual relationship, but might be a relationship of cooperative nature and be characterized by asymmetric information and differing goals (see figure 11).

---

132 In his interview with the FCIC, Roubini argues that increased complexity and the repeal of Glass-Steagall have increased agency problems within financial institutions (Roubini 2010).

133 Following Hobbes, one can argue that there is an implicit social contract between a government and its peoples. This principle might be applied to regulators and regulatees, too. By operating in a certain country and paying taxes, firms implicitly accept governmental control and enter into a quasi-contractual relationship with the state. In addition, regulators and regulatees sign (not legally enforceable) memoranda of understanding. Regulators do in fact enter into contractual relationships, e.g. in the area of waste disposal and private prisons. These firms act in a double role, as (a) regulatees, and (b) contractors. The Tradeworx case in this text provides a good example here, as the company is supervised by and works for the SEC (see Willke, Becker and Rostásy 2013).

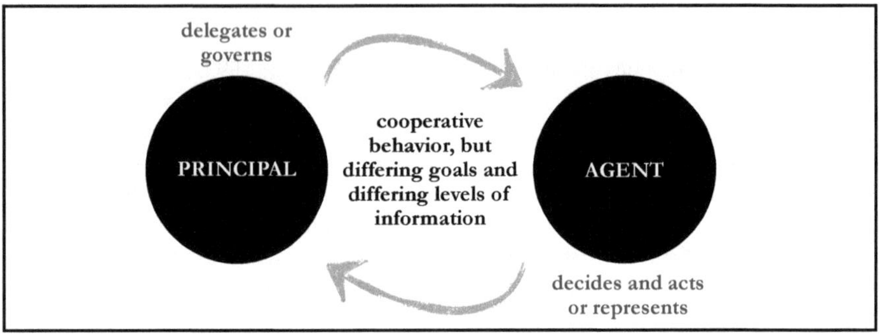

Figure 11: Principal-agent relationships.

As Eisenhardt points out, agency theory captures two problems of agency relationships – first, the *agency problem* that can be observed when "(a) the desires or goals of the principal and agent conflict and (b) it is difficult or expensive for the principal to verify what the agent is actually doing"; and second, the *problem of risk sharing* that occurs whenever principal and agent have different attitudes towards risk (Eisenhardt 1989, 58; see also Jensen and Meckling 1976). According to agency theory, the principal should be more affine to risk than his agent because he is able to diversify it. Third, agency relationships are characterized by the fact that the agent possesses *better or more information* than the principal (Ross 1973) – either because of the work that has been delegated to him and the resulting experience, or as a condition to his appointment (we will later see that Max Weber makes the same observation for knowledge). A fourth important point is that actors can take on *both roles simultaneously*, being agent and principal at the same time (Shapiro 2005, 267), either to different actors or even to each other. Last but not least, principal-agent relationships are characterized by their *degree of programmability*. According to Eisenhardt, programmability can be defined "as the degree to which appropriate behavior by the agent can be specified in advance" (Eisenhardt 1989, 62). All but the second aspect are relevant to our analysis of information and knowledge asymmetries between regulators and regulatees.

As already indicated, some basic assumptions have to be modified when transferring agency theory from economics to political sciences (Shapiro 2005, 270f.). Nevertheless, and despite of its economic restrictions, agency theory invites us to think about *principal-agent phenomena in the area of politics*: Politicians are citizens' agents, bureaucrats are politicians' agents, and bureaucratic employees are the agents of their superiors. "The whole of politics", as Moe argues, "is therefore structured as a chain of principal-agent relationships, from citizen to politician to bureaucratic superior" (Moe 1984, 765; see also Kiser 1999; Mitnick 1984). Agency theory in political science mostly focuses on legislatures and policy implementation, and, in the tradition of Max Weber, related problems of control and "bureaucratic drift"; Weber emphasized the expertise-based predominance of bureaucratic agents over their democratic or aristocratic sovereigns (see Weber 1922, 671; 673f.; Kiser 1999, 154; Weingast 1984; for an opposing standpoint, see Niskanen 2007; Wilson 1980; see also Mitnick 1984, for an outdated but nevertheless interesting and detailed overview). [134] Even though the general relevance of regulatees is acknowledged in some agency texts – Kiser, for example, highlights the importance of third parties in political agency theory (Kiser 1999, 156) – only few texts approach regulators and regulatees with agency theory (Mitnick 1984).

It is in fact intuitive *and* counterintuitive to model these relationships as principal-agent relationships: They are characterized by information asymmetries and differing goals – the regulatee has an informational advantage towards the regulator and obviously pursues other interests (simplified, the *preservation of public goods vs. profit seeking)* – however, the regulatee neither works for nor represents its regulator. Therefore, the contractual nature of classic agency relationships must be modified for an application to regulatory and supervisory relationships (Moe 1984). Mitnick accordingly defines regulation as

> relationships in which regulators (principal) interfere in the choices available to regulatees (agent) such that the regulatee is caused to act for some goals held by the regulator. Furthermore, the regulator does not actually perform the agent's activity; he seeks to control or influence the agent's activities as a party outside the agent's normal activity set. (Mitnick 1982, 447; see also Mitnick 1975)

Moe asks how bureaucratic superiors can control their subordinates, and whether politicians (principals) are able to control bureaucrats (agents) (Moe 1984, 758ff.). With regard to regulators and regulatees, and against the backdrop of the financial crisis of 2007ff., the following question becomes even more pressing: Are financial regulators capable of controlling how well the entities they control comply with their rules and regulations? The recent scandals indicate that they are not. One might even ask whether regulatees have managed to turn their principals into their agents. Many observers of the recent financial crisis, among them academics as Simon Johnson and policymakers as Elisabeth Warren, would most certainly agree. Grossman and Helpman illustrate how interest groups may act as principles, designing incentive schemes to push their agents – politicians – towards certain policy decisions (Grossman and Helpman 2001, ch. 8.1). As already indicated, one of the interesting aspects in applying principal-agent theory to financial regulation is

134 The original text says: "stets befindet er [der Herrscher, EB] sich den im Betrieb der Verwaltung stehenden geschulten Beamten gegnüber in der Lage des 'Dilettanten' gegenüber dem 'Fachmann'. Diese Überlegenheit des berufsmäßig Wissenden sucht jede Bürokratie noch durch das Mittel der *Geheimhaltung* ihrer Kenntnisse und Absichten zu steigern" (Weber 1922, 671).

that both regulator and regulatee can be modeled as principals, building a two-way agency relationship.[135]

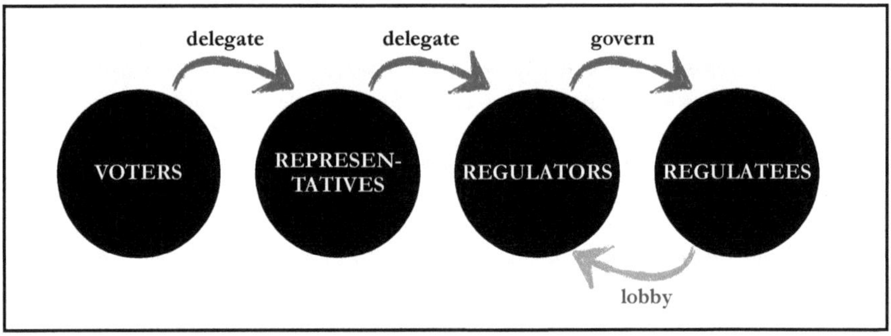

Figure 12: Principal-agent relationships in politics.

Agency theory supports our analysis so far: Not only do economic theories indicate that information asymmetries exist among (private or institutional) market participants, but also between regulators and regulatees.[136] The stronger the information asymmetry, the more the regulator relies on the information and expertise of the regulatee. In view of the developments described in chapter two and three – first and foremost increased complexity – Mitnick's basic principle is likely to be true: "Agency failure to some degree (as judged by the principal) is the norm, not the exception" (Mitnick 1984, 5). What Morgan claims for banks holds true for other financial institutions as well: Trading positions can change quickly and certain products, such as loans and OTC derivatives, are difficult to evaluate from outside. As a result, financial institutions are, from the viewpoint of their regulators, "black holes at the center of the financial universe, powerful and influential, but [...] to some degree, unfathomable" (Morgan 2002, 888). Complexity increases the information asymmetries that are inherent to all markets.

135 Laffont and Tirole argue that federal agencies have the resources to seek information about an industry while Congress does not; Congress therefore relies on the agency to provide information, and the agency can deliberately hide it from Congress (Laffont and Tirole 1993, 477).

136 US regulators traditionally place examiners inside the banks. Agency theory supports this strategy, as "it seems reasonable that when principals and agents engage in a long-term relationship, it is likely that the principal will learn about the agent [...] and so will be able to assess behavior more readily. Conversely, in short-term agency relationships, the information asymmetry between principal and agent is likely going to be greater" (Eisenhardt 1989, 62). Not only the crisis but also a number of scandals succeeding the crisis demonstrated that even if examiners are placed inside financial institutions, as was the case at JPMorgan, supervisors' ability to assess the banks' risks are quite limited. We will get back to this important point in chapter six.

One might conclude that, compared to other policy fields, information asymmetries are of a special importance in the regulation of the global and highly complex financial market of the 21st century. The financial crisis of 2007ff. did indeed make one point quite clear: "Although there is still considerable controversy over the root causes of the Financial Crisis [...], there is little dispute that regulators, policy-makers, and the financial industry did not have ready access to information" (Bisias et al. 2012, 38).

A Four-Category-Framework of Information Asymmetries

While Stiglitz assumes that there is "an infinite number of ways in which information can be imperfect" (Stiglitz 2001, 486), the FSB and the IMF identify data/information gaps in three areas of the financial market: First with regard to the overall *build-up of risk* in the financial system; secondly in the context of *cross-border linkages* via financial products and firms; and the third identified gap concerns the *vulnerability* of national economies to shocks (Financial Stability Board and International Monetary Fund 2009, 10). Even though it provides a good starting point, the FSB/IMF approach has major shortcomings: It is not systematic in the sense that it remains unclear why certain types of gaps are excluded and others included. Moreover, the nature of these gaps is quite vague. Using an actor-centered approach, Becker/Willke distinguish types of information asymmetries according to the institutions or actors involved: While there is usually a financial institution on the informed side, we can find regulators, private consumers and other financial institutions, such as institutional investors, on the other. Their approach also takes into account the information asymmetries within financial institutions that are usually not taken into account and that became visible in the JP Morgan London Whale case. As we will see, it relates to major arguments in economic theory. The four types of information are:

(1) *Sufficient information to regulate the financial system*, referring to information asymmetries between regulatees and regulators;
(2) *sufficient information to protect consumers*, referring to information gaps between financial institutions and customers;
(3) *sufficient information to keep the market going*, referring to information asymmetries among financial institutions (inter-organizational information gaps); and
(4) sufficient information about systemically important institutions within these institutions themselves, which we want to label *internal information asymmetries* (Becker and Willke 2013).

In the US, measures have been put in place since 2010 to address all four types of information asymmetries. Becker/Willke name a variety of different policy responses, such as new reporting forms for financial advisors (form PF), or living wills and stress tests for financial institutions. On the following pages, we want to use and further elaborate their four-category-framework of information asymmetries. In order to better understand the nature of the described problems, as well as the manifold policy responses, we refer to examples wherever we can.

(1) Sufficient information to regulate the financial system: It would be outright wrong to say that supervisors and regulators had no access to information during the crisis; compared to the information available to the general public, their access was much better (Engle 2010). This does however not imply that it was sufficient. Bernanke, as chairman of the Federal Reserve Bank, described how during the crisis "supervisory expertise and information have repeatedly proved invaluable in helping us to address potential systemic risks involving specific financial institutions and markets and to effectively fulfill our role as lender of last resort" (Bernanke 2009c). Information gaps might be an obstacle to effective long-term regulation; but as the crisis demonstrated, they make it especially difficult to design and implement ad hoc measures, let them be bailouts or no-bailouts or Fed lending programs. Looking at interconnectedness, derivatives provide a good example: It is widely agreed that derivatives are a good and important tool to hedge financial risk and as such they have a long-standing history. The basic problem in 2008 was that regulators had no information on (a) the types of derivatives that existed and (b) the exposure of US counterparties, because the majority of derivatives was negotiated privately and traded over-the-counter. After the crisis, supervisors accordingly argued that "authorities need detailed information on derivatives transactions and bilateral positions to assess evolving market risks and to execute their financial stability responsibilities" (Yellen 2013a).

Interestingly, several pre-crisis statements imply that regulators *wanted* to collect certain information, but were *not authorized* to do so. Bernanke for instance argues that the information available to regulators had been limited due to "gaps in statutory authority" and a "lack of preexisting reporting and supervisory relationships [that] hindered systematic gathering of information that might have helped policymakers in the early days of the crisis" (Bernanke 2012) – a view that is supported by Tarullo who identified a "lack of authority to collect and analyze information from unregulated entities" (Tarullo 2010b, 12). Dodd-Frank fills these gaps, at least to a certain degree: It requires, for example, certain derivatives contracts to be traded via registered trading platforms and to be centrally cleared by registered derivatives clearing houses (Danielsson and Vries 2008; Schwarcz 2009). As a result, information on derivatives volumes and counterparties should be accessible and useable in the future. In addition, stress tests and living wills provide data and information to regulators. With Dodd-Frank fully implemented, the information gathering efforts of US financial regulators, via the OFR and the Fed, will therefore increase massively. The newly established reporting requirements, as well as the broader work of the OFR, might provide the basis for ad hoc policy responses in a future crisis. As discussed in chapter four, Dodd-Frank even provides the OFR with subpoena power to get the information it wants. As early as 1999, Tietmayer demanded better information for systemic risk regulation; the *efficient use of information* was one of the challenges he named, especially from a global financial governance perspective. Again, data and information were mostly national, while risks and markets had become increasingly global (Tietmeyer 1999). In 2008, these problems persisted:

> I would say… the information was available maybe in a piecemeal or patchwork fashion not in a … – *aggregated?* – yeah, exactly. So, they have this vision for an agency whose job is to basically be in the information gathering and examination business. (Interview with Andreas Lehnert, December 05, 2012, Washington)

Against the background of recent policy measures, the important point however is that, even with the OFR up and running, it is highly unlikely that the US government will ever be *fully informed* about the banks' counterparts and trading positions. In line with this argument, Stiglitz argues that regulators should take their informational disadvantage as a given and design financial rules and regulations in ways that take into account the existing information asymmetries (Stiglitz 2009b, 13). To some extent, the Basel accords followed this dictum, or rather acknowledged it implicitly: Since the 1990s, banks were allowed to use their own internal risk models to evaluate the risk of their assets.[137] According to Admati/Hellwig, regulators at the time "realized that banks generally have better and more up-to-date information about these risks, as well as better techniques for evaluating them" (Admati and Hellwig 2013, 184), and therefore delegated the risk assessment to the entities they oversaw. *Regulators rely on regulatees to provide the information they need.*[138]

137 According to David Einhorn's FCIC interview, the same applied to the SEC: "The SEC really allowed everybody to just do their own calculations. And it is not at all clear that the SEC did anything to actually monitor the calculations. To test them the way, you know, like a bank examiner would. And so you had a lot of self-reported stuff which led to enormous abuse. I can't account for why the SEC behaved this way, other than it just might have been their political philosophy at the time to really allow the market to sort all this stuff out" (Einhorn 2010).

138 Following Luhmann, it can be argued that policymakers' information gathering efforts are "more an indication of having lost confidence than a means to gain it" (Luhmann 2008, 154). The information gathering efforts of US regulators as required by Dodd-Frank have massively increased. Put differently, policymakers' pre-crisis desire to be uninformed might be understood as the result of a dangerous degree of overconfidence in the system and its financial institutions.

(2) Sufficient information for consumers: The crisis revealed at the side of policymakers the basic belief that if only private consumers buying financial products or signing mortgage contracts had had better information, they would have made better – meaning better informed, but also more rational – decisions. This is, again, an interesting premise with regard to buyers' bounded rationality, but we'll leave that aside for the moment and have a closer look on the nature of these information asymmetries instead.

As we have argued in the introduction to this chapter, information asymmetries between sellers and buyers are inherent to every market, and it is not possible to fully overcome them. Two points are important here: First, it cannot be denied that some buyers are *better informed than others*, leading to different degrees or levels of information. This brings us to peoples' ability to assess information. In this context, Anabtawi and Schwarcz coined the term *cognizant complexity*: Information might just not be available because "things are just too complex to understand" (Anabtawi and Schwarcz 2011, 41) – meaning that people could not access information about the risks related to their assets.[139] Second, and even more importantly, the fact that certain information is provided does not mean that it is actually *taken into account*. As the following example from the field of mortgage-backed securities (MBS) demonstrates, this holds true for institutional as well as for private investors: Fligstein and Goldstein show exemplarily that institutional investors had access to information about the very low creditworthiness of borrowers whose mortgages provided the basis for the MBSs they bought – in this case, GSAMP 2006-N2C – but bought it nevertheless (Fligstein and Goldstein 2010). The problem here is the degree of "people's willingness to undertake the costs necessary to become informed about and assess the low-probability risks" (Anabtawi and Schwarcz 2011, 41). It raises the question of whether people wanted to know about the risks related to these assets or not. Besides, psychological research indicates that more information leads to a significant increase in decision makers' confidence concerning the accuracy of a conclusion, but that they do not increase the accuracy of the conclusion itself (Oskamp 1965).

---

139 Gary Cohn of Goldman Sachs argues that all of Goldman's counterparties understood what they were doing: "*I want to get to the question of what is an informed investor and what isn't. And it strikes me that you guys are playing at a league where you do understand things that a whole bunch of people in the market, that are qualified investors, whatever that means, may not understand. Is that your perception?* […] I totally believe that our clients and our counterparties knew what they did. – *At all levels of knowledge?* – Meaning they knew the kinds of bets they were making, the implications for themselves? I am shaking my head, so the answer is yes. We have enough discussion with our clients to be very comfortable that they all knew what they were doing. And just so you know: The clients created these products. […] The nature of our business is to stand ready and be able to facilitate" (Cohn 2010). Goldman's Lloyd Blankfein basically makes the same argument, stating that "We only sold to, […] we only dealt with people who knew what they were buying. And of course when you look at, after the fact, someone is going to come along and say 'we really didn't know'" (Blankfein 2010).

Both phenomena – a *lack of willingness* and a *lack of ability* – have to be taken into account when we look at information asymmetries between financial institutions and private consumers. To our knowledge, the specific decision-making behavior of institutional and private investors is not a widely discussed issue – neither in academia nor in policymaking. We however find a few analyses, revealing interesting insights: Barber and Odean demonstrate that private investors buy *attention grabbing stocks*, meaning stocks that are in the news or stocks with very high trading volumes (while their selling of stocks is not attention-driven). As they argue, stock buyers usually face search problems before they can make a buying decision:

> There are thousands of common stocks from which to choose. Human beings have bounded rationality. There are cognitive – and temporal – limits to how much information we can process. [...] One way to make the search for stocks to purchase more manageable is to limit the choice set. (Barber and Odean 2008, 786)

Keloharju et al. are able to show a link between individuals' choices in the product market and the stock market, essentially arguing that investors *buy what they know* (Keloharju, Knüpfer, and Linnainmaa 2012). Besides, the issue of *financial literacy* has been on the agenda of academics and policymakers for some time now. Several years before the recent financial crisis with its devastating consequences for many private households, Braunstein/Welch warned that bad money management would "result in behaviors that make consumers vulnerable to severe financial crises" (Braunstein and Welch 2002, 445).[140] Based on the assumption that well-informed, knowledgeable consumers are not only able to make better decisions, but are also "essential to an effective and efficient marketplace" (Hilgert, Hogarth, and Beverly 2003, 309), *financial education* has gained a lot of attention. Herbert Simon's groundbreaking work on the bounded rationality of economic actors provides a theoretical framework for these studies. As we will discuss in greater detail towards the end of this chapter, Simon argues that the human mind is constrained by its limited capacity to process information (Simon 1997 [1947]) – a fact that applies to private investors as well as to regulators and policymakers. In line with Simon, Stiglitz argues that "[t]he problem with many derivatives was that they were so complex that even if all the information about them had been disclosed, most market participants would not have been able to assess their real value" (Stiglitz 2009b, 15). Against this background, the establishment of the Consumer Financial Protection Bureau (CFPB) in the US is an especially interesting venture. It was

140 Yet, Elizabeth Warren warns that the question to what degree borrowers understood the contracts they signed or whether they observed the changes that took place in the mortgage originating business presents an under-researched issue (Warren 2010).

installed as a response to information asymmetries between consumers and providers of financial products; it is tasked with enforcing the law, gathering and analyzing information on consumers as well as providers, and educating consumers – as the "informed consumer is the first line of defense against abusive practices" (Group of Thirty 2009).

(3) Sufficient information to keep the market going: One can assume that, when the crisis hit in 2007/2008, the major banks had – compared to regulators and private investors – a higher level of knowledge and expertise concerning their business and market. They were however not immune to the information asymmetries that, together with direct and indirect exposures between these banks, ultimately led to the freeze of the interbank market. The interbank market is one of the most liquid markets in normal times (Heider, Hoerova, and Holthausen 2009); in 2008, however, banks stopped lending to each other and started hoarding liquidity instead. Following Heider et al., we want to argue that information asymmetries are inherent to the interbank market and not problematic during normal times – however, after an initial systemic shock, they amplify the friction that results from increased counterparty risks (ibid.). According to Danielsson/de Vries, extreme information asymmetries between banks during the crisis prevented them from lending to each other, a problem that could not be solved by such government responses as money injections, lower interest rates or bank recapitalization. The two economists recommended *breaking the information asymmetry* and solving the interbank freeze by pressuring the market participants to "open their books to their counterparts, in a manner similar to bank mergers, [so that] banks would be able to confidently lend to each other, or refuse lending with good reason" (Danielsson and Vries 2008). Calls for more transparency were widespread: In line with Heider et al., the de Larosière Report and the G30 Report recommend greater transparency (Group of Thirty 2009; High Level Group on Financial Supervision in the EU 2009).

To provide a look into the banks' books, Dodd-Frank established semi-annual or annual stress tests for certain institutions, and requires the OFR "to evaluate and report on stress tests or other stability-related evaluations of financial entities overseen by the member agencies" (Sec. 154(c)). As we saw in chapter four, the stress tests proved to be highly efficient in the US, yet they could not solve the problems in the EU. The FSOC's designation of systemically important financial institutions also provides useful information for other financial institutions: Doing business with a US SIFI is supposedly less risky than with a non-SIFI, as it is (a) closely supervised by the Fed, and (b) not allowed to fail, at least not in a chapter 11 bankruptcy process. During normal and crisis times, SIFIs might accordingly be the more reliable business partners. In uncertain times, financial institutions have to be able to trust each other in order to do business with each other – either because they have reliable information about the other institution's safety and soundness, or because someone, in this case the government, acts as a guarantor for it.

(4) Sufficient internal information: The fourth type of information-related problem does not describe an information asymmetry between two parties – let them be regulator and bank, or customer and bank, or bank and bank – instead, it refers to the information that a bank possesses about its own counterparties, organizational entities and dealings. In comparison to the other types of information asymmetries, the information gaps within the banks, especially within the highly professionalized and global SIFIs, were perhaps the biggest surprise during the crisis. The best example in this context is certainly the investment bank Lehman Brothers, where many data were available, but in a piecemeal fashion that made it impossible to access and process them. JPMorgan's London Whale scandal provided us with another example – Jamie Dimon's demand to *see everything* included. Both cases raise the question of whether "the executives and chief risk officers of these financial institutions have the data or the analytics to really understand what is going on in their balance sheets" (Interview with Allan Mendelowitz, December 03, 2012, Washington). Internal information gaps have raised the issue of *too complex to manage institutions* that we discussed at-length in chapter three. The question was also discussed in the FCIC interviews with regard to Citigroup: Are complex financial institutions able to gather and organize information about their business operations in a way that makes it possible to handle and use them, or not? (Prince 2010). It also feeds into the debate of breaking up certain institutions: If these banks cannot govern themselves, who else would be able to control them? Following Herring and Carmassi (2012), one might ask whether resolving internal information asymmetries is too complex, or just too costly.

The orderly resolution plans or living wills that are required by Dodd-Frank for certain financial institutions tackle this exact problem: They force the banks to plan and prepare for their own collapse by aggregating data and gathering information that would support an orderly resolution, and to provide these information to the Fed and the FDIC: Which subsidiaries could be sold in the case of bankruptcy? What are the most important business lines? The initial orderly resolution plan published by Deutsche Bank revealed that the DB Group consisted of approximately 2,906 active legal entities (1,113 subsidiaries and 733 special purpose entities) in 72 countries (Deutsche Bank 2012b). These numbers give us an idea of the size and complexity of SIFIs. The objective behind living wills is actually two-fold: The collection of standardized data and information should improve the risk management of the firms themselves; secondly, the plans should enable regulators to wind down the institutions (Tarullo 2010b, 7). The SIFIs themselves face major challenges when preparing the resolution plans. According to an Ernst & Young analysis, they have to rethink their IT systems, which have been designed to fulfill business needs and usually do not take into account legal-entity lines; a second problem results from the fact that financial institutions book transactions not by legal entities, but by business units (Kumar and Mangaraj 2012).

To summarize the information provided so far, the following table summarizes all four categories of information asymmetries and assigns exemplary measures taken in the US (and elsewhere) to address them.

Category	**Problem**	**Exemplary measure**
Information asymmetries between regulatees and regulators	Regulators cannot assess crisis situations adequately	Establishment of OFR
Information asymmetries between financial institutions and consumers	Consumers do not know the risks associated to the products they buy, e.g. mortgages	Establishment of the CFPB
Inter-organizational information asymmetries	Banks cannot assess each others' creditworthiness and stop lending to each other	Stress tests
Internal information asymmetries or gaps	Financial institutions do not have adequate information about their business operations and structure	Resolution plans

Table 4: Four-category-framework of information asymmetries (table based on Becker and Willke 2013).

The short excursus on agency theory at the beginning of this chapter should have made one point quite clear: Information asymmetries exist between all principals and agents; they can therefore be found between regulators and regulatees in other industries – between the US Food and Drug Administration (FDA) and a pharmaceutical company, to name just one example – and also inside every other, non-financial organization. Drawing on our analysis in chapter two and three, we however want to argue that a very high complexity at three levels – the product level, the organizational level and the system level, has exacerbated all four types of information asymmetries in the financial sector. The problem looms large against the background of TBTF: Financial regulators are confronted with TBTF institutions on the one hand and an overwhelming degree of complexity on the other. Taken together they threaten to undermine the political legitimacy of the democratic nation state.

5.2.3 Knowledge Asymmetries: Regulatees Racing Ahead

Analyzing the nature of knowledge asymmetries in financial regulation is, compared to data and information related problems, easier for two central reasons: First, the phenomenon itself is much more distinct: While we have to distinguish between different types of information asymmetries, there is only one type of knowledge asymmetry that is relevant to our work.[141] Secondly, while policymakers and supervisors often confuse data and information related problems, many descriptions of knowledge deficiencies are surprisingly clear. In the current section, we draw on speeches, papers, interviews and statements by government officials, but also on selected literature from the fields of political science, economics and sociology.

As we argued at the beginning of chapter five, there are crucial differences between data and information on the one hand and knowledge on the other: All knowledge is closely tied to experience and practice (Becker and Willke 2013); it accordingly requires human capabilities to create knowledge, and it is much more difficult to transfer knowledge than to exchange data and information. While information is often defined as the *know what*, knowledge means to *know how* a system works, and it might even comprise the ability to control it (Ackoff 1989; Machlup 1980, draws this distinction without explicitly applying it to information and knowledge). Being a precondition to systems control, knowledge enables humans to "make distinctions, choices and decisions" (Zeleny 1987, 63). Our definition of knowledge gives us a hint at the problems resulting from knowledge asymmetries: They are hard to overcome and they hamper any form of governance. Yet knowledge asymmetries are, as we will show in this section, inherent to all relationships between regulator and regulatee. We learn from Max Weber that they are no recent phenomenon. As we argue against the background of financial system complexity, they have become especially problematic in the area of financial regulation, putting the sovereign nation state under immense pressure. The more distinct and specified the knowledge of financial experts gets, the bigger are the

141 We do not want to assert that only one type of knowledge asymmetry exists: Knowledge asymmetries between consumers and financial institutions clearly exist, as do knowledge asymmetries within financial institutions; in addition, some financial institutions – e.g. Goldman Sachs and JPMorgan – were perceived as being more competent than others (cf. Cohn 2010). However, none of these knowledge asymmetries were identified as problematic by either policymakers or regulators during the crisis, while inter-organizational and intra-organizational information asymmetries were identified as such, and directly addressed.

risks posed by non-knowledge and uncertainty to society as a whole (Willke and Willke 2012).

Academia on Knowledge Asymmetries in Financial Regulation

Academic literature has dealt with the issue of knowledge asymmetries in regulation for some time, but rather indirectly or implicitly. Diverse research traditions, such as public choice and agency theory, touch the issue, but are usually characterized by the same definitional inaccuracy that we find in the statements of policymakers and regulators on data and information: Information and knowledge are seldom distinguished and rarely defined. They are nevertheless described, especially in sociological texts, and we can hence base our analysis on the classic works of Max Weber, Charles Lindblom, and Robert E. Lane, and also draw on more recent texts from Renate Mayntz, Helmut Willke and Robert Weber. Last but not least, Mitnick provides us with a helpful matrix to distinguish between problems rooted in information and knowledge asymmetries. Some of these authors will be important in the following chapter on knowledge capture, too. There are surely many more to refer to; however, as our focus lies on the practical implications of knowledge asymmetries, and their appearance during the recent financial crisis, we restrict ourselves to the texts we assume to be most central.

As already mentioned in the preceding section on information asymmetries, Max Weber described the relationship between sovereign and bureaucracy as an agency relationship. Concerning information and expertise, regulators accordingly outperform their constituents. In this context, Weber distinguishes between bureaucrats' technical knowledge (*Fachwissen*) and a certain type of knowledge acquired through the conduct of office (*Dienstwissen*), resulting in regulators' "domination through knowledge" (Weber 1922, 129).[142] Central to our argument is that Weber identifies a second knowledge asymmetry, emphasizing the pre-dominance of private over bureaucratic knowledge:

> Only the expert knowledge of private economic interest groups in the field of 'business' is superior to the expert knowledge of the bureaucracy. This is so because the exact knowledge of facts in their field is of direct significance for economic survival. [...] For this reason alone authorities are held within narrow boundaries when they seek to influence economic life in the capitalist epoch, and very frequently their measures take an unforeseen and unintended course or are made illusory by the superior expert knowledge of the interest groups. (Weber 1968, 994)[143]

142 Translations taken from or based on: Max Weber (1968): Economy and Society. Edited by Guenther Roth and Claus Wittich. Berkeley a.o.: University of California Press, p. 225.

143 The original text says: "Ueberlegen ist der Sachkenntnis der Bürokratie nur die Sachkenntnis der privatwirtschaftlichen Interessen auf dem Gebiet der 'Wirtschaft'. Diese deshalb, weil für sie die genaue

Following a capitalistic logic, Weber argues that regulatees' knowledge must be superior to regulators' knowledge because it is existential. In view of the fate of the US Office of Thrift Supervision (OTS), which was closed in 2010 because it had failed to supervise and police US savings and loan associations, we want to point out that information and knowledge can be existential for regulators, too. Every banking scandal sheds new light on the (in)ability of supervisors and regulators to monitor financial institutions, undermining the legitimacy of the remaining US financial agencies – most prominently, the SEC, the CFTC, the OCC, and also the Fed. We nevertheless adopt Weber's central argument that *the dominance of private over bureaucratic knowledge hampers regulators' ability to control industries.*

Charles Lindblom, in his seminal work on *Politics and Markets*, observed that "because every person in high authority needs information, he comes to be in some degree the *captive of knowledge specialists*" (Lindblom 1977, 120, emphasis added) who constrain the authority of undemocratic and democratic leaders alike.[144] Like Weber, Lindblom refers to legislative and executive knowledge gaps. The basic mechanism he describes is central to all knowledge societies: As society increasingly relies on specialized knowledge, experts possessing that knowledge become more and more influential: "They do not demand influence; they simply achieve it by reason of what they know" (Lindblom 1977, 187). We want to highlight the importance of Lindblom's arguments for regulator-regulatee relationships: Here, too, *experts expand their influence simply by reason of what they know.* If and to what degree they demand influence is yet another, quite controversial issue, and we will get back to it in chapter six in the context of current capture diagnoses.

Lindblom himself draws on the works of Daniel Bell and Robert E. Lane. Lane models politics on a continuum between pure politics and pure knowledge, and identifies a trend towards more rational, meaning less ideological, politics:

> If one thinks of a domain of 'pure politics' where decisions are determined by calculations of influence, power, or electoral advantage, and a domain of

---

Tatsachenkenntnis auf ihrem Gebiet direkt wirtschaftliche Existenzgrundlage ist […]. Schon deshalb ist die behördliche Beeinflussung des Wirtschaftslebens im kapitalistischen Zeitalter an so enge Schranken gebunden und entgleisen die Maßregeln des Staats auf diesem Gebiete so oft in unvorhergesehene und unbeabsichtigte Bahnen oder wurden durch die überlegene Sachkenntnis der Interessenten illusorisch gemacht" (Weber 1922, 673).

144 Under the heading of dual leadership, Lindblom argues that the importance of a well-functioning market is so central to democracies that businessmen will be granted a privileged position by government officials: "He does not have to be bribed, duped, or pressured to do so. Nor does he have to be an uncritical admirer of businessmen to do so. He simply understands […] that public affairs in market-oriented systems are in the hands of two groups of leaders, government and business, who must collaborate and that, to make the system work government leadership must often defer to business leadership. Collaboration and deference between the two are at the heart of politics" (Lindblom 1977, 175).

> 'pure knowledge' where decisions are determined by calculations of how to implement agreed-upon values with rationality and efficiency, it appears to me that the political domain is shrinking and the knowledge domain is growing, in terms of criteria for decisions, kinds of counsel sought, evidence adduced, and nature of the 'rationality' employed. (Lane 1966, 657f.)

Consequently, *the power to influence politics is based on specialized, potentially but not necessarily self-interested knowledge* (ibid., 658). We agree with Lane that the importance of specialized knowledge has increased in tandem with the growing importance of highly technical areas of regulation – the EU regulation REACH (for Registration, Evaluation, Authorisation and Restriction of Chemicals), which took seven years to pass and is widely perceived as the most complex EU regulation ever (Rettman 2007), provides a good, non-financial example here. Industry and its supervision and regulation evolve in parallel, and as described in chapter two, so does their degree of complexity. In one important point, however, we disagree with Lane: Beneath the distinction of *pure politics* and *pure knowledge* lies a counterfactual belief in an absolute truth. In the tradition of the *correspondence theory of truth* that goes back to Aristotle and Plato, and that George Soros explicitly refers to in his recent book on the financial crisis and financial paradigms (Soros 2008), there exists the world as it is – the absolute truth, or truth consisting in relation to reality – and political decisions can, at least theoretically, correspond with it. Following this argument, scientific knowledge makes politics truer, meaning better. Even if we would agree with this claim (which we do not), the question remains whether it applies to all policy areas, including financial policies. We argue that *the financial system, as a complex and self-referential network of interactions and interconnections, produces "true facts" of its own*: Whether a statement is true or false depends upon its correspondence with other statements, instead of its relation to the world (*coherence theory of the truth*), or, as Millo and McKenzy have convincingly argued, upon its relevancy and usefulness for particular groups – market participants, as well as regulators (Millo and MacKenzie 2009).[145] Here, the market follows a simple logic that has been described by March and Simon for organizations: "In organizational communication, evidence is replaced with conclusions drawn from […] evidence, and these conclusions then become the 'facts' on which the rest of the organization acts" (March and Simon 1993 [1958], 176).

Relevant to our understanding of regulator-regulatee knowledge asymmetries is also the work of German sociologist Renate Mayntz. She not only depicts information asymmetries between these two entities, but also argues that *policy-*

145 In line with Millo and McKenzy, Preda claims, "neoclassical economics is not a theory. It is a social practice and, as such, it is not merely true: it is lived" (Preda 2001, 16). Mark-to-market accounting provides a good example here: Fair value asset prices do not reflect the true or absolute prices of assets, but the current valuations of these assets.

makers are heavily dependent on the knowledge of those affected by financial regulation. More importantly, she describes how gaps in agency information and knowledge result in uncertainty about side effects and long-term consequences of new rules and regulations. The belief that "to regulate effectively, you need information on how it is going to affect the entities that you regulate" (Barkow 2013) is widespread among policymakers and regulators. The horror scenarios and "grim picture[s] of the economic consequences of restrictive regulation" (Mayntz 2012, 22) conjured up by industry experts – loss of jobs, less credit for small and medium-sized enterprises, financial sector downturn – temper enthusiasm for financial reform (Mayntz 2010b; see also Lindblom 1977, 178; Admati and Hellwig 2013). A New York Times article written by Senator Charles E. Schumer and Michael R. Bloomberg in 2006 demonstrates the relevance of such fears. Under the heading "To Save New York, Learn from London", Schumer and Bloomberg warned that New York as a financial center had been losing ground to its UK and Asian competitors. They reported that New York had hired a consulting firm to identify "the specific variables that are negatively impacting our financial-services industry" and to develop a plan for corrective action (Schumer and Bloomberg 2006). The consulting firm identified the US regulatory enforcement style as a major obstacle to financial institutions, describing it as "punitive and overly public" (Bloomberg and Schumer 2007, 17). The British Financial Services Authority (FSA), Schumer's and Bloomberg's role model for financial supervision and regulation, was dissolved in 2013 due to its perceived failure to police the UK financial services industry; the negative scenarios summoned by the US financial industry – a medium-term financial sector downturn – did not stem from too much regulation, but rather from too little supervision.

Contrary to many policymakers and experts, Mayntz is critical towards calls for more transparency (and accordingly, more information), based on the assumption that it rests upon a *false belief in fully informed and self-regulatory markets* (Mayntz 2010a, 184; we will revert to that thought in the chapter on regulators as boundedly rational agents). As a third important point, she puts the incongruence between national financial regulation and the global financial system center stage – assuming that political governance is possible in principle, but has become increasingly difficult during the second half of the 20th century, inter alia because the state followed a neo-liberal paradigm and deliberately withdrew from the market (Mayntz and Scharpf 2005). Willke emphasizes the incongruence of national policies on the one hand, and a globalized financial market on the other (Willke and Willke 2012). Looking at the global level, he observes a lack of system governance, as well as an overestimation of the existing global institutions with regard to their ability to control the system (Willke, Becker, and Rostásy 2013, 48). Based on Kahneman, he argues that that same overconfidence can also be found at the level of financial experts. Finance professionals are indeed experts for their respective working areas, but they largely misunderstand or ignore the systems characteristics of the complex financial system they operate in, and generally underestimate the risks resulting from complexity, interconnectedness and emergent properties:

> Governments, lawmakers and regulators appear to depend on the very experts who contributed to precipitating the financial crisis or failed to prevent it from happening. Emergent properties and counter-intuitive systems dynamics do not only hinder an understanding of the financial system's inherent systemic risks; unfortunately, these traits also lead actors, namely experts, astray in devising *obvious* solutions. (ibid., 54)

Robert Weber's text on knowledge asymmetries in financial regulation is certainly one of the most relevant publications for our work (Weber 2012). Published in the American Business Law Journal, it argues that "regulators face a *structural, widening epistemic gap between what they are able to know and what they need to know* in order to administer the statutory mandates of their agencies" (ibid., 644f., emphasis added). Based on this observation, Weber develops a comprehensive concept of complexity capture that we want to discuss at length in the following chapter.

We want to end our short literature review with the agency theory work of Mitnick. In his four-field matrix (see figure 13), Mitnick distinguishes between the ability of a principal to *observe* his agent's behavior, and the ability of the principal to *judge* the optimality of his agent's behavior. Juxtaposed with our concept of data, information and knowledge, one could well say that Mitnick's two categories coincide with knowing what (*information, including data*) and knowing how (*knowledge*). Put differently, agency relationships like the one persisting between regulator and regulatee are characterized by two types of asymmetries: A data and information asymmetry that *constrains the regulator's ability to observe the regulatees' behavior*, and a knowledge asymmetry that *limits the regulator's ability to judge the regulatee's behavior, and intervene.*

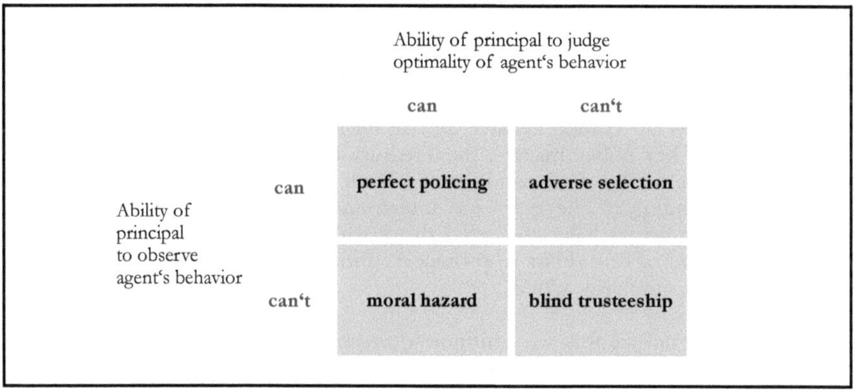

Figure 13: Core agency problems (Mitnick 1984, 20)

Shortly summarized, these texts provide us with the following arguments: Based on their superior knowledge (specialized knowledge, or *Fachwissen* in Max Weber's sense), regulatees are in a dominant position towards their respective regulators. During the recent financial crisis, it has in fact become increasingly evident that regulators depend on their regulatees' knowledge. As a result, industry experts can expand their influence, simply by reason of what they know. Based on these observations, one can conclude that the power to influence politics is increasingly based on specialized (potentially, but not necessarily) self-interested knowledge. Private interests accordingly threaten to undermine agency decision-making. Looking at the nature of this knowledge, we argue that it is not absolute in the sense that it corresponds with given facts or truths. Instead, we claim that the financial system produces its own truths. Herein, we follow Knorr-Cetina and Bruegger who argue for trading markets that "market reality is knowledge generated, that is, has no existence independent from the informational representation of the market on screen that is provided by news agencies, analysts, and traders themselves" (Knorr-Cetina and Bruegger 2002, 915). The ability of private non-profit groups to build up counter-expertise must therefore be limited. The faster the financial system evolves, the farther financial regulators fall behind. The gap between regulators' and regulatees' expertise is therefore growing, at least in the area of financial regulation. It limits regulators' abilities to judge or control their regulatees.

Policymakers and Regulators on Knowledge Asymmetries

To support our argument that knowledge asymmetries between regulators and regulatees hamper financial supervision and regulation and played a major role in the recent financial crisis, we provide the following six quotes from the Financial

Crisis Inquiry Commission, from Janet L. Yellen, now President of the Federal Reserve Bank, from former Fed President Ben Bernanke, from economist Viral Acharya, from FSOC member John Ducrest, and from the de Larosière Report:

> There was no comprehensive and strategic plan for containment, because they [the key policy makers: the Treasury Department, the Federal Reserve Board, and the Federal Reserve Bank of New York] lacked a *full understanding* of the risks and interconnections in the financial markets. Some regulators have conceded this error. We had allowed the system to *race ahead of our ability* to protect it. (Financial Crisis Inquiry Commission 2011, xxi, emphasis added)

> We must ensure that we continue to *increase our expertise* so it is properly matched with the problems and challenges we will face in both our bank supervisory role and in meeting our traditional financial stability mandate. (Bernanke 2009a, emphasis added)

> The financial regulatory system as it was structured at that time was ill-prepared to manage this crisis, lacking the necessary tools and *more importantly, the knowledge of the risks and operations* of the largest financial firms. We also lacked the ability to monitor and contain nonbank firms that were able to take large risks but had no prudential standards or supervision over certain parts of their operations. (Ducrest 2012, emphasis added)

> Insufficient supervisory and regulatory resources combined with an *inadequate mix of skills* [...] made the situation worse. (High Level Group on Financial Supervision in the EU 2009, 11)

> But as we learned during the recent crisis, the financial system has also grown much larger and more complex, and *our efforts to understand and influence it* have, at best, only kept pace. (Yellen 2013a, emphasis added)

> There's also a knowledge issue which is that a lot of times regulators are constantly catching up with newer products, newer organizational forms in the markets. Things like *OFR could potentially help with that.* (Interview with Viral Acharya, November 28, 2012, New York)

While all of these observers support our argument that a knowledge asymmetry exists between regulators and regulatees, two points are of special importance: First, knowledge asymmetries between regulators and regulatees are rooted in the complexity and fast development (often referred to as *financial innovation*) of the financial system – but they are also rooted in the structure of the knowledge itself: We have argued that, distinct from data and information, knowledge cannot be transferred. Acharya refers to the OFR that is provided by Dodd-Frank with subpoena power to get access to highly relevant data. Dodd-Frank also requires certain financial institutions to submit stress tests and resolution plans. However, regulators cannot ask financial firms to *report knowledge*, or *hand over knowledge*, or *re-organize knowledge* by implementing measures that are of the same basic nature as stress-tests or living wills. Instead, regulators have to pursue other strategies to gain expertise – a dilemma that the SEC's Gregg Berman described well when he said "the best way to understand high frequency trading might be to become a high frequency trader" (Berman 2011, 11).

The SEC is an agency that acknowledges and evidently struggles with the identified knowledge gaps. After having been heavily criticized for its lack of expertise and enforcement rigor before the crisis, it has gone through notable changes. The former SEC chairwomen Mary Schapiro and Elisse Walter have both described the agency's recent knowledge building efforts:

> So, when I look at where we are today I feel pretty good about it. You know, we're work in progress as every institution always should be, but we've brought in incredible talent with very current Wall Street experience, and financial services experience. We have ETF [exchange-traded funds] experts at the SEC for the first time, we have quants at the SEC for the first time, *we have people right from trading desks, directly from operations in major financial institutions, from credit rating agencies.* So we've brought in great talent, we've really focused on one of the core criticisms of the agency, which was a lack of cross-divisional cooperation and collaboration. Stovepipes that allow things like Madoff to become a problem out of control, and we've done lots of work internally through [...] our cross-border working group that brings people from all over the agency to tackle a problem. (Schapiro 2012, emphasis added)

> I do think it's very important for an agency like this to have a mix of people working for it, and *they bring in an expertise that they have in the private sector*, which is very much for the benefit of the agency and for the benefit of investors. In turn, it has been my experience, that those people who have spent time at the Commission end up understanding very well the importance of our mission, and the importance of compliance with the law, and when they leave, they bring a culture of compliance to the private entities they work for. (Walter 2013, emphasis added)

As one of our interview partners from the SEC put it, in accordance with Walter's and Schapiro's statements, the agency wants to employ people with "real financial knowledge" and "street knowledge" (Interview with an SEC official, December 05, 2012, Washington) – meaning with practical experience – because directly engaging in high-frequency trading is for obvious reasons no viable option for the Commission (Berman 2011, 11). Besides its human resources efforts, the SEC has built a new department that investigates major trading errors and incidents. It collaborates with market insiders, such as the high-frequency-trading firm Tradeworx, to get access to current technology and the related expertise (see Willke, Becker, and Rostásy 2013, for more information on the "Tradeworx case") and to enable the SEC "to detect whether trading firms are overwhelming the market's plumbing when they rapidly submit and cancel orders" (Popper and Protess 2012). The SEC was criticized for engaging one of the companies it oversees – but against our working definition of knowledge, we have to ask where else it could have turned for such highly specialized knowledge? Here, regulators and supervisors are obviously confronted with another Hobbson's choice. As the chief executive officer of Tradeworx put it: "Where else are they going to be able to get these capabilities? [...] They are not available from anywhere other than high-speed trading firms. We're the only ones who possess it" (Narang, quoted by Popper and Protess 2012).

Going back to the six quotes at the beginning of this section, a second point is important. With regard to our definition of knowledge in the first part of this chapter, Yellen's assessment is the most interesting: Following Ackoff, knowledge is "what makes possible the transformation from information into instructions" and "makes the control of a system possible" (Ackoff 1989, 4). Controlling complex systems is an impossible task. Trying to *understand and influence* it might be within the realms of possibility. As the respective quote shows, Acharya identifies the OFR as potentially helpful in this context. In addition to its data and information collection efforts, the office basically pursues a twofold strategy for knowledge creation: First, it conducts its own research. Among the first publications from the OFR is, as an example, an extensive study on systemic risk analytics, comparing 31 quantitative measures of systemic risk (Bisias et al. 2012). Second, Section 152 of Dodd-Frank advises the OFR to establish a fellowship program for academics and professionals who are not only supposed to carry out research, but should also provide training for the Office staff. Together with the data and information gathering efforts of the OFR, and against the background of the DIK(W)-hierarchy, these attempts sound very reasonable. The question, then, is how the Office translates its mission into action. So far, the OFR seems to have a strong focus on data and systemic risk measurements.

Taken together, both academic and non-academic assessments support our case that knowledge asymmetries are inherent to regulation, and against the background of increased financial complexity and the TBTF phenomenon, they have become especially pressing in the area of financial regulation. While Dodd-Frank directly addresses data and information asymmetries, it remains mostly silent on knowledge asymmetries. The OFR provides answers to all three problems, but again focuses on data and information gathering efforts. From our problem descriptions we can conclude that these tasks are less challenging than building up knowledge. The Fed has underscored its commitment to data collection and analysis many times (see for example Bernanke 2010b, 2010a; Yellen 2013a). Yet, other regulatory and supervisory entities – the SEC, to name one example – address the knowledge asymmetries they experience, independent of Dodd-Frank. Beneath lies the counterfactual claim that these asymmetries can be addressed and essentially overcome.

5.2.4 Feigned and Factual Non-Knowledge

The financial crisis confronted us with different types of non-knowledge. One was of a strategic nature – people who could have been held responsible for decisions that contributed to the crisis chose to rather hide behind ignorance in their interviews and testimonies. The following long excerpt from an FCIC interview with Thomas Maheras (2010), Citigroup's former Chief of Fixed Income, illustrates the point:

> Q: Do you recall any discussions with senior management from 2003 to 2006 about the CDO business at Citi? [...]
> A: As I sit here, no. To the extent that it could have possibly come up within the purview of this broader structured credit priority that I mentioned, it could have come up. I don't recall any discussion around CDOs.
> Q: Did you do anything to prepare for today's interview?
> A: Yes.
> Q: What was that?
> A: I met with my counsel on a couple of occasions, and that is it.
> Q: Did you review any documents to prepare for today?
> A: I was shown a couple of documents, I think just a couple of documents.
> Q: What documents were you shown?
> A: I don't recall.
> Q: Do you recall the nature of those documents?
> A: They looked like internal management reports or presentations. And again it was just, I think we only looked at a couple. I would defer to counsel on this because I don't recall exactly what I saw. I am sorry; I did look at the, I looked at the testimony that I provided two years ago to a probe by the SEC. I looked at a transcript.
> Q: Did you look at any exhibits accompanying that transcript?
> A: No.
> Q: How long ago were these preparatory meetings for today?
> A: In the last week.
> Q: And you don't recall what documents you saw?
> A: By name or title, no.
> Q: By substance?
> A: By substance, what I recall is that I saw a couple of presentations that I can say were not prepared by me, so I would say that I actually saw a couple of single pages. I didn't see full presentations or look at full presentations.
> Q: Did they refresh your recollection at all about your experiences with the CDO business from 2003 to 2007?
> A: Those documents?

> Q: The documents and the preparatory sessions that you had for today, reviewing the SEC testimony that you gave?
> A: To the extent that it refreshed my memory of the testimony of two years ago, it refreshed my recollection in some areas.

The interview culminates in a statement by Thomas Maheras that he does not know what a CDO squared is (Maheras 2010). Similar conversations can be found in other FCIC interviews, too. At the same time, market insiders who were not afraid of prosecution boasted in their interviews about their insights and expertise, and how few people actually understand the markets as they do (see for example Das 2010a). When we look at the risks resulting from *known and unknown unknowns*, we therefore have to be careful not to underestimate, based on such interviews, the knowledge possessed by market insiders. However, even though people like Thomas Maheras certainly knew and understood more than they later pretended, the analysis so far clearly indicates that significant parts of the financial markets were neither understood nor well known, especially not by policymakers and regulators. The so-called shadow banking system, comprising opaque organizations, products and trades, presents a case in point. The reason is threefold: First, as knowledge and non-knowledge grow in tandem, more and more specialized expertise on increasingly complex products resulted in even greater unknowns (Willke and Willke 2012; Willke 2007, 2002). Second, as illustrated at the beginning of this book, components in complex systems interact in ways that are not foreseeable, resulting in the growth of what Willke terms *systemic non-knowledge* (*systemisches Nichtwissen*): Non-knowledge of the logic, operations and dynamic of a complex and tightly coupled financial system (Willke 2002, 30). Third, opaque and unregulated markets provide a competitive advantage for the financial firms that operate in them. As Cohn emphasizes in his FCIC interview, dark markets exist not despite, but *because* they are dark (Cohn 2010). Whenever the transparency of a business or market is increased through regulation, certain operations and trades will therefore move into some other, darker corner of the market.

As already argued, regulators fail to address the resulting uncertainty. To deal with systemic risk, regulators have to acknowledge and address these unknowns, while knowing at the same time that they cannot possibly be eliminated. Against the background of this paradox problem, Soros warns regulators that financial regulation must be imperfect, "subject to regulatory arbitrage and lack of foresight"; he goes on that

> regulation should recognize its own imperfection. That's a very important point – do you think that the failure to do so … is because of the nature of the regulatory process or because the influence of firms whose interests – all of the above! First of all, it is inherent in the human condition. […] Second, regulation by their nature are [sic!] static and will always lag behind reality, it

> is always, the markets are much faster in recognizing reality than bureaucrats. Thirdly, political influence is, regulations are subject to politics. [...] the fact that markets need to be regulated does not mean that the regulations will do the job they are supposed to do, in fact they will always fail. And if this is recognized, then the regulations themselves will prove to be flexible enough that they might have a better chance of catching up with the new developments. (Soros 2010)

We will further discuss these points in the following sections on regulators' bounded rationality and on the privatization of legitimacy through the rise of private financial experts, and will then turn to the question whether of the US regulators can (partly) overcome such problems with the help of the OFR.

5.3 Boundedly Rational Financial Regulators

Let us assume that the establishment of the OFR brings about fully informed supervisors and regulators. The CFPB achieves an increase in average financial literacy; as fraudulent behavior is prosecuted, the overall quality of products and product-related information increases. Systemically important financial institutions aggregate internal data and information of high quality through the preparation of living wills; and banks receive reliable information on other banks from regular stress tests. In this hypothetical post-crisis world, with all new mechanisms and institutions up and running perfectly, would all participants – supervisors, regulators, financial institutions, consumers – make better (meaning better informed) decisions?

In the context of data-, information- and knowledge-related problems, we have distinguished between two schools of thought: School number one argues that standardized, aggregated financial market data would increase the ability of US supervisors to monitor market developments closely, to spot trends and to mitigate systemic risk. Some even believe in the general feasibility to forecast market behavior, drawing a comparison of weather forecasting on the one hand and financial forecasting on the other. Members of the second school are less optimistic: As they argue, data are just the starting point. More specifically, the bigger and resource-intensive challenge is to build up expertise that is needed to mitigate systemic risk and to prevent systemic crises. We want to juxtapose these two perspectives with Herbert Simon's concept of *bounded rationality* as it challenges both. Without delving too deeply into the backgrounds of rational choice and bounded rationality theory, we argue that Dodd-Frank comprises an overly-optimistic view of human and organizational information processing capabilities and, more generally, overestimates the value of financial data and information.[146] What looks like a reasonable policy change to address data and information gaps at first sight might in fact have dangerous side effects: The focus on data and information gathering efforts distracts attention from even bigger problems, namely: The over-complexity of the financial sector, and the inability of financial supervisors and regulators to build-up the knowledge required to react to major developments in the financial sector, such as the emergence of shadow-banking and the nature and the proliferation of CDOs.

Simon argues that no organism is capable of (1) attaching definite pay-offs to outcomes of decisions, (2) specifying the nature of these outcomes, (3) bringing the pay-offs into a consistent order, and (4) defining the probabilities of the respective outcomes (Simon 1955, 103f.). He comes to the conclusion that no such thing as *global rationality* exists: Human decision makers are agents with bounded rationality. Simon contrasts his concept with what is often referred to as *traditional economic theory*. Here, *economic men* have unlimited data or information processing capabilities, and they operate in an information environment that "is free of noise and friction" – information is not only well-structured but also easily accessible (Boisot and Canals 2004, 49). Based on "knowledge of the relevant aspects of [their] environment which, if not absolutely complete, is at least impressively clear and voluminous" (Simon 1955, 99), economic men are able to make *rational decisions*. Three points are of central importance here: Economic men are not only assumed to have access to all relevant information, in addition, decision-makers are expected to weigh up means and ends systematically, and make rational, fully-informed choices. Also, motivations deviating from self-interest are widely excluded. Yet Simon questions the human ability to process information and come to rational conclusions "in situations of any complexity" (ibid., 104).[147] To describe the process of decision-making, Simon coins the term *satificing*: Agents do not search for the optimal, but for a satisfying solution to a problem (Simon 1956, 129; March and Simon 1993 [1958], 162). His approach has thus been described as the "more realistic theory of human decision making" (Selten 2002, 16).

Interestingly, the concept of economic men not only asks how decisions are taken, but also explains what we pursue (see Persky 1995, 223). It assumes that men are not only rational agents, but also *utility maximizers*: Accordingly, businessmen,

146 Simon's theory can be well applied to organizations: They are not only characterized by diverse and diverging internal and external interests, but also by insufficient information and knowledge (Perrow 2007, 292).

147 As Haldane and Madouros point out, finance research and practice has also been dominated by rational expectations theory. Going back to Muth (1961) the theory argues "that information collection is close to costless and that agents have cognitive faculties sufficient to weight probabilistically all future outturns" (Haldane and Madouros 2012, 2). They contrast rational expectations theory with the approaches of Keynes, Hayek, Friedman and also Simon, who "placed imperfections in information and knowledge centre-stage" (ibid.).

politicians, bureaucrats and voters generally aim at maximizing their own good – pursuing either private profit, reelection or variations of it, such as future job prospects.[148] In economics, this approach is termed *homo economicus*; it is opposed by the *behavioral approach*, which includes psychological traits that undermine the rational view of human decision-making (Aikman et al. 2011, 7). While we leave it to others to challenge the utility maximizing principle – many have done so, to be clear – the idea of the rational decision-maker is central to our analysis. Simon aims at replacing the widely accepted paradigm of the rational agent with, as he argues, "a kind of rational behavior that is compatible with the access to information and computational capacities that are *actually possessed by organisms*, including man, in the kinds of environments in which such organisms exist" (Simon 1955, 99, emphasis added).

Simon's seminal text on bounded rationality dates back to the 1950s. It set off a wide range of research in different disciplines, and it has influenced (behavioral) economists and social psychologists alike (see for example Gigerenzer 2002; Kahneman 2003; Thaler 1991). Kahneman and Tversky for example have explored biases and heuristics in human decision-making, choices under risk (which led them to develop their *prospect theory*), and framing effects (Kahneman 2003, 1449; see also Kahneman and Tversky 1984; 2011). Based on a wide range of experiments, they have advanced Simon's concept and argue that "[t]he central characteristic of agents is not that they reason poorly but that they often act intuitively. And the behavior of these agents is not guided by what they are able to compute, but by what they happen to see at a given moment" (Kahneman 2003, 1469). More recent behavioral research supports Simon's central point, showing that "the availability of data does not always lead to effective communication and knowledge" (Barr, Mullainathan, and Shafir 2009, 26). Against this background, it is all the more surprising that the bounded rationality of regulators and supervisors only played a minor role in the post-crisis debate of roots and causes.[149]

As we show, policymakers and academics have discussed the role of data, information and knowledge gaps at length. Recent policy responses, such as the establishment of the OFR and the CFPB, reflect the fact that the US government perceived insufficient data and information as a major cause of supervisory and regulatory failure prior to and during the crisis. In the tradition of Herbert Simon, one might ask whether financial supervisors are "rational agents of the classical

148 This idea of the *homo economicus* is of course an oversimplification: For purposes of modeling, the theory focuses on extrinsic motivation, but it does not exclude intrinsic motivation per se. Assuming that someone values the wellbeing of others more than his own, he might indeed seek to maximize other peoples' wellbeing. Thaler, who states that the homo economicus must become more emotional, convincingly argues that "[b]uilding models of rational, unemotional agents is easier than building models of quasi-rational emotional humans" (Thaler 2000, 140).

149 Several recent papers explore the role of financial agents' bounded rationality in the financial crisis; due to space constraints, these are left aside here.

theory, who make well informed, carefully considered, and fully controlled choices" (ibid.), or rather boundedly rational agents in Simon's sense. Yet, to our knowledge, only one recent paper – Weber's *Structural Regulation as Antidote to Complexity Capture* (2012) – explicitly takes into account that "regulators, like all agents charged with tasks, are limited by their bounded rationality; in other words, they possess limited capacities to process information, maintain their attention, and calculate" (Weber 2012, 644).[150] However, one cannot assess the role of data, information and knowledge in financial regulation without taking into account what the concept of bounded rationality indicates for decision-making in financial crises: While medium- and long-term policymaking is a complex process of bargaining and logrolling, during 2007 and 2008 – and supposably also during the negotiations between Fed, government, and private banks in the LTCM crisis – we were able to observe a completely different type of political decision-making, where a group of very few, sleep-deprived people made ad hoc decisions with far-reaching, long-term consequences. As long as the TBTF phenomenon exists, a small group of supervisors will have to decide whether it wants to bail out a SIFI or not. At the critical moment when the decision is made, these regulators act as bounded agents. Similar, but less far-reaching situations occur in the day-to-day supervision of financial institutions. Now we could argue that, due to technological progress, our computational capacities have increased in a way that Herbert Simon could not possibly have imagined. But while this certainly holds true, we also experienced a major increase in overall complexity. The resulting question is: What evolves faster: Financial market complexity, or the human ability to handle it?

According to Robert Weber,

> under conditions of complexity regulators may find themselves in situations where they lack the basic access to information on which to exercise their discretion in a rational manner, whether to pursue self-regarding profit or their public-regarding regulatory goals. Regulators' bounded rationality becomes the defining characteristic of the regulatory program. (ibid., 656f.)

Recent developments indicate that financial complexity increases at high speed, but data processing capabilities do not keep pace. What does this mean for the US policy responses to the crisis? The collection of financial data and information is

150 The problem is in fact not new, nor is the academic debate dealing with it. Richard B. Stewart discussed it under the headline *The Diagnosis of Imbalance in Representation* in 1975: Regulated interests, he argued, had several advantages in agency decision-making. One was based upon the fact that "the information upon which the agency must ultimately base its decision must come to a large degree from the groups being regulated. In theory", he went on, "the agency staff can gather information of its own, but agency staff resources are normally limited" (Stewart 1975, 1714). The crucial point is that even if they were not limited – and neither resources nor rationality were constricted – the idea of a fully informed regulator is not realistic. In addition, information is only the first step; what is required is knowledge of financial business.

certainly a step into the right direction, but two aspects have to be kept in mind here: *First, data and information are just a starting point. Second, supervisors and regulators are boundedly rational agents: Their data and information processing abilities are in fact limited.*[151]

5.4 Representatives vs. Experts: The Privatization of Legitimacy

Max Weber warned of the dominance of experts in general (Weber 1922). While private interest groups have played a central role in the policy arena for decades, and have therefore traditionally been a major subject in the political science literature (Olson 1965), they recently gain a lot of attention because of special relevance of such groups in global financial regulation. The underlying logic is quite simple, and arises from the developments described so far: The more complex the financial system gets, the more do policymakers and regulators rely on the increasingly specified and dispersed knowledge of financial experts. Hence, as Tsingou argues convincingly, financial firms assume "a privileged position as knowledge holders. Public authorities lag behind in terms of technical capabilities and expertise" (Tsingou 2007, 216). While financial supervision and regulation share with other policy fields their high degree of complexity – when it comes to climate policy, policymakers are also confronted with a global, complex system – differences arise from (a) *the behavioral aspects of finance*, including panics and herding behavior (Schwarcz 2009), and (b) the *near absence of well-organized private, not-for-profit interest groups*, the latter being highly relevant in the context of this book. While policymakers can, before they set the limit for carbon dioxide

151 A question that directly hinges on the bounded rationality of supervisors and regulators is whether the whole enterprise of informing and educating financial consumers is doomed to fail. Based on the discussion so far, we can already rule out that consumers are or are to become economic men in the classical understanding, meaning "(1) that all the alternatives of choice are 'given'; (2) that all the consequences attached to each alternative are known […]; (3) that the rational man has a complete utility-ordering (or cardinal function) for all possible sets of consequences" (March and Simon 1993 [1958], 159). This does however on no account mean that consumers' decision-making cannot be improved, and result in *satisfying choices* of mortgages or investments. The disclosure policy of the SEC is in fact based on the assumption that private decision makers can make rational choices: "Since the Depression, the […] rationale was that a disclosure regime […] would contribute to informed choices by market participants, furthering efficiency both in the paper economy and in the real economy. […] Managements would be deterred from behavior unsustainable in the light of day, and the monitoring and disciplining of managements by shareholders, as well as the market for corporate control, would be facilitated" (Hu 2012, 1606). Recent research questions the effectiveness of the SEC's disclosure regime. Beshears et al. examine the effect of recent changes in disclosure rules, introducing a simplified Summary Prospectus for mutual fund investors. They find no evidence that user-friendly information leads to better investment decisions (Beshears et al. 2009, 13). Experiments have also shown that bubbles can arise even though investors know that the assets are overrated (Weber 2012, 694, referring to experiments by physicist Doyne Farmer).

emissions in the EU, consult with renowned NGOs (e.g. Greenpeace) and well-established industry experts (e.g. the German Bundesverband der Deutschen Industrie e.V., or BDI), it is much less clear where to turn for expertise and opinion when it comes to capital ratios for banks or to the central clearing and netting of derivatives contracts. In finance, private, not-for-profit expertise is quite rare. This problem became explicit with the establishment of the Brussels based NGO Finance Watch. It was initiated when a group of members of the European Parliament published a *Call for a Finance Watch* in 2010, describing the need for a "counter-weight to the lobbying power of the financial industry" (Finance Watch 2010). The MEPs expressed their concerns that:

> the asymmetry between the power of this lobbying activity and the *lack of counter-expertise* poses a *danger to democracy* [...]. As European elected officials in charge of financial and banking regulations, we therefore call on civil society [...] to organize to create one (or more) non-governmental organization(s) capable of developing a counter-expertise on activities carried out on financial markets by the major operators [...] and to convey effectively this analysis to the media. As elected officials from different political families we may differ on the measures to be taken. But we are all together in wanting to create greater awareness in the public opinion on this risk for the quality of democracy. (ibid., emphasis added)[152]

Three years after its establishment, Finance Watch ran an office in Brussels; it had 41 member organizations, it had adopted an official mission, and it had published its first annual report for 2011 and 2012 (Finance Watch 2013). Yet it will take some time until Finance Watch has built up the expertise and gained the reputation of established NGOs in other policy fields.[153] Until then, and supposedly long after, the *dominance of private for-profit interests over private non-profit interests* and the lack of *counter-knowledge* (Willke 2007, 110) remains alarming, a point that will be central in chapter six of this book. That policymakers and regulators base their decisions on the data, information and expertise of private interest groups is, as we argue, neither new nor a threat to democracy: Officials rely on industry expertise in various policy fields, and besides, experts from industry groups *and* NGOs suffer from "cognitive biases" and imperfect information (Levitin 2011, 448). The crucial

152 Jones illustrates the importance of counter-expertise in his FCIC interview: "If you're going to challenge banks in the supervisory process in terms of say stress tests, you need to have an alternative model that you can bring to the table. If you just walk in to one of those discussions and are presented with a bunch of model results, you don't have a basis for, you can't just say 'oh I think this number is too low', you need to have an alternative model that you can pull out to say 'look, our model says, you know, comes up with a number of three to four times as big as your number', that's how you have an interesting dialogue, otherwise you're at a disadvantage" (Jones 2010).

153 To give just two examples from other policy fields: The Red Cross was founded in the early 20th century, and Greenpeace in the 1960s/1970s.

question is whether these officials have different experts to consult, if they can form their own opinion on a matter and decide independently which policy to pursue. If they do not, fears that "private interests may have severely undermined the authority of public actors to formulate financial and regulatory policies in line with the broader public interest" (Underhill and Zhang 2008, 553) are indeed justified.

Underhill and Zhang identify "a diffusion of power in favour of private actors" that roots in global financial integration (Underhill and Zhang 2008, 535), while Pozner et al. observe a *privatization of legitimacy* specifically in financial regulation (Pozner, Stimmler, and Hirsch 2010, 197). Private experts do not derive their legitimacy from any formal process (election or training), but exclusively from the knowledge they possess (*Herrschaftswissen*). In line with Finance Watch, Willke and Willke warn that groups who derive their legitimacy from their expertise threaten to undermine legitimacy through democratic processes (Willke and Willke 2012, 136). As already indicated, financial institutions have strong incentives not only to exploit, but to further increase financial market complexity (Stiglitz 2009b, 11). One could argue that being faster and better informed than regulators was more a strategy than a side effect during the years leading up to the crisis. Mayntz identifies complexity and speed as two major strategies for financial firms to circumvent regulation.[154] She argues that, based on their experience of regulators relying on the expertise of regulatees, market participants deliberately exploit information asymmetries. Opponents of financial reform are thus able to invoke horror scenarios about the future of banking and the wider economy, caused by regulation (Mayntz 2010b, 9f.). A recent study by the Institute of International Finance on the *Cumulative Impact in the Global Economy of Changes in the Financial Regulatory Framework* estimated that the suggested financial reforms might lead to a 3.2 percent decrease of GDP over five years for the US, the EMU, Japan, the UK and Switzerland (Institute of International Finance 2011). As the report highlights, that "would imply a combined 7.5 million jobs foregone in those countries alone" (ibid, introduction). Who would want to impose new regulation that hinders economic recovery?[155]

---

154 Schwarcz makes the opposite argument that "Complexity is not an end in itself but usually is a by-product of salutary goals such as seeking to transfer risk to parties better positioned to hold the risk and reducing the cost of funding businesses" (Schwarcz 2009, 239).

155 Admati and Hellwig identify the assertion that "[e]very dollar of capital is one less dollar working in the economy" (Norris 2010, quoting a member of the lobbyist group Financial Serives Roundtabl, see also Admati and Hellwig 2013) as an example for a widely discussed yet fundamentally flawed argument. It relates to the debate about the side effects of higher capital standards for banks: Would they directly reduce credits for consumers and businesses as it is implied in the short quote, or are the side-effects of higher capital standards rather small? The problem, now, is the common view that to regulate, policymakers "need information on how it is going to affect the entities that you regulate – so where do you get that? […] the question is: does the agency have the intelligence, the data at needs to second-guess that" (Barkow 2013).

5.5 Keeping Pace with the Market, or: Can the OFR Enlighten Regulators?

Looking back, we see that the problem of inadequate financial data and information is not new. Tufano argues that until the early twentieth century, companies disclosed only very little credible information until market forces, as well as governmental action, increased the overall quantity and quality of financial information (Tufano 2004, 13). Confronted with a truly complex financial system, regulators and policymakers face new problems posed by non-knowledge and uncertainty. As the financial crisis triggered new disclosure requirements for financial firms, it can be concluded that market complexity and information-gathering efforts evolve in tandem; they however cannot be increased endlessly. Even with the recent measures in place, financial firms remain black boxes for regulators, consumers and to a certain degree also for the management of these firms. Subsuming the current chapter, we discuss on the following pages the constraints of financial data and information collection, and then proceed to the limitations of knowledge-based regulation to ultimately ask whether the OFR can enlighten US regulators.

Data and Information Collection Efforts, and their Limits

In the context of data and information collection, several questions were raised during this chapter: (1) whether regulators have unlimited data and information processing capabilities (*the rational regulator*), (2) given that adequate processing capabilities exist, whether regulators and policymakers actually take these data and information into account when making decisions, and (3) whether financial data and information are in fact sufficient for financial regulation (*sufficiency argument*), or do they present just the starting point.

With regard to the ideal of the rational regulator, Simon's work on bounded rationality indicates that the computational capabilities of supervisors and regulators (as well as of consumers and financial institutions) are in fact quite limited. Even though complexity and processing skills evolve in tandem, recent developments and events in financial markets bear evidence that products, organizations, and the system itself have become overly complex, at least from the perspective of regulators and supervisors. While many theories find their way into policies – the EMH provides an example here – Simon's concept of bounded rationality surprisingly did not play a role in the debate about policy responses to systemic risk. Weber, whose work will be discussed in greater detail in the following chapter, provides an (academic) exception here: Looking at data and information based regulation, he argues that the bounded rationality of financial regulators "becomes the defining characteristic of the regulatory program" (Weber 2012, 656).

In view of *bounded rationality*, *herd behavior* and *irrational exuberance* on the one hand and highly complex products on the other, the CFPB's belief that "the informed consumer is the first line of defense" (Consumer Financial Protection Bureau 2014) appears politically legitimate, but quite naïve.[156] This brings us to the second question of whether financial data and information are actually taken into account by policymakers and regulators. The recent crisis showed that data and information were either not available or not accessible. Against this background, both regulators and financial institutions started to strengthen their data and information bases. Yet, a future crisis might well reveal that data were available *and* accessible, but simply not taken into account. Some FCIC interviews do indeed point into that direction (see for example Tett 2010). Ignorance towards relevant data and information might be rooted in a lack of expertise – to extract information, one needs the respective knowledge – but it could also be an issue of IT, of time or staff constraints, or ultimately of too much data (*data overload*), a problem that remains very much underestimated to this day.[157] The case of Brooksley Born gives a hint into yet another direction, and in his testimony before the House Financial Services Committee, Levitin criticized regulators' and policymakers' ignorance towards certain information:

> They don't want to see if there is a problem, because they are too scared that if there is a problem, they are going to have to do something about it. And that is rather disturbing, but basically this is, you know, *let's stick our head in the sand and hope that there isn't a problem.* Because the prime directive coming out of Treasury is: protect the banks. Don't let anything happen that prevents the banks from recognizing their losses over retained earnings over the next decade. (Levitin 2010b)

Again, a political rationale comes into play. Data and information alone obviously do not provide answers to the pressing questions in financial policymaking: The vision of data and information based policymaking hits its limits where financial paradigms and politics come into play. This brings us back to our definition of systemic risk in chapter two, which introduced a *political logic to the merely economic concept of systemic risk.* When we look at the Lehman case, we see that

156 In the world as it is it is highly unlikely that a majority of consumers can be informed to a degree that leads to optimal, economic decision-making. We do not want to imply that policymakers and regulators should not aim at financial education and literacy: These are very important tasks, but as already argued, we ought to be aware of their limitations. The CFPB might in fact be able to enlighten those consumers who are willing to make well-informed choices, and it can also police and reduce fraud, but it will not be able to turn US Americans into *rational consumers.*

157 Barry Zubrow from JPMorgan Chase is one of the view commenters who mentions the risks resulting from data overload. In his FCIC interview, he warns of the "enormous flow of information. And in that flow of information it's very important,[...] that you can overwhelm any organization with too much data and not enough information"; according to his report, JPMorgan is "constantly trying to think about how we make sure that the reports we are generating and looking at [...] are a better reflection of what is really happening in the business than just something, lots of data" (Zubrow 2010).

the decision not to save the investment bank ultimately followed a political logic – while windows of opportunity opened up for some financial institutions, they did not open up for others. Would a similar decision be "rationalized" by additional information? Data and information might support a governmental decision to rescue a financial institution, given that systemic relevance could be proven, but they might as well be outweighed by moral or political arguments. Luhmann argues that political decision-making depends on time, "on favourable moments [...] with the risk of reacting too early or too late" (Luhmann 2008, 173). The *time dependency* in crises naturally limits the ability of the government to decide rationally.

Finally, we get to the third question of whether data and information are sufficient for financial regulation. Based on our analysis so far, the answer is clearly no. We agree with other non-optimistic observers, such as Acharya and Gensler, that data and information gathering efforts are a first and important step, while regulators either have to ultimately build up their own, independent knowledge or support private, non-profit groups as Finance Watch and rely on their expertise and advice instead. The data and information collection efforts of the OFR might in fact create new problems, including a *false sense of security* at the side of policymakers and regulators (and shareholders as well – stress tested banks must not be controlled as much as non-tested banks by their boards and shareholders), accompanied by *ignorance towards problems related to non-knowledge and uncertainty*.

Pace-Keepers vs. Pace-Reducers: Knowledge-Based Regulation and its Limitations

Throughout this chapter, we argued that information asymmetries constrain regulators' ability to observe the behavior of regulatees, while knowledge asymmetries limit regulators' ability to judge and intervene. As a result of knowledge asymmetries, specialists gain influence simply because of what they know and their influence gains legitimacy based on their highly specialized expertise. In the absence of private, non-profit experts in the area of finance, industry experts lack a significant counter-balance. Therefore, financial institutions have strong incentives and good opportunities to exploit knowledge asymmetries, undermining democratic policymaking and ultimately posing a threat to democracy (Finance Watch 2010). But what should regulators do to counteract the described developments?

Again, we can distinguish between two basic schools of thought (Kwak 2012b). Proponents of the first school of thought argue that regulators should try to keep pace with the financial system; we therefore want to label it the *pace-keeping school*. From this point of view, the responsible agencies are just too underfunded and incentives to work in the public sector are just too small, but generally, regulators should try to keep up with market developments and innovations. The second, contrasting school of thought asserts that, instead of adjusting the regulatory bodies and rules to the highly complex system, one should adjust the system to the (limited) possibilities, or rationality, of the regulators. What is needed, they argue, is a reduction of overall system complexity. We therefore want to name this group the *pace-reducing school*. Former CEO of Citigroup Sandy Weill, in his interview with the FCIC, illustrates how regulators might keep up with their regulatees:

> I think the Federal Reserve is a very good regulator of markets. But it is very hard to be a perfect regulator of markets when they only have about 30 percent of the information. And I think now, with the investment banks becoming banks and being regulated by the Fed, and all of the hedge funds and private equity funds saying that they would accept more regulation, and all of their activities are cleared by people that are regulated to an extent by the Federal Reserve, you know, I think we will be able to have a better system. Could the regulators have done better? I think the answer is yes. But I think they were terribly handicapped by a lack of information. And by the direction that people wanted to go at that point in time. (Weill 2010)

Andrew Haldane is a prominent opponent of the pace-keeping school. He argues that in order to enable regulators to effectively govern and supervise the system, a reduction of its complexity might be needed; what should be avoided in any case is counteracting financial complexity with regulatory complexity:

> Modern finance is complex, perhaps too complex. Regulation of modern finance is complex, almost certainly too complex. That configuration spells trouble. As you do not fight fire with fire, you do not fight complexity with complexity. Because complexity generates uncertainty, not risk, it requires a regulatory response grounded in simplicity, not complexity. (Haldane and Madouros 2012, 19)

Looking at current financial regulation, Dodd-Frank is not only highly complex, but also inherits elements of both schools. On the one hand, there is the establishment of the OFR with its mandate for data collection and the build-up of expertise, as well as the introduction of stress tests and living wills. On the other hand, the yet to be implemented Volcker rule aims at separating proprietary trading from classic banking, and the untangling (or, as the Europeans say, ringfencing) of these two intertwined business areas clearly constitutes a reduction of bank complexity.

At the beginning of this chapter, we introduced the term *knowledge-based regulation*. Two aspects are important here. We termed the first the *necessity argument*, based on the question of whether policymaking, supervision and regulation require detailed, technical knowledge of the regulated industry, business or product (Landis 1947 [1938]). The Call for a Finance Watch, published by policymakers, indicates that this is the case. The second aspect relates to the design of such regulations – as we will discuss in greater detail in chapter seven, the degree of expertise needed for regulation depends on the type of regulation employed.[158] We want to leave both aside for the moment and turn to the limitations of knowledge-based regulation. Hayek made the important argument that

> If man is not to do more harm than good in his efforts to improve the social order, he will have to learn that in this, as in all other fields where essential complexity of an organized kind prevails, he *cannot acquire the full knowledge which would make mastery of the events possible*. He will therefore have to use what knowledge he can achieve, not to shape the results as the craftsman shapes his handiwork, but rather to cultivate a growth by providing the appropriate environment, in the manner in which the gardener does this for his plants (Hayek 1974, emphasis added).

This implies for financial regulators that they have to realize that, as Willke et al. argue, "it is impossible to control or direct the financial system in its entirety. The regimes, models, instruments and principles of regulation, therefore, must be chosen very carefully in view of vast areas of uncertainty, including *unknown unknowns*" (Willke, Becker, and Rostásy 2013, 57). Our analysis to this point indicates that financial regulators are confronted with a *basic paradox*: Confronted with an increasingly complex financial system, their knowledge is necessarily limited. Yet, given the fact that complexity has become an industry strategy to circumvent regulation, they must strive to address dark and unknown areas of the market. The OFR, as a single supervisory body required solely to enhance data, information and knowledge, is in the right position to fulfill such a task. Whether the problems described here are on the Office's agenda is highly unlikely. The developments so far suggest that the OFR might get lost in microprudential data collection.

A Short Note on the Idea of the Learning Regulator

Against the background of the financial crisis of 2007ff., some observers formulate their vision of a *flexible regulatory system* (Stiglitz 2010, 50) that quickly adapts to a changing market environment and can accordingly not be tricked by new products and services, inhabited by *learning regulators* (Ford 2013; Schneiberg and Bartley

158 Put simply, and following the basic idea of bureaucrats brought forward by Max Weber, regulation sets the frame without diving too deeply into the technical details. One of our interview partners used the metaphor of football referees to make this argument clear: In football, simple ground rules are needed. To call a game, a referee does not have to be a very experienced football player – he only has to know the rules, and to follow the game closely. As convincing as it is at first sight, this metaphor has obvious limitations: First of all, *financial regulation exceeds supervision*, as it includes rulemaking. Secondly, the referee is in a very special position, being in the middle of the game and shadowing the players, supported by his linesmen. While the possibilities of game supervision become more elaborate over the years, for example through the use of goal line technology, the game itself basically stays the same.

2010) that are able to see both micro- and macroprudential problems, that understand the risks resulting from interconnectedness and contagion, that are intelligent in Willke's understanding (Willke 2007), and that have an eye on the system as such (Senge 1996). They are needed vis-à-vis a financial sector that is "organized for continual innovation and creative destruction", and where "it is not entirely clear what the right rules or measures are, whether these will hold over time, and how future innovation might exploit their loopholes" (Schneiberg and Bartley 2010, 293). The de Larosière report even demanded that regulators should analyze and make public their failures, "so that lessons can be learnt and future supervisory behaviour improved" (High Level Group on Financial Supervision in the EU 2009, 40), and according to Levitt and March, learning organizations do indeed translate "inferences from history into routines that guide behavior" (Levitt and March 1988, 319). However, the fact that future crises differ from past crises makes it difficult to learn from the recent financial breakdown (Black 2012), and when asked about lessons learned from the crisis, several FCIC interviewees could not even give an answer. At the beginning of this chapter, we emphasized the fact that knowledge cannot be as easily transferred as data and information. Hence it appears that regulators must either be or become learning organizations. The resulting challenge is to collect data and information, but to not get lost in them; and to build one's own, independent knowledge, but keeping one's own non-knowledge in mind. And last but not least, supporting the private not-for-profit build up of expertise is highly important. As we discuss at-length in the following chapter, experts can easily capture regulators in complex policy areas.

6 Knowledge Capture: A Theoretic Framework

When the crisis hit in 2008, and when it became clear that supervision and regulation had their part in it, many observers identified *regulatory capture* as the underlying cause. Such capture is said to occur when an "agency is more responsive to the desires of an entity that it is supposed to be regulating than it is to the general public" (Financial Crisis Inquiry Commission 2011, xviii). The argument is as follows: Such as a ship that is captured by pirates, Congress, courts and financial regulators were captured by special interest groups (in this case: the financial industry), and because the culture and rules on deck served special, short-term interests, the crew maneuvered the financial system right into a global financial crisis. One might object that this crisis narrative is overly simplistic, and for good reasons. However, as we will show in section 6.2, renowned experts argue that capture was and remains a major reason for inefficient financial regulation (see for example A. Baker 2010b; Kwak 2013). They assume that regulatory capture led to lax financial supervision and regulation, both domestically and internationally. Looking back at decades of (bi-partisan) neo-liberal policymaking and regulation in the US, major decisions – e.g. to repeal the Glass-Steagall Act in 1999 – indeed seemed to favor industry interests over public welfare. Have policymakers and financial regulators been captured by financial institutions?

The aim of influencing politics is certainly as old as politics itself. The argument that special interests or factions shape US policymaking can be traced back to James Madison's Federalist Paper No. 10, and has been discussed ever since (Novak 2013; see Schlozman and Tierney 1986, supra note 6, ch. 1, for an overview of special interest literature). As we will see in section 6.1, it evolved into a major economics research strand in the 1970s, when George Stigler published his "Theory of Economic Regulation" (Stigler 1971) and set off a wave of publications (see for example Becker 1983; Laffont and Tirole 1991; Peltzman 1976). His contribution reflected a basic mistrust towards economic regulation as it was embraced by left and right wing academics and policymakers at the time (Etzioni 2009; Novak 2013). That the government might not be the solution to societal and economic problems, but instead be the problem itself, has become common parlance ever since.[159]

159 In his first inaugural address, Ronald Reagan famously stated that "government is not the solution to our problem, government is the problem" (Reagan 1981). That same year, Quirk described in his book

Regulation was perceived as being too costly in two respects: It imposed costs on taxpayers because regulations had to be written and enforced; and it imposed compliance costs on the regulated industries. Regulatory capture was a third point of critique: In the 1970s, Jaffe described how US agencies had become "the whipping boy of the American governmental establishment for the last 20 years" for being "the 'captive' of the industries which they are charged with regulating" (Jaffe 1970, 565). Current suspicions of regulatory capture are accordingly far from new. Yet, the financial crisis of 2007ff. shed new light on regulatory capture, and the role and relevance of special interests in policymaking and regulation has re-entered the public agenda. Simon Johnson, former chief economist at the IMF, has become a major advocate of the capture critique:

> In the past twenty years, it has turned around. It is all about capture. It is all about ideas. It is coming from Wall Street, Wall Street influencing the New York Fed, unduly having this excessive power in the Federal Reserve system. (Johnson 2013)

As we will see throughout this chapter, Capture Theory has again become a multifaceted and lively research strand. In 1991, Laffont and Tirole distinguished between six types of capture according to the means of the capturing interest group, including capture by (1) monetary bribes, (2) future job prospects for public servants in the private sector (*the so called revolving door*), (3) personal relationships in general, (4) public pressure through public critique, (5) monetary contributions to officials and (6) the activation by interest groups of bigger "grass roots" interest groups with overlapping interests (Laffont and Tirole 1991, 1090f.; see also Landis 1960, ch.1/D).[160] Since the onset of the financial crisis of 2007ff., new concepts of capture have evolved, including *self capture* (Masciandaroa, Nietob, and Quintync 2011), *methodological/theoretical* and *political/doctrinal /policy* capture (Kennedy 2001), as well as types of *cognitive or psychological capture* as described by Barth et al. (Barth, Caprio, and Levine 2012) and by Baker (A. Baker 2010b). In chapter six, focusing on *information capture* (Wagner 2010) and *complexity capture* (Weber 2012), we provide an overview of *current capture diagnoses* (section 6.2) and *recent capture frameworks* (section 6.3) against the

on regulatory capture "an unusual, if not unprecedented, antiregulatory mood" (Quirk 1981, x). Reagan went on: "From time to time, we have been tempted to believe that society has become too complex to be managed by self-rule, that government by an elite group is superior to government for, by, and of the people. But if no one among us is capable of governing himself, then who among us has the capacity to govern someone else?" (Reagan 1981). In light of the financial crisis, and of later incidents such as the "London Whale" scandal, this is a very remarkable statement, evoking the question: Are global complex financial institutions capable of governing themselves?

160 Some of them apply to the legislative branch, and others to the executive branch. Monetary contributions, for example, are common in the form of campaign contributions but are illegal when given to public servants. Future job prospects are mainly discussed in the context of federal agencies.

background of *classic Capture Theory*, including Stigler's *Theory of Economic Regulation* (section 6.1).

While we will only have a short look on the majority of these approaches, information and complexity capture will be discussed at-length: They build the basis for what we want to term *knowledge capture* – a phenomenon that can be traced back to (1) an increasingly complex, global financial system, (2) the data, information and knowledge asymmetries in financial regulation as described in chapter five, (3) the absence of private, not-for-profit expertise in the financial sector, (4) the bounded rationality of financial regulators, and (5) the process of regulation as such (section 6.4). Again, we draw on literature from several research strands: *Capture Theory* provides the theoretical frame for chapter six. As it is "undoubtedly the source of policy failure most discussed in the academic literature" (Quirk and Nesmith 2005, 298), the number of possibly relevant publications in the field is vast. We focus on the roots of Capture Theory in economics literature – mainly on Stigler's and the Chicago School's contributions – and then look at more recent capture approaches. While legal scholars and political scientists are behind some of the works, half of these contributions stem from economists. For numbers on contacts between regulatory agencies on the one hand, and interest groups on the other, we rely on central US *interest group literature*. As Furlong reports, the majority of studies examines attempts to influence Congress (Furlong 2005, 295). Yet we are able to find ample evidence supporting our hypotheses on executive branch lobbying. Contributions in the field of *Public Service Motivation* (PSM), juxtaposed with Simon's concept of bounded rationality, help us to provide a realistic picture of the public servant. Last but not least, we rely on our interview analysis and a selection of media articles dealing with the financial crisis.

6.1 Introduction to the Theory of Economic Regulation

Stigler's *Theory of Economic Regulation* of 1971 discusses the fundamental question *why* governments intervene in markets by regulating industries. At the time, two major approaches dominated the debate (Levine and Forrence 1990; Posner 1971; Noll 1985): *Public Interest Theory* argues that governments, acting in the interest of society and pursuing public welfare or the public good, correct inadequate market practices or "failures in industrial adjustment" (Pigou 1924, 298). From a Public Interest viewpoint, regulation is not only costless, but simply necessary to correct market failure. Economic regulation hence takes place because the public demands it (Posner 1974), e.g. in the area of anti-monopolistic policies or environmental legislation. The second argument evolved in the broader context of

Public Choice Theory.[161] It stood in the tradition of political scientists such as Bentley (1967 [1908]) and Truman (1971 [1951], especially ch. XI) who examined the role of pressure or interest groups in US policymaking, and it was then picked up by economist George Stigler.[162] Stigler approached regulation as a *merely economic phenomenon* that could be described in terms of *supply and demand*: Industries demand and seize regulation because they profit from it (Owen and Braeutigam 1978, 2), and the state provides regulation because industries acquire it (Stigler 1971, 3).[163] What became known as *Capture Theory* argues in a somewhat Marxist tradition that economic regulation ultimately serves industry interests and assumes that policymakers and regulators are industry advocates (Posner 1974).[164] In the Theory of Economic Regulation, political entities are "rationally employed" by special interest groups (Laffont and Tirole 1993, 503).

Several points are central to Stigler's approach. First, the state is perceived as "a potential resource or threat to every industry in the society" because it "can and does selectively help or hurt a vast number of industries" (Stigler 1971, 3), e.g. by establishing entry barriers for new market participants. From the viewpoint of classic Capture Theory, *regulation means redistribution*: Some industries receive subsidies, while taxes and tariffs are imposed on others. Second, to get favorable regulation, *industry groups provide policymakers with what they desire* – in the context of policymakers, this means "votes and resources", either directly as campaign contributions or related services, or indirectly, e.g. by employing party workers (ibid., 12). Later contributions to Capture Theory examined other factors,

161 Capture Theory raises the basic question of what to prefer: A captured agency regulating the economy, or an unregulated industry with a tendency to monopolize and misallocate? Even advocates of economic regulation admit that "authorities are liable alike to ignorance, to sectional pressure and to personal corruption by private interest" (Pigou 1924, 301), and drawing on Herbert Simon, we basically took the same stand: Even incorruptible regulators are boundedly rational agents. What distinguishes proponents of classic Capture Theory from those of Public Interest Theories is the belief that government imperfections might be even greater than those of the market, opting "not to regulate economic monopolies and to suffer their bad effects, rather than to regulate them and suffer the effects of political imprfections [sic!]" (Becker 1958, 109).

162 Kamieniecki, in his book on *Corporate America and Environmental Policy*, provides a detailed and recent overview over interest group literature in the US (Kamieniecki 2006, ch. 2).

163 Against the background of Public Interest Theory, Owen and Braeutigam distinguish between two types of capture theory: "In the first, regulatory agencies are established for 'public interest' purposes, but subsequently they become the tools of the industry they regulate. [...] The other version of the theory is that regulatory agencies are in fact created to serve the interests of the industry they regulate" (Owen and Braeutigam 1978, 11).

164 Pigou himself was not blind to the idea of capture. Instead, he described it broadly in his chapter on government intervention, arguing that one "cannot expect that any State authority will attain, or will even whole-heartedly seek, that ideal. Such authorities are liable alike to ignorance, to sectional pressure and to personal corruption by private interest. [...] companies, particularly when there is continuing regulation, may employ corruption, not only in the getting of their franchise, but also in the execution of it" (Pigou 1924, 301).

especially with regard to executive capture, such as the role of future job prospects for public servants and of future budget increases for agencies (Quirk 1981).[165] As policymakers are assumed to maximize their campaign contributions, and as public officials are assumed to enhance their private gains, each of them "is a potential opportunity for some form of self-interest arrayed against the common interest" (Pigou 1924, 302, quoting from a Report to the National Civic Federation; see exemplary Downs 1957). Following that same logic, it is most rational for interest groups to influence policymakers and regulators to implement interest group-friendly rules and regulations. Third, in neo-liberal tradition, Capture Theory assumes that *both market participants and regulators are rational utility maximizers* in the fashion of homo economicus – which is why regulators are open to capture attempts in the first place. Fourth, as Weber emphasizes, Capture Theory implicitly "assumes that *regulators understand the markets they regulate*" (Weber 2012, 657, emphasis added) – because if they did not, they could not withhold strategic information from their principal, Congress, and effectively pursue their own interests. Fifth, regulatees aim at *more regulation instead of deregulation*; traditional capture accordingly has to be distinguished from more recent capture diagnoses of corrosive capture (Carpenter 2013a), where industry groups demand less or weaker regulation. And last but not least, proponents of classic Capture Theory identify a *hierarchical order of influence*: Organized interests are in a better position to influence regulation than the unorganized, general public and compared to industry interest groups, non-industry interest groups are in a weak position to influence legislation and regulation because they are constrained by their limited resources, meaning limited budget, personnel and information.

Theoretical and Empirical Shortcomings of Classic Capture Theory

Capture Theory is based on four main premises: That interest groups *attempt to influence* policymaking and regulation; that policymakers and public servants are self-interested, *rational utility maximizers*; that interest groups, especially industry interest groups, not only overcome the collective action problem (Olson 1965), but have *something to offer* that helps or enables policymakers and public servants to meet their needs; and that these policymakers and public servants *reward interest groups* for what they offer with interest group-friendly policymaking and regulation. We briefly discuss each premise, before we move on to current capture diagnoses.[166] With regard to the first premise, sufficient evidence can be found that interest groups do seek influence (see for example Baumgartner and Leech 2001). This quickly brings us to the second premise. From a theoretical viewpoint, the

165 Arthur Levitt, former chairman of the SEC, does indeed describe how future budget constraints were used as a threat to influence SEC rulemaking (Levitt 2010).

166 For a more detailed discussion we refer to Croley who, in his extensive and explicitly cynical analysis, decomposes the theoretical underpinnings of Capture Theory (Croley 2008).

assumption that a sufficiently large fraction of policymakers and public servants trades regulation for personal gain seems to be a strong oversimplification. It is contested empirically by research in the field of Public Service Motivation (PSM). Here, we can find evidence that public servants "are a mix of motives, exhibiting combinations of values over a lifetime and focusing on different motives at various points in their careers" (Perry and Wise 1990, 369). More specifically, public service is characterized to a notable degree by a specific public service ethic, including intrinsic motivational factors such as altruism and self-sacrifice (Perry, Hondeghem, and Wise 2010). While some policymakers and regulators are certainly self-interested, it would be wrong to state that the public service is per se corruptible. Yet, *classic Capture Theory fails to explain how capture might occur in the absence of self-interested public officials*. The third premise, that industry groups have something to offer that helps or enables policymakers and public servants to meet their needs, implies that (a) there is something to offer to policymakers and regulators, and (b) that industry interest groups can make better offers than public interest groups. Future job prospects, which are usually discussed under the notion of the *revolving door* between private and public sector, are a classic example here. However, while industry interest groups do in fact dominate in Washington, other interests are also represented (Furlong 2005; Coglianese 1994). Jaffe argues convincingly that

> One of the defects of the capture theory is the premise that the object of regulation is always a more or less gigantic corporate combination to whose pressure and power the agency is predominately subject. This of course is a simplified derivative of the classic Marxian analysis. [...] each agency operates within a complex of powers which is peculiar to that agency, and that even for any single agency there is rarely a single interest which can dominate. (Jaffe 1970, 567f.)

Especially with regard to policymaking (as distinguished from regulation), Capture Theory does not reflect the complexity of decision-making: Decisions are usually the outcome of a long process of bargaining and logrolling, they are made by many, and influenced by an even greater number of actors. NGOs play a minor, yet central role. With regard to the fourth premise that policymakers and regulators reward industry groups with industry-friendly policies and regulations, the evidence is mixed. Here, Capture Theory is often criticized for its weak empirical basis. As Landis put it more than 50 years ago, the "tendency toward industry orientation is subtle and difficult to deal with" (Landis 1960, 51). Yet, the number of general studies on Capture is endless; some found evidence for and some found evidence against a pro-industry bias in the US executive and legislative branches (see Yackee and Yackee 2006, providing not only a literature overview but also a study finding strong evidence for such a bias). Capture Theory goes in line with Olson's argument that "the organized and active interest of small groups tend to triumph over the unorganized and unprotected interests of larger groups" (Olson 1965, 144). Numerous studies are able to show the dominance of industry interest groups over public interest groups in Washington D.C., at least in quantitative terms: Baumgartner and Leech analyzed 19,000 reports filed in 1996 under the Lobbying Disclosure Act of 1995. They are able to show that industry interest groups "are by far the best endowed and the most active" groups in the US (Baumgartner and Leech 2001, 1196; see also Schlozman and Tierney 1986, 70 and Kamieniecki 2006, 26f. for an overview of studies examining the degree of industry and private interest influence). Furlong (2005) finds ample evidence that business groups and trade associations dominate executive branch lobbying, while public interest groups focus on legislative branch lobbying. Schlozman and Burch (2005) demonstrate that organized and represented interests are foremost economic interests. Taken together, these studies show that (1) the number of business lobbyists exceeds the number of public interest lobbyists by far, (2) business lobbyists participate more often in filing rulemaking comments than do public interest groups, and (3) they have far more informal contacts with regulators (Shapiro 2012, 117).

Recent research on the revolving door principle shows that the situation is less clear than expected: While interest groups may try to get access to the legislative via campaign contributions, this is neither legal nor possible in the context of regulatory agencies. Future job prospects of public servants are commonly seen as a sort of indirect contribution to gain access. In their study on revolving door effects in the SEC, deHaan et al. investigate whether there is a correlation between the efficiency and independence of the Commission's enforcement actions, and the future job options of its employees. The authors develop a *human capital hypothesis* and a *rent-seeking hypothesis*. The first assumes that public servants are hired by private sector organizations because of their expertise. In view of future job prospects, they will therefore try to enhance and demonstrate their capabilities by enforcing regulation aggressively. The second hypothesis assumes that public servants, aiming at highly paid jobs in the future, will act pro-industry during their tenure. deHaan and his colleagues found out that, in the period of 1990 to 2007, 31 percent of the SEC's lawyers quit their jobs and joined private law firms (deHaan et al. 2012, 3)3. They are able to show that, contrary to what is commonly expected, there is no evidence that these SEC lawyers enforce regulation less aggressively then their colleagues. Thirty years earlier, Quirk had already found evidence that vigorous enforcement actions by public servants are generally rewarded with better job opportunities in the future (Quirk 1981, 149).[167]

167 The question is in fact why industries should entice industry-friendly public servants, as they best serve the industry when working at the agency.

Many empirical studies of capture are problematic: Capture Theory distinguishes between organized, pro-industry interests on the one hand and the public interest on the other, but this distinction is vague insofar as it remains unclear what *the social welfare* or *the public interest* is (Schlozman and Tierney 1986, supra note 17, ch. 2; Downs 1957). While public interest remains a vague concept, Quirk was able to show that only a minority of public servants has pro-industry attitudes. He examined whether (a) high-rank agency officials are appointed according to their pro-industry attitude, (b) agencies act industry-friendly to increase their budget in the long term, and whether (c) agency officials, having future job prospects in mind, have a pro-industry tendency; he finds no or only weak evidence supporting any of these hypotheses (Quirk 1981). Yet, evaluating regulation against the public interest, and comparing it to a hypothetical public interest achieved by other regulation remains a difficult task. Besides, while many studies examine if regulators have a pro-industry bias, the process of regulation itself remains a black box; while it is quite common to look at the motivations of public servants, "capture theories do not explicitly consider the relationships among actors in the governmental process nor the mechanisms by which the acts of regulators are made to conform to the desires of organized subgroups" (Levine and Forrence 1990, 170). What is missing is "a better understanding of what actually occurs in this relationship" (Furlong 2005, 293).

6.2 Capture Diagnoses in the Recent Financial Crisis

Kennedy warns rightly that "too often claims of 'capture' are simply ways of disagreeing with the policies which have been made" (Kennedy 2001, 747). Besides, explaining financial crises with regulatory capture bears the risk of oversimplification, leaving aside the deeper political forces that shape financial policies (Interview with Philip Wallach, December 05 2012, Washington; see also Schlozman and Tierney 1986, 346). Capture has become a buzzword, and it actually is an easy-to-make accusation. Yet, renowned academics and financial experts have identified capture as a major reason for the financial crisis of 2007ff. To name just a few, Etzioni finds "[a]mple evidence […] that regulatory capture is indeed widespread and takes a variety of forms" (Etzioni 2009, 319; see also Helleiner and Porter 2009); Kwak and Johnson do not get tired warning of financial capture in the US (see for example Johnson 2012; Kwak 2012a); and Admati and Hellwig observe capture in many regulated industry sectors, but argue that "it is particularly striking in banking and finance" (Admati and Hellwig 2013, 194). Addressing capture has accordingly been identified as a central task on the post-crisis, macroprudential reform agenda:

> To implement effective macroprudential regulation, the question of possible 'capture' of the regulatory process by private actors needs to be addressed more squarely. Macroprudential regulation requires regulators to take a strong stance against market trends [...]. If regulators' relationships with private market actors are too cosy, this role cannot be performed well. (Helleiner 2010a, 16)

Many US citizens believe that their policymakers and regulators are captured or corrupted by Wall Street. Krawiec has analyzed the comment letters on Volcker Rule implementation sent to the FSOC; the following comment stands exemplary for many:

> We understand the relationship between the money big business gives elected officials and the laws that are written and we are sick and tired of laws being written by and for big business at the expense of human beings. (Rachel Kaplan, as quoted by Krawiec 2013, 25)

The notion of the "Wall Street-Treasury complex" dates back to the 1990s, and describes a powerful network in Washington of "like-minded luminaries among the powerful institutions" (Bhagwati 1998, 11); consisting of banks as well as of domestic and international regulatory bodies, it is "unable to look much beyond the interest of Wall Street" (ibid., 12). Close ties between Wall Street firms and regulators across the globe, but especially between Goldman Sachs and the U.S. Treasury, have gained lots of attention during the crisis. A "flow of Goldman Sachs officers into high levels of government" (McDonnell 2012, 122) has evoked terms like "Government Sachs" (see for example Creswell and White 2008; Kavoussi 2012) and "the Goldman Sachs connection" (Blackden 2012); they account for the fact that important public servants – such as Hank Paulson, Neel Kashkari and Robert K. Steel – worked for Goldman Sachs before they moved into positions at Treasury.

It is common sense that, by moving back and forth from the public to the private sector, people on both sides gain valuable expertise for their jobs. Our definition of knowledge, being rooted in communities of practice and closely tied to working experience, supports this argument. According to a study from 1986, nearly 90 percent of all Washington-based interest groups employed someone who had previously worked for the federal government (Schlozman and Tierney 1986, 269). At the same time, it is clear that this same expertise enables the private sector organizations to increase their influence, as they do not only know how things in the regulatory agencies work, but they also know the "right people" inside these agencies, as well as the relevant rules and regulations. While public sector expertise in private sector organizations is largely perceived by the public as a negative and distorting phenomenon, private sector expertise in the public sector is widely seen as helpful, if not necessary for effective regulation. From 2007 on, the crisis has clearly fuelled the debate about the role of capture, especially in the United States. Interestingly, while the capture argument plays a major role in the debate about the causes of the US crisis, it is far less important in Europe. One reason might lie in the traditionally high degree of permeability between the private and the public sector in the US.[168] As Kwak puts it, the normalcy of changing sides and the numbers of people passing through the revolving door "imply that the regulators and the representatives of financial institutions are really the same people" (Kwak 2013, 83; see also Barkow 2013). McDonell argues that the revolving door policy "places many industry insiders at the heart of agency decision-making" and "that this revolving door goes a long way towards explaining the excessive deregulation which set the stage for the financial crisis" (McDonnell 2012, 117). This raises the question of why financial regulation in particular should be especially prone to regulatory capture.

6.3 New Perspectives on Regulation: Information and Complexity Capture

Many observers describe the US political system as being strongly captured, or even "crudely corrupt" (Kay 2012). The importance of campaign contributions for re-election, combined with a culture of revolving doors and a strong presence of interest groups on Capitol Hill, do indeed create a fertile ground for such assumptions. In comparison, EU policymaking is said to be much more technical and independent from special interests. Even so, such interests appear to find their way into European politics, too. Here, critics identify a special type of capture:

> The European position is better described as *intellectual capture*. Regulators come to see the industry through the eyes of market participants rather than the end users they exist to serve, because market participants are the only source of the *detailed information and expertise* this type of regulation requires. (ibid., emphasis added)

This brings us to the notion of information capture, building the grounds for both complexity capture and knowledge capture as discussed on the following pages. As we will see, information capture differs from Capture Theory in the tradition of Stigler and the Chicago School in four central points: (1) it does not ask *why economic regulation occurs*, but *how it actually works*, focusing on the mechanism of capture; (2) it highlights the importance of administrative law, thereby replacing the foremost economic perspective of Capture Theory with a legal-procedural one;

168 Compared to other countries, the United States has a strong *revolving door* culture: Throughout their careers, employees, public servants and elected officials move back and forth from the private to the public sector.

(3) it puts information asymmetries center-stage, introducing a principal-agent logic to Capture Theory, and (4) it does not assume that capture requires the regulatees' intention to influence: Distinct from classic Capture, information capture can occur unintentionally.

A Brief Introduction into the Information Capture Approach

Drawing on the works of Landis (1960), Jaffe (1970), Owen and Braeutigam (1978), Quirk (1981) and Coglianese (1994), Wagner develops a distinguished concept of *information capture*. The starting point for her analysis is US administrative law, which is characterized by a strong commitment to *transparency and open government* (Wagner 2010, 1325). Open Government, which has recently become a buzzword in public management literature, has a long tradition in the US: Going back to Louis Brandeis, advocates for informational freedom argue that policy-making and regulation should be transparent.[169] Access to information – for lay citizens, as well as for organized interest groups – is seen as a prerequisite for the functioning of the democratic state, as well as of the economy (see for example Nader 1981; Brandeis 1914). Yet, following Wagner's argument, current administrative law falls short of its initial objectives: It invites the public to participate in the rulemaking process – however, based on the belief that "more information is better than less" (Paredes 2003), it does not require interest groups to *self-process and filter the information* they provide (Wagner 2010, 1325). Therefore, US administrative law leads to information capture, which Wagner defines as follows:

> In the regulatory context, information capture refers to the excessive use of information and related information costs as a means of gaining control over regulatory decisionmaking in informal rulemakings. (ibid.)

Providing comments to a proposed rule is "one of the most popular ways in which interest groups can directly lobby administrative agencies" (Furlong 2005, 288). The mechanism that Wagner describes is quite simple: Interest groups and interested individuals submit vast and unfiltered amounts of information to regulatory agencies, while these agencies are required by law to consider all comments concerning a proposed rulemaking: Section 553 of the Administrative Procedure Act (APA) demands agencies to issue a "concise general statement" of the rule's basis and purpose; if an agency does not obey, its rule is likely to be rejected by court (Wagner 2010).[170]

169 As Louis Brandeis put it: "Publicity is justly commended as a remedy for social and industrial diseases. Sunlight is said to be the best of disinfectants; electric light the most efficient policeman" (Brandeis 1914).

170 One example provided by Wagner makes the point quite clear. In United States v. Nova Scotia Food Products Corp (568 F.2d 240, 2d Cir. 1977), judge Gurfein argued that the "[a]ppellants [...] attack the 'concise general statement' required by APA [...] as inadequate. We think that, in the circumstances, it

Central elements and arguments of Wagner's concept have been discussed in capture and special interest literature for decades. To start with, the fact that policymakers and regulators rely on information provided by regulated industries is commonly accepted:

> Limited agency resources imply that agencies must depend on outside sources of information [...]. This outside input comes primarily from organized interests, such as regulated firms, that have a substantial stake in the substance of agency policy and the resources to provide such input. (Stewart 1975, 1686; see also Coglianese 1994, and ch. 5.2.2 of this book)

As a result, groups that provide "accurate, detailed and pertinent information will find officials more responsive" to their needs (Schlozman and Tierney 1986, 97), and these are usually the industry interest groups (Furlong 2005). As emphasized by Quirk, an "exclusive reliance on industry for information might lead to decisions predominantly favoring industry interests" (Quirk 1981, 17). The following table illustrates the point that, at least in notice-and-comment rulemaking, industry interest groups dominate the rulemaking process.

	Mean number of comments (average number of comments provided by each interest group type)	Mean percentage (average percentage of total comments received for each regulation)
Business groups	20.96	**30.23**
Trade associations	8.14	19.36
Unions	0.31	0.45
Public Interest Groups	1.84	4.88
Government groups	6.35	22.72
Other	25.29	22.47

Table 5: Participation in the notice-and-comment rulemaking process (Furlong 2005, 289).

In the interest group literature, information is perceived as a key to the executive branch. Many have made the observation that regulatees can affect policy decisions by controlling the flow of information to Congress or the responsible agency

was less than adequate. It is not in keeping with the rational process to leave vital questions, raised by comments which are of cogent materiality, completely unanswered." Interestingly, judicial review of agency rulemakings was initially implemented to protect these decisions against capture by interest groups (Coglianese 1994, 4).

(Owen and Braeutigam 1978, 4) – either by providing or hiding certain information or through information overload (ibid).[171] Taking a normative viewpoint, some even argue that the access of interest groups to agency decision-making is in the public interest, precisely because they provide important information for and about the agencies and thereby increase the rationality of agency decisions: "if interest groups can bring new information about the agency's activity, it may be socially desirable to increase their stakes in regulatory decisions so as to induce them to acquire information and make regulation more efficient" (Laffont and Tirole 1993, 500).[172]

According to Wagner, however, none of these texts covers the full meaning of information capture, because they do not account for the role of administrative law in the capture process:

> The problem is not just that interested parties can strategically bombard the agency with information in order to overwhelm them. It is that the administrative system is so completely oblivious to information costs that it not only neglects requiring some information filtering, but also collectively creates strong incentives for this information excess. (Wagner 2010, 1339)

Ironically, the opaqueness resulting from information overload is not only ignored by administrative law, but actually produced and amplified by the rules that originally aim at increasing transparency and accountability in the policymaking process.

The following figure illustrates Wagner's concept. It puts administrative *filter failure* center-stage. Due to filter failure, information costs increase for all participants – including interest groups as well as the agency itself – causing a distortion in the competition of private interests: The number of participating groups narrows down to the ones that are well-resourced – information capture shares with Capture Theory the argument that the better organized, funded and informed an interest group is, the better it can influence agency decision-making. In fact, information capture increases the costs for all interest groups. As Wagner argues, the groups with the smaller budget, or resources in general, are likely to fall out: "In regulatory settings characterized by escalating information costs, it is generally (but perhaps not always) the public interest groups that find themselves on the short end of the participation stick" (ibid., 1378). Information capture occurs

---

171 Information overload is also a widely discussed issue in information management and social psychology literature (see for example Paredes 2003, discussing information overload in the context of securities regulation).

172 Note that Laffont and Tirole define inefficient regulation as regulation where the information asymmetries between regulatee and Congress are huge. In line with Laffont and Tirole, one EPA staff member argues that "[t]he more information [outside groups] can help us with, the better the rule will turn out – in their interest as well as everyone else's" (Coglianese 1994, 39, quoting from an interview with an EPA staff member).

– resulting in the imbalanced representation of interests in the decision-making process.

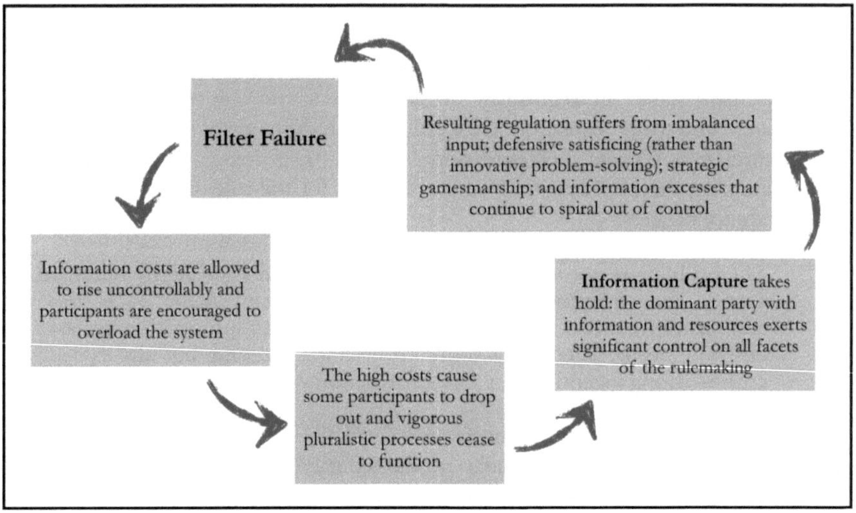

Figure 14: Flowchart of filter failure and information capture (see Wagner 2010, 1333).

Information capture is accordingly contradictory to the ideal of a pluralistic decision-making process. The consequences as outlined by Wagner are (1) a loss of pluralistic oversight, (2) the repression of creative policymaking, (3) limited agency accountability, and (4) information excesses difficult to reverse once they have started (Wagner 2010). Interest groups with sufficient resources can use information strategically to bury regulators in information, e.g. to slow down regulatory processes or to superimpose information by other interest groups:

> Information excess can then be a *conscious strategy deployed by resourceful participants* to exhaust their adversaries, reduce the accountability of the rulemakings outside of the immediate circle of those in the know, and browbeat the agency into capitulating to many of their demands by reinforcing each technical complaint and criticism with a credible threat of litigation. (ibid., 1339)

However, information capture does not require anyone's intention to capture a rulemaking, which is an important difference to classic Capture Theory: It may in fact occur *inadvertently*. Besides, while Capture Theory assumes that public servants are rational utility maximizers pursuing their own good, information capture sees public officials as they presumably are: Some are corruptible while others are strongly committed to civic virtue and the public good. As Wagner argues quite rightly, "If the soul of the regulatory official is not for sale, then this traditional form of agency capture is ineffectual" (ibid., 1336f.; see also Croley 2008), which is not the case in the context of information capture. A second point is of great importance: According to Wagner, information capture follows a *self-reinforcing logic*: Once an interest group has provided relevant information to an agency, or sued an agency, a dependency relationship evolves – either because the agency relies on information or because it fears litigation. As agency rulemaking is based on more and more information, highly technical knowledge is required to oversee and understand the rulemaking landscape and again, certain groups are left behind (Wagner 2010).

While some have suggested abolishing agency regulation and replacing it with free markets in order to fight capture (see Stewart 1975, 1689ff. for a brief discussion), Wagner suggests a set of strategies to overcome information capture, or at least counteract it – among them are (1) make the rulemaking process more pluralistic, e.g. by requiring courts to evaluate rulemakings according to the engagement of various groups in the process and by establishing limits to the information each participant is allowed to submit, (2) create a phase in the rulemaking process where agencies develop first drafts of rules free from interest group input and pressure, termed *policy-in-the-raw*, and (3) implement structural reforms to increase competition between like-minded interest groups (Wagner 2010, ch. IV). We will revert to them when discussing solutions at the end of this chapter.

While Wagner's seminal paper is very important for our line of argument, it has two shortcomings with regard to this book: First, Wagner applies her concept to environmental rulemaking in the US, and she unfortunately spares financial regulation. While most of her findings can be transferred from environmental to financial rulemaking – both are highly technical and complex and require specialized knowledge, while media interest for the details of regulation is generally low – a striking difference lies in the number of well-organized, highly professional environmental NGOs, and the absence of such organizations in financial regulation (see Finance Watch 2010).[173] The imbalance of private interests (*industry vs. public*) in agency participation that Wagner criticizes in the area of environmental rulemaking is much bigger in the field of finance. Secondly, being an expert for administrative law and regulation, Wagner does not distinguish between data, information and knowledge. Moreover, she clearly focuses on information-related problems. We therefore want to turn to Robert Weber's concept of complexity capture: It takes into account the increased complexity in the financial system, and

173 Dodd-Frank received much media attention, as did the Basel accords; when it gets to the detailed rules, e.g. concerning derivatives trading, media interest generally fades.

is based on the observation of an epistemic gap between financial regulators and financial institutions.

Weber's Concept of Complexity Capture

Just like Wagner, Weber published his paper – *Structural Regulation as Antidote to Complexity Capture* – in a law journal. Yet, while information capture has its roots in US administrative law, Weber's understanding of *complexity capture* stands in the tradition of Simon (1997 [1947], 1962, 1992), Perrow (1984, 2007), and Weick and Sutcliffe (2001). Weber reexamines US financial regulation against the background of increased financial complexity to discuss whether financial regulation, aiming at a more resilient, robust and modular financial system, should be primarily structural or behavioral. He integrates findings from various fields of research, while providing a detailed analysis of current reform efforts.

With regard to financial system complexity, Weber distinguishes three elements of financial networks: *Legal entity networks*, referring to large, complex financial institutions as discussed in chapter 3.2 of this book; *market networks*, consisting of the contractual obligations (*links*) between market participants (*nodes*), and building "networks of claims in their own right" (Weber 2012, 684); and *network effects of regulation and trading strategies* (ibid., 689f.), leading to positive feedback loops and cyclicality. Weber observes increased complexity on all three levels, and emphasizes the fact that financial markets are "authentically complex, rather than merely complicated or difficult to understand" (ibid., 645). Drawing on Simon, he argues that regulators "are limited by their bounded rationality; in other words, they possess limited capacities to process information, maintain their attention, and calculate" (ibid., 644). As a result, confronted with complex financial conglomerates, contracts and products,

> regulators face a *structural, widening epistemic gap* between what they are able to know and what they need to know in order to administer the statutory mandates of their agencies. This epistemic gap results from dramatic increases over the past two decades in the complexity of the markets and institutions regulators are charged with overseeing. (ibid., 644f., emphasis added)

This epistemic gap is neither rooted in administrative law (Wagner 2010) nor in agency funding (Gensler 2013): As a structural problem, it is inherent to all types of regulation, and grows in tandem with the complexity of the regulated entities. It can accordingly not be overcome (see Weber 2012, 645).

While Weber draws on recent complexity research, he does not differentiate between data-, information- and knowledge-related problems. Information asymmetries, or rather a reliance of regulators on regulatees to provide information, are a central element of Weber's approach. However, the problem that he describes exceeds information asymmetries: "To the extent regulators rely on industry itself to provide the information they require to make a good-faith effort at performing their mandates, they risk *complexity capture – a soft, hegemonic capture of even virtuous, public-regarding regulators who are resistant to traditional capture*" (ibid., emphasis added). Complexity capture accordingly occurs when boundedly rational regulators deal with highly complex problems.

Both Wagner and Weber disagree with classic Capture Theory in two central points: The first is the somewhat simplifying idea of the public servant as a homo economicus: Public servants might be strongly devoted to the public good and be captured nevertheless. Hence, neither of the two newer versions of Capture Theory allows normative finger-pointing at the executive branch; even the most professional and respectable public servants would not be able to disengage from information and complexity capture. Secondly, both Wagner and Weber avoid the question of why economic regulation occurs (*perspective of supply and demand*) – they instead focus on the question how special interests, especially industry interests, find their way into regulation.

In view of post-crisis financial regulation – living wills and stress tests, as well as Basel III capital requirements – Weber discusses two regulatory paradigms, *structural* and *behavioral regulation*, and we will revert to both in chapter seven:

> A question lurks in the background of recent financial regulatory reform debates: whether to adopt a *behavioral regulatory regime* that reacts via incremental, ad hoc responses to a complex industrial logic subject to significant uncertainty or instead to adopt a *structural regulatory regime* that shapes, by adjusting financial market network structures, the industrial logic itself so as to minimize its vulnerability to perturbation. (ibid., 706, emphasis added)

Capital requirements provide a good example here, as they can be an instrument of structural as well as of behavioral regulation, depending on the details. Weber cites the Basel III risk-based capital requirements as an example of behavioral regulation. Here, capital requirements are not set in an absolute manner (*one size fits all regulation*), but depend on the risks borne by each bank. Complexity capture seeks to explain this fact: Confronted with information and knowledge asymmetries, regulators delegated the task of setting the ratios to the banks themselves (*internal ratings-based approach*). From a principal-agent viewpoint, financial regulators act as principals, as they delegate the assessment of capital ratios to their regulatees. Despite the crisis experience, the Basel accords do still rely heavily on the banks' internal risk models. Weber assumes that "[w]hen charged with regulating an industry characterized by complexity, regulators face a structural dilemma: they can either conduct regulatory policy by, in effect, guessing at what optimal rules and enforcement would be, or they can delegate their duties to industry itself" (ibid.,

660). In the context of Basel II and III, regulators pursued the second strategy. Living wills provide another example. They aim at reducing information asymmetries, yet they increase regulators' vulnerability to complexity capture (ibid., 734). Weber finds many more examples to demonstrate that "regulators have been overwhelmed by market complexity" (ibid., 731).

With his complexity capture concept, Weber provides an interesting explanation of why capture occurs; yet he remains vague on the specific characteristics of complexity capture: Distinct from Wagner's concept of information capture, the mechanism of complexity capture largely remains a black box. Weber's contribution to capture literature is central because it takes into account increased complexity, identifies a growing epistemic gap between regulators and regulatees, and is applicable to financial regulation where capture appears to be a pressing problem. Unfortunately, Weber does not discuss when and under which circumstances complexity capture occurs or does not occur.

6.4 Knowledge Capture: Experts Hijacking Regulators

When formulating his Economic Theory of Regulation, Stigler argued that "[t]o explain why many industries are able to employ the political machinery to their own ends, we must examine the nature of the political process in a democracy" (Stigler 1971, 3). Today, Stigler's basic assumption still holds true – in the 21st century, however, it has to be reformulated to account for recent developments. To explain why certain industries are able to employ the political machinery to their own ends, we must examine the nature of the policymaking and regulation process in a world that is *global and interconnected, innovative and fast, and complex as opposed to "merely complicated"* (Weber 2012, 645). Doing so, we are able to observe a phenomenon that is likely to become increasingly dominant, particularly in financial regulation and particularly at the global level – a specific type of regulatory capture that we want to term *knowledge capture*.

Capture Theory in the tradition of Stigler argues that regulation can be perceived as a phenomenon of supply and demand: Policymakers and regulators provide rules and regulations according to the needs of the firms and industries. Distinct from Capture Theory, knowledge capture neither aims at explaining the causes nor the effects of economic or financial regulation as such; it instead focuses on the mechanism by which capture operates that has been identified as a major research desiderate in the field of capture theory (see for example Carpenter 2013b). As we will show, several experts and academics have, implicitly and explicitly, described the developments and mechanisms contributing to knowledge capture. Yet, these have not been integrated in a comprehensive framework. Bringing together theoretical arguments and empirical evidence, and drawing heavily on the works of Wagner and Weber, we want to fill this gap. Academics in the tradition of classic Capture Theory discuss the role of campaign contributions, personal favors, future job prospects, future agency budget developments and even bribes on policymaking and regulation. While these factors do all play a role, we argue that, compared to knowledge capture, their overall impact is in fact quite limited. We will first describe the basic capture mechanism, and then look at the question of evidence for knowledge capture.

The Basic Mechanism of Knowledge Capture

Brown has made the important statement that the crucial point in policymaking and regulation is "not so much corruption, it's who we listen to" (Brown 2013). Knowledge capture is not about corruption – it is about experts hijacking regulators. It can therefore only be understood against the background of increased financial system complexity (see chapter three of this book). As illustrated in figure 15, financial regulators increasingly rely on data, information and knowledge provided by non-political actors (see chapters four and five of this book). As Richard Breeden of the SEC illustrates, neither examiners nor "the decision makers above them have crystal balls. And if CitiCorp or Goldman Sachs or Bank of America tells you 'oh, this is our view where the markets are going to go over the next two years' you may think it sounds optimistic, but you can't disprove it either" (Breeden 2010). Dodd-Frank does not provide supervisors with crystal balls. While the new measures in place are able to fill certain data and information gaps, e.g. through the establishment of the OFR in the United States and of Finance Watch in the EU, as well as through stress tests and living wills in both the US and the EU, they cannot fully overcome them – especially not with regard to financial knowledge, as knowledge cannot be collected or transferred, but has to be acquired through practice. This development gives rise to lobbying through expertise, which has to be distinguished from other forms of lobbying, e.g. from types of grassroots lobbying often employed by NGOs and public interest groups. As Weber describes,

> under conditions of complexity regulators may find themselves in situations where they lack the basic access to information on which to exercise their discretion in a rational manner, whether to pursue self-regarding profit or their public-regarding regulatory goals. *Regulators' bounded rationality becomes the defining characteristic of the regulatory program.* (Weber 2012, 656, emphasis added)

As a result, international expert elites and policy circles gain power over financial policymaking and regulation at the national and global level, leading to a dominance of the better informed, highly experienced industry interest groups over public interest groups and NGOs, and resulting in knowledge capture of financial regulators by the entities they are supposed to supervise or regulate. Contrary too

Capture Theory, knowledge capture does not depend on a specific perception of the public servant: Captured government employees might either be strongly civic-minded or rational utility maximizers.

As Landis remarks, agency contacts with industry groups are not only necessary, but "frequent and generally productive of intelligent ideas. Contacts with the public, however, are rare and generally unproductive of anything except complaint" (Landis 1960, 51). While this is a strong oversimplification, it is most certainly true that traditionally, industry and public interest group contacts to legislators and the executive branch are of a different nature: Having a better access to data and information, industry interest groups are "more likely to join in agency rulemaking proceedings that require the type of technical expertise needed for effective participation" (Furlong 2005, 288). Stiglitz described well that "[t]oo often, the regulatory system gets captured by those that are supposed to be regulated. They are, after all, the 'experts' who understand the system" (Stiglitz 2009b, 18). As regulatees exploit and foster the existing data, information and knowledge asymmetries, a spiral of ever increasing complexity is set off, and it reinforces the mechanism of knowledge capture. Baker argues that capture in financial regulation has "evolved through a life-cycle that moved in parallel with the long financial boom of the late 1990s and 2000s" (A. Baker 2010b, 648). While the innovation and industry friendly beliefs and paradigms of the time certainly did play a role, we want to take a different position: *Capture in financial regulation evolved in tandem with financial system complexity.* Using a simple game theoretic model of financial regulation, McCarty reaches the same conclusion (McCarty 2013). As we shall see throughout this chapter, additional factors are important, however we will focus on complexity for the moment.

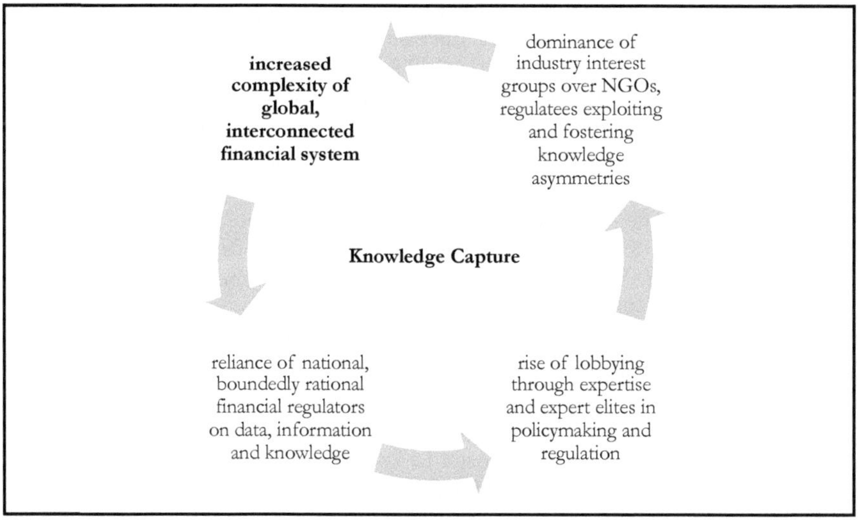

Figure 15: Knowledge capture in financial regulation.

Even though the distinction is not made, the general fact that regulators rely on data, information and knowledge provided by non-state actors is widely accepted: Kamieniecki argues that "[t]he rulemaking process has become increasingly open and information driven, thereby providing stakeholders an opportunity to influence the final outcome of the process" (Kamieniecki 2006, 107). Tsingou (2007) draws on Lindblom, who describes the mechanism by which authorities become "captive of knowledge specialists" in different policy fields (Lindblom 1977, 120). In her case study on the Group of Thirty, she explains the particular importance of non-state experts in the area of finance with the central role of expertise in global financial market governance; she identifies a "transnational policy community at the heart of complex policy processes" (Tsingou 2007, 224). Admati and Hellwig describe the close connection between the expertise that is needed to supervise and regulate an industry on the one hand and the revolving door phenomenon on the other; as they argue, both lead to regulatory capture (Admati and Hellwig 2013, 205). And Underhill and Zhang identify a trend towards self-regulation in financial governance, which they explain with "common professional norms, the *specialized and technical nature of expertise in the financial sector*, and the shared need to maintain public confidence in the financial system itself" (Underhill and Zhang 2008, 541, emphasis added) between regulators and regulatees; together, these factors provide the industry with "the opportunity to influence the nature of financial governance, but also the potential to capture regulatory processes"(ibid.). Helleiner and Porter examine the close ties between the private interest group

Institute of Finance (IIF) and the Basel Committee and come to the conclusion that "The loose, elite, and highly technical character of regulatory networks provide [sic!] privileged access points for business" (Helleiner and Porter 2009, 20). They attribute core points of Basel II, such as the use of the banks' internal risk models, to the influence of the IFF experts (ibid.). Yet, *what the financial industry wants and what it gets is a different thing.* The difficulty about capture is to ascertain when an industry is and when it is not able to push through its interests against the interests of the public (see Stigler 1971). In 1981, Quirk criticized that even though many causal factors for capture have been discussed, little effort has been made "to determine which of the suggested causal factors actually operate, and under what conditions" (Quirk 1981, ix) Before we turn to the question of empirical evidence, we have to look at the *conditions under which knowledge capture operates.*

In line with Carpenter and Moss (2013), we distinguish between strong and weak forms of capture: Knowledge capture prevails in various fields of regulation, but to different degrees. Moreover, not all agency decisions, not even in capture-prone policy fields, can be traced back to knowledge capture by industry interest groups. We hypothesize that anti-industry rules and regulations can be explained by (1) *diverse experts* resulting in pluralistic interpretations of the situation and the relevant facts, (2) *small knowledge asymmetries* between regulators and regulatees, resulting from a comparatively low complexity of the policy field (see Schlozman and Tierney 1986, 298), (3) a generally *slow pace of innovation* and progress on the side of the regulatees, (4) a *slowdown of the pace of innovation* and progress in generally fast-moving industries, e.g. during a crisis, and (5) a *strong public interest* in the rulemaking, confronting regulators not only with increased attention by the media and the legislative, but also with dissenting interpretations of the situation and the relevant facts (McDonnell 2013). If these hypotheses hold true, knowledge capture is highly likely to occur in financial governance. While logical deduction indicates that this is the case, only further empirical research can prove the point.[174]

Especially the first and the fifth point – the plurality of experts, and the degree of public interest – are important here, as they point to the unique features of financial regulation. A comparison with another policy field illustrates the point: Coglianese, in his study on EPA rulemaking in the 1980s, provides important evidence concerning the symbiotic relationship between regulators and regulatees in the area of environmental regulation. Regulators do heavily rely on industry expertise:

> We try to bring them [the regulatees] in as early as possible on what we are required to do and request their help very early on and usually this is

174 Kamieniecki examines if and how public opinion, party control (Republican or Democrat majorities in the US case), campaign spending, countermobilization and overall economic conditions affect the environmental policymaking agenda of the US Congress (Kamieniecki 2006, chapters three and four).

> appreciated because that way they have input as opposed to EPA unilaterally going out and looking at various textbooks and writing rules that are ridiculous because we don't fully understand what the hell we are regulating. So it works out better by working very closely with the people that we are going to regulate and we do this in various ways. We meet with them, we have industry-agency workgroups that will meet together. (Coglianese 1994, 38f., quoting an EPA staff member)

> Typically the industry participants will come at the issue from a very practical standpoint. They will have the data, because they're in the business, to back up their positions. They will have fairly detailed alternatives to propose and reasons for that. (ibid., 49, quoting from an interview with a corporation's general counsel)

One might be able to transfer these findings to financial regulation. Yet, the important difference between environmental and financial policymaking and regulation is that the former is characterized by *pluralistic interests*: Non-industry groups, though fewer and weaker in terms of resources, counterbalance the impact of industry groups. Furthermore, these NGOs have been able to awaken *public interest and awareness* in environmental issues. In financial regulation, this is not the case.

Advocates of lobbying argue that policymakers and regulators should and could consult different sources of information, weigh their arguments, and make a balanced (meaning legitimate) decision. The following quotes from interviews with US legislative staff, again from an environmental context, illustrate the point.

> Everybody has a vested interest, and it's reflected in what they're telling you. But I honestly find it easier to deal with information when you know there's a vested interest, because you can interpret that information according to the bias, which is easier in some cases than testing the accuracy of the data itself. (passage from an interview with US legislative staff conducted by Susan E. Fallows as quoted in Schlozman and Tierney 1986, 298)

> If we don't know about an issue or a technology, we talk to everyone we can about it. […] The industry and environmental groups are always anxious to see you […]. We know we're getting biased information from everybody. But in just about every case we can pretty well figure out what the direction of that bias is and what effect it's likely to have on the data. We look for areas of agreement and assume that stuff is valid. One the things where disagreement exists, you keep going to other sources to try to finally elucidate the common ground and the area of dispute. Then in that area, we have to use our judgment. (ibid., 299)

However, when industry interest groups are the only reliable source of data, information and expertise, the ideal of a competition of interests and arguments as brought forward by Wagner cannot be upheld. As McCarty points out, one of the challenges of financial regulation is that expertise can only be acquired through industry training, which limits the ability of both regulators and NGOs to build up the respective knowledge (McCarty 2013, 102; Willke 2002).

Knowledge Capture Cycles

Baker argues that capture is "relatively easy during boom periods, but becomes much harder when regulation is repoliticized in the context of a crisis" (A. Baker 2010b, 652). While it is true that crises and downturns increase public interest for financial markets and financial regulation, resulting in *pluralistic interpretations of the situation*, regulators do strongly rely on financial institutions for data, information and expertise once a crisis hits. MBSs, CDOs and CDSs, as well as SPVs, played a strong role in the financial crisis of 2007ff., yet policymakers and regulators relied on financial experts to explain to them the nature and role of such products and entities. Knowledge capture therefore occurs in cycles: During boom times, complexity grows in tandem with innovation and regulators are captured by their regulatees. Then, once a crisis hits, industry influence grows further – but only for a short period. Once the situation is under control and long-term policy responses and reforms are formulated, policymakers and regulators stand under increased public scrutiny, and as a result public interest groups and academics gain influence vis-à-vis the financial industry. Yet, when regulators come to the technical details of regulation, such as the definition of swaps or the exact formulation of the Volcker rule, industry interest groups do again provide the needed expertise, and as the following figure illustrates, knowledge capture recurs.

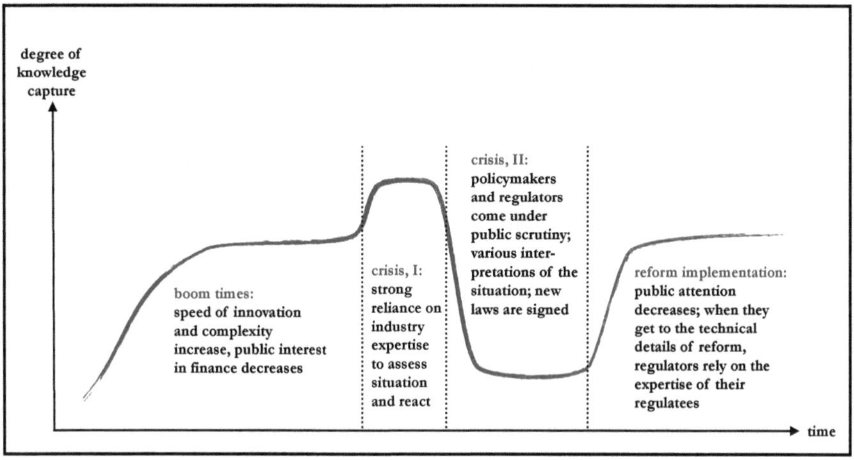

Figure 16: Knowledge capture cycles.

Cultural or Cognitive Capture as Variations of Knowledge Capture

The financial crisis has triggered a lively debate about a phenomenon termed cultural or cognitive capture. It reflects the fact that in hindsight, policymakers and regulators alike struggle to explain and justify the pre-crisis course of financial governance. How could it be, for instance, that Congress constrained the CFTC's ability to investigate the role and nature of the OTC derivatives market in 2000? Why did the Fed not see the crisis coming, even though it had its supervisors placed in every major financial institution? The members of the US Financial Crisis Inquiry Commission could not accept

> that regulators lacked the power to protect the financial system. They had ample power in many arenas and they chose not to use it. [...] Too often, they lacked the *political will* – in a political and ideological environment that constrained it – as well as the fortitude to critically challenge the institutions and the entire system they were entrusted to oversee. (Financial Crisis Inquiry Commission 2011, xviii, emphasis added)

While some argue that policymakers and regulators were afraid to address certain risks (see for example Levitin 2010b, Interview with an OCC official, December 06, 2012, Washington), others identify *groupthink or cultural capture* as the main cause: Stigler, in his Economic Theory of Regulation, emphasized the fact that public servants who have worked for an industry in the past keep their industry's perspective (Stigler 1971, 10). Helleiner describes the "broader belief systems that can emerge among tightly networked regulators working closely with the private sector" (Helleiner 2010a, 17), Baker observes "the personnel of leading banks heavily influencing the thinking and mindsets of regulators" (A. Baker 2010b, 653), while Mayntz warns of a "coalition of financial and policy elites" (Mayntz 2012, 22) in the United States. Barkow defines intellectual or cultural capture as a "set of economic, political, intellectual, and cultural forces", creating a "general mindset that private market actors are good and dynamic while regulation is generally bad and stultifying" (Barkow 2013). Supporting her argument, Adair Turner describes how during the 1980s and 1990s, the EMH and the Washington Consensus had taken hold of policy elites to ultimately become "like a religion" (Turner as quoted in Gieve et al. 2009). He distinguishes between "overt lobbying power" on the one hand, and "regulatory capture through the intellectual zeitgeist" on the other (ibid.).[175] The following quote from McDonnell summarizes the arguments brought forward by many:

> Intellectual capture, in turn, also relates to the 'groupthink' that has taken hold in the making of financial policy. Regulatory and supervisory arrangements are discussed and agreed in expert and apolitical terms, bringing like-minded individuals who, whether in the official, private or academic sphere, can reach common understandings based on shared training, practice and access to economic ideas. Both in the national arena and, increasingly, in the international fora around the Basel process, such networks are technocratic, informal, politically unaccountable and have a narrowly defined understanding of financial policy. They are also often decoupled from other economic considerations or broader questions about the role of finance. (McDonnell 2012, 124)

Cultural capture analyses provide important insights from other research fields, especially from social psychology (see for example Kwak 2013) – yet cultural capture alone is a too narrow concept to explain recent developments in financial governance.[176] Two points are important in this respect: First, while the financial crisis must be perceived as a turning point in terms of paradigms and core beliefs (see chapter two of this book) – a fact that is reflected not only in governmental reports and comments by central policymakers, but also in new legislation – Dodd-

175 The FCIC interview with British journalist Gillian Tett is very interesting in this regard. Tett, an anthropologist by training, not only describes what she terms the narratives and the exclusive language of derivatives experts. She also illustrates the difficulties she experienced when taking an innovation-critical position during 2005 and 2006 (Tett 2010).

176 March and Simon have described the mechanisms by which interpretations of facts and situations are reinforced once they have taken hold of someone: "Reinforcement through selective perception and rationalization and reinforcement through in-group communication serve to explain how a particular definition of the situation, once it becomes established in an individual or group, maintains itself with great stability and tenacity. These mechanisms do not explain, however, what particular definitions of the situation will *become* established in particular environments – they explain behavior persistence and not the origins of behavior" (March and Simon 1993 [1958], 175).

Frank implementation fails to live up to the expectations that the initial policy debate has given rise to. Many observers make out a cultural change at the major US financial regulators; however, *where it gets technical, capture seems to persist.* Second, cultural capture fails to explain why capture strongly prevails in certain policy fields, while it appears to be weak in others. Kwak, himself a proponent of cultural capture, argues that financial regulators were not captured in the "strict sense" – but rather "persuaded by the argument that free financial markets were good for the public" (ibid., 93). He adds: "Where the underlying theories require highly specialized expertise [...] and are empirically contested, it would be naïve to expect policy debates to turn solely on the intellectual merits of the parties' positions" (ibid.). The developments he describes to strengthen his argument – rapid financial innovation, increased financial system complexity, and a disproportionate growth of industry lobbying activities since the 1970s – all point towards a phenomenon that we have termed knowledge capture. Wilson made the important point that, if capture theory is correct, "it is unreasonable to assume that only business firms would be able to capture an agency. [...] If we assume that the airline companies will try to capture the Civil Aeronautics Board, it makes sense to assume that professors will try to capture the National Science Foundation" (Wilson 1980, ix). This holds true if we do not take complexity and data, information and knowledge asymmetries into account. If we do take them into account, it appears obvious why certain interest groups are more powerful than others, and why capture is more dominant in some policy fields than in others.

The Complexity Paradox

The question of whether the financial sector works better with or without government intervention lies at the heart of the systemic risk debate. A central argument throughout this book is that regulatees possess better data, information and knowledge than their regulators – and at first sight, this point appears to support capture scholars who argue that no regulation is a more viable option than regulation by captured regulators. Levitt, himself not a strong believer in self-regulation, advocates self-regulation "to the extent to which government lacks the resources, the insights to do the job" (Levitt 2010). Do data, information and knowledge asymmetries point to the fact that ultimately, financial institutions should be self-regulated? To see why this is not the case, we have to pay particular attention to the known and unknown unknowns of 21st century financial institutions. Confronted with systemic risk (see ch. two of this book), the data, information and expertise of SIFIs is in fact quite limited. Inter-organizational information gaps and too big to manage institutions (see ch. three of this book) indicate that financial organizations are experts in their respective fields, but do not understand the overall markets they create significantly better than their regulators (Weber 2012, 661). This is what we want to term the *complexity paradox*:

Regulators, confronted with a complex financial system, turn to their regulatees to get the relevant data and information. Yet, when it comes to systemic complexity, regulators and regulatees are both confronted with non-knowledge and uncertainty: First, data, information and knowledge have a price both for regulators and financial institutions – and the "understanding of complex transactions in, and obscure corners of, financial markets is often prohibitively expensive" (ibid., 652). Second, non-knowledge and uncertainty in complex systems cannot be fully overcome, but are instead about to increase (Willke 2002).

6.5 Solutions to Knowledge Capture Problems

As illustrated in the preceding section, knowledge capture is rooted in (1) an increasingly complex, global financial system, (2) data, information and knowledge asymmetries in financial regulation, (3) the absence of private, not-for-profit expertise in the financial sector, (4) the bounded rationality of financial regulators, and (5) the process of regulation as such. The fact that all knowledge is closely tied to communities of practice does also play a role (Willke 2007). Interestingly, the very idea of the independent US agency was based on a perceived need of expert decision-making, insulated from political pressure (Barkow 2010, 19f.) – however, these same agencies are strongly lobbied by financial institutions and interest groups (Furlong 2005), who gain access based on the information they provide (Wagner 2010). As a result of the developments elaborated in this book, these agencies are increasingly driven by their processing constraints instead of their mandates (Wilson 1989).

The academic literature discusses various solutions to capture problems, and some of those can be very well applied to knowledge capture. A first set of suggestions either *limits the role of industry interest groups* in the rulemaking process, or *enhances the role of non-industry interest groups* (NGOs, academia) (Kwak 2013; McCarty 2013). A second set of reforms aims to *strengthen public sector expertise*, e.g. by attracting talents through higher salaries, and by developing career paths for public servants that explicitly incorporate learning (McCarty 2013, 119f.). McCarty, in his game theoretic model of regulation in complex policy environments, draws a simple yet central conclusion:

> Unless the agency is willing and able to commit significant resources to building its own expertise, it can learn about the policy environment only through monitoring the firm. This learning, however, is imperfect, and the information obtained from monitoring declines in the complexity of the policy environment. (ibid. 103)

Some academics recommend *increased control*, e.g. through external reviews of the information and analysis underlying all agency decision-making, potentially through the Office of Information and Regulatory Affairs (OIRA) (Kwak 2013; Livermore and Revesz 2013), and to slow down or block the revolving door between the private and public sector (Kwak 2013). Other interesting approaches suggest the establishment of *advocates of public interest* in every rulemaking process (ibid.), of *personnel and ethics policies* to mitigate pro-industry biases (McCarty 2013), or to increase *awareness towards the danger of being captured* (Zingales 2013). Wagner suggests a set of strategies to counteract capture: to make the rulemaking process more pluralistic, to create a phase in the rulemaking process where agencies develop first drafts of rules free from interest group input and pressure, and to increase competition between like-minded interest groups (Wagner 2010, ch. IV). Looking at our analysis so far, it becomes evident substantial counter-expertise, either by regulators or by public interest groups, is required for and enables most of these reform ideas.

As illustrated in chapter four, Dodd-Frank aims at increasing public sector expertise by establishing the FSOC, the OFR and the CFPB (even though the CFPB focuses on consumer protection, and research and monitoring are only means to this end). Some tools, especially living wills and stress tests, should also enhance the database of financial regulators. Given the case they reveal that certain institutions are too complex to be resolved in an orderly manner, or too complex to manage, and therefore pose a severe threat to financial stability in the US, Dodd-Frank provides regulators with the authority to ultimately break up the institutions. Yet, whether US regulators will make use of this authority is highly questionable. Dodd-Frank neither constrains the influence of financial institutions in US policymaking and regulation, nor does it significantly enhance the impact of public interest groups and academics. When we look at recent financial reform from a knowledge capture perspective, it becomes apparent that Dodd-Frank acknowledges data and information gaps on the side of regulators, and identifies them as a major problem prior to and during the crisis; yet, the severe problems resulting from non-knowledge and uncertainty remain largely unaddressed: As Richard Breeden from the SEC emphasizes, "our sophistication has given us tools that give us false confidence while we really can't predict where the next risk is coming from" (Breeden 2010).

7 Conclusion: Policy Implications and Future Research

"If man is not to do more harm than good in his efforts to improve the social order, he will have to learn that in this, as in all other fields where essential complexity of an organized kind prevails, he cannot acquire the full knowledge which would make mastery of the events possible. He will therefore have to use what knowledge he can achieve, not to shape the results as the craftsman shapes his handiwork, but rather to cultivate a growth by providing the appropriate environment, in the manner in which the gardener does this for his plants."

(Hayek 1974)

The financial crisis of 2007ff. triggered far-reaching financial reforms in the United States, in Europe and at the global level. The long-term policy responses to the crisis are characterized by an overall paradigm shift from micro- to macroprudential supervision and regulation and present a turning point with regard to the deregulatory policy environment of the past decades. Stiglitz argues that the financial crisis marks an end for market fundamentalism (Stiglitz 2008). While it remains to be seen if this is truly the case, policymakers and regulators have acknowledged that they had been charmed by the market over the years leading up to the crisis, and that gaps in financial regulation played an important role in causing the crisis.[177] Today, newly established systemic risk watchdogs – among them the FSOC, the ESRB and the FSB – are mandated to guard systemic risk and to enhance macroprudential supervision and regulation.

The crisis experience resulted in major changes in the regulatory architecture on both sides of the Atlantic. Yet, the political debate and the policy responses triggered by the crisis differ fundamentally in the EU and the US. Even though the crisis of 2007ff. was a financial crisis of global reach, it does make sense to distinguish between a US and an EU crisis. A comparative perspective reveals that the US financial crisis was not only perceived as a crisis of the financial system, but also as a regulatory crisis of inadequate financial data, information and knowledge:

177 Kane criticizes that "[t]he nub of the problem is that government regulators' conception of systemic risk neglects the pivotal role they themselves play in generating it" (Kane 2011, 9). Looking at recent financial reform and at the governmental reports that built the basis for reform in the EU and elsewhere, we strongly disagree. To end TBTF, Dodd-Frank limits the Fed's ability to lend to specific financial institutions. Yet, as Bernanke himself admits, TBTF persists as long as the market believes it is still in effect (Warren 2013).

Financial data were either not available or not accessible.[178] Financial institutions, despite constant on-site examinations, turned out to be black boxes. When he was asked by the FCIC whether his 50 on-site examiners at Citigroup were able to "keep on top of the situation at Citibank", the OCC's Lyons admits that regulators rely

> very heavily on what the bank is doing and providing us, because there is no way I can have enough people to look at every (unclear), it's just not possible. You know, audit [the audit department at Citigroup, EB] alone has several 1000 people, I have 50. So we rely very heavily on the work of the control functions within the company, and then our job is to go in and periodically test and validate that they're actually doing what they say they're doing. And that we can rely on the information they're giving us. (Lyons 2010)[179]

Data, information and knowledge asymmetries between regulators and financial institutions are not a new issue. However, the degree to which policymakers and regulators were forced to fly blind throughout the crisis came as a huge surprise, and the gap that has opened up between regulatees and regulators appears to be wider than ever before (Levitt 2010). While the EU reform debate focuses on the restructuring of the supervisory architecture, including the three ESAs and the European Banking Union, the US initiatives are, based on the crisis narrative as a crisis of data, information and knowledge, characterized by their strong focus on data and information gaps. Especially the establishment of the Office of Financial Research, an institution that is equipped with subpoena power and mandated to provide US financial regulators with better data and information on the financial system, presents a unique policy response to the crisis.

When we look at the state of today's financial system, there is good and bad news. The good news is that it is widely agreed that, vis-à-vis a global financial system, international coordination is needed more than ever; major challenges, such as the resolution of systemically important, globally operating financial institutions, require a common understanding and close cooperation. While we still do not have a global financial regulator overseeing and policing global financial institutions, the crisis has strengthened efforts to establish a global financial governance regime through the FSB, through Basel III and also through bilateral cooperation and memoranda of understanding. In addition, the crisis has sharpened our

178 As illustrated in the preceding chapter, a second distinctive point is of great importance: The US crisis provoked a lively debate in academia and in the media on regulatory capture; in the EU, capture remained a minor issue both on the public and the academic agenda.

179 Charles Prince, former CEO of Citigroup, states the opposite: "Our regulators were for the most part embedded in the organization. They had offices at the company. They were there full-time. I met with the regulators on a very frequent basis. They met with our directors, with the audit committee. They met with our auditors. They met with Dave Bushnell [the chief risk officer, EB] frequently. There was nothing that we were doing that wasn't fully transparent to the regulators" (Prince 2010).

understanding of systemic risk and broadened the debate. And last but not least, the crisis opened a window of opportunity for financial reform. Unfortunately, it soon started to close again – but while it was still wide open, policymakers raised the question of whether the benefits of financial innovation did actually exceed the costs. Fundamental reforms were discussed. This brings us to the bad news: From our point of view, the biggest challenge for financial regulation did not receive enough attention – *financial complexity and knowledge capture*, and how they ought to be addressed.

7.1 Tackling Complexity Through Regulation

Once they are TBTF, financial institutions have no intrinsic reason whatsoever to reduce financial complexity (Herring 2009). If it does in fact pose a major threat to financial stability and therefore to society as a whole, policymakers and regulators have to make a decision as to whether they want to *build upon or eliminate financial complexity* (Porter 2009). As elaborated in this book, policymakers and regulators have three basic options: (1) to try to eliminate or at least reduce financial complexity, e.g. through size caps for financial institutions, (2) to accept the degree of complexity but try to limit the resulting risks, e.g. through much higher capital requirements[180], or (3) to accept the degree of complexity, but try to keep pace with it, e.g. through the central clearing of derivatives and through living wills.[181] Against the background of current domestic and international reform efforts, we can assert that policymakers pursue a mix of all three strategies. Section 165 of the Dodd-Frank Act authorizes the Fed and the FDIC to "jointly impose more stringent capital, leverage, or liquidity requirements, or restrictions on the growth, activities, or operations of the company, or any subsidiary thereof" (Sec. 165(d)) if an NFC or a BHC is unable to submit a sufficient living will. Basel III requires financial institutions to hold more capital and be less leveraged, especially when they are SIFIs. Examples for attempts to keep pace with financial complexity are manifold,

180 Weber refers to forest fire management (firebreaks), utility service management (latencies), disease control (quarantines, travel restrictions) and avalanche prevention (avalanche blasting) (Weber 2012, 709). Schwarcz sees only one option, the establishment of a (privately financed) liquidity provider of last resort: "Because it is impossible to predict precisely how complexities might cause future evolving financial markets to fail, this Article offers no general prescriptive framework for regulating complexity per se. Nonetheless, the analysis has shown that regulators can generally mitigate the consequences of these failures by creating a market liquidity provider of last resort to decouple the risk of failures being systemically transmitted" (Schwarcz 2009, 263).

181 Certain measures, for instance living wills, fall under more than one category: Living wills help the Fed and the FDIC to keep pace with the complexity of financial institutions, while at the same time, they open up the possibility for regulators to change the structure of such institutions in order to reduce their complexity.

ranging from stand-alone measures such as living wills to the establishment of the OFR as a new government body that explicitly aims at reducing data and information gaps.

The establishment of the OFR by the US government certainly presents a step into the right direction, and the OFR initiatives to this date, as well as its annual reports and research papers, cover a range of very important issues. Working together with the FSOC, and based on its Dodd-Frank authorities, the Office does indeed bear the potential to shape the US financial system. In a little thought experiment, we might ask how the Brooksley Born case would have evolved with both entities in place: Born could have publicly brought the issue of OTC derivatives on the Council's agenda. She could have asked the OFR for data support and, alarmingly, data were – as we know now – not available. As emphasized by Lehnert, based on the FSOC annual report, agency heads that underestimate risks to the financial system are held responsible for inaction (Interview with Andreas Lehnert, December 05, 2012, Washington). So even if the FSOC would have decided that it did not want to follow up on the issue, Born's doubts had been out in the public. However, even with the OFR up and running, major problems remain: (a) the overall *degree of complexity persists* and is likely to grow; (b) *recent policy responses are likely to further increase knowledge capture in the US supervisory and regulatory system;* and (c) with the OFR up and running, we must assume that *US regulators will be blinded by the data and information collection successes and become ignorant of the knowledge-related problems that remain, including unknown and known unknowns.*

We have discussed the problem of financial complexity at-length in the third chapter of this book: While complexity was already growing over the pre-crisis decades, the crisis mergers and acquisitions have, orchestrated and supported by the US government, resulted in even bigger financial conglomerates – and unfortunately, size and complexity grow in tandem. Haldane, an outspoken critic of financial and regulatory complexity, advocates the explicit regulation of complexity (Haldane and Madouros 2012, 14). While he acknowledges that stress tests and livings wills are a first step in this direction, he calls for a complexity tax for too big to manage institutions and also proposes imposing a levy on cross-system complexity, i.e. on linkages in the system (ibid., 17f.). Both approaches would, if they were successful in tackling complexity, directly reduce the likelihood and degree of knowledge capture. The second category of policy responses – accepting the degree of complexity but trying to limit the resulting risks, e.g. through much higher capital requirements – appears to be a viable option to protect taxpayers and the economy without getting lost in the details. However, such buffers would have to be very large, and the problem with all far-reaching reform initiatives is that the international community, in the absence of a global government, has to agree on a common denominator. Very high capital requirements in a single country or market are likely to trigger a move of financial institutions to countries that are more business-friendly. Again, the incongruence between national policies and global finance presents a major problem. All measures that fall under the third category – regulators trying to keep pace with the market – risk knowledge capture as described and defined in the previous chapter. When we look at recent reforms from the perspective of knowledge capture, it becomes clear that regulators have *delegated important tasks in the field of financial supervision to their regulatees, exactly because these regulatees possess the data, information and expertise that are needed.* Living wills provide a case in point: Regulators must hope that financial institutions take the task seriously, and if they do not, the Fed and the FDIC will hopefully be in the position to realize and police it. The same also basically applies to stress tests.

Stress tests, while increasing financial market transparency and restoring trust, also create a sense of security that might not only be dangerous but also false. Altogether, the safety and soundness tests and disclosure requirements that are now in place are likely to make policymakers and regulators believe that the beast – meaning systemic risk – has been tamed.[182] The crisis has taught us the basic yet fundamental lesson that the financial system cannot be outsmarted – neither by market participants, nor by policymakers and regulators. It reminded us of the fact that policymakers and regulators are confronted with a truly global, highly complex financial system. It consists of innumerable links between complex nodes, some of which are global super-spreader organizations and have become even bigger throughout the crisis, characterized by their non-linear, reciprocal behavior. Small changes in the system might have big effects, while major changes might have no effects. The resulting uncertainty and non-knowledge remain largely unaddressed by recent financial reforms.

7.2 Future Financial Reform

The ability to regulate the financial system is necessarily limited: As illustrated in chapter two, it evolves in ways that are impossible to predict and control – systemic breakdowns are inevitable, and even if we learn our lessons from these breakdowns, they do not necessarily help us to prevent the next: Each financial crisis differs from the last crises (Schwarcz 2009). And yet, we do not mean to give the impression that financial regulation is ineffective, or useless, and bound to fail completely. Even though it appears that there is no "magical, technical step-change that

182 The same basic phenomenon could be well observed in the pre-crisis period: Based on triple-A credit ratings, the control mechanisms installed to protect shareholders and customers from losses, e.g. corporate boards, failed miserably. Dodd-Frank might therefore directly lead into the next major crisis.

regulation can do [...] that can sort of harness private sector innovation and create simply better regulation that is going to make everyone happy" (Seabrooke and Tsingou 2010, 321), the success of regulation is after all not a question of yes or no, but of degree. That principle also applies to systemic financial crises: They cannot be fully prevented but can surely be mitigated. This raises the question of how financial regulation must be designed if future policymakers and regulators do not want to give in to financial complexity. Turner concludes that, despite the limitations of financial regulation, policymakers and regulators should "give well-reasoned proposals for reform a try", and look at new policies from a perspective of "trial and error" (P. Turner 2010, 47). The OFR presents such a trial: If it gets lost in its data collection efforts, it might turn out to be ineffective, yet it bears the potential to widen it's scope of analysis and work on a closely related, but different set of problems, namely the challenges posed by uncertainty and non-knowledge vis-à-vis a truly complex financial system.

Against the background of knowledge capture, it is apparent that certain forms of regulation are more adequate for finance than others. In chapter two, we made the important distinction between behavioral and structural narratives of the financial crisis. According to the former, the crisis can be traced back to human misbehavior. Investigating this narrative, many FCIC interviews focus on the role that mortgage fraud and financial sector incentive structures played in causing the breakdown. According to the latter, the crisis rooted in the weaknesses of the system, and can be categorized as a *natural accident* in Perrow's sense (1981). Robert Weber makes a similar distinction in the context of regulation. Based on his analysis of systemic risk, financial complexity and regulators' bounded rationality, he emphasizes the value of structural as opposed to behavioral regulation: Compared to behavioral regulation, he argues, it is much more independent from private sector expertise. As the following table illustrates, regulators in structural regulation regimes establish fixed rules (e.g. size caps for financial institutions) and monitor compliance, while regulators in behavioral regulation regimes react to undesirable industry behavior by implementing detailed rules; however, as they lack the expertise to effectively set up and run such a regulatory system, they are forced to delegate central responsibilities to their regulatees (e.g. the Basel capital requirements).[183]

183 Agency theory supports this strategy: As "information and knowledge asymmetries [...] are characteristic of many agency relationships, and because agency relationships are exceptionally opaque [...] and relatively inaccessible to surveillance, self-regulation (drawing on inside information and expertise) plays an important monitoring role" (Schapiro 2005, 280).

Regulatory paradigm	Basic mechanism	Attitude towards complexity	Examples	
Behavioral Regulation	Counteracts or mitigates incentives for undesirable behavior	Regulators accept the degree of complexity and delegate primary responsibilities to their regulatees	Basel II capital requirements[184]	Risk is assessed by financial institutions themselves
			Resolution plans	Resolution is prepared by financial institutions
Structural Regulation	Restricts firms' size or scope of activities	Regulators reduce complexity to strengthen their position	Bank break-ups	Size is reduced
			Ban on proprietary trading by commercial banks	Moral hazard is reduced

Table 6: Differences between behavioral and structural regulation (table based on Weber 2012; see also Volcker 2010).

Weber argues that, in view of the existing knowledge asymmetries between regulators and regulatees, the focus should lie on structural instead of behavioral regulation. The argument is in fact quite simple: When designing, implementing and monitoring financial rules and regulations, regulators' dependence on industry experts increases the deeper they dive into the details and complexities of financial issues. The more an agency relies on the knowledge of its regulatees, the more it is confronted with classic agency problems, among them problems of control:

> The goal of structural regulation is to address market failure by deploying public power to set up a system that largely can run on its own; the need for ongoing supervision is diminished because the system has been structured so that secured regulatory objectives occur organically through self-interested transacting parties. By contrast, proposals to regulate behavior within existing complex network structures pose a microengineering

184 Capital ratios are not a behavioral tool per se. In the second Basel accords, however, capital requirements depend on the risks taken by each financial institution. They therefore present a behavioral regulatory tool (see Weber 2012).

> problem of how to construct finely tuned rules that foster regulatory objectives. (Weber 2012, 707)

An approach that partly overlaps with Weber's idea of structural regulation, and that is widely discussed in academia and in the policy arena, is principles-based regulation (PBR). The example of New York's Senator Schumer and Mayor Bloomberg as described in chapter two, who suggested that US regulators should adopt the British FSA's approach to financial supervision and regulation, provides a case in point, as the now abolished FSA made strong use of PBR (Black 2008).[185] PBR is based on a framework of general, outcome-oriented principles (e.g. private borrowers must understand the mortgage they buy). Each regulator has to decide how to reach the goals set by PBR (e.g. regular internal audits of the understanding of the mortgages sold, based on interviews with mortgage customers), and non-compliance can lead to enforcement actions even in cases where no rules were breached (ibid.). PBR in the area of finance sets the basic frame for conducting financial business, but leaves the details and technicalities to the experts, namely the financial institutions themselves. However, major problems and paradoxes remain, which is why Black terms PBR a *regulatory Utopia*:

> In this regulatory Utopia, regulation is targeted and focused, and preferably harmonized across jurisdictions, regulated firms are given the flexibility they need to get on with running their businesses, and consequently regulatory outcomes are achieved with no undue cost to business. It is a world in which regulators have sufficient perspective on and understanding of the problems and issues that they confront to be selective and to identify the key issues on which regulation should focus, [...] and in which regulated firms are given the flexibility and responsibility to develop their own systems for ensuring that the regulatory principles are adhered to [...]. (ibid., 430)

Black identifies seven paradoxes of PBR, of which the most important one is termed the "trust paradox": PBR aims to build mutual trust between regulators and regulatees, yet it also requires trust for principles-based regimes to work in the first place (Black 2008). She concludes that PBR is a "highly complex form of regulation, belying its rhetoric of simplicity" (ibid., 456). Willke and Willke acknowledge the shortcomings of PBR, yet they identify it as "the best available approach" for policymakers and regulators confronted with a highly complex financial system (Willke and Willke 2012, 105). They also argue that PBR is "necessary but not sufficient" (ibid.): Even though Willke and Willke stress the importance of a global financial governance regime, they suggest that PBR should incorporate the political principle of *subsidiarity*, and must also be "supported by stringent *learning*

185 Black distinguishes between four types of PRB; her approach comprises formal, substantive, full and polycentric PRB (Black 2008).

procedures which enable both sides of the regulatory relation to adapt continuously to new challenges" (ibid., 103, emphasis added). In view of the severe knowledge asymmetries described in chapter five and six, the idea that policymakers and regulators define the common principles of finance based on the desired outcomes and effects and delegate the details to the financial institutions themselves is in fact convincing. Besides, a principles-based approach makes regulatory arbitrage much more difficult: The principles are usually neither complex, nor do they contain any loopholes that allow financial institutions to circumvent regulation. Schwarcz is nevertheless critical of PBR, based on the observation that it requires common interpretations of the principles by regulators and regulatees, and without such "shared assumptions and procedures, regulated parties will be unable to predict the consequences of their actions" (Schwarcz 2009, 264). The resulting uncertainty for financial institutions is a closely related counterargument brought forward by the institutions' lawyers (Black 2008). From the perspective of knowledge capture, it can also be argued that the more details regulators delegate to their regulatees, the further they lag behind in terms of financial expertise, resulting in an ever increasing epistemic gap. Against this background, it is also questionable whether regulators have the data, information and expertise to (a) design good principles, and (b) conduct sufficient supervision and enforcement actions. However, based on the fact that complex systems "respond to changes of relevant parameters in their environment, that is, 'contextual conditions', although they respond within their own language and operational logic", meaning that financial governance "needs to respect the internal operational modes of these entities and must avoid imposing an extraneous logic on them" (Willke and Willke 2012, 40), PBR might present a deficient, yet viable option. In the last chapter of this book, we finally examine the paradox that financial regulation has to stay out of the technical details of regulation, while it must at the same time counteract knowledge capture, by (1) building up its own expertise, (2) supporting private sector, non-profit groups that might, in the future, provide counter-expertise, (3) and directly tackling complexity through measures as the ones brought forward by Haldane.[186]

This brings us back to private, non-profit expertise in the financial sector. As early as 1975, Stewart demanded that "more effective representation for unorganized 'public' interests" be provided as an antidote to organized industry interests: "If such representation could be provided, policy choices would presumably reflect an appropriate consideration of all affected interests" (Stewart 1975, 1715). As shown in the section on solutions to knowledge capture problems, several scholars bring forward the argument that the integration of interest groups in the process of policymaking and regulation would result in more balanced rules

186 As a response to the financial crisis, US financial experts – including Sheila Bair, Brooksley Born, Simon Johnson and Paul Volcker – have set up the Systemic Risk Council (SRC). The SRC monitors the regulatory reforms addressing systemic risk.

and decisions. International organizations such as the United Nations have shown that it is in fact possible to set up structures and processes that guarantee or at least allow many voices to be heard, and as illustrated in chapter four, the ESRB also tries to enhance transparency and NGO participation (even though public interest groups criticize that the transformation process progresses too slowly). Taking into account not only the knowledge capture framework as introduced in this book, but also the short discussion of different regulatory regimes, we can conclude that problems arise in complex and innovative policy fields (a) where regulators strongly rely on expertise that is not possessed by the public sector, (b) when non-industry counter-expertise is not available, and (c) when the regulation itself is structured in a way that requires regulators to dive deep into the technical details of the regulated entity. The Call for a Finance Watch provides some evidence that this is the case in finance (Finance Watch 2010). Policymakers and regulators should support such initiatives, because in the future, they might prove to be an important, if not indispensable ally.

Another prerequisite of successful financial regulation is, regardless of the question of whether it is principles-based or not, a basic awareness of the limitations of financial regulation. The focal point is whether policymakers and regulators can overcome their "delusion of omnipotence" (Willke 2007, 116), engage in "critical self-reflection" (Black 2012, 44) and acknowledge the shortcomings inherent to financial regulation and governance. Hayek warns us not to act upon the belief that we possess the knowledge to shape society entirely (Hayek 1974); as the crisis has shown, that same warning also applies to financial regulation. JPMorgan's London Whale incident reminded us of the fact that, no matter how elaborated regulators' data collection efforts are, complex financial institutions remain just what they are – complex financial institutions operating in a highly complex environment, to a certain degree black boxes for investors, for their regulators and for the management of these institutions.[187] Returning to the quote at the beginning of this chapter, we have to keep in mind that "[i]f man is not to do more harm than good in his efforts to improve the social order, he will have to learn that [...] he cannot acquire the full knowledge which would make mastery of the events possible. He will therefore have to use what knowledge he can achieve, [...] to cultivate a growth by providing the appropriate environment, in the manner in which the gardener does this for his plants" (ibid.). Can the OFR unbound the US policymakers that come together at the FSOC meetings? Unfortunately, the answer is no: "Politics has insufficient universal knowledge; above all, it has no knowledge of the future. It must therefore make risky decisions. However, in the

187 The OCC, which was responsible for overseeing the CIO, had approximately 65 staff members located inside JPMorgan, and the Fed had placed another 40 examiners at the investment bank, yet the trades "failed to raise alarms for the regulator even as of late April, well after the initial media reports surfaced" (Hu 2012, 1677f.; United States Senate 2013).

politicized conflict between decision makers and affected parties it cannot very well present its decisions for what they are – risky" (Luhmann 2008, 155).

7.3 Future Research

This book touches upon a variety of issues. In this final section, we turn to some of the questions that were raised but not answered throughout this book and briefly discuss some aspects that, from our point of view, require further research.

As already argued, the framework of knowledge capture developed and described in this book is based primarily on *academic literature and logical deduction and only partly on empirical research.* Unfortunately, only a relatively small number of interviews on the financial crisis discusses problems in financial regulation resulting from financial complexity, and we were only able to focus on such problems in our own interviews, conducted in an early phase of the research project. While classic Capture Theory has triggered much empirical research, the concepts brought forward by Wagner and Weber, both being central to our line of argument, have not yet been empirically tested. A study by Jason and Susan Webb Yackee (2006) indicates where the difficulties lie: The authors examined 40 rules published by four different US agencies over a seven-year period. While the study confirms an industry bias in rulemaking, it refutes the hypothesis that business insiders prevail because of their level of information or expertise. To measure the level of information and expertise provided in a comment, they asked whether (1) the commenter described himself as an expert, (2) the comment was short or long, (3) the commenter attached any documents, e.g. scientific studies, (4) the number of changes proposed exceeded one, and if (5) the commenter was a renowned Washington insider (Yackee and Yackee 2006, 136). The authors themselves admit that these five variables are imperfect to evaluate the level of information and expertise; more importantly, they fail to distinguish between the two. Taking their study as a starting point, and following Wagner's approach to environmental rulemaking, it would be interesting to look at concrete examples of Dodd-Frank rulemaking, e.g. the definition of derivatives by the CFTC. Yet, as Quirk warns for classic Capture, "[j]udging the validity of this accusation with respect to particular agencies can become quite complex and uncertain […] because an allegation of industry influence usually rests on an (often unstated) assumption about what the *agency would* have done in the absence of industry influence – an assumption that tends to derive from what the critic thinks *should have* been done" (Quirk 1981, 4).[188] We provided in chapter six a set of hypothetical factors that we assume to

188 A study by Croley (2008) on the role of public interests in US regulation illustrates the point: In his pre-crisis case study, the author argues that consumers benefit from financial reforms pushed forward by

either support or hamper knowledge capture, and even though it might be difficult, each of them invites empirical testing.[189] In the context of data, information and knowledge asymmetries in finance, we also shortly touched upon other types of information asymmetries, e.g. within financial institutions. Recent Research (Hu 2012) and several FCIC interviews indicate that the *siloing of information in complex financial conglomerates*, for instance Citigroup, presented and remains a major problem (Kohlhagen 2010). It is closely intertwined with the complexity of financial institutions, most of which did not grow organically but through numerous mergers and acquisitions. It would be especially interesting to look at the data and information, as well as the knowledge management systems of financial institutions, and if and how they were modified after the financial crisis.

In our analysis, we mostly constrained ourselves on *financial regulation in the United States, and did not discuss if and how knowledge capture occurs at the European and global level* – even though publications in the field of global financial governance put much emphasis on the technical nature of international rulemaking, and the important role that private expertise plays in this context (Tsingou 2007; Willke and Willke 2012). Besides, what is still missing is a comparative analysis of the details of recent reform efforts: Why did US stress tests work well, while the EU stress tests are widely perceived as being ineffective? First publications on differences and commonalities of the FSOC and the ESRB have been quite valuable (Kern and Lantz 2012), but this field does certainly require further investigation.

Willke et al. discuss how systemic risk undermines democratic governance (Willke, Becker, and Rostásy 2013). Also, the Call for a Finance Watch by members of the European Parliament describes a fear by policymakers that the *lack of counter-expertise* that they experience *presents a danger to democracy* (Finance Watch 2010). That governments are hijacked by collapsing SIFIs is only one aspect of the problem; the subsection on *too big to jail institutions* in chapter three provides evidence that some financial institutions have in fact become too big to be prosecuted, undermining the judiciary authority. Regulators appear to be caught in

the OCC despite the opposition by parts of Congress – they enhance competition between insurance companies, banks and other financial services firms, thereby increasing financial efficiency (Croley 2008, 236). As we know today, efforts to liberalize the banking sector, especially the ones promoted by the OCC, did not necessarily correspond with the public interest. Croley conducted the case study to support his argument that "organized and well-funded interests [...] were unable to use the administrative process to change the course of ambitious regulatory initiatives that advanced general interests but imposed costs on them" (ibid., 282f.), and that regulators neither rely on information nor expertise provided by their regulatees: "The idea that regulated interests can fool agencies fails to consider the considerable infrastructure agencies have developed to generate and process information" (ibid., 294).

189 Croley argues that the US agency decision-making process, including peer reviews and cost-benefit analyses, was structured and designed to prevent *informational capture*. He however admits that it is "not impossible that agencies are (nevertheless sometimes) 'captured' by the information supplied by self-interested groups" (Croley 2008, 50).

Kane's regulatory dialectic – they address some of problems revealed by the crisis, but whatever they do creates new and even bigger risks (Kane 1986). As brought forward by Cohn, dark markets exists not despite, but because they are dark (Cohn 2010). Unfortunately, regulators counteract financial complexity with regulatory complexity (Haldane and Madouros 2012). A *complex system of rules and regulations serves certain groups* – among them lawyers and accountants who are said to be the biggest profiteers of the crisis – but also the financial institutions that manage to lobby loopholes into every piece of legislation, and circumvent regulation (Commodity Futures Trading Commission 2012). Kane warns that this "offers numerous opportunities for the regulatory community to misread its authority or otherwise miss its marks" (Kane 2011, 3f.). Dodd-Frank, signed into law in 2010 to protect taxpayers from future bank bailouts, presents two steps forward; its lengthy and fragmented implementation presents one step back. Against this background, it would be interesting to look at *democratic policymaking from the background of knowledge capture*, discussing not only the role of *legitimacy through expertise*, but also the changing role of various experts in different policy fields.

As we warned at the beginning of this book, we base our argument on contributions from a set of disciplines; this invites criticism from all of them. The knowledge capture framework is embedded in arguments and theories from economic, political, sociologic and law scholarship, and subsequent research by experts in each of these academic fields would certainly help to specify and improve it.

Stiglitz (2008) argues that the financial crisis was to market fundamentalism what the Berlin Wall meant for Communism: The end. This book illustrates that, as long as financial market complexity persists, policymakers and regulators will not be able to emancipate themselves from the dominant interpretation of the facts by market experts whose interests are strongly intertwined with the interests of their industry, and who neglect the risks resulting from high-speed innovation and growth. Counterevidence would be highly welcome.

References

Abolafia, Mitchel Y. (1996): *Making Markets. Opportunism and Restraint on Wall Street.* Cambridge and London: Harvard University Press.

——— (2005): Interpretative Politics at the Federal Reserve. In *The Sociology of Financial Markets*, eds. Karin Knorr-Cetina and Alex Preda. Oxford: Oxford University Press. 207-228.

Acharya, Viral V, Thomas Cooley, Matthew Richardson, and Ingo Walter, eds (2011): *Dodd-Frank: One Year On.* VoxEu.org ebook, July 2011.

Acharya, Viral V., Deniz Anginer, and A. Joseph Warburton (2013): The End of Market Discipline? Investor Expectations of Implicit State Guarantees. *Available at SSRN:* http://ssrn.com/abstract=1961656.

Acharya, Viral V., Thomas Cooley, Matthew Richardson, Richard Sylla, and Ingo Walter (2010a): A Bird's-Eye View. In *Regulating Wall Street. The Dodd-Frank Act and the New Architecture of Global Finance*, eds. Viral V. Acharya, Thomas Cooley, Matthew Richardson, Richard Sylla and Ingo Walter. New Jersey: John Wiley & Sons. 1-32.

———, eds (2010b): *Regulating Wall Street. The Dodd-Frank Act and the New Architecture of Global Finance.* New Jersey: John Wiley & Sons.

Acharya, Viral V., Lasse H. Pedersen, Thomas Philippon, and Matthew Richardson (2010): Measuring Systemic Risk. *Federal Reserve Bank of Cleveland: Working Paper* 10-02.

Ackoff, Russel L. (1989): From Data to Wisdom. Presidential Address to ISGSR, June 1988. *Journal of Applied Systems Analysis* 16: 3-9.

Admati, Anat, and Martin Hellwig (2013): *The Bankers' New Clothes. What's Wrong with Banking and What to Do About It.* Princeton and Oxford: Princeton University Press.

Ahmed, Shamima, and David M. Potter (2006): *NGOs in International Politics.* Bloomfield: Kumarian Press.

Aikman, David, Philip Barrett, Sujit Kapadia, Mervyn King, James Proudman, Tim Taylor, Iain de Weymarn, and Tony Yates (2011): Uncertainty in Macroeconomic Policy Making: Art or Science? *Philosophical Transactions of the Royal Society* A 2011: 4798-4817.

Akay, Ozgur, Zeynep Senyuz, and Emre Yoldas (2013): Hedge Fund Contagion and Risk-Adjusted Returns: A Marko-Switching Dynamic Factor Approach. *Office of Financial Research Working Paper Series* 0006 (March 13, 2013).

Alblescu, Henry (2010): "Interview with the Financial Crisis Inquiry Commission." FCIC. http://fcic-static.law.stanford.edu/cdn_media/fcic-audio/2010-05-14 FCIC staff audiotape of interview with Henry Alblescu, Standard & Poor's.mp3 (March 25, 2014).

Alvarez, Scott, Bill English, Kieran Fallon, and Bill Nelson (2010): "Interview with the Financial Crisis Inquiry Commission." FCIC. http://fcic-static.law.stanford.edu/cdn_media/fcic-audio/2010-07-29 FCIC staff audiotape of interview with Scott Alvarez, Bill English, Kieran Fallon and Bill Nelson, Federal Res~1.mp3 (March 26, 2014).

Alvarez, Scott G., Richard M. Ashton, Kieran J. Fallon, Mark E. Van Der Weide, and Sophia H. Allison (2009): *Memorandum According the Authority of the Federal Reserve to Provide Extensions of Credit in Connection with a Commercial Paper Funding Facility (CPFF).*

Anabtawi, Iman, and Steven Schwarcz (2011): Regulating Systemic Risk: Towards an Analytical Framework. *Notre Dame Law Review* 86 (4): 1349-1412.

Angelides, Phil (2012): "Interview with Mark Crumpton." Bloomberg TV. http://www.bloomberg.com/video/it-s-time-to-break-up-the-biggest-banks-angelides-C9nAa6gpTs61Nrj~R3H70g.html (March 10, 2014).

Aven, Terje (2012): A Conceptual Framework for Linking Risk and the Elements of the Data-Information-Knowledge-Wisdom (DIKW) Hierarchy. *Reliability Engineering and System Safety* 111 (2013): 30-36.

Avgouleas, Emilios, Charles Goodhart, and Dirk Schoenmaker (2010): Living Wills as a Catalyst for Action. *DSF Policy Paper Series* 4 (2010).

Bair, Sheila (2012a): *Bull by the Horns. Fighting to Save Main Street from Wall Street and Wall Street from Itself.* New York a.o.: Free Press.

——— (2012b): "Why It's Time to Break up the 'Too Big to Fail' Banks." CNN Money. http://finance.fortune.cnn.com/2012/01/18/big-banks-break-up- bair/ (March 10, 2014).

——— (2013): "Financial Stability and the Problem of Too-Big-to-Fail Financial Institutions." Peterson Institute for International Economics. http://www.iie.com/events/event_detail.cfm?EventID=265 (May 13, 2014).

Baker, Andrew (2010a): Mandate, Accountability and Decision Making Issues to Be Faced by the FSB. In *The Financial Stability Board: An Effective Fourth Pillar of Global Economic Governance?*, eds. Stephany Griffith-Jones, Eric Helleiner and Ngaire Woods. Waterloo, Ontario, Canada: CIGI. 19-22.

——— (2010b): Restraining Regulatory Capture? Anglo-America, Crisis Politics and Trejectories of Change in Global Financial Governance. *International Affairs* 86 (3): 647-663.

Baker, Dean (2010): "Interview with the Financial Crisis Inquiry Commission." FCIC. http://fcic-static.law.stanford.edu/cdn_media/fcic-audio/2010-08-18 FCIC staff audiotape of interview with Dean Baker, Center for Economic & Policy Research.mp3 (March 04, 2014).

Baker, Dean, and Travis McArthur (2009): "The Value of the 'Too Big to Fail' Big Bank Subsidy." Center for Economic and Policy Research. http://www.cepr.net/documents/publications/too-big-to-fail-2009-09.pdf (September 24, 2013).

Bank for International Settlements (2009): *Issues in the Governance of Central Banks. A Report from the Central Bank Governance Group.* Basel: BIS.

——— (2010): "80th Annual Report." BIS. http://www.nextnewdeal.net/sites/default/files/wp-content/uploads/2010/07/ar2010e.pdf (September 19, 2013).

Barber, Brad M., and Terrance Odean (2008): All That Glitters: The Effect of Attention and News on the Buying Behavior of Individual and Institutional Investors. *The Review of Financial Studies* 21 (2, 2008): 785-818.

Barkow, Rachel E. (2010): Insulating Agencies: Avoiding Capture through Institutional Design. *New York University School of Law Public Law & Legal Theory Research Paper Series* Working Paper No. 10-82.

——— (2013): "Regulatory State, Capture, and Financial Regulatory Reform." Presented at the Political Economy of Financial Regulation Conference, Washington.

Barofsky, Neil (2013): "Geithner Doctrine Lives on in Libor Affair." Financial Times online. http://www.ft.com/intl/cms/s/0/0c39210e-6ebb-11e2-9ded-00144feab49a.html-axzz2MlFV u1EQ (September 20, 2013).

Barr, Michael S. (2013): "Keynote Address." Presented at the Conference on the Political Economy of Financial Regulation. George Washington University Law School, Center for Law, Economics & Finance (C-LEAF). http://vimeo.com/user9108723/review/60270641/2035e8e136 (May 13, 2014).

Barr, Michael S., Sendhil Mullainathan, and Eldar Shafir (2009): The Case for Behaviorally Informed Regulation. In *New Perspectives on Regulation*, eds. David Moss and John Cisternino. Cambridge: The Tobin Project. 25-61.

Barrett, Devlin (2013): "Justice Department Plans New Crisis-Related Cases." The Wall Street Journal online. http://online.wsj.com/news/articles/SB1000 1424127887323423804579025262544041336?mg=reno64-wsj&url=http%3A%2F%2Fonline.wsj.com%2Farticle%2FSB1000142412 7887323 423804579025262544041336.html (February 04, 2014).

Barth, James R., Gerard Caprio, and Ross Levine (2012): *Guardians of Finance: Making Regulators Work for Us*. Cambridge: MIT press.

Baumgartner, Frank R., and Beth L. Leech (1998): *Basic Interests. The Importance of Groups in Politics and in Political Science*. Princeton: Princeton University Press.

——— (2001): Interest Niches and Policy Bandwagons: Patterns of Interest Group Involvement in National Politics. *The Journal of Politics* 63 (4, Nov. 2001): 1191-1213.

Baxter, Lawrence G. (2013): "The Future Direction of Financial Regulation after the 2012 Election." George Washington University, Center for Law, Economics & Finance (C-LEAF). http://vimeo.com/user9108723/review/60276063/00647ee6e2 (May 13, 2014).

Beale, Nicholas, David G. Rand, Heather Battey, Karen Croxson, Robert M. May, and Martin A. Nowak (2011): Individual Versus Systemic Risk and the Regulator's Dilemma. *Available at* http://www.pnas.org/cgi/doi/10.1073/pnas.1105882108.

Becker, Eva, and Helmut Willke (2013): A Demonstrably Fragile Financial System. Information and Knowledge Asymmetries in the Global Financial Crisis. In *Fragile Stabilität – Stabile Fragilität*, eds. Stephan A. Jansen, Eckhard Schröter and Nico Stehr. Wiesbaden: VS Verlag. 219-242.

Becker, Gary S. (1958): Competition and Democracy. *Journal of Law and Economics* Vol. 1 (Oct. 1958): 105-109.

——— (1983): A Theory of Competition among Pressure Groups for Political Influence. *The Quarterly Journal of Economics* 98 (3, August 1983): 371-400.

Begg, Ian (2009): Regulation and Supervision of Financial Intermediaries in the EU: The Aftermath of the Financial Crisis. *Journal of Common Market Studies* 47 (5): 1107-1128.

Benoit, Bertrand, and James Wilson (2008): "Germany Guarantees Savings." Financial Times online. http://www.ft.com/intl/cms/s/0/d895ef54-92ef-11dd-98b5-0000779fd18c.html-axzz2iLTw Kjgx (October 21, 2013).

Bentley, Arthur F. (1967 [1908]): *The Process of Government*. Cambridge: The Belknap Press of Harvard University Press.

Berman, Gregg E. (2011): "Market Structure: What We Know, and What We Need to Know." Presented at the 12th Annual SIFMA Market Structure Conference, New York.

——— (2013): "The Fat-Finger Problem." Markets in Motion (Vol. 4 No. 25), published by Financial Technologies Knowledge Management Company Limited. http://www.ftkmc.com/newsletter/Vol4-25-Sep2-2013.pdf (March 03, 2014).

Bernanke, Ben (2007a): "Regulation and Financial Innovation." Presented at the Federal Reserve Bank of Atlanta's 2007 Financial Markets Conference, Sea Island.

——— (2007b): "Testimony of Ben Bernanke, Chairman of Federal Reserve System, on the Economic Outlook, March 28 2007." U.S. Congress, Joint Economic Committee. http://www.federal reserve.gov/newsevents/testimony/bernanke20070328a.htm (June 12, 2014).

——— (2009a): "Financial Reform to Address Systemic Risk. Speech at the Council on Foreign Relations, Washington D.C." Federal Reserve Board of Governors. http://www.federalreserve.gov/newsevents/speech/bernanke20090310a.htm (September 23, 2013).

——— (2009b): "Financial Regulation and Supervision after the Crisis: The Role of the Federal Reserve." Presented at the Federal Reserve Bank of Boston 54th Economic Conference, Chatham, Massachusetts.

——— (2009c): "Lessons of the Financial Crisis for Banking Supervision." Presented at the Federal Reserve Bank of Chicago Conference on Bank Structure and Competition, Chicago, Illinois.

——— (2010a): "Interview with Scott Pelley." CBSNews. http://www.cbsnews.com/8301-504803_162-20024635-10391709.html (June 12, 2013).

——— (2010b): "Remarks on the Squam Lake Report." Presented at the Squam Lake Conference, New York.

——— (2010c): "Testimony of Ben Bernanke, Chairman of the Federal Reserve System, on the Causes of the Recent Financial and Economic Crisis, September 02 2010." Financial Crisis Inquiry Commission. http://www.federalreserve.gov/newsevents/testimony/bernanke20100902a.htm (May 16, 2014).

——— (2012): "Some Reflections on the Crisis and the Policy Response." Presented at the Russell Sage Foundation and The Century Foundation Conference on Rethinking Finance, New York.

Bernardino, Gabriel (2013): "Introductory Statement: Public Hearing on the Financial Supervision in the EU on 24 May 2013." EIOPA. https://eiopa.europa.eu/fileadmin/tx_dam/files/Press-Room/speeches/2013-05-24_Public_hearing_on_Financial_Supervision.pdf (August 22, 2013).

Berner, Richard (2013a): "Remarks." Presented at the the 14th Annual Risk Management Convention of the Global Association of Risk Professionals (GARP), New York.

——— (2013b): "Testimony of Richard Berner, Director of the Office of Financial Research, on Who Is Too Big to Fail? GAO's Assessment of the Financial Stability Oversight Council and the Office of Financial Research, March 14 2013." U.S. House of Representatives, Financial Services Subcommittee on Oversight and Investigations. http://www.

treasury.gov/press-center/press-releases/Pages/jl1883.aspx (December 11, 2013).

Bernstein, Donald S., John L. Douglas, Marshall S. Huebner, and Daniel J. Ehrmann (2011): "A Creditor's Guide to the FDIC's Orderly Liquidation Authority." Davis Polk & Wardwell LLP. http://www.davispolk.com /files/uploads/OLA.Presentation.11.30.11.pdf (August 02, 2013).

Bernstein, Jay H. (2009): The Data-Information-Knowledge-Wisdom Hierarchy and Its Antithesis. *Proceedings North American Symposium on Knowledge Organization* 2: 68-75.

Beshears, John, James J. Choi, David Laibson, and Brigitte C. Madrian (2009): How Does Simplified Disclosure Affect Individuals' Mutual Fund Choices? *NBER Working Paper Series* Working Paper 14859.

Bhagwati, Jagdish (1998): The Capital Myth: The Difference between Trade in Widgets and Dollars. *Foreign Affairs* Volume 77 (No. 3): 7-12.

BIS Archives (7.18(15)): The Use of Prudential Measures in the International Banking Markets. *Papers Lamfalussy* LAM25/F67.

Bisenius, Donald J. (2010): "Interview with the Financial Crisis Inquiry Commission." FCIC. http://fcic-static.law.stanford.edu/cdn_media/fcic-audio/2010-09-29 FCIC staff audiotape of interview with Donald J. Bisenius, Freddie Mac.mp3 (March 10, 2014).

Bisias, Dimitrios, Mark D. Flood, Andrew W. Lo, and Stavros Valavanis (2012): A Survey of Systemic Risk Analytics. *Office of Financial Research Working Paper Series* 1.

Black, Julia (2008): Forms and Paradoxes of Principles-Based Regulation. *Capital Markets Law Journal* 3 (4): 425-457.

——— (2012): Restructuring Global and EU Financial Regulation: Character, Capacities, and Learning. In *Financial Regulation and Supervision. A Post-Crisis Analysis*, eds. Eddy Wymeersch, Klaus J. Hopt and Guido Ferrarini. Oxford: Oxford University Press. 3-47.

Blackden, Richard (2012): "Mark Carney: The Goldman Sachs Connection." The Telegraph online. http://www.telegraph.co.uk/finance/newsbysector/banksandfinance/9704522/Mark-Carney-The-Goldman-Sachs-connection.html (April 09, 2013).

Blankfein, Lloyd (2010): "Interview with the Financial Crisis Inquiry Commission." FCIC. http://fcic-static.law.stanford.edu/cdn_media/fcic-audio/2010-06-16 FCIC staff audiotape of interview with Lloyd Blankfein, Goldman Sachs.mp3 (February 11, 2014).

Blinder, Alan (2010): "Interview with the Financial Crisis Inquiry Commission." FCIC. http://fcic-static.law.stanford.edu/cdn_media/fcic-audio/2010-09-

17 FCIC staff audiotape of interview with Alan Blinder, Princeton University.mp3 (March 07, 2014).

Bloomberg (2013a): "Bank Lobbyists Dispute $83 Billion Subsidy. They're Wrong." Bloomberg.com. http://www.bloomberg.com/news/2013-03-12/lobbyists-dispute-our-83-billion-argument-they-re-wrong.html (September 20, 2013).

——— (2013b): "Why Should Taxpayers Give Big Banks $83 Billion a Year?" Bloomberg.com. http://www.bloomberg.com/news/2013-02-20/why-should-taxpayers-give-big-banks-83-billion-a-year-.html (September 20, 2013).

Bloomberg, Michael R., and Charles E. Schumer (2007): "Sustaining New York's and the US' Global Financial Services Leadership." The City of New York. http://www.nyc.gov/html/om/pdf/ny_report_final.pdf (December 06, 2013).

Blyth, Mark (2003): The Political Power of Financial Ideas: Transparency, Risk, and Distribution in Global Finance. In *Monetary Orders: The Political Foundations of Twenty-First Century Money*, ed. Jonathan Kirshner. Ithaca: Cornell University Press. 239-259.

Board of Governors of the Federal Reserve System (2011): "Federal Reserve Board Approves Final Rule Implementing the Resolution Plan Requirement of the Dodd-Frank Act." October 17, 2011. http://www.federalreserve.gov/newsevents/press/bcreg/20111017a.htm (August 01, 2013).

——— (2013a): "Credit and Liquidity Programs and the Balance Sheet." May 09, 2014. http://www.federalreserve.gov/monetarypolicy/bst_recenttrends.htm (May 16, 2014).

——— (2013b): "Designated Financial Market Utilities." February 21, 2014. http://www.federalreserve.gov/paymentsystems/designated_fmu_about.htm (May 16, 2014).

——— (2013c): "Federal Reserve Releases Summary Results of Bank Stress Tests (March 2013)." March 07, 2013. http://www.federalreserve.gov/newsevents/press/bcreg/20130307a.htm (July 25, 2013).

——— (2013d): "List of Financial Holding Companies under the Bank Holding Company Act." February 24, 2014. http://www.federalreserve.gov/bankinforeg/fhc.htm (May 16, 2014).

Boisot, Max, and Agustí Canals (2004): Data, Information and Knowledge: Have We Got It Right? *Journal of Evolutionary Economics* 2004 (14): 43-67.

Bookstaber, Rick (2007): "The Myth of Noncorrelation." September 23, 2007. http://rick.bookstaber.com/2007/09/myth-of-noncorrelation.html (October 28, 2013).

——— (2012): Using Agent-Based Models for Analyzing Threats to Financial Stability. *Office of Financial Research Working Paper Series* 0003 (December 21, 2012).

Bookstaber, Rick, Jill Cetina, Greg Feldberg, Mark Flood, and Paul Glasserman (2013): Stress Tests to Promote Financial Stability: Assessing Progress and Looking to the Future. *Office of Financial Research Working Paper Series* 0010 (July 18, 2013).

Borio, Claudio, Mathias Drehmann, and Kostas Tsatsaronis (2012): Stress-Testing Macro Stress Testing: Does It Live up to Expectations? *Bank for International Settlements Working Paper Series* 369 (January 2012).

Born, Brooksley (2009): "The Warning." Interview conducted by Frontline/PBS. http://www.pbs.org/ wgbh/pages/frontline/warning/interviews/born.html (June 14, 2012).

Braithwaite, Tom (2012): "DoJ Holds 'Sword of Damocles' over HSBC." Financial Times online. http://www.ft.com/intl/cms/s/0/dc80fcf2-43cc-11e2-84 4c-00144feabdc0.html?siteedition=intl (November 06, 2013).

Brandeis, Louis D. (1914): "Other People's Money." The University of Louisville Louis D. Brandeis School of Law. http://www.law.louisville.edu/ library/collections/brandeis/node/191 (Sep-tember 27, 2013).

Braunstein, Sandra, and Carolyn Welch (2002): Financial Literacy: An Overview of Practice, Research, and Policy. *Federal Reserve Bulletin* 88 (11, November 2002): 445-457.

Breeden, Richard (2010): "Interview with the Financial Crisis Inquiry Commission." FCIC. http://fcic-static.law.stanford.edu/cdn_media/fcic-audio/2010-10-14 FCIC staff audiotape of interview with Richard Breeden, Securities and Exchange Commission.mp3 (April 02, 2014).

British Academy (2009): "Letter Send to Her Majesty the Queen on July 22." British Academy. http://www.britac.ac.uk/templates/asset-relay.cfm?frmAsset FileID=8285 (November 25, 2013).

Brown, Sherrod (2013): "Financial Stability and the Problem of Too-Big-to-Fail Financial Institutions. Panel Discussion at the Peterson Institute for International Economics, Washington D.C." IIE. http://www.iie.com /events/event_detail.cfm?EventID=265 (September 20, 2013).

Bruner, Robert F. (2008): "The Financial Panic of 1907: Running from History. Interview with Abigail Tucker." Smithsonian.com. http://www.smith sonianmag.com/history-archaeology/1907_Panic. html (May 16, 2014).

Brush, Silla (2012): "CFTC Approves Swap Definition Triggering Dodd-Frank Rules." Bloomberg.com. http://www.bloomberg.com/news/2012-07-10/cftc-votes-4-1-to-approve-swap-definition-starting-overhaul-1-.html (October 22, 2013).

Buffett, Warren E. (2002): "Letter to the Shareholders of Berkshire Hathaway Inc." Berkshire Hathaway. http://www.berkshirehathaway.com/letters/2002 pdf.pdf (April 05, 2013).

——— (2010): "Interview with the Financial Crisis Inquiry Commission." FCIC. http://fcic-static.law.stanford.edu/cdn_media/fcic-audio/2010-05-26 FCIC staff audiotape of interview with Warren Buffett, Berkshire Hathaway.mp3 (February 18, 2014).

Bush, George (2008): "Christopher Demuth: A Conversation with President Bush." American Enterprise Institute. http://www.aei.org/speech/society-and-culture/free-enterprise/a-conversation-with-p resident-bush/ (March 27, 2013).

Calomiris, Charles (2010): "Interview with the Financial Crisis Inquiry Commission." FCIC. http://fcic-static.law.stanford.edu/cdn_media/fcic-audio/2010-09-10 FCIC staff audiotape of interview with Charles Calomiris, Columbia University.mp3 (March 12, 2014).

Campbell, John L. (2010): Neoliberalism in Crisis: Regulatory Roots of the U.S. Financial Meltdown. In *Markets on Trial. The Economic Sociology of the US Financial Crisis.*, eds. Michael Lounsbury and Paul M. Hirsch. 367-403.

Campbell, John Y., Howell E. Jackson, Brigitte C. Madrian, and Peter Tufano (2011): Consumer Financial Protection. *Journal of Economic Perspectives* 25 (1, Winter 2011): 91-114.

Carpenter, Daniel (2013a): Corrosive Capture? The Dueling Forces of Autonomy and Industry Influence in FDA Pharmaceutical Regulation. In *Preventing Regulatory Capture. Special Interest Influence and How to Limit It*, eds. Daniel Carpenter and David A. Moss. Cambridge: Cambridge University Press. 152-172.

——— (2013b): Detecting and Measuring Capture. In *Preventing Regulatory Capture: Special Interest Influence and How to Limit It*, eds. Daniel Carpenter and David Moss. Cambridge: Cambridge University Press. 57-68.

Carpenter, Daniel, and David Moss (2013): Introduction. In *Preventing Regulatory Capture: Special Interest Influence and How to Limit It*, eds. Daniel Carpenter and David Moss. Cambridge: Cambridge University Press. 1-22.

Carpenter, David H. (2014): "The Consumer Financial Protection Bureau (CFPB): A Legal Analysis." Congressional Research Service. http://www.fas.org/sgp/crs/misc/R42572.pdf (March 20, 2014).

Castro, Gregorio Martín de, Pedro López Sáez, José Emiliio Navas López, and Raquel Galindo Dorado (2007): *Knowledge Creation Processes.* Basingstoke and New York: palgrave macmillan.

Cetorelli, Nicola, and Linda S. Goldberg (2014): Measures of Complexity of Global Banks. *Federal Reserve Bank of New York Economic Policy Review* 20 (2, March 2014).

Cetorelli, Nicola, James McAndrews, and James Traina (2014): Evolution in Bank Complexity. *Federal Reserve Bank of New York Economic Policy Review* 20 (2, March 2014).

Chen, Nan, Paul Glasserman, Behzad Nouri, and Markus Pelger (2013): CoCos, Bail-in, and Tail Risk. *Office of Financial Research Working Paper Series* 0004 (January 23, 2013).

Clark, Alastair, and Andrew Large (2011): *Macroprudential Policy: Addressing the Things We Don't Know*. Washington: Group of Thirty.

Clement, Piet (2010): The Term 'Macroprudential': Origins and Evolution. *BIS Quarterly Review* March 2010: 59-67.

Clinton, Bill (1994): "Remarks to the National Association of Realtors in Anaheim, California, on November 5, 1994." The American Presidency Project. http://www.presidency.ucsb.edu/ws/? pid=49450 (September 10, 2013).

Clowers, A. Nicole (2013): "Testimony of A. Nicole Clowers, Director Financial Markets and Community Investment at the Government Accountability Office, on Who Is Too Big to Fail? GAO's Assessment of the Financial Stability Oversight Council and the Office of Financial Research, March 14 2013." House of Representatives, Committee on Financial Services, Subcommittee on Oversight and Investigations. http://www.gao.gov /assets/660/653013.pdf (September 04, 2013).

Coffee, John C. (2012): The Political Economy of Dodd-Frank: Why Financial Reform Tends to Be Frustrated and Systemic Risk Perpetuated. In *The Regulatory Aftermath of the Global Financial Crisis*, eds. Eilís Ferran, Niamh Moloney, Jennifer G. Hill and John C. Coffee. Cambridge: Cambridge University Press. 301-372.

Coglianese, Cary (1994): *Challenging the Rules: Litigation and Bargaining in the Administrative Process*. Dissertation Submitted in Partial Fulfillment of the Requirements for the Degree of Doctor of Philosophy in the University of Michigan.

Cohan, William (2010): "Interview with the Financial Crisis Inquiry Commission." FCIC. http://fcic-static.law.stanford.edu/cdn_media/fcic-audio/2010-07-30 FCIC staff audiotape of interview with William Cohan, Author.mp3 (April 14, 2014).

Cohn, Gary (2010): "Interview with the Financial Crisis Inquiry Commission." FCIC. http://fcic-static.law.stanford.edu/cdn_media/fcic-audio/2010-06-16 FCIC staff audiotape of interview with Gary Cohn, Goldman Sachs.mp3 (March 01, 2014).

Cole, Margret (2006): "The UK FSA: Nobody Does It Better?" Financial Services Authority. http://www.fsa.gov.uk/library/communication/speeches/2006/1017_mc.shtml (November 06, 2013).

Committee to Establish the National Institute of Finance (2012): "Does the OFR Represent Any Kind of Threat to Personal Privacy?" CE-NIF. http://www.ce-nif.org/faqs-role-of-the-nif/office-of-financial-research (August 24, 2012).

Commodity Futures Trading Commission (2012): "Open Meeting to Consider Final Rule on Further Definition of the Term 'Swap', Final Rule on the End-User Exeption to Clearing, and Proposed Rule to Exempt from Clearing Certain Swaps by Cooperatives." CFTC. http://www.cftc.gov/ucm/groups/public/@swaps/documents/dfsubmission/dfsubmission11_071012-trans.pdf (October 22, 2013).

Commodity Futures Trading Commission, and Securities and Exchange Commission (2012): "Further Definition of 'Swap,' 'Security-Based Swap,' and 'Security-Based Swap Agreement'; Mixed Swaps; Security-Based Swap Agreement Recordkeeping." SEC. https://http://www.sec.gov/rules/final/ 2012/33-9338.pdf (February 20, 2014).

Congressional Budget Office (2009): "The Troubled Asset Relief Program: Report on Transactions through December 31, 2008." CBO. http://www.cbo.gov/publication/41754 (May 16, 2014).

——— (2010): "CBO's Budgetary Treatment of Fannie Mae and Freddie Mac." CBO. http://www.cbo. gov/publication/41887 (May 16, 2014).

Consumer Financial Protection Bureau (2013): "Financial Literacy Annual Report." CFPB. http://files. consumerfinance.gov/f/201307_cfpb_report_financial-literacy-annual.pdf (July 25, 2013).

——— (2014): "About Us." April 09, 2014. http://www.consumerfinance.gov/the-bureau/ (May 16, 2014).

Cooley, Thomas, Kermit Schoenholtz, George David Smith, Richard Sylla, and Paul Wachtel (2010): The Power of Central Banks and the Future of the Federal Reserve System. In *Regulating Wall Street. The Dodd-Frank Act and the New Architecture of Global Finance.*, eds. Viral V. Acharya, Thomas F. Cooley, Matthew Richardson and Ingo Walter. New Jersey: John Wiley & Sons, Inc. 51-71.

Corkery, Michael (2014): "Citigroup Fails Federal Reserve's Stress Test for 2nd Time in 3 Years." The New York Times online. http://dealbook.nytimes.com/2014/03/26/fed-rebuffs-citigroup-on-capital-plans/?_php=true&_type=blogs&_r=0 (March 27, 2014).

Cowen, Tyler (2008): "Bailout of Long-Term Capital: A Bad Precedent?" The New York Times online. http://www.nytimes.com/2008/12/28/business/economy/28view.html?_r=0 (September 13, 2013).

Creswell, Julie, and Ben White (2008): "The Guys from 'Government Sachs'." The New York Times online. http://www.nytimes.com/2008/10/19/business/19gold.html?pagewanted=all&_r=0 (May 16, 2014).

Crittenden, Michael R., and Jeffrey Sparshott (2013): "Banks Are Pressed to Expand 'Living Wills'." The Wall Street Journal online. http://online.wsj.com/article/SB10001424127887324345804578425131915554450.html (July 26, 2013).

Croley, Steven P. (2008): *Regulation and Public Interest. The Possibility of Good Regulatory Government.* Princeton and Oxford: Princeton University Press.

Danielsson, Jon, and Casper de Vries (2008): "Money Market on Strike." The Financial Times online. http://blogs.ft.com/economistsforum/2008/11/money-market-on-strike/ (June 25, 2013).

Darling, Alistair (2009): "Letter to Miroslav Kalousek 'European Financial Regulation and Supervision'." HM Treasury. http://data.parliament.uk/DepositedPapers/Files/DEP2009-0735/DEP2009-0735.pdf (August 6, 2013).

Das, Satyajit (2008): "Interview with Ira Glass." This American Life: Another Frightening Show About the Economy. http://www.thisamericanlife.org/radio-archives/episode/365/transcript (May 16, 2014).

——— (2010a): "Interview with the Financial Crisis Inquiry Commission, Part 1." FCIC. http://fcic-static.law.stanford.edu/cdn_media/fcic-audio/2010-05-07 FCIC staff audiotape of interview with Satyajit Das, (Interview 1).mp3 (March 31, 2014).

——— (2010b): "Interview with the Financial Crisis Inquiry Commission, Part 2." FCIC. http://fcic-static.law.stanford.edu/cdn_media/fcic-audio/2010-08-24 FCIC staff audiotape of interview with Satyajit Das, (Interview 2).mp3 (April 03, 2014).

Davenport, Thomas H., and Larry Prusak (1998): *Working Knowledge: How Organizations Manage What They Know.* Boston: Harvard Business School Press.

Davidoff, Steven M., and David Zaring (2009): Regulation by Deal: The Government's Response to the Financial Crisis. *Administrative Law Review* 61 (3, Summer 2009).

Davis, E. Philip (1995): *Debt, Financial Fragility, and Systemic Risk.* Oxford: Oxford University Press.

De Bandt, Olivier, and Philipp Hartmann (2000): Systemic Risk. A Survey. *European Central Bank Working Paper Series* (35, November 2000).

deHaan, Ed, Simi Kedia, Kevin Koh, and Shivaram Rajgopal (2012): Does the Revolving Door Affect the SEC's Enforcement Outcomes? *Available at SSRN:* http://ssrn.com/abstract=2125560.

Demyanyk, Yuliya, and Otto Van Hemert (2011): Understanding the Subprime Mortgage Crisis. *The Review of Financial Studies* 24 (6): 1848-1880.

Depillis, Lydia (2014): "A Watchdog Grows Up: The Inside Story of the Consumer Financial Protection Bureau." Washington Post online. http://www.washingtonpost.com/blogs/wonkblog/wp/2014/01/11/a-watchdog-grows-up-the-inside-story-of-the-consumer-financial-protection-bureau/ (March 20, 2014).

Deutsche Bank (2012a): "Deutsche Bank Announces Strategic and Financial Aspirations for 2015 and Beyond." Deutsche Bank online. https://http://www.db.com/medien/en/content/3862_4199.htm (February 28, 2014).

——— (2012b): "Deutsche Bank Resolution Plan: Section 1 (Public Section)." Board of Governors of the Federal Reserve Bank. http://www.federalreserve.gov/bankinforeg/deutsche-bank-2012070 3.pdf (August 10, 2012).

Deutscher Wetterdienst (2009): *Wie gut sind Wettervorhersagen? Qualitätsprüfung beim DWD*. Offenbach: DWD.

Dichev, Ilia D. (1998): Is the Risk of Bankruptcy a Systematic Risk? *The Journal of Finance* 53 (3): 1131-1147.

Donnelly, Shawn (2012): Institutional Change at the Top: From the Financial Stability Forum to the Financial Stability Board. In *Crisis and Control. Institutional Change in Financial Market Regulation*, ed. Renate Mayntz. Frankfurt: Campus. 263-277.

Douglas, Danielle (2013): "As Dodd-Frank Turns 3, It Remains a Work in Progress." The Washington Post online. http://www.washingtonpost.com/business/economy/as-dodd-frank-turns-3-it-remains-a-work-in-progress/2013/07/19/ac802820-efcf-11e2-a1f9-ea873b7e0424_story.html (July 25, 2013).

Downs, Anthony (1957): An Economic Theory of Political Action in a Democracy. *Journal of Political Economy* 65 (2, Apr., 1957): 135-150.

Draghi, Mario (2009): "Challenges to Financial Stability and the Proposals of the Financial Stability Board." Presented at the 12th Conference of the ECB-CFS Research Network: Learning from the Crisis – Financial Stability, Macroeconomic Policy and International Institutions, Rome.

——— (2013): "Hearing before the Committee on Economic and Monetary Affairs of the European Parliament on July 08 2013: Introductory

Statement." ESRB. http://www.esrb.europa.eu/news/pr/2013/html/is 130708.en.html (August 29, 2013).
Ducrest, John (2012): "Speech at the Graduate School of Banking." Louisiana State University, Baton Rouge. http://www.csbs.org/news/presentations/ Documents/FinalDucrestLSUSpeech.pdf (June 26, 2013).
Dudley, William C. (2012): "Solving the Too Big to Fail Problem. Remarks at the Clearing House's Second Annual Business Meeting and Conference, New York City." Federal Reserve Bank of New York. http://www. newyorkfed.org/newsevents/speeches/2012/dud121115.html (March 21, 2014).
Duffie, Darrell, and Nicolae Gârleanu (2001): Risk and Valuation of Collateralized Debt Obligations. *Financial Analysts Journal* January/February 2001.
Duhigg, Charles (2008): "Loan-Agency Woes Swell from a Trickle to a Torrent." The New York Times online. http://www.nytimes.com/2008/07/11/ business/11ripple.html?pagewanted=1&_r=0&ei=5124&en=8ad220403fc fdf6e&ex=1373515200&partner=permalink&exprod=permalink (September 04, 2013).

Eavis, Peter (2013): "Fed Still Owes Congress a Blueprint on Its Emergency Lending." The New York Times online. http://dealbook.nytimes.com/ 2013/04/22/fed-still-owes-congress-a-blueprint-on-emergency-lending- to-banks/ (August 05, 2013).
Eavis, Peter, and Ben Protess (2013): "Banks Pass Fed's Tests; Critics Say It Was Easy." The New York Times online. http://query.nytimes.com/gst/ fullpage.html?res=9D04E5DB1039F93BA35750C0 A9659D8B63&ref=supervisorycapitalassessmentprogram (July 25, 2013).
Edelman, Murray (1970): *The Symbolic Uses of Politics*. Urbana a.o.: University of Illinois Press.
Eichler, Alexander (2012): "CFTC Head Gary Gensler: Congress 'Sides with Wall Street'." TheHuffingtonPost.com. http://www.huffingtonpost.com/ 2012/06/08/gary-gensler-cftc-congress_n_1580860.html (August 28, 2012).
Eigen, Manfred, and Ruthild Winkler (1981): *Laws of the Game. How the Principles of Nature Govern Chance*. New York: Alfred A. Knopf.
Einhorn, David (2010): "Interview with the Financial Crisis Inquiry Commission." FCIC. http://fcic-static.law.stanford.edu/cdn_media/fcic-audio/2010-11- 09 FCIC staff audiotape of interview with David Einhorn, Greenlight Capital.mp3 (February 22, 2014).
Eisenhardt, Kathleen M. (1989): Agency Theory: An Assessment and Review. *The Academy of Management Review* 14 (1, January 1989): 57-74.

Elliott, Douglas J., Greg Feldberg, and Andreas Lehnert (2013): The History of Cyclical Macroprudential Policy in the United States. *Office of Financial Research Working Paper Series* 0008 (May 15, 2013).

Engle, Robert (2010): "Testimony of Robert Engle, Stern School of Business, New York University, on Equipping Financial Regulators with the Tools Necessary to Monitor Systemic Risk, February 12 2010." U.S. Senate, Committee on Banking, Housing & Urban Affairs. http://www.banking.senate.gov/public/index.cfm?FuseAction=Hearings.Testimony&Hearing_ID=5478a8c8-6616-4a35-bd74-8fd5adeb1268&Witness_ID=274909c2-7fb4-4ce7-ad68-1832bf78ec52 (May 16, 2014).

Etzioni, Amitai (2009): The Capture Theory of Regulations – Revisited. *Society* 46 (4): 319-323.

European Banking Authority (2011): "Work Programme 2012." EBA. http://www.eba.europa.eu/documents/10180/15748/EBA-BS-2011-137-Final-EBA-work-programme-for-2012-FINAL.pdf /cbe1d67b-c5fd-400c-ab4c-23fb5279a3f9 (August 19, 2013).

——— (2012a): "Annual Report 2012." EBA. http://www.eba.europa.eu/documents/10180/233831/EBA+2012+Annual+Report.pdf/50e3883d-0392-4ace-8af9-789f289dde0b (August 23, 2013).

——— (2012b): "Work Programme 2013." EBA. http://www.eba.europa.eu/documents/10180/15745/EBA-BS-2012-163-FINAL--EBA-work-programme-for-2013-.pdf/d235718d-b11f-496a-8fd3-82daee8a1a80 (August 19, 2013).

——— (2013): "About Us: Organisation." EBA. http://www.eba.europa.eu /about-us/organisation (August 21, 2013).

European Central Bank (2010): "Lessons Learned from the Financial Crisis: Paths Towards Macro-Prudential Supervision and Regulation and the Role of the ECB and the ESCB." Presented at the 23rd Annual Conference of the Group of Banking Supervisors from Central and Eastern Europe (BSCEE), Ohrid.

European Commission (2009): "Communication from the Commission: European Financial Supervision Com(2009) 252 Final." European Commission. https://eiopa.europa.eu/fileadmin/tx_dam/files/pressreleases/Background-Communication-European-Commission-2009.pdf (June 12, 2014).

European Insurance and Occupational Pensions Authority (2012): "Annual Report." EIOPA. https://eiopa.europa.eu/publications/annual-reports/index.html (August 20, 2013).

European Parliament and Council of Ministers (2010a): Regulation (EU) No 1092/2010 of the European Parliament and of the Council of 24 November 2010 on European Union Macro-Prudential Oversight of the Financial System and Establishing a European Systemic Risk Board.

——— (2010b): Regulation (EU) No 1093/2010 of the European Parliament and of the Council of 24 November 2010 Establishing a European Supervisory Authority (European Banking Authority), Amending Decision No 716/2009/EC and Repealing Commission Decision 2009/78/EC.

——— (2010c): Regulation (EU) No 1094/2010 of the European Parliament and of the Council of 24 November 2010 Establishing a European Supervisory Authority (European Insurance and Occupational Pensions Authority), Amending Decision No 716/2009/EC and Repealing Commission Decision 2009/79/EC.

——— (2010d): Regulation (EU) No 1095/2010 of the European Parliament and of the Council of 24 November 2010 Establishing a European Supervisory Authority (European Securities and Markets Authority), Amending Decision No 716/2009/EC and Repealing Commission Decision 2009/77/EC.

European Securities and Markets Authority (2011): "Annual Report." ESMA. http://www.esma.europa. eu/system/files/esma-2011.pdf (August 20, 2013).

——— (2012): "Annual Report." ESMA. http://www.esma.europa.eu/system /files/esma_annual_report _2012_final_2.pdf (August 20, 2013).

European Systemic Risk Board (2012): "Annual Report 2011." ESRB. http://www. esrb.europa.eu/pub/pdf/ar/2011/esrbar2011en.pdf?132b000c3b1411095 0da82b4380bcc01 (May 16, 2014).

——— (2013a): "Annual Report 2012." ESRB. http://www.esrb.europa. eu/pub/pdf/ar/2012/esrbar2012en.pdf?96b4542b34daa72b48e66f4e2711 44c8 (August 09, 2013).

——— (2013b): "High-Level Group on the ESRB Review." ESRB. http://www.esrb.europa.eu/pub/ pdf/other/130708_highlevelgroupreport.pdf?f7070ff8a4a7f651aae0ed2e2 b2bd1d3 (August 29, 2013).

Faber, David (2010): "Interview with the Financial Crisis Inquiry Commission." FCIC. http://fcic-static.law.stanford.edu/cdn_media/fcic-audio/2010-11-19 FCIC staff audiotape of interview with David Faber, CNBC.mp3 (April 09, 2014).

Fama, Eugene F. (1964): *The Behavior of Stock Market Prices. Dissertation Submitted to the Faculty of the Graduate School of Business in Candidacy for the Degree of Doctor of Philosophy*. Chicago: Department of Economics, Graduate School of Business, University of Chicago.

——— (1970): Efficient Capital Markets: A Review of Theory and Empirical Work. *The Journal of Finance* 25 (2): 383-417.

——— (1980): Agency Problems and the Theory of the Firm. *Journal of Political Economy* 88 (2, April 1980).

Fatovic, Clement (2004): Constitutionalism and Presidential Prerogative: Jeffersonian and Hamiltonian Perspectives. *American Journal of Political Science* 48 (3, July 2004): 429-444.

Federal Deposit Insurance Corporation (2011): The Orderly Liquidation of Lehman Brothers Holdings Inc. Under the Dodd-Frank Act. *FDIC Quarterly* 5 (2).

Federal Deposit Insurance Corporation, and Bank of England (2012): "Resolving Globally Active, Systemically Important, Financial Institutions." FDIC. http://www.fdic.gov/about/srac/2012/ gsifi.pdf (August 02, 2013).

Federal Deposit Insurance Corporation, and Board of Governors of the Federal Reserve System (2013): "Guidance for 2013 §165(D) Annual Resolution Plan Submissions by Domestic Covered Com-panies That Submitted Initial Resolution Plans in 2012." Federal Reserve Board of Governors. http://www.federalreserve.gov/newsevents/press/bcreg/bcreg20130415c2.pdf (August 01, 2013).

Federal Register Vol. 76, No. 144 (July 27, 2011): Financial Stability Oversight Council: 12 CFR Chapter XIII and Part 1320, RIN 4030–Aa01, Authority to Designate Financial Market Utilities as Systemically Important, Final Rule.

Federal Register Vol. 77, No. 70 (April 11, 2012): Financial Stability Oversight Council: 12 CFR Part 1310 RIN 4030–Aa00, Authority to Require Supervision and Regulation of Certain Nonbank Financial Companies, Final Rule and Interpretive Guidance.

Fenton-O'Creevy, Mark, Nigel Nicholson, Emma Soane, and Paul Willam (2005): *Traders. Risks, Decisions, and Management in Financial Markets.* Oxford: Oxford University Press.

Ferran, Eilis (2011): Understanding the New Institutional Architecture of EU Financial Market Supervision. *University of Cambridge Legal Studies Research Paper Series* Paper No. 29/2011.

——— (2012a): Crisis-Driven EU Financial Regulatory Reform. *University of Cambridge Legal Studies Research Paper Series* 06/2012 (March 2012).

——— (2012b): Understanding the New Institutional Architecture of EU Financial Market Supervision. In *Financial Regulation and Supervision. A Post-Crisis Analysis*, eds. Eddy Wymeersch, Klaus J. Hopt and Guido Ferrarini. Oxford: Oxford University Press. 111-158.

Ferran, Eilis, and Alexander Kern (2011): *Can Soft Law Bodies Be Effective? Soft Systemic Risk Oversight Bodies and the Special Case of the European Systemic Risk Board.* Cambridge: University of Cambridge. Paper No. 36/2011.

Finance Watch (2010): "Call for a Finance Watch." Finance Watch. http://www.finance-watch.org/ifile/FW_governance_docs/Text-of-the-Initial-Call-for-a-Finance-Watch1.pdf (June 28, 2013).

——— (2013): "Annual Report for 2011 and 2012." Finance Watch. http://www.finance-watch.org/ifile/FW_governance_docs/Annual_report_2011_and_2012.pdf (May 16, 2014).

Financial Crisis Inquiry Commission (2011): *The Financial Crisis Inquiry Report. Final Report of the Nation Commission on the Causes of the Financial and Economic Crisis in the United States*. Washington D.C.: Government Printing Office.

Financial Services Authority (2009): *The Turner Review: A Regulatory Response to the Global Banking Crisis*. London: Financial Services Authority.

Financial Stability Board (2009): "Charter." June 19, 2012. http://www.financial stabilityboard.org/publications/r_090925d.pdf (September 03, 2013).

——— (2011a): "FSB Announces Policy Measures to Address Systemically Important Financial Institutions (Sifis) and Names Initial Group of Global Sifis." FSB. http://www.financial stabilityboard.org/press/pr_111104cc .pdf (March 27, 2014).

——— (2011b): "Shadow Banking: Strengthening Oversight and Regulation. Recommendations of the Financial Stability Board." FSB. http://www.financialstabilityboard.org/list/fsb_publications/tid_150/index.htm (October 27, 2011).

——— (2012): "Report to the G20 Los Cabos Summit on Strengthening FSB Capacity, Resources and Governance." FSB. http://www.financialstability board.org/publications/r_120619c.pdf (Septem-ber 03, 2013).

——— (2013): "Report to the G20 Finance Ministers and Central Bank Governors on Progress in Reforming Resolution Regimes and Resolution Planning for Globally Systemically Important Financial Institutions (G-Sifis)." FSB. http://www.financialstabilityboard.org/publications/r _130419b.pdf (March 27, 2014).

——— (2014): "Key Standards for Sound Financial Systems." FSB. http://www.financialstabilityboard.org/cos/key_standards.htm (March 26, 2014).

Financial Stability Board, and International Monetary Fund (2009): "The Financial Crisis and Information Gaps." IMF. http://www.imf.org/external/np/g20/pdf/102909.pdf (June 04, 2013).

——— (2011): "Financial Crisis and Information Gaps. Implementation Progress Report." IMF. http://www.imf.org/external/np/g20/pdf/063011.pdf (June 04, 2013).

Financial Stability Oversight Council (2011a): "Annual Report." U.S. Department of the Treasury. http://www.treasury.gov/initiatives/fsoc/Documents/FSOCAR2011.pdf (April 04, 2012).

——— (2011b): "FSOC Budget Information." U.S. Department of the Treasury. http://www.treasury. gov/initiatives/fsoc/Documents/6a Principles Meeting Budget ONE PAGER FINAL.pdf (September 23, 2012).

——— (2012a): "Annual Report." U.S. Department of the Treasury. http://www.treasury.gov/initiatives/fsoc/Documents/2012Annual Report.pdf (March 10, 2014).

——— (2012b): "Minutes of the Financial Stability Oversight Council Meeting on July 8, 2012." U.S. Department of the Treasury. http://www.treasury.gov /initiatives/fsoc/Documents/July 18 FSOC Meeting Minutes.pdf (July 12, 2013).

——— (2012c): "Proposed Recommendations Regarding Money Market Mutual Fund Reform." U.S. Department of the Treasury. http://www.treasury. gov/initiatives/fsoc/Documents/Proposed Recommendations Regarding Money Market Mutual Fund Reform - November 13, 2012.pdf (July 16, 2013).

——— (2013a): "Annual Report." U.S. Department of the Treasury. http://www. treasury.gov/initiatives/fsoc/Documents/FSOC2013 Annual Report.pdf (July 05, 2013).

——— (2013b): "FSOC Budget Information." U.S. Department of the Treasury. http://www.treasury. gov/initiatives/fsoc/Documents/FY 2013 FSOC Budget.pdf (April 30, 2013).

——— (2013c): "Meeting Minutes of the July 8, 2013 Meeting." U.S. Department of the Treasury. http://www.treasury.gov/initiatives/fsoc/council-meetings/Documents/July 8, 2013, Notational Votes.pdf (July 12, 2013).

Financial Times (2013): "Fat Finger Errors." Financial Times Online Lexicon. http://lexicon.ft.com/ Term?term=fat-finger-error (September 10, 2013).

Fisher, Richard W. (2013): "Ending 'Too Big to Fail'. Remarks before the Conservative Political Action Conference." Federal Reserve Bank of Dallas. http://www.dallasfed.org/news/speeches/fisher/2013/fs130316 .cfm (May 13, 2014).

Fisher, Richard W., and Harvey Rosenblum (2012): "How Huge Banks Threaten the Economy." The Wall Street Journal online. http://online. wsj.com/article/SB10001424052702303816504577311211082 1340648.html (September 20, 2013).

Flannery, Mark J., Paul Glasserman, David K.A. Mordecai, and Cliff Rossi (2012): Forging Best Practices in Risk Management. *Office of Financial Research Working Paper Series* 0002 (March 26, 2012).

Fligstein, Neil, and Adam Goldstein (2010): The Anatomy of the Mortgage Securitzation Crisis. In *Markets on Trial: The Economic Sociology of the U.S. Financial Crisis*, eds. Michael Lounsbury and Paul Hirsch. Bingley, UK: Emerald Group. 27-68.

Flood, Mark D., and George G. Korenko (2013): Systematic Scenario Selection. *Office of Financial Research Working Paper Series* 0005 (February 07, 2013).

Flood, Mark, H. V. Jagadish, Albert Kyle, Frank Olken, and Louiqa Raschid (2010): »Using Data for Systemic Financial Risk Management.« Presented at the Conference on Innovative Data Systems Research (CIDR), Asilomar, California.

Fonteyne, Wim, Wouter Bossu, Luis Cortavarria-Checkley, Alessandro Giustiniani, Alessandro Gullo, Daniel Hardy, and Seán Kerr (2010): Crisis Management and Resolution for a European Banking System. *IMF Working Paper Series* 10/70.

Ford, Cristie (2013): "Regulatory State, Capture, and Financial Regulatory Reform." Presented at the Political Economy of Financial Regulation Conference at George Washington University Law School, Washington D.C.

Fox, Justin (2009): *The Myth of the Rational Market: A History of Risk, Reward, and Delusion on Wall Street.* New York: HarperCollins Publishers.

Frické, Martin (2009): The Knowledge Pyramid: A Critique of the DIKW Hierarchy. *Journal of Information Science* 35 (2): 131-142.

Fuld, Richard S. (2008): "Testimony of Richard S. Fuld, Jr. on the Causes and Effects of the Lehman Brothers Bankruptcy. October 06, 2008." U.S. House of Representatives, Committee on Oversight and Government Reform. http://online.wsj.com/public/resources/documents/fuldtestimony20081006.pdf (May 16, 2014).

——— (2010): "Interview with the Financial Crisis Inquiry Commission." FCIC. http://fcic-static.law.stanford.edu/cdn_media/fcic-audio/2010-08-24 FCIC staff audiotape of interview with Richard (Dick) S. Fuld, Lehman Brothers.mp3 (March 12, 2014).

Furlong, Scott R. (2005): Exploring Interest Group Participation in Executive Policymaking. In *The Interest Group Connection*, eds. Paul S. Herrnson, Ronald G. Shaiko and Clyde Wilcox. Washington D.C.: CQ Press. 282-297.

Gadinis, Stavros (2012): The SEC and the Financial Industry: Evidence from Enforcement against Broker-Dealers. *The Business Lawyer* 67 (May 2012): 679-728.

——— (2013): The Financial Stability Board: The New Politics of International Financial Regulation. *Texas International Law Journal* 48 (2).

Gai, Prasanna (2013): *Systemic Risk. The Dynamics of Modern Financial Systems.* Oxford: Oxford University Press.

Gai, Prasanna, Andrew Haldane, and Sujit Kapadia (2011): Complexity, Concentration and Contagion. *Journal of Monetary Economics* Vol. 58 (5): 453-470.

Gai, Prasanna, and Sujit Kapadia (2010): Contagion in Financial Networks. *Proceedings of the Royal Society* A 2010 446: 2401-2423.

Garber, Peter M. (1989): Tulipmania. *Journal of Political Economy* 97 (3, June 1989): 535-560.

Geithner, Timothy (2004): "Changes in the Structure of the U.S. Financial System and Implications for Systemic Risk." Federal Reserve Bank of New York. http://www.newyorkfed.org/newsevents/speeches/2004/gei041001.html (April 24, 2013).

——— (2009a): "How We Tested the Big Banks." The New York Times online. http://www.nytimes. com/2009/05/07/opinion/07geithner.html?ref=supervisorycapitalassess mentprogram&_r=0 (July 25, 2013).

——— (2009b): "Press Briefing by Treasury Secretary Tim Geithner on the G20 Meetings in Pittsburgh, Pennsylvania." The White House, Office of the Press Secretary. http://www.whitehouse.gov /the-press-office/press-briefing-treasury-secretary-geithner-g20-meetings (September 02, 2013).

——— (2011): "Interview with Evan Davis." BBC. http://news.bbc.co.uk /today/hi/today/newsid _9404000/9404150.stm (September 21, 2012).

——— (2012): "Letter to FSOC Members on Necessary Money Market Fund Reforms." U.S. Department of the Treasury. http://www.treasury.gov/ connect/blog/Documents/Sec.Geithner. Letter.To.FSOC.pdf (July 16, 2013).

Gensler, Gary (2012): "Interview with Adam Johnson." Bloomberg TV. http://www.ustream.tv/recorded /23309286 (September 18, 2012).

——— (2013): "Testimony of Gary Gensler, Chairman of the U.S. Commodity Futures Trading Commission, Wall Street Reform: Oversight of Financial Stability and Consumer and Investor Protections, February 14 2013." U.S. Senate, Committee on Banking, Housing & Urban Affairs. http://www. banking.senate.gov/public/index.cfm?FuseAction=Hearings.Testimony& Hearing_ID=84abcfc3-9dd8-49ec-b5c0-2f75c618f075&Witness_ID= 5889a57a-fc51-4ed6-89b8-8677fc6f8b16 (June 11, 2013).

Gerlach, Stefan (2009): *Defining and Measuring Systemic Risk.* Brussels: European Parliament, Directorate General for Internal Policies, Policy Department A: Economic and Scientific Policies.

Gieve, John, Jonathan Ford, Gillian Tett, and Paul Woolley (2009): "How to Tame Global Finance. Interview with Adair Turner." Prospect Magazine.

http://www.prospectmagazine.co.uk/ magazine/how-to-tame-global-finance/ - .UiS1LxaeT-Y (September 02, 2013).

Gigerenzer, Gerd (2002): The Adaptive Toolbox. In *Bounded Rationality: The Adaptive Toolbox*, eds. Gerd Gigerenzer and Reinhard Selten. Cambridge: MIT Press. 37-50.

Glasserman, Paul, Chulmin Kang, and Wanmo Kang (2013): Stress Scenario Selection by Empirical Likelihood. *Office of Financial Research Working Paper Series* 0007 (April 9, 2013).

Glasserman, Paul, and H. Peyton Young (2013): How Likely Is Contagion in Financial Networks? *Office of Financial Research Working Paper Series* 0009 (June 21, 2013).

Goffmann, Erving (1974): *Frame Analysis. An Essay on the Organization of Experience.* Cambridge: Harvard University Press.

Goldman Sachs (2012): "Summary of Resolution Plan." Board of Governors of the Federal Reserve System. http://www.federalreserve.gov/bankinforeg/goldman-sachs-20120703.pdf (August 01, 2013).

Goldstein, Morris, and Nicolas Véron (2011): Too Big to Fail: The Transatlantic Debate. *Peterson Institute for International Economics Working Paper* 11-2 (01/2011).

Goodman, Laurie S., Douglas J. Lucas, and Frank J. Fabozzi (2007): Financial Innovations and the Shaping of Capital Markets: The Case of CDOs. *The Journal of Alternative Investments* Summer 2007.

Gorton, Gary (2012): "Finding Balance. Interview by Paula Green." Global Finance Magazine. http://www.gfmag.com/archives/159-september-2012/11969-global-salon-gary-gorton-yale.html - axzz2vmf6Yab1 (March 10, 2014).

Gray, Alistair (2013): "Discord Dogs EU Insurance Rules Shake-Up." Financial Times online. http://www.ft.com/intl/cms/s/0/e1c01a1c-d770-11e2-8279-00144feab7de.html?siteedition=intl-axzz2cg7Ep0no (August 22, 2013).

Greenberger, Michael (2013): "Panel Discussion: The Future Direction of Financial Regulation after the 2012 Election." George Washington University, Center for Law, Economics & Finance (C-LEAF). http://vimeo.com/ user9108723/review/60276063/00647ee6e2 (May 16, 2014).

Greenspan, Alan (1995): "Remarks." Presented at the Conference of Risk Measurement and Systemic Risk, Washington D.C.

——— (1998): "Testimony of Alan Greenspan, Chairman of the Federal Reserve System, on Private-Sector Refinancing of the Large Hedge Fund, Long-Term Capital Management, October 01 1998." U.S. House of Representatives, Committee on Banking and Financial Services.

http://www.federalreserve.gov/boarddocs/testimony/1998/19981001.htm (September 13, 2013).
——— (2010): "Interview with the Financial Crisis Inquiry Commission." FCIC. http://fcic-static.law.stanford.edu/cdn_media/fcic-docs/2010-03-31 FCIC memo of staff interview with Alan Greenspan Interview, Federal Reserve Board.pdf (March 31, 2014).
Griffith-Jones, Stephany, Eric Helleiner, and Ngaire Woods, eds (2010): *The Financial Stability Board: An Effective Fourth Pillar of Global Economic Governance? Special Report. The Centre for International Governance Innovation.* Waterloo, Ontario: CIGI.
Grossman, Gene M., and Elhanan Helpman (2001): *Special Interest Politics.* Cambridge and London: MIT Press.
Group of Thirty (1997): *Global Institutions, National Supervision and Systemic Risk. A Study Group Report.* Washington D.C.: Group of Thirty.
——— (2009): *Financial Reform. A Framework for Financial Stability.* Washington, D.C.: Group of Thirty.
Group of Twenty (2009): "Global Plan Annex: Declaration on Strengthening the Financial System. Statement Issued by the G20 Leaders in London, April 2, 2009." Group of Twenty. http://www. g20.utoronto.ca/2009/ 2009ifi.html (September 03, 2013).
Grynbaum, Michael M. (2008): "Fed Plans to Lend $200 Billion to Banks." The New York Times online. http://www.nytimes.com/2008/03/11/business /11cnd-fed.html (July 03, 2013).
Guillén, Mauro, and Sandra Suárez (2010): The Global Crisis of 2007-2009: Markets, Politics, and Organizations. In *Markets on Trial. The Economic Sociology of the US Financial Crisis*, eds. Michael Lounsbury and Paul Hirsch. Bingley, UK: Emerald Group. 255-277.

Haldane, Andrew G. (2009): "Rethinking the Financial Network." BIS. http://www.bis.org/review/r0905 05e.pdf?frames=0 (May 16, 2014).
——— (2010): "The $100 Billion Question. Speech at the Institute of Regulation & Risk, Hong Kong." Bank of England. http://www.bankofengland.co.uk /publications/Documents/speeches/2010/speech433.pdf (September 24, 2013).
——— (2011): "On Tackling the Credit Cycle and Too Big to Fail." Institute of International and European Affairs. http://www.iiea.com/event/ download_powerpoint?urlKey=andrew-haldane-on-fixing-finance (November 25, 2013).
——— (2012): "On Being the Right Size." Presented at the Institute of Economic Affairs' 22nd Annual Series 2012 Beesley Lectures, Pall Mall.

Haldane, Andrew G., and Vasileios Madouros (2012): "The Dog and the Frisbee." Presented at the Federal Reserve Bank of Kansas City's 366th economic policy symposium: "The changing policy landscape", Jackson Hole, Wyoming.

Haldane, Andrew G., and Robert M. May (2011): Systemic Risk in Banking Ecosystems. *Nature* 469 (20 January 2011): 351-355.

Haldane, Andrew G., and Benjamin Nelson (2012): "Tails of the Unexpected." Presented at the Conference on Credit Crisis Five Years On: Unpacking the Crisis, University of Edinburgh Business School.

Hamada, Robert S. (1972): The Effect of the Firm's Capital Structure on the Systematic Risk of Common Stocks. *The Journal of Finance* 27 (2): 435-452.

Hansen, Lars Peter (2013): Challenges in Identifying and Measuring Systemic Risk (Draft of May 23, 2013). In *Risk Topography: Systemic Risk and Macro Modeling*, eds. Markus K. Brunnermeier and Arvind Krishnamurthy. Chicago: University of Chicago Press.

Hanson, Samuel G., Anil K Kashyap, and Jeremy C. Stein (2011): A Macroprudential Approach to Financial Regulation. *Journal of Economic Perspectives* 25 (1, Winter 2011): 3-28.

Harrison, J. Michael, and David M. Kreps (1978): Speculative Behavior in a Stock Market with Heterogeneous Expectations. *The Quarterly Journal of Economics* 92 (2, May 1978): 232-336.

Hayek, Friedrich A. von (1945): The Use of Knowledge in Society. *The American Economic Review* XXXV (4): 519-530.

——— (1974): The Pretence of Knowledge. *Prize Lecture to the Memory of Alfred Nobel, December 11, 1974.*

——— (2007 [1967]): The Theory of Complex Phenomena. *E:CO* 9 (1-2 2007): 143-165.

Heider, Florian, Marie Hoerova, and Cornelia Holthausen (2009): Liquidity Hoarding and Interbank Market Spreads. The Role of Counterparty Risk. *ECB Working Paper Series* 1126 (December 2009).

Helbing, Dirk (2010): "Systemic Risks in Society and Economics." International Risk Governance Council. http://www.futurict.eu/sites/default/files/ Systemic risks in society and economics.pdf (January 22, 2014).

Helleiner, Eric (2010a): The Financial Stability Board and International Standards. *CIGI G20 Papers* 1 (June 2010).

——— (2010b): Governance Issues Relating to the FSB and International Standards. In *The Financial Stability Board: An Effective Fourth Pillar of Global Economic Governance? Special Report. The Centre for International Governance Innovation*, eds. Stephany Griffith-Jones, Eric Helleiner and Ngaire Woods. Waterloo, Ontario: CIGI. 28-31.

Helleiner, Eric, and Tony Porter. 2009. "Making Transnational Networks More Accountable." In *Dialogue on Globalization. Occasional Paper No. 42*, ed. Friedrich Ebert Stiftung. New York: Friedrich Ebert Stiftung. 14-24.

Henderson, Brian J., and Neil D. Pearson (2009): The Dark Side of Financial Innovation. *EFA 2009 Bergen Meetings Paper. Available at* http://ssrn.com/abstract=1342654.

Henriques, Diana B. (2008): "Treasury to Guarantee Money Market Funds." The New York Times online. http://www.nytimes.com/2008/09/20/business/20moneys.html (October 21, 2013).

Henry, David (2013): "U.S. Government Selling Last of Its Citigroup Bailout Securities." Reuters. http://www.reuters.com/article/2013/09/10/us-citigroup-bailout-idUSBRE98918Q20130910 (November 29, 2013).

Herring, Richard, and Jacopo Carmassi (2012): "The Corporate Structure of International Financial Conglomerates: Complexity and Its Implications for Safety and Soundness." In *The Oxford Handbook on Banking*, eds. Allen N. Berger, Philip Molyneux and John O. S. Wilson. http://www.oxfordhandbooks.com/view/10.1093/oxfordhb/9780199640935.001.0001/oxfordhb-9780199640935: Oxford Handbooks Online.

Herring, Richard J. (2009): Wind-Down Plans as an Alternative to Bailouts. *PEW Briefing Paper Series* 15.

High Level Group on Financial Supervision in the EU, chaired by Jacques de Larosière (2009): *Report*. Brussels: European Commission.

Hilgert, Marianne A., Jeanne M. Hogarth, and Sondra G. Beverly (2003): Household Financial Management: The Connection between Knowledge and Behavior. *Federal Reserve Bulletin* 89 (7, July 2003): 309-322.

Hirshleifer, Jack, and John G. Riley (1979): The Analytics of Uncertainty and Information – an Expository Study. *Journal of Economic Literature* 17 (4, December 1979): 1375-1421.

Hodson, Dermot, and Lucia Quaglia (2009): European Perspectives on the Global Financial Crisis: Introduction. *Journal of Common Market Studies* 47 (5): 939-953.

Hoenig, Thomas M. (1999): "Financial Industry Megamergers and Policy Challenges." Federal Reserve Bank of Kansas City. http://www.kc.frb.org/publicat/econrev/PDF/3q99hoen.pdf (November 11, 2013).

Holder, Eric H. (2013): "Testimony and Hearing of Eric H. Holder, Attorney General of the United States, on Oversight of the U.S. Department of Justice, March 06 2013." U.S. Senate Committee on the Judiciary. http://www.judiciary.senate.gov/hearings/hearing.cfm?id=e0c4315749c10b 084028087a4aa80a73 (September 23, 2013).

Horne, Stephen C. (2010): "Testimony of Stephen C. Horne, Vice President, Master Data Management and Integration Services, Dow Jones Business &

Relationship Intelligence, on Equipping Financial Regulators with the Tools Necessary to Monitor Systemic Risk, February 12 2010." U.S. Senate, Committee on Banking, Housing & Urban Affairs, Subcommittee on International Trade and Finance. http://www.banking.senate.gov/public/index.cfm?FuseAction=Hearings.Testimony&Hearing_ID=5478a8c8-6616-4a35-bd74-8fd5adeb1268&Witness_ID=1b09ca13-7caf-4d80-8593-57bdbfa0d1b8 (June 12, 2013).

Hu, Henry T. C. (2009): "Testimony of Henry T.C. Hu, Allan Shivers Chair in the Law of Banking and Finance University of Texas School of Law, on over-the-Counter Derivatives: Modernizing Oversight to Increase Transparency and Reduce Risks, June 22 2009." U.S. Senate, Banking Committee, Subcommittee on Securities, Insurance, and Investment. http://www.banking.senate.gov/public/index.cfm?FuseAction=Hearings.Testimony&Hearing_ID=34ee16e5-5bf4-4bb1-85db-d05d911c08a0&Witness_ID=5136d3f7-fabd-400f-995d-e584eda3acdc (September 27, 2013).

——— (2012): Too Complex to Depict? Innovation, 'Pure Information,' and the SEC Disclosure Paradigm. *Texas Law Review* 90 (7): 1601-1715.

Institute of International Finance (2011): »Cumulative Impact in the Global Economy of Changes in the Financial Regulatory Framework.« IIF. http://www.iif.com/download.php?id=oXT67gHVBJk= (December 16, 2013).

International Monetary Fund (2008): *Global Financial Stability Report. Containing Systemic Risks and Restoring Financial Soundness.* Washington D.C.: IMF.

——— (2009): *Global Financial Stability Report: Responding to the Financial Crisis and Measuring Systemic Risks.* Washington DC: IMF.

——— (2010): *Central Banking Lessons from the Crisis.* Washington D.C.: IMF.

——— (2013a): "European Union: Publication of Financial Sector Assessment Program Documentation – Technical Note on European Banking Authority." IMF. http://www.imf.org/external/pubs/ft/scr/2013/cr1374.pdf (August 19, 2013).

——— (2013b): "European Union: Publication of Financial Sector Assessment Program Documentation – Technical Note on European Insurance and Occupational Pensions Authority Assessment." IMF. http://www.imf.org/external/pubs/ft/scr/2013/cr1373.pdf (August 21, 2013).

——— (2013c): "European Union: Publication of Financial Sector Assessment Program Documentation – Technical Note on European Securities and Markets Authority." IMF. http://www.imf.org/external/pubs/ft/scr/2013/cr1369.pdf (August 20, 2013).

International Monetary Fund, Bank for International Settlements, and Financial Stability Board (2009): "Report to G20 Finance Ministers and Governors: Guidance to Assess the Systemic Importance of Financial Institutions, Markets and Instruments: Initial Considerations." BIS. http://www.bis.org/publ/othp07.pdf (September 11, 2013).

International Organization of Securities Commissions (2011): Mitigating Systemic Risk. A Role for Securities Regulators. *OICU-IOSCO Discussion Papers* 02/2011 (February 2011).

International Risk Governance Council (2010): *The Emergence of Risks: Contributing Factors.* Geneva: IRGC.

Jackson, Howell E. (2001): The Role of Credit Rating Agencies in the Establishment of Capital Standards for Financial Institutions in a Global Economy. In *Regulating Financial Services and Markets in the Twenty First Century*, eds. Eilís Ferran and Charles Goodhart. Oxford and Portland: Hart Publishing. 311-322.

Jaffe, Louis L. (1970): The Federal Regulatory Agencies in Perspective: Administrative Limitations in a Political Setting. *Boston College Industrial and Commercial Law Review* 11 (4, May 1970): 565-570.

Jenkins, Patrick (2012): "EBA Chief Plots Path to Banking Union." Financial Times online. http://www.ft.com/intl/cms/s/0/574c19ac-cd1d-11e1-b78b-00144feabdc0.html-axzz2cnNXs Bvn (August 23, 2013).

Jenkins, Patrick, and Brooke Masters (2013): "EBA Set to Opt for Pragmatism over Publicity." Financial Times online. http://www.ft.com/intl/cms/s/0 /b0bd83dc-50d0-11e1-ab40-00144feabdc0.html-axzz2cnNXsBvn (August 23, 2013).

Jenkins, Robert (2012): "Let's Make a Deal. Speech at the Worshipful Company of Actuaries, Haberdasher's Hall, London." The Bank of England. http://www.bankofengland.co.uk/publi cations/Documents/speeches/2012/speech593.pdf (September 20, 2013).

Jensen, Michael C., and William H. Meckling (1976): Theory of the Firm: Managerial Behavior, Agency Costs and Ownership Structure. *Journal of Financial Economics* 3 (4, October 1976): 305-360.

Jickling, Mark, and Edward V. Murphy (2010): *Who Regulates Whom? An Overview of U.S. Financial Supervision. CRS Report for Congress. Prepared for Members and Committees of Congress.* Washington D.C.: Congressional Research Service.

Johnson, Simon (2012): "The Market Has Spoken – and It Is Rigged." The Baseline Scenario. http://baselinescenario.com/2012/07/12/the-market-has-spoken-and-it-is-rigged/ (January 15, 2014).

——— (2013): "Keynote Address." Presented at the Conference on the Political Economy of Financial Regulation, George Washington University Center for Law, Economics & Finance (C-LEAF), The George Washington University Law School.

Jones, David (2010): "Interview with the Financial Crisis Inquiry Commission." FCIC. http://fcic-static.law.stanford.edu/cdn_media/fcic-audio/2010-10-19 FCIC staff audiotape of interview with David Jones, Federal Reserve Board.mp3 (April 01, 2014).

JP Morgan Chase (2012): "JP Morgan Chase & Co. Resolution Plan, Public Filing." Board of Governors of the Federal Reserve System. http://www.federalreserve.gov/bankinforeg/jpmorgan-chase-20120703.pdf (August 01, 2013).

Kahneman, Daniel (2003): Maps of Bounded Rationality: Psychology for Behavioral Economics. *The American Economic Review* 93 (5, Dec. 2003): 1449-1475.

——— (2011): *Thinking, Fast and Slow*. London: Penguin Books.

Kahneman, Daniel, and Amos Tversky (1984): Choices, Values, and Frames. 1983 APA Award Adress. *American Psychologist* 39 (4): 341-350.

Kamieniecki, Sheldon (2006): *Corporate America and Environmental Policy*. Stanford: Stanford University Press.

Kane, Edward J. (1986): Technology and the Regulation of Financial Markets. In *Technology and the Regulation of Financial Markets*, eds. Anthony Saunders and Lawrence J. White. Lexington: Lexington Books. 187-193.

——— (2011): Missing Elements in US Financial Reform: A Kübler-Ross Interpretation of the Inadequacy of the Dodd-Frank Act. *Available at SSRN:* http://ssrn.com/abstract=1654051.

Kashkari, Neel (2010): "Interview with the Financial Crisis Inquiry Commission." FCIC. http://fcic-static.law.stanford.edu/cdn_media/fcic-audio/2010-11-02 FCIC staff audiotape of interview with Neel Kashkari, Department of the Treasury.mp3 (February 19, 2014).

Kaufman, George G. (1996): Bank Failures, Systemic Risk, and Bank Regulation. *The Cato Journal* 16 (1, Spring/Summer 1996): 17-45.

Kavoussi, Bonnie (2012): "Andrew Williams, Ex-Treasury Spokesman, Headed to Goldman Sachs." The Huffington Post online. http://www.huffington post.com/2012/07/12/andrew-williams-gold man-sachs_n_1669021.html (April 09, 2013).

Kay, John (2012): "Finance Needs Stewards, Not Toll Collectors." The Financial Times online. http://www.ft.com/intl/cms/s/0/f61fe69a-d27b-11e1-8700-00144feabdc0.html-axzz31srn6JAC (May 16, 2014).

Keloharju, Matti, Samuli Knüpfer, and Juhani Linnainmaa (2012): Do Investors Buy What They Know? Product Market Choices and Investment Decisions. *The Review of Financial Studies* 25 (10, 2012): 2921-2958.

Kennedy, David (2001): The Politics of the Invisible College: International Governance and the Politics of Expertise. *European Human Rights Law Review* (5 2001): 463-497.

Kennedy, Leonard J., Patricia A. McCoy, and Ethan Bernstein (2012): The Consumer Financial Protection Bureau: Financial Regulation for the Twenty-First Century. *Cornell Law Review* 97: 1141-1176.

Kern, Steffen, and Sarah Lantz (2012): Macro-Prudential Financial Supervision in the US. The Financial Stability Oversight Council (FSOC). *Deutsche Bank Research: Current Issues* April 2012.

Kiser, Edgar (1999): Comparing Varieties of Agency Theory in Economics, Political Science, and Sociology: An Illustration from State Policy Implementation. *Sociological Theory* 17 (2, July 1999): 146-170.

Kissinger, Henry (2009): "The Chance for a New World Order." The New York Times online. http://www.nytimes.com/2009/01/12/opinion/12iht-edkissinger.1.19281915.html?page wanted=2 (June 19, 2013).

Knight, Frank H. (1964): *Risk, Uncertainty and Profit.* New York: Augustus M. Kelley.

Knorr-Cetina, Karin (2005): How Are Global Markets Global? The Architecture of a Flow World. In *The Sociology of Financial Markets*, eds. Karin Knorr-Cetina and Alex Preda. Oxford: Oxford University Press. 38-61.

Knorr-Cetina, Karin, and Urs Bruegger (2002): Global Microstructures: The Virtual Societies of Financial Markets. *American Journal of Sociology* 107 (4): 905-950.

Knorr-Cetina, Karin, and Alex Preda, eds (2005): *The Sociology of Financial Markets.* Oxford: Oxford University Press.

Kohlhagen, Steve (2010): "Interview with the Financial Crisis Inquiry Commission." FCIC. http://fcic-static.law.stanford.edu/cdn_media/fcic-audio/2010-05-24 FCIC staff audiotape of interview with Steve Kohlhagen, University of California Berkeley.mp3 (April 13, 2014).

Krawiec, Kimberly D. (2013): Don't 'Screw Joe the Plummer': The Sausage-Making of Financial Reform. *Duke Law Journal* 55 (0): 2-31.

Krugman, Paul (2010): "Too Big to Fail Fail?" The New York Times online. http://krugman.blogs. nytimes.com/2010/01/11/too-big-to-fail-fail-2/ (September 20, 2013).

Kumar, Dilip, and Sandeep Mangaraj (2012): "Living Wills: The IT Implications." Bank Systems & Technology. http://www.banktech.com/risk-manage ment/living-wills-the-it-implications/24000

5236?queryText=Living+wills%3A+the+IT+implications (November 21, 2013).
Kwak, James (2012a): "Can Financial Regulation Be Fixed?" The Baseline Scenario. http://baseline scenario.com/2012/07/25/fixing-financial-regulation/ (January 15, 2014).
——— (2012b): "Simple or Complex?" The Baseline Scenario. http://baseline scenario.com/2012/09/14/simple-or-complex/ (November 11, 2013).
——— (2013): Cultural Capture and the Financial Crisis. In *Preventing Regulatory Capture. Special Interest Influence and How to Limit It*, eds. Daniel Carpenter and David A. Moss. Cambridge: Cambridge University Press. 71-98.

Lacker, Jeffrey M. (2013): "Testimony of Jeffrey M. Lacker, President and Chief Executive Officer, Federal Reserve Bank of Richmond, on Examining How the Dodd-Frank Act Could Result in More Taxpayer-Funded Bailouts, June 26 2013." U.S. House of Representatives, Committee on Financial Services. https://http://www.richmondfed.org/press_room/speeches/president_jeff_ lacker/2013/lacker_testimony_20130626.cfm (August 01, 2013).
Laffont, Jean-Jacques, and Jean Tirole (1993): *A Theory of Incentives in Procurement and Regulation*. Cambridge and London: The MIT Press.
Laffont, Jean-Jaques, and Jean Tirole (1991): The Politics of Government Decision-Making: A Theory of Regulatory Capture. *The Quarterly Journal of Economics* November 1991: 1089-1127.
Lagarde, Christine (2013): "The Global Financial Sector – Transforming the Landscape." Presented at the Frankfurt Finance Summit, March 19, 2013, Frankfurt.
Lamson, Donald N., and Sylvia Favretto (2013): "FSOC's Risky Push for Money-Market Fund Reform." American Banker online. http://www.americanbanker.com/bankthink/fsocs-risky-push-for-mo ney-market-fund-reform-1056877-1.html (July 16, 2013).
Landis, James M. (1947 [1938]): *The Administrative Process*. New Haven: Yale University Press.
——— (1960): "Report on Regulatory Agencies to the President-Elect". SECHistorical.org. http://3197d6d14b5f19f2f440-5e13d29c4c016cf96cbbfd197c579b45.r81.cf1.rackcdn.com/collection/papers/1960/1960_1221_Landis_report.pdf (November 26, 2013).
Lane, Robert E. (1966): The Decline of Politics and Ideology in a Knowledgeable Society. *American Sociological Review* 31 (5, October 1966): 649-662.

Langevoort, Donald C. (1992): Theories, Assumptions, and Securities Regulation: Market Efficiency Revisited. *University of Pennsylvania Law Review* 140 (3, January 1992): 851-920.

Langley, Monica (2012): "Inside J.P. Morgan's Blunder." The Wall Street Journal online. http://online.wsj.com/article/SB10001424052702303448404577410341236847980.html (September 27, 2013).

Lerner, Josh (2009): "The Litigation of Financial Innovations." Hardvard Business School. http://www.people.hbs.edu/jlerner/FinPatLit.09222009.pdf (October 22, 2013).

Levine, Michael E., and Jennifer L. Forrence (1990): Regulatory Capture, Public Interest, and the Public Agenda: Toward a Synthesis. *Journal of Law, Economics, & Organization* 6, Special Issue (April 1990): 167-198.

Levitin, Adam J. (2010a): "Interview with the Financial Crisis Inquiry Commission." FCIC. http://fcic-static.law.stanford.edu/cdn_media/fcic-audio/2010-10-28 FCIC staff audiotape of interview with Adam Levitin, Georgetown University.mp3 (February 19, 2014).

——— (2010b): "Testimony and Questioning of Adam J. Levitin, Professor of Law Georgetown University Law Center, on Robo-Singing, Chain of Title, Loss Mitigation, and Other Issues in Mortgage Servicing, November 18 2010." U.S. House of Representatives, Financial Services Committee, Subcommittee on Housing and Community Opportunity. http://www.youtube.com /watch?v=ibgdgl0PoBw (December 20, 2013).

——— (2011): In Defense of Bailouts. *The Georgetown Law Journal* 99 (2): 437-514.

Levitt, Arthur (2010): "Interview with the Financial Crisis Inquiry Commission." FCIC. http://fcic-static.law.stanford.edu/cdn_media/fcic-audio/2010-10-01 FCIC staff audiotape of interview with Arthur Levitt, Securities and Exchange Commission.mp3 (April 24, 2014).

——— (2013): "Interview with Tom Keene and Ken Prewitt." Bloomberg.com. http://media.bloomberg.com/bb/avfile/vVBhcf5t_xpk.mp3 (May 13, 2014).

Levitt, Barbara, and James G. March (1988): Organizational Learning. *Annual Review of Sociology* 1988 (14): 319-340.

Lewis, Michael (2011): *The Big Short. Inside the Doomsday Machine. With a New Afterword.* New York: W. Nortin & Company.

Liberto, Jennifer (2013): "Living Wills for Megabanks Released." CNN Money. http://money.cnn.com/2012/07/03/news/economy/bank-living-wills/index.htm (August 01, 2013).

Lindblom, Charles (1977): *Politics and Markets. The World's Political-Economic Systems.* New York: Basic Books.

Livermore, Michael A., and Richard L. Revesz (2013): Can Executive Review Help Prevent Capture? In *Preventing Regulatory Capture. Special Interest Influence and How to Limit It*, eds. Daniel Carpenter and David A. Moss. Cambridge: Cambridge University Press. 420-450.

Lo, Andrew W. (2011): Fear, Greed, and Financial Crises: A Cognitive Neurosciences Perspective (Draft). *Available at SSRN:* http://ssrn.com/abstract=1943325

Lounsbury, Michael, and Paul Hirsch, eds (2010): *Markets on Trial: The Economic Sociology of the U.S. Financial Crisis.* Bingley, UK: Emerald Group.

Lowenstein, Roger (2008): "Bleakonomics." The New York Times online. http://www.nytimes.com/2008/03/30/magazine/30wwln-lede-t.html (July 03, 2013).

Lubben, Stephen J. (2011): "The F.D.I.C.'S Lehman Fantasy." The New York Times online. http://deal book.nytimes.com/2011/04/29/the-f-d-i-c-s-lehman-fantasy/?_r=0 (August 02, 2013).

——— (2013): Resolution, Orderly and Otherwise: B of A in OLA. *University of Cincinnati Law Review* 81 (2013): 1-35.

Ludwig, Eugene (2010): "Interview with the Financial Crisis Inquiry Commission." FCIC. http://fcic-static.law.stanford.edu/cdn_media/fcic-audio/2010-09-02 FCIC staff audiotape of interview with Eugene Ludwig, Promotory Financial Group.mp3 (April 05, 2014).

Luhmann, Niklas (2008): *Risk. A Sociological Theory.* New Brunswick, London: Transaction Publishers.

Luttrell, David, Tyler Atkinson, and Harvey Rosenblum (2013): Assessing the Costs and Consequences of the 2007-09 Financial Crisis and Its Aftermath. *Federal Reserve Bank of Dallas Economic Letter* 8 (7, September 2013).

Lyons, John (2010): "Interview with the Financial Crisis Inquiry Commission." FCIC. http://fcic-static.law.stanford.edu/cdn_media/fcic-audio/2010-03-12 FCIC staff audiotape of interview with John Lyons, Office of the Comptroller of the Currency.mp3 (April 01, 2014).

Machlup, Fritz (1980): Knowledge and Knowledge Production. In *Knowledge: Its Creation, Distribution, and Economic Significance, Vol. 1*, ed. Fritz Machlup. Princeton: Princeton University Press.

——— (1984): The Economics of Information and Human Capital. In *Knowledge: Its Creation, Distribution, and Economic Significance, Vol. 3*, ed. Fritz Machlup. Princeton: Princeton University Press.

MacKenzie, Donald (2005): How a Superportfolio Emerges: Long-Term Capital Management and the Socoiology of Arbitrage. In *The Sociology of Financial Markets*, eds. Karin Knorr-Cetina and Alex Preda. Oxford: Oxford University Press. 62-83.

MacKenzie, Donald, Fabian Muniesa, and Lucia Siu, eds (2007): *Do Economists Make Markets? On the Performativity of Economics*. Princeton: Princeton University Press.

Maheras, Thomas (2010): "Interview with the Financial Crisis Inquiry Commission." FCIC. http://fcic-static.law.stanford.edu/cdn_media/fcic-docs/2010-03-10 transcript of FCIC staff interview with Thomas Maheras, Citigroup.pdf (March 25, 2014).

Malkiel, Burton G. (2003): The Efficient Market Hypothesis and Its Critics. *The Journal of Economic Perspectives* 17 (1, Winter 2003): 59-82.

Mamudi, Sam (2008): "Lehman Folds with Record $613 Billion Debt." Market Watch. http://www.marketwatch.com/story/lehman-folds-with-record-613-billion-debt?siteid=rss (August 10, 2012).

Mandelker, Gershon N., and S. Ghon Rhee (1984): The Impact of the Degrees of Operating and Financial Leverage on Systematic Risk of Common Stock. *Journal of Financial and Quantitative Analysis* 19 (01): 45-57.

Mankiw, Greg (2010): "Interview with the Financial Crisis Inquiry Commission." FCIC. http://fcic-static.law.stanford.edu/cdn_media/fcic-audio/2010-10-27 FCIC staff audiotape of interview with Greg Mankiw, Harvard University.mp3 (March 18, 2014).

Manzoor, Sarfraz (2013): "Quants: The Maths Geniuses Running Wall Street." The Telegraph online. http://www.telegraph.co.uk/finance/10188335/Quants-the-maths-geniuses-running-Wall-Street.html (September 04, 2013).

March, James G., and Herbert A. Simon (1993 [1958]): *Organizations*. Cambridge: Blackwell.

Markose, Sheri, Simone Giansante, Mateusz Gatkowski, and Ali Rais Shaghaghi (2010): Too Inter-connected to Fail: Financial Contagion and Systemic Risk in Network Model of CDS and Other Credit Enhancement Obligations of US Banks. *University of Essex, Department of Economics Discussion Paper Series* 683 (February 2010).

Markowitz, Harry (2010): "Interview with the Financial Crisis Inquiry Commission." FCIC. http://fcic-static.law.stanford.edu/cdn_media/fcic-audio/2010-09-13FCIC staff audiotape of interview with Harry Markowitz, University of California San Diego.mp3 (April 06, 2014).

Masciandaroa, Donato, Maria J. Nietob, and Marc Quintync (2011): Exploring Governance of the New European Banking Authority – a Case for Harmonization? *Journal of Financial Stability* 7 (2011): 204-214.

Masters, Brooke (2013a): "ESMA Criticises Agencies' Rating Methods." Financial Times online. http://www.ft.com/intl/cms/s/0/7dd71cc8-8fca-11e2-9239-00144feabdc0.html?siteedition=intl-axzz2cnNXsBvn (August 23, 2013).

——— (2013b): "ESMA Probes Agencies' Views on Banks." Financial Times online. http://www.ft.com Z/intl/cms/s/0/93b049e0-c359-11e1-966e-00144feabdc0.html-axzz2cnNXsBvn (August 23, 2013).

Matz, Debbie (2012): "Interview with Jennifer Openshaw." The Wall Street Journal, Market Watch. http://www.marketwatch.com/story/credit-unions-offer-consumer-choices-2012-06-06 (May 13, 2014).

Mayer, Thomas (1975): Should Large Banks Be Allowed to Fail? *The Journal of Financial and Quantitative Analysis* 10 (4, November 1975).

Mayntz, Renate (2010a): Die Handlungsfähigkeit des Nationalstaats bei der Regulierung der Finanzmärkte. *Leviathan* 38: 175–187.

——— (2010b): Die transnationale Ordnung globalisierter Finanzmärkte. Was lehrt uns die Krise? *MPIfG Working Paper* 10/8.

——— (2013): Financial Market Regulation in the Shadow of the Sovereign Debt Crisis. *MPIfG Discussion Paper* 13/11.

———, ed. (2012): *Crisis and Control. Institutional Change in Financial Market Regulation*. Frankfurt: Campus.

Mayntz, Renate, and Fritz W. Scharpf (2005): Politische Steuerung – Heute? *MPIfG Working Paper* 05/1.

McCarty, Nolan (2013): Complexity, Capacity, and Capture. In *Preventing Regulatory Capture. Special Interest Influence and How to Limit It*, eds. Daniel Carpenter and David A. Moss. Cambridge: Cambridge University Press. 99-123.

McCarty, Nolan, Keith T. Poole, and Howard Rosenthal (2013): *Political Bubbles: Financial Crises and the Failure of American Democracy*. Princeton: Princeton University Press.

McConnell, Mitch (2013): "McConnell, 42 Senators Demand Accountability and Transparency at the Consumer Financial Protection Bureau." CFPB Monitor. http://www.cfpbmonitor.com/files/2013/02/Senate-Republican-Leader-McConnell-42-Senators-Demand-Accountability-and-Transparency-at-the-Consumer-Financial-Protection-Bureau-Full-Text-of-February-2013-and-May-2011-Letters-to-President-Obama.pdf (March 20, 2014).

McCurry, Justin (2005): "Too Fat, Too Fast. The £1.6bn Finger." The Guardian online. http://www.the guardian.com/business/2005/dec/09/japan.internationalnews (September 11, 2013).

McDade, Bart (2010): "Interview with the Financial Crisis Inquiry Commission." FCIC. http://fcic-static.law.stanford.edu/cdn_media/fcic-audio/2010-08-09 FCIC staff audiotape of interview with Bart McDade, Lehman Brothers.mp3 (February 01, 2014).

McDonnell, Brett H. (2012): Financial Regulation Reform and Too Big to Fail. *American University Business Law Review, Forthcoming; Minnesota Legal Studies Research Paper No. 12-08.*

——— (2013): "Capture Dynamics in Agencies." George Washington University, Center for Law, Economics & Finance (C-LEAF). http://vimeo.com/user9108723/review/60464466/188777 60d1 (May 12, 2014).

Mendelowitz, Allan, and John Liechty (2010): "Testimony of Allan Mendelowitz, Founding Member of the Committee to Establish the National Institute of Finance, and John Liechty, Associate Professor of Marketing and Statistics Smeal College of Business, Penn State University and Founding Member, the Committee to Establish the National Institute of Finance, on Providing Financial Regulators with the Data and Tools Needed to Safeguard Our Financial System, February 20 2010." U.S. Senate, Committee on Banking, Housing and Urban Affairs, Subcommittee on Security, International Trade and Finance. http://banking.senate.gov/public/index.cfm?FuseAction=Hearings.Testimony&Hearing_ID=5478a8c8-6616-4a35-bd74-8fd5adeb1268&Witness_ID=aa87c6ca-a422-4767-a692-71684195da33 (January 08, 2013).

Merton, Robert C. (1995): Financial Innovation and the Management and Regulation of Financial Institutions. *Journal of Banking & Finance* 19 (1995): 461-481.

Miller, Mary J. (2013): "Testimony of Mary J. Miller, under Secretary for Domestic Finance, on Wall Street Reform: Oversight of Financial Stability and Consumer and Investor Protections, February 14 2013". U.S. Senate, Committee on Banking, Housing & Urban Affairs. http://www.banking.senate.gov/public/index.cfm?FuseAction=Hearings.Testimony&Hearing_ID=84abcfc3-9dd8-49ec-b5c0-2f75c618f075&Witness_ID=fe527d6b-a158-4222-82da-df1e735e5d71 (June 26, 2013).

Miller, Robert (2006): "You Bet: Tokyo Recovers from Fat Fingers." The Telegraph online. http://www.telegraph.co.uk/finance/2930992/You-bet-Tokyo-recovers-from-fat-fingers.html (September 11, 2013).

Millo, Yuval, and Donald MacKenzie (2009): The Usefulness of Inaccurate Models: Towards an Understanding of the Emergence of Financial Risk Management. *Accounting, Organizations and Society* 34 (2009): 638-653.

Mitnick, Barry M. (1975): The Theory of Agency: The Policing 'Paradox' and Regulatory Behavior. *Public Choice* 24 (1, Winter 1975): 27-42.

——— (1982): Regulation and the Theory of Agency. *Review of Policy Research* 1 (3, February 1982): 442-453.

——— (1984): "Agency Problems and Political Institutions." Presented at the Sixth Annual Research Conference of the Association for Public Policy Analysis and Management, New Orleans.

——— (1992): The Theory of Agency and Organizational Analysis. In *Ethics and Agency Theory: An Introduction*, eds. Norman E. Bowie and R. Edward Freeman. New York: Oxford University Press. 75-96.

Moe, Terry M. (1984): The New Economics of Organization. *American Journal of Political Science* 28 (4, November 1984): 739-777.

Momani, Bessma (2010): The IMF and FSB: Intractable Political Reality and Organizational Mismatch. In *The Financial Stability Board: An Effective Fourth Pillar of Global Economic Governance? Special Report. The Centre for International Governance Innovation*, eds. Stephany Griffith-Jones, Eric Helleiner and Ngaire Woods. Waterloo, Ontario: CIGI. 36-38.

Moody's (2011): "Rating Action: Moody's Downgrades Bank of America Corp. To Baa1/P-2; Bank of America N.A. To A2, P-1 Affirmed." Moody's. http://www.moodys.com/research/Moodys-downgrades-Bank-of-America-Corp-to-Baa1P-2-Bank--PR_226511 (August 01, 2013).

Moore, Heidi N. (2008): "Dick Fuld's Vendetta against Short-Sellers – and Goldman Sachs." The Wall Street Journal online. http://blogs.wsj.com/deals/2008/10/07/dick-fulds-vendetta-against-short-sellers-and-goldman-sachs/ (March 10, 2014).

Morgan, Donald P. (2002): Rating Banks: Risk and Uncertainty in an Opaque Industry. *The American Economic Review* 92 (4): 874-888.

Morgan, Donald P., and Kevin J. Stiroh (1999): Bond Market Discipline of Banks: Is the Market Tough Enough? *Federal Reserve Bank of New York Staff Reports* No. 95 (December 1999).

——— (2005): Too Big to Fail after All These Years. *Federal Reserve Bank of New York Staff Reports* No. 220 (September 2005).

Moschella, Manuela (2012): Designing the Financial Stability Board: A Theoretical Investigation of Mandate, Discretion, and Membership. *Journal of International Relations and Development* 16: 380-405.

Mosley, Layna, and David Andrew Singer (2009): The Global Financial Crisis: Lessons and Opportunities for International Political Economy. *International Interactions: Empirical and Theoretical Research in International Relations* 35 (4): 420-429.

Muth, John F. (1961): Rational Expectations and the Theory of Price Movements. *Econometrica* 29 (3): 315-335.

Nader, Ralph (1981): Don't Let the Sunshine In. *The Nation* November 7, 1981: 470-473.

Nakamoto, Michiyo, and David Wighton (2007): "Citigroup Chief Stays Bullish on Buy-Outs." The Financial Times online. http://www.ft.com/intl/cms/s/0/80e2987a-2e50-11dc-821c-0000779fd2ac.html-axzz2takxoZLZ (February 18, 2014).

Neyer, Ulrike, and Thomas Vieten (2013): Die neue Europäische Bankenaufsicht: Eine kritische Würdigung. *DICE Ordnungspolitische Perspektiven* 45 (July 2013).

Nier, Erlend W. (2009): Financial Stability Frameworks and the Role of Central Banks: Lessons from the Crisis. *IMF Working Paper* 09 (70).

Niskanen, William A. (2007): *Bureaucracy and Representative Government.* New Brunswick and London: Transaction Publishers.

Noll, Roger G. (1985): Government Regulatory Behavior: A Multidisciplinary Survey and Synthesis. In *Regulatory Policy and Social Sciences*, ed. Roger G. Noll. Berkeley a.o.: University of California Press. 9-64.

Norris, Floyd (2010): "A Baby Step toward Rules on Bank Risk." The New York Times online. http://www.nytimes.com/2010/09/17/business/17norris.html?dbk (June 26, 2013).

Novak, William J. (2013): "A Revisionist History of Regulatory Capture." In *Preventing Regulatory Capture: Special Interest Influence and How to Limit it*, ed Daniel Carpenter and David Moss. Cambridge: Cambridge University Press. 25-48.

O'Hara, Maureen, and Wayne Shaw (1990): Deposit Insurance and Wealth Effects: The Value of Being 'Too Big to Fail'. *The Journal of Finance* 45 (5, Dec. 1990): 1587-1600.

O'Toole, James (2013): "Five Years Later, Lehman Bankruptcy Fees Hit $2.2 Billion." CNN Money. http://money.cnn.com/2013/09/13/news/companies/lehman-bankruptcy-fees/ (April 04, 2014).

Obama, Barack (2009): "Remarks by the President on 21st Century Financial Regulatory Reform." The White House Office of the Press Secretary. http://www.whitehouse.gov/the_press_office/Remarks-of-the-President-on-Regulatory-Reform/ (May 15, 2014).

——— (2010): "Remarks by the President at Signing of Dodd-Frank Wall Street Reform and Consumer Protection Act." The White House Office of the Press Secretary. http://www.whitehouse.gov/ the-press-office/remarks-president-signing-dodd-frank-wall-street-reform-and-consumer-protection-act (April 23, 2013).

——— (2013): "Remarks by the President on the Confirmation of Richard Cordray as Director for CFPB." The White House Office of the Press Secretary. http://www.whitehouse.gov/the-press-office/2013/07/17/remarks-president-confirmation-richard-cordray-director-cfpb (July 25, 2013).

OECD Global Science Forum (2009): "Applications of Complexity Science for Public Policy: New Tools for Finding Unanticipated Consequences and Unrealized Opportunities." OECD. http://www.oecd.org/sti/sci-tech/43891980.pdf (May 15, 2014).

Office of Financial Research (2012a): "Annual Report." U.S. Department of the Treasury. http://www.treasury.gov/initiatives/wsr/ofr/Documents/OFR_Annual_Report_071912_Final.pdf (August 28, 2012).
——— (2012b): "Annual Report to Congress on Human Capital Planning." U.S. Department of the Treasury. http://www.treasury.gov/initiatives/ofr/about/Documents/OFR_HR_Report_Web_ final.pdf (July 17, 2013).
——— (2012c): "Office of Financial Research Fellowship Opportunities." U.S. Department of the Treasury. http://www.treasury.gov/initiatives/ofr/about/Documents/OFRFellowship Program Flyer_Nov2012_FINAL.pdf (July 18, 2013).
——— (2013a): "Annual Report." U.S. Department of the Treasury. http://www.treasury.gov/initiatives/ofr/about/Documents/OFR_AnnualReport2013_FINAL_12-17-2013_Accessible.pdf (March 15, 2014).
——— (2013b): "LEI Primer." U.S. Department of the Treasury. http://www.treasury.gov/initiatives/ofr/data/Documents/LEI Primer_June2013_FINAL.pdf (September 05, 2013).
Olson, Mancur (1965): *The Logic of Collective Action. Public Goods and the Theory of Groups*. Cambridge: Harvard University Press.
Orts, Eric W. (1995): Reflexive Environmental Law. *Northwestern University Law Review* 89 (4, Summer 1995): 1227-1340.
Oskamp, Stuart (1965): Overconfidence in Case-Study Judgements. *Journal of Consulting Psychology* 29 (3): 261-265.
Ötker-Robe, I□ nci, Aditya Narain, Anna Ilyina, and Jay Surti (2011): The Too-Important-to-Fail Conundrum: Impossible to Ignore and Difficult to Resolve. *IMF Staff Discussion Notes* May 27, 2011 (SDN/11/12).
Owen, Bruce M., and Ronald Ray Braeutigam (1978): *The Regulation Game: Strategic Use of the Administrative Process*. Cambridge: Ballinger.

Palmer, Donald, and Michael Maher (2010): A Normal Accident Analysis of the Mortgage Meltdown. In *Knowledge and Liquidity: Institutional and Cognitive Foundations of the Subprime Crisis*, eds. Michael Lounsbury and Paul Hirsch. Bingley, UK: Emerald Group. 217-254.
Panetta, Fabio (2013): "Macroprudential Tools – Where Do We Stand? Remarks by Fabio Panetta, Deputy Director General of the Bank of Italy, During the Presentation of the 2013 Financial Stability Review, Central Bank of Luxembourg, Luxembourg, 14 May 2013." Bank for International Settlements. http://www.bis.org/review/r130527a.pdf (February 28, 2014).
Paredes, Troy A. (2003): Blinded by the Light: Information Overload and Its Consequences for Securities Regulation. *Washington University in St.*

Louis School of Law, Faculty Working Paper Series 03-02-02 (June 1, 2003).

Partnoy, Frank (2010): "Do C.D.O.'s Have Social Value?" The New York Times. http://roomfordebate. blogs.nytimes.com/2010/04/27/do-c-d-o-s-have-social-value/?_r=0 (September 24, 2013).

Patterson, Scott (2010): *The Quants: How a New Breed of Math Whizzes Conquered Wall Street and Nearly Destroyed It.* New York: Crown Business.

Pauly, Louis (2008): Financial Crisis Management in Europe and Beyond. *Contributions to Political Economy* 27 (2008): 73-89.

——— (2009): The Old and the New Politics of International Financial Stability. *Journal for Common Market Studies* 47 (5): 955-975.

——— (2010): The Financial Stability Board in Context. In *The Financial Stability Board: An Effective Fourth Pillar of Global Economic Governance? Special Report. The Centre for International Governance Innovation*, eds. Stephany Griffith-Jones, Eric Helleiner and Ngaire Woods. Waterloo, Ontario: CIGI. 13-18.

Peltzman, Sam (1976): Toward a More General Theory of Regulation. *NBER Working Paper Series* Working Paper No. 133.

Perrow, Charles (1981): Normal Accident at Three Mile Island. *Society* 18 (5): 17-26.

——— (1984): *Normal Accidents: Living with High-Risk Technologies.* New York: Basic Books.

——— (2007): *The Next Catastrophe. Reducing Our Vulnerabilities to Natural, Industrial, and Terrorist Disasters.* Princeton and Oxford: Princeton University Press.

——— (2010): The Meltdown Was Not an Accident. In *Knowledge and Liquidity: Institutional and Cognitive Foundations of the Subprime Crisis*, eds. Michael Lounsbury and Paul Hirsch. Bingley, UK: Emerald Group. 307-330.

Perry, James L., Annie Hondeghem, and Lois Recascino Wise (2010): Revisiting the Motivational Bases of Public Service: Twenty Years of Research and an Agenda for the Future. *Public Administration Review* September/October 2010: 681-690.

Perry, James L., and Lois Recascino Wise (1990): The Motivational Bases of Public Service. *Public Administration Review* May/June 1990: 367-373.

Persky, Joseph (1995): Retrospectives: The Ethology of Homo Economicus. *The Journal of Economic Perspectives* 9 (2, Spring 1995): 221-231.

Pfinsgraff, Martin (2012): "Supervision Matters." Presented at the Risk Magazine Credit Risk Conference, New York.

Philips, Matthew (2012): “Knight Shows How to Lose $440 Million in 30 Minutes.” Bloomberg Business-week. http://www.businessweek.com/articles/2012-08-02/knight-shows-how-to-lose-440-million-in-30-minutes (September 11, 2013).

Pianalto, Sandra (2013): “Financial Stability: Lessons from Monetary Policy.” Presented at the Cleveland Fed and OFR Conference on Financial Stability Analysis, Washington D.C.

Pigou, Arthur Cecile (1924): *The Economics of Welfare*. London: Macmillan and Co., Limited.

Pisani-Ferry, Jean, and André Sapir (2010): Banking Crisis Management in the EU: An Early Assessment. *Economic Policy* 25 (62 (April 2010)): 341-373.

Popper, Karl R. (1994): *Alles Leben ist Problemlösen. Über Erkenntnis, Geschichte und Politik*. Darmstadt: Wissenschaftliche Buchgesellschaft.

Popper, Nathaniel (2012): “Changes to Money Market Funds Stalls.” The New York Times online. http://www.nytimes.com/2012/08/23/business/sec-calls-off-vote-on-fund-regulation.html?_r=2&pagewanted=1&ref=business (June 16, 2013).

Popper, Nathaniel, and Ben Protess (2012): “To Regulate Rapid Traders, S.E.C. Turns to One of Them.” The New York Times online. http://www.nytimes.com/2012/10/08/business/sec-regulators-turn-to-high-speed-trading-firm.html?smid=tw-share (September 10, 2012).

Porter, Tony (2009): “Global Governance Theories, Complexity, and the Post-Crisis Internatinal Financial Architecture.” Presented at the International Studies Association Annual Meeting, New York.

Porter, William (2013): “Interview with Cushla Sherlock.” Credit Suisse. https://http://www.credit-suisse.com/ch/en/news-and-expertise/news/economy/global-trends.article.html/article/pwp/ news-and-expertise/2013/10/en/the-crisis-is-not-over-its-gone-underground.html (May 05, 2014).

Posner, Richard A. (1971): Taxation by Regulation. *The Bell Journal of Economics and Management Science* 2 (1, Spring 1971): 22-50.

——— (1974): Theories of Economic Regulation. *The Bell Journal of Economics and Management Science* 5 (2): 335-358.

Pozner, Jo-Ellen, Mary Stimmler, and Paul Hirsch (2010): Terminal Isomorphism and the Self-Destructive Potential of Success: Lessons from Subprime Mortgage Origination and Securitization. In *Markets on Trial: The Economic Sociology of the U.S. Financial Crisis*, eds. Michael Lounsbury and Paul Hirsch. Bingley, UK: Emerald Group. 181-216.

Preda, Alex (2001): Sense and Sensibility: Or, How Should Social Studies of Finance Behave, a Manifesto. *Economic Sociology: European Electronic Newsletter* 2 (2, January 2001): 15-18.

Pressler, Jessica (2012): "122 Minutes with Jamie Dimon: The JPMorgan Chase CEO Is Really, Really, Really Sorry. Except When He's Not." New York Magazine. http://nymag.com/news /intelligencer/encounter/jamie-dimon-2012-8/ (March 13, 2014).

Prince, Charles (2010): "Interview with the Financial Crisis Inquiry Commission." FCIC. http://fcic-static.law.stanford.edu/cdn_media/fcic-docs/2010-03-17 transcript of FCIC staff interview with Charles Prince, Citigroup.pdf (March 28, 2014).

Protess, Ben, and Jessica Silver-Greenberg (2012): "HSBC to Pay $1.92 Billion to Settle Charges of Money Laundering." The New York Times online. http://dealbook.nytimes.com/2012/12/10/hsbc-said-to-near-1-9-billion-settlement-over-money-laundering/?ref=todayspaper (September 23, 2013).

Quaglia, Lucia (2008): Explaining the Reform of Banking Supervision in Europe: An Integrative Approach. *Governance: An International Journal of Policy, Administration, and Institutions* 21 (3, July 2008): 439-463.

Quirk, Paul J. (1981): *Industry Influence in Federal Regulatory Agencies*. Princeton: Princeton University Press.

Quirk, Paul J., and Bruce F. Nesmith (2005): Who Serves Special Interests? The President, Congress, and Interest Groups. In *The Interest Group Connection*, eds. Paul S. Herrnson, Ronald G. Shaiko and Clyde Wilcox. Washington D.C.: CQ Press. 298-318.

Rakoff, Jed S. (2014): "The Financial Crisis: Why Have No High-Level Executives Been Prosecuted?" The New York Review of Books. http://www.nybooks.com/articles/archives/2014/jan/09/financial - crisis-why-no-executive-prosecutions/ (February 04, 2014).

Reagan, Ronald (1981): "First Inaugural Address on January 20, 1981." PBS. http://www.pbs.org/wgbh/americanexperience/features/primary-resources/reagan-inaugural-1981/ (September 10, 2013).

Reed, John (2010): "Interview with the Financial Crisis Inquiry Commission." FCIC. http://fcic-static.law.stanford.edu/cdn_media/fcic-audio/2010-03-24 FCIC staff audiotape of interview with John Reed, Citigroup.mp3 (April 08, 2014).

Reed, Matthew (2014): "Legal Entity Identifier System Gains Global Momentum." U.S. Department of the Treasury. http://www.treasury.gov/connect/blog /Pages/Legal-Entity-IdentifierSystem-Gains-Global-Momentum.aspx (March 19, 2014).

Rehm, Barbara A. (2012): "What Ex-Comptroller Walsh Really Thinks About the State of Banking." American Banker online. https://http://www.american

banker.com/issues/177_168/what-ex-comptroller-walsh-really-thinks-about-the-state-of-banking-1052256-1.html?pg=2 (November 05, 2013).

Reinert, Hugo, and Erik S. Reinert. (2006): "Creative Destruction in Economics: Nietzsche, Sombart, Schumpeter." In *Friedrich Nietzsche (1844–1900)*, eds. Jürgen Backhaus and Wolfgang Drechsler. New York: Springer. 55-85.

Reinhart, Carmen M., and Kenneth S. Rogoff (2009): *This Time Is Different: Eight Centuries of Financial Folly*. Princeton: Princeton University Press.

Rettman, Andrew (2007): "EU's REACH Chemicals Law Begins Life in Helsinki." euobserver.com. http://euobserver.com/economic/24169 (December 06, 2013).

Roca, Paco (2014): "Freut euch nicht zu früh (Illustrations for an Article by Lorenz Wagner and Alexander Hagelüken)." Süddeutsche Zeitung Magazin (12/2014).

Rosen, James (2012): "New Federal Agency OFR Stirs 'Orwellian' Fears." FoxNews.com. http://www.foxnews.com/politics/2012/04/19/new-federal-agency-ofr-stirs-orwellian-fears/ (August 24, 2012).

Rosengreen, Eric S. (2013): "Letter to the Financial Stability Oversight Council Concerning the FSOC's Proposed Recommendations Regarding Money Market Mutual Fund Reform." Federal Reserve Bank of Boston. http://www.bostonfed.org/news/press/2013/pr021213-letter.pdf (July 17, 2013).

Ross, Stephen A. (1973): The Economic Theory of Agency: The Principal's Problem. *The American Economic Review* 63 (2, May 1973): 134-139.

Roubini, Nouriel (2010): "Interview with the Financial Crisis Inquiry Commission." FCIC. http://fcic-static.law.stanford.edu/cdn_media/fcic-audio/2010-11-15 FCIC staff audiotape of interview with Nouriel Roubini, New York University.mp3 (March 19, 2014).

Rowley, Jennifer (2007): The Wisdom Hierarchy: Representations of the DIKW Hierarchy. *Journal of Information Science* 33 (2): 163-180.

Rumsfeld, Donald (2002): "Department of Defence News Briefing – Secretary Rumsfeld and General Myers on February 12, 2002" http://www.defense.gov/transcripts/transcript.aspx?transcriptid =2636 (April 05, 2013).

Saari, Christopher Paul (1977): The Efficient Capital Market Hypothesis, Economic Theory and the Regulation of the Securities Industry. *Stanford Law Review* 29 (5, May 1977): 1031-1076.

Sassen, Saskia (1996): *Losing Control?: Sovereignty in an Age of Globalization*. New York, Chichester: Columbia University Press.

Schammo, Pierre (2012): EU Day-to-Day Supervision or Intervention-Based Supervision: Which Way Forward for the European System of Financial Supervision? *Oxford Journal of Legal Studies* 32 (4 (2012)): 771-797.

Schapiro, Mary (2009): "Testimony of Mary Schapiro, Chairman of the U.S. Securities and Exchange Commission, on Establishing a Framework for Systemic Risk Regulation, July 23 2009." U.S. Senate, Committee on Banking, Housing & Urban Affairs. http://www.banking.senate.gov/public/index.cfm?FuseAction=Hearings.Testimony&Hearing_ID=dabb299b-02c3-4e4b-a116-0767 b04768ff&Witness_ID=5f1a3238-4489-4c36-a371-4816c3b47bd5 (September 20, 2013).

——— (2012): "Interview with Mellody Hobson." Investment Company Institute. http://vimeo.com/ 42647174 (September 18, 2012).

Schlozman, Kay Lehman, and Traci Burch (2005): Political Voice in an Age of Inequality. In *America at Risk. Threats to Liberal Self-Government in an Age of Uncertainty*, eds. Robert Faulkner and Susan Shell. Ann Arbor: The University of Michigan Press. 140-173.

Schlozman, Kay Lehman, and John T. Tierney (1986): *Organized Interests and American Democracy*. New York: Harper & Row Publishers.

Schmidt, Robert (2010): "The Treasury's New Research Office." Bloomberg Businessweek. http://www.businessweek.com/magazine/content/10_37/b4194026970590.htm (August 24, 2012).

Schneiberg, Marc, and Tim Bartley (2010): Regulating or Redesigning Finance? Market Architectures, Normal Accidents, and Dilemmas of Regulatory Reform. In *Knowledge and Liquidity: Institutional and Cognitive Foundations of the Subprime Crisis*, eds. Michael Lounsbury and Paul Hirsch. Bingley, UK: Emerald Group. 279-306.

Schnidman, Evan (2011): Why the Federal Reserve Is Dodd-Frank's Big Winner. *Harvard Business Law Review Online* 1 (2011): 88-93.

Schoenholtz, Kermit, and Paul Wachtel (2010): "Dodd-Frank and the Fed." NYU Stern University, Leonard N. Stern School of Business. http://w4.stern.nyu.edu/blogs/regulatingwallstreet/2010/ 07/doddfrank-and-the-fed-kermit-s.html (August 05, 2013).

Schoenmaker, Dirk (2011): *The Financial Trilemma*. Amsterdam: Duisenberg School of Finance, University of Amsterdam., Tinbergen Institute Discussion Paper No. TI 11-019/DSF 7.

Schuck, Peter H. (1992): Legal Complexity: Some Causes, Consequences, and Cures. *Duke Law Journal* 42 (1, October 1992): 1-52.

Schuermann, Til (2013): "The Fed's Stress Tests Add Risk to the Financial System." The Wall Street Journal online. http://online.wsj.com/article/SB10001424127887324532004578362543899 602754.html (July 25, 2013).

Schultz, Stefan (2008): "Merkel und Steinbrück im Wortlaut: 'Die Spareinlagen sind Sicher'." Spiegel Online. http://www.spiegel.de/wirtschaft/merkel-und-steinbrueck-im-wortlaut-die-spareinlagen-sind-sicher-a-582305.html (October 21, 2013).

Schumer, Charles E., and Michael R. Bloomberg (2006): "To Save New York, Learn from London." The Wall Street Journal online. http://online.wsj.com/news/articles/SB116234404428809623 (No-vember 05, 2013).

Schwarcz, Steven L. (2002): Private Ordering of Public Markets: The Rating Agency Paradox. *University of Illinois Law Review* 1 (2002): 1-28.

——— (2008): Systemic Risk. *The Georgetown Law Journal* 97 (1): 194-249.

——— (2009): Regulating Complexity in Financial Markets. *Washington University Law Review* 87 (2): 211-268.

Scism, Leslie, and Alan Zibel (2012): "Prudential Heads toward 'Systemically Important' Tag." The Wall Street Journal online. http://online.wsj.com /article/SB10000872396390444734804578066960730974162.html (October 08, 2012).

Scott, Hal S. (2012): "Interconnectedness and Contagion." Committee on Capital Markets Regulation. http://www.capmktsreg.org/pdfs/2012.11.20_Inter connectedness_and_Contagion.pdf (March 10, 2014).

Seabrooke, Leonard, and Eleni Tsingou (2010): Responding to the Global Credit Crisis: The Politics of Financial Reform. *The British Journal of Politics and International Relations* 12: 313-323.

Securities and Exchange Commission (2013a): "Administrative Proceeding File No. 3-15570 in the Matter of Knight Capital Americas LLC Respondent." SEC. http://www.sec.gov/litigation/admin/ 2013/34-70694.pdf (March 03, 2014).

——— (2013b): "SEC Proposes Money Market Fund Reforms." SEC. http://www.sec.gov/news/press/ 2013/2013-101.htm (July 17, 2013).

Selten, Reinhard (2002): What Is Bounded Rationality? In *Bounded Rationality: The Adaptive Toolbox*, eds. Gerd Gigerenzer and Reinhard Selten. Cambridge: MIT Press. 13-36.

Senge, Peter M. (1996): *Die Fünfte Disziplin. Kunst und Praxis der Lernenden Organisation*. Stuttgart: Klett-Cotta.

Shannon, Claude (1993): The Lattice Theory of Information. Originally Published In: IRE Transactions Information Theory, No. 1 (Feb. 1950). In *Claude Elwood Shannon: Collected Papers*, eds. N.J.A. Sloane and Aaron D. Wyner. New York: The Institute of Electrical and Electronics Engineers. 180-183.

Shapiro, Sidney A. (2012): The Complexity of Regulatory Capture: Diagnosis, Causality and Remediation. *Roger Williams University Law Review* 102 (1, 2012).

Shapiro, Susan P. (2005): Agency Theory. *Annual Review of Sociology* 31 (2005): 263-284.

Shiller, Robert J. (1989): *Market Volatility*. Cambridge: MIT Press.

——— (2003): From Efficient Markets Theory to Behavioral Finance. *Journal of Economic Perspectives* 17 (1, Winter 2003): 83–104.

——— (2010): "Interview with the Financial Crisis Inquiry Commission." FCIC. http://fcic-static.law.stanford.edu/cdn_media/fcic-audio/2010-09-22 FCIC staff audiotape of interview with Robert Shiller, Yale University.mp3 (February 28, 2014).

Siddique, Sabeth (2010): "Interview with the Financial Crisis Inquiry Commission." FCIC. http://fcic-static.law.stanford.edu/cdn_media/fcic-audio/2010-09-09 FCIC staff audiotape of interview with Sabeth Siddique, Federal Reserve Board (Part 1).mp3 (April 01, 2014).

Silver-Greenberg, Jessica, and Nelson D. Schwartz (2012): "'Living Wills' for Too-Big-to-Fail Banks Are Released." The New York Times online. http://www.nytimes.com/2012/07/04/business/living-wills-of-how-to-unwind-big-banks-are-released.html?_r=0 (July 26, 2013).

Simon, Herbert A. (1955): A Behavioral Model of Rational Choice. *The Quarterly Journal of Economics* 69 (1, February 1955): 99-118.

——— (1956): Rational Choice and the Structure of the Environment. *Psychological Review* 63 (2, 1956): 129-138.

——— (1962): The Architecture of Complexity. *Proceedings of the American Philosophical Society* 106 (6, December 12, 1962): 467-482.

——— (1997 [1947]): *Administrative Behavior. A Study of Decision-Making Processes in Administrative Organizations*. New York: The Free Press.

Simon, Herbert A., Massimo Egidi, Robin Marris, and Riccardo Viale (1992): *Economics, Bounded Rationality and the Cognitive Revolution*. Edited by Herbert A. Simon. Aldershot: Edward Elgar.

Skeel, David A. (2010): The New Financial Deal: Understanding the Dodd-Frank Act and Its (Unintended) Consequences. *University of Pennsylvania Law School, Institute for Law and Economics Research Paper* 10-21.

Sorkin, Andrew Ross (2010): *Too Big to Fail. Inside the Battle to Save Wall Street.* London: Penguin.

——— (2013): "Realities Behind Prosecuting Big Banks." The New York Times online. http://dealbook. nytimes.com/2013/03/11/big-banks-go-wrong-but-pay-a-little-price/ (September 23, 2013).

Soros, George (2008): *The New Paradigm for Financial Markets. The Credit Crisis of 2008 and What It Means*. New York: PublicAffairs.

——— (2010): "Interview with the Financial Crisis Inquiry Commission." FCIC. http://fcic-static.law.stanford.edu/cdn_media/fcic-audio/2010-10-04

FCIC staff audiotape of interview with George Soros, Soros Fund Management, LLC.mp3 (March 19, 2014).
Spiro, Leah Nathans (1998): "Inside the Long Term Capital Management Bailout." Business Week online. http://www.businessweek.com/bwdaily/dnflash/sep1998/nf80925d.htm (September 13, 2013).
Stehr, Nico (2007): Societal Transformations, Globalisation and the Knowledge Society. *Journal of Knowledge and Learning* 3 (2/3, 2007): 139-153.
Stern, Gary H., and Ron J. Feldman (2004): *Too Big to Fail: The Hazards of Bank Bailouts.* Washington D.C.: Brookings Institution Press.
Stewart, Richard B. (1975): The Reformation of American Administrative Law. *Harvard Law Review* 88 (8, June 1975): 1667-1813.
Stigler, George J. (1971): The Theory of Economic Regulation. *The Bell Journal of Economics and Management Science* 2 (1): 3-21.
Stiglitz, Joseph E. (1974): Incentives and Risk Sharing in Sharecropping. *The Review of Economic Studies* 41 (2, April 1974): 219-255.
——— (2001): "Information and Change in the Paradigm in Economics. Nobel Prize Lecture." Nobelprize.org. http://www.nobelprize.org/nobel_prizes/economics/laureates/2001/stiglitz-lec ture.pdf (June 10, 2013).
——— (2002): Information and the Change in the Paradigm in Economics. *The American Economic Review* 92 (3, June 2002): 460-501.
——— (2008): "Interview with Nathan Gardels." The Huffington Post online. http://www.huffington post.com/nathan-gardels/stiglitz-the-fall-of-wall_b_126911.html (February 28, 2014).
——— (2009a): Moving Beyond Market Fundamentalism to a More Balanced Economy. *Annals of Public and Cooperative Economics* 80 (3, 2009): 345-360.
——— (2009b): Regulation and Failure. In *New Perspectives on Regulation*, eds. David Moss and John Cisternino. Cambridge: The Tobin Project. 11-23.
——— (2010): Government Failure vs. Market Failure: Principles of Regulation. In *Government and Markets. Toward a New Theory of Regulation*, eds. Edward J. Balleisen and David A. Moss. New York: Cambridge University Press. 13-51.
Streeck, Wolfgang (2011): The Crisis in Context. Democratic Capitalism and Its Contradictions. *MPIfG Discussion Paper* 11/15.
——— (2013): The Politics of Public Debt: Neoliberalism, Capitalist Development and the Restructuring of the State. *MPIfG Discussion Paper* 13/7.
Strongin, Steve, Amanda Hindlian, Sandra Lawson, Jorge Murillo, Koby Sadan, and Balakrishna Subramanian (2013): "Measuring the TBTF Effect on Bond Pricing." Goldman Sachs Global Market Institute. http://www.goldmansachs.com/our-thinking/public-policy/regulatory-reform/measuring-tbtf-doc.pdf (September 20, 2013).

Svetlova, Ekaterina, and Henk van Elst (2012): How Is Non-Knowledge Represented in Economic Theory? *Available at* http://arxiv.org/pdf/1209.2204.

Systemic Risk Council (2012): "Prompt, Full Funding of the SEC and CFTC Is Essential to Reducing Systemic Risk." Pew Chariatble Trust. http://www.pewtrusts.org/news_room_detail.aspx?id=85899435227 (January 22, 2013).

Taibbi, Matt (2011): "Why Isn't Wall Street in Jail? Financial Crooks Brought Down the World's Economy – but the Feds Are Doing More to Protect Them Than to Prosecute Them." RollingStone Magazine. http://www.rolling stone.com/politics/news/why-isnt-wall-street-in-jail-20110216 (October 26, 2012).

Taleb, Nassim Nicholas (2007): *The Black Swan: The Impact of the Highly Improbable*. New York: Random House.

——— (2012a): *Antifragile: Things That Gain from Disorder*. New York: Random House.

——— (2012b): "Report on the Effectiveness and Possible Side Effects of the Office of Financial Research (OFR)." United States House Committee on Financial Services. http://financialservices.house.gov/uploadedfiles/071411nassim.pdf (March 19, 2014).

Tankersley, Jim (2013): "As Washington's Top Risk Seeker, Richard Berner Crunches Numbers to See around Dark Corners in the Economy." Washington Post online. http://www.washingtonpost. com/business/wall-street-veteran-heads-new-federal-office-tasked-with-making-better-economic-forecasts/2013/04/05/bc9c912e-9ad6-11e2-9a79-eb5280c81c63_story_2.html (April 01, 2014).

Tarullo, Daniel K. (2008): *Banking on Basel: The Future of International Financial Regulation*. Washington D.C.: Peterson Institute for International Economics.

——— (2010a): "Financial Regulatory Reform. Speech at the U.S. Monetary Policy Forum, New York." Board of Governors of the Federal Reserve System. http://www.federalreserve.gov/newsevents /speech/tarullo20100226a.htm (November 06, 2013).

——— (2010b): "Testimony of Daniel K. Tarullo, Governor on the Board of Governors of the Federal Reserve System, on Equipping Financial Regulators with the Tools Necessary to Monitor Systemic Risk, February 12 2010." U.S. Senate, Banking Subcommittee on Security and International Trade and Finance. http://banking.senate.gov/public /index.cfm?FuseAction=Hearings.Testimony&Hearing_ID=5478a8c8-

6616-4a35-bd74-8fd5adeb1268&Witness_ID=512 ecda5-e98e-4668-9fce-4684e30f7a5a (January 08, 2013).

Taylor, John B. (2009): The Financial Crisis and the Policy Responses: An Empirical Analysis of What Went Wrong. *NBER Working Paper Series* 14631 (January 2009).

——— (2010): "Interview with the Financial Crisis Inquiry Commission." FCIC. http://fcic-static.law.stanford.edu/cdn_media/fcic-audio/2010-09-23 FCIC staff audiotape of interview with John Taylor, Stanford University (Part 2).mp3 (April 07, 2014).

Tett, Gillian (2010): "Interview with the Financial Crisis Inquiry Commission." FCIC. http://fcic-static.law.stanford.edu/cdn_media/fcic-audio/2010-10-28 FCIC staff audiotape of interview with Gillian Tett, Financial Times.mp3 (February 22, 2014).

Thaler, Richard (1991): *Quasi Rational Economics.* New York: Russell Sage Foundation.

——— (2000): From Homo Economicus to Homo Sapiens. *The Journal of Economic Perspectives* 14 (1, Winter 2000): 133-141.

The Economist (2008): "Paulson's Bazooka." The Economist online. http://www.economist.com/blogs/freeexchange/2008/09/paulsons_bazooka (July 04, 2013).

The New York Times Editorial Board (2013): "The Good Guy Wins." The New York Times online. http://www.nytimes.com/2013/07/22/opinion/the-good-guy-wins.html?_r=0 (July 25, 2013).

The Royal Swedish Academy of Sciences (2013): "The Sveriges Riksbank Prize in Economic Sciences in Memory of Alfred Nobel 2013: Eugene F. Fama, Lars Peter Hansen, Robert J. Shiller." October 14, 2013. http://www.nobelprize.org/nobel_prizes/economic-sciences/laureates/2013/press.html (May 15, 2014).

The Wall Street Journal (2008): "Paulson's Bazooka: A Weapon to Be Remembered?" The Wall Street Journal Online. http://blogs.wsj.com/economics/2008/09/24/paulsons-bazooka-a-weapon-to-be-remembered/ (July 04, 2013).

The Warwick Commission (2009): *The Warwick Commission on International Financial Reform: In Praise of Unlevel Playing Fields. The Report of the Second Warwick Commission.* Coventry: The University of Warwick.

Thurner, Stefan (2011): "Systemic Financial Risk: Agent Based Models to Understand the Leverage Cycle on National Scales and Its Consequences." OECD/IFP Project on Future Global Shocks. http://www.futurict.eu/sites/default/files/Report commissioned by the OECD on Systemic Risk, by Stefan Thurner.pdf (February 12, 2014).

Tietmeyer, Hans (1999): Report on International Cooperation and Coordination in the Area of Financial Market Supervision and Surveillance. *BIS Review* 21 (1999).

Transparency International (2009): "G20 Regulatory Efforts Must Be Transparent, Include Civil Society." November 05, 2009. http://www.transparency.org/news/pressrelease/20091105_g20_regulatory_efforts_must_be_transparent_include_civil_society (September 03, 2013).

Trichet, Jean-Claude (2009): "Remarks on the Future of European Financial Regulation and Supervision. Keynote Address by Jean-Claude Trichet, President of the ECB at the Committee of European Securities Regulators (CESR) Paris, 23 February 2009." European Central Bank. http://www.ecb.europa.eu/press/key/date/2009/html/sp090223.en.html (August 30, 2013).

——— (2010): State of the Union: The Financial Crisis and the ECB's Response between 2007 and 2009. *Journal of Common Market Studies* 48 (Annual Review): 7-19.

——— (2011): "Hearing on the ESRB before the Committee on Economic and Monetary Affairs of the European Parliament: Introductory Statement by Jean-Claude Trichet, Chair of the ESRB, Brussels, 07 February 2011." ESRB. http://www.esrb.europa.eu/news/pr/2011/html/sp110207.en.html (August 29, 2013).

Truman, David B. (1971 [1951]): *Governmental Process. Political Interests and Public Opinion.* New York: Alfred A. Knopf.

Tsingou, Eleni (2007): The Role of Policy Communities in Global Financial Governance: A Critical Examination of the Group of Thirty. In *Towards a Cognitive Mode in Global Finance. Perspectives on the Governance in the Knowledge-Based Economy* eds. Torsten Strulik and Helmut Willke. Frankfurt, New York: Campus. 213-237.

Tufano, Peter (2004): "Financial Innovation. Text Prepared for the Handbook of the Economics of Finance (North Holland), Edited by George Constantinides, Milt Harris and René Stulz." Harvard Business School. http://www.people.hbs.edu/ptufano/fininnov_tufano_june2002.pdf (October 22, 2013).

Turner, Adair (2010): "Too Much 'Too Big to Fail'?" Project Syndicate. http://www.project-syndicate.org/commentary/too-much--too-big-to-fail-- (September 23, 2013).

Turner, Philip (2010): Macroprudential Policies and the Cycle. In *The Financial Stability Board: An Effective Fourth Pillar of Global Economic Governance?*, eds. Stephany Griffith-Jones, Eric Helleiner and Ngaire Woods. Waterloo, Ontario: CIGI. 42-48.

U.S. Department of the Treasury (2008): "Treasury Announces Temporary Guarantee Program for Money Market Funds." September 29, 2008. http://www.treasury.gov/press-center/press-releases/Pages/hp1161.aspx (July 12, 2013).

——— (2012): "Nonbank Financial Company Designations Final Rule and Interpretive Guidance Fact Sheet." U.S. Department of the Treasury. http://www.treasury.gov/press-center/press-releases/Documents/Nonbank Financial Company Designations Final Rule and Interpretive Guidance Fact Sheet.pdf (July 09, 2013).

Ueda, Kenichi, and Beatrice di Mauro (2012): Quantifying Structural Subsidy Values for Systemically Important Financial Institutions. *IMF Working Paper* 12/128. May 2012.

Underhill, Geoffrey R. D., and Xiaoke Zhang (2008): Setting the Rules: Private Power, Political Underpinnings, and Legitimacy in Global Monetary and Financial Governance. *International Affairs* 84 (3, 2008): 535-554.

United States Senate, Permanent Subcommittee on Investigations, Committee on Homeland Security and Governmental Affairs (2013): "JPMorgan Chase Whale Trades: A Case Hirstory of Derivatives Risks and Abuses. Majority and Minority Staff Report." U.S. Senate. http://www.google.de/url?sa=t&rct=j&q=&esrc=s&source=web&cd=1&ved=0CCUQFjAA&url=http%3A%2F%2Fwww.hsgac.senate.gov%2Fdownload%2Freport-jpmorgan-chase-whale-trades-a-case-history-of-derivatives-risks-and-abuses-march-15-2013&ei=pLWaU9XSJ-Wy7AaJtIGIAQ&usg=AFQjCNH7jwCaDEiz9w9e0th6P-tshKLe8w&bvm=bv.68911936,d.ZGU (June 12, 2014).

Valukas, Anton R. (2010): "Lehman Brothers Holdings Inc. Chapter 11 Proceedings Examiner Report." Jenner & Block LLP. http://jenner.com/lehman/VOLUME 1.pdf (May 15, 2014).

Vanoli, Alejandro (2010): FSB: Current Structure and Proposals for a More Balanced Representation. In *The Financial Stability Board: An Effective Fourth Pillar of Global Economic Governance?*, eds. Stephany Griffith-Jones, Eric Helleiner and Ngaire Woods. Waterloo, Ontario: CIGI. 23-27.

Veblen, Thorstein (1898): Why Is Economics Not an Evolutionary Science? *Quarterly Journal of Economics* 12 (4): 373-397.

Vermeule, Adrian (2009): Our Schmittian Administrative Law. *Harvard Law Review* 122: 1095-1149.

Vitali, Stefania, James Glattfelder, and Stefano Battiston (2011): The Network of Global Corporate Control. *PLoS ONE 6(10): e25995.*

Volcker, Paul (2009): "Interview with Alan Murray." The Wall Street Journal: Future of Finance Initiative. http://online.wsj.com/article/SB10001424052748704825504574586330960597134.html (June 18, 2013).
——— (2010): "How to Reform Our Financial System." The New York Times online. http://www.ny times.com/2010/01/31/opinion/31volcker.html?pagewanted=all&_r=0 (November 25, 2013).

Wagner, Wendy E. (2010): Administrative Law, Filter Failure, and Information Capture. *Duke Law Journal* 59: 1321-1432.
Wallach, Philip (2010): "Policy Responses to the Financial Crisis of 2008 and the Rule of Law." Presented at the Annual Meeting of the American Political Science Association, Washington D.C.
Wallison, Peter J. (2013): *Bad History, Worse Policy: How a False Narrative About the Financial Crisis Led to the Dodd-Frank Act.* Washington D.C.: American Enterprise Institute for Public Policy Research.
Walter, Andrew (2010): Can the FSB Achieve Effective Surveillance of Systemically Important Countries? In *The Financial Stability Board: An Effective Fourth Pillar of Global Economic Governance? Special Report. The Centre for International Governance Innovation*, eds. Stephany Griffith-Jones, Eric Helleiner and Ngaire Woods. Waterloo, Ontario: CIGI. 32-35.
Walter, Elisse (2013): "A Closer Look with Arthur Levitt." Bloomberg TV. http://media.bloomberg.com/bb/avfile/News/Surveillance/vAQGKAngLrmU.mp3 (June 26, 2013).
Walton, John (1992): Making the Theoretical Case. In *What Is a Case? Exploring the Foundations of Social Enquiry*, eds. Charles C. Ragin and Howard S. Becker. Cambridge: Cambridge University Press. 121-137.
Warren, Elizabeth (2007): Unsafe at Any Rate. *Democracy Journal* 5 (Summer 2007).
——— (2010): "Interview with the Financial Crisis Inquiry Commission." FCIC. http://fcic-static.law.stanford.edu/cdn_media/fcic-audio/2010-09-16 FCIC staff audiotape of interview with Elizabeth Warren, Congressional Oversight Panel.mp3 (February 22, 2014).
——— (2013a): "Questioning of Ben Bernanke on TBTF before the Senate Banking Committee." February 26, 2013. http://www.youtube.com/watch?v=y7X3uac0lzw (June 26, 2013).
——— (2013b): "Senators Warren, Mccain, Cantwell, and King Introduce 21st Century Glass-Steagall Act." July 11, 2013 . http://www.warren.senate.gov/?p=press_release&id=178 (March 13, 2014).
Watzlawick, Paul, Janet Beavin, and Don Jackson (1969): *Menschliche Kommunikation.* Bern: Huber.

Weber, Max (1922): *Wirtschaft und Gesellschaft.* Tübingen: Verlag von J. C. B. Mohr (Paul Siebeck).

——— (1968): *Economy and Society. An Outline of Interpretive Sociology. Edited by Guenther Roth and Claus Wittich. Three Volumes.* New York: Bedminster Press.

Weber, Robert F. (2012): Structural Regulation as Antidote to Complexity Capture. *American Business Law Journal* Volume 49 (Issue 3): 643-738.

Weber, Rolf H., and Dominic N. Staiger (2014): Financial Stability Board: Mandate and Implementation of Its Systemic Risks Standards. *International Journal of Financial Studies* 2 (1): 82-102.

Weick, Karl, and Kathleen Sutcliffe (2001): *Managing the Unexpected: Assuring High Performance in an Age of Complexity.* San Francisco: Jossey-Bass.

Weidmann, Jens (2013): "Striving for a Stable Framework for Monetary Union – an Old Debate Revisited. Speech to the Ambassadors Conference in Berlin on 26 August 2013." Deutsche Bundesbank. http://www.bundesbank.de/Redaktion/EN/Reden/2013/2013_08_26_weidmann.html (August 30, 2013).

Weil, Jonathan (2012): "Let Justice Be Done, Though a Huge Bank Falls." Bloomberg.com. http://www.bloomberg.com/news/2012-12-20/let-justice-be-done-though-a-huge-bank-falls.html (November 06, 2013).

Weill, Sandy (2010): "Interview with the Financial Crisis Inquiry Commission." FCIC. http://fcic-static.law.stanford.edu/cdn_media/fcic-audio/2010-10-04 FCIC staff audiotape of interview with Sandy Weill, Citigroup.mp3 (April 03, 2014).

Weingast, Barry R. (1984): The Congressional-Bureaucratic System: A Principal Agent Perspective (with Applications to the SEC). *Public Choice* 44: 147-191.

Wigand, James R. (2013): »Statement on Improving Cross Border Resolution to Better Protect Taxpayers and the Economy before the Subcommittee on National Security and International Trade and Finance, U.S. Senate.«. http://www.fdic.gov/news/news/speeches/spmay1513_2.html (August 02, 2013).

Wigand, James R., and Richard J. Osterman (2013): "Who Is Too Big to Fail? Examining the Application of Title I of the Dodd-Frank Act before the Subcommittee on Oversight and Investigations; Committee on Financial Services; U.S. House of Representatives on April 16, 2013." FDIC. http://www.fdic.gov/news/news/speeches/spapr1613.html?source=govdelivery (July 26, 2013).

Willke, Helmut (2002): *Dystopia. Studien Zur Krisis des Wissens in der Modernen Gesellschaft.* Frankfurt: Suhrkamp.

——— (2006): *Global Governance.* Bielefeld: transcript.

——— (2007): *Smart Governance. Governing the Global Knowledge Society.* Frankfurt: Campus.

Willke, Helmut, Eva Becker, and Carla Rostásy (2013): *Systemic Risk. The Myth of Rational Finance and the Crisis of Democracy.* Frankfurt and New York: Campus.

Willke, Helmut, and Gerhard Willke (2012): *Political Governance of Capitalism. A Reassessment Beyond the Global Crisis.* Cheltenham a.o.: Edward Elgar.

Wilmarth, Arthur E. (2002): The Transformation of the U.S. Financial Services Industry, 1975-2000: Competition, Consolidation, and Increased Risks. *University of Illinois Law Review* 2002 (2): 215-476.

——— (2013): Turning a Blind Eye. Why Washington Keeps Giving in to Wall Street. *University of Cincinnati Law Review* 81 (2013): 1283-1446.

Wilson, James (2011): "ESRB to Use 'Moral Authority' in Curbing Risk." Financial Times online. http://www.ft.com/intl/cms/s/0/ec986daa-24b6-11e0-a919-00144feab49a.html-axzz2dMnPgiTj (August 29, 2013).

Wilson, James Q. (1980): The Politics of Regulation. In *The Political Economy. Readings in the Politics and Economics of American Public Policy*, eds. Thomas Ferguson and Joel Rogers. 82-103.

——— (1989): *Bureaucracy: What Government Agencies Do and Why They Do It.* New York: Basic Book.

Wilson, Woodrow (1913): "The New Freedrom. A Call for the Emancipation of the Generous Energies of a People." Gutenberg Project. http://www.guten berg.org/files/14811/14811-h/14811-h.htm (November 27, 2013).

Woolley, John T., and J. Nicholas Ziegler (2012): The Two-Tiered Politics of Financial Reform in the United States. In *Crisis and Control. Institutional Change in Financial Market Regulation*, ed. Renate Mayntz. Frankfurt: Campus. 29-65.

Wymeersch, Eddy (2012): The European Financial Supervisory Authorities or ESAs. In *Financial Regulation and Supervision. A Post-Crisis Analysis*, eds. Eddy Wymeersch, Klaus J. Hopt and Guido Ferrarini. Oxford: Oxford University Press. 232-320.

Xiong, Wei (2013): Bubbles, Crises, and Heterogeneous Beliefs. In *Handbook on Systemic Risk* eds. Jean-Pierre Fouque and Joseph A. Langsam. Cambridge: Cambridge University Press. 663-713.

Yackee, Jason Webb, and Susan Webb Yackee (2006): A Bias Towards Business? Assessing Interest Group Influence on the U.S. Bureaucracy. *The Journal of Politics* 68 (1, February 2006): 128-139.

Yellen, Janet L. (2010): "Interview with the Financial Crisis Inquiry Commission." FCIC. http://fcic-static.law.stanford.edu/cdn_media/fcic-audio/2010-11-

15 FCIC staff audiotape of interview with Janet Yellen, Federal Reserve Board.mp3 (March 06, 2014).
——— (2013a): "Interconnectedness and Systemic Risk: Lessons from the Financial Crisis and Policy Implications." Presented at the American Economic Association/American Finance Association Joint Luncheon, San Diego.
——— (2013b): "Testimony and Questioning of Janet L. Yellen, Confirmation Hearing as Chairman of the Federal Reserve System, November 14 2013." U.S. Senate, Committee on Banking, Housing & Urban Affairs. http://live.wsj.com/video/yellen-fed-not-prisoner-of-the-markets/6904CE7D-2945-471C-AAFF-DA40445952A8.html-!6904CE7D-2945-471C-AAFF-DA40445952A8 (May 16, 2014).

Zeleny, Milan (1987): Management Support Systems: Towards Integrated Knowledge Management. *Human Systems Management* 7 (1987): 59-70.

Zibel, Alan (2013): "Consumer Bureau's Director Confirmed after Long Delay." The Wall Street Journal online. http://online.wsj.com/article/SB10001424127887323664204578609801504103648.html (July 25, 2013).

Zingales, Luigi (2013): Preventing Economists' Capture. In *Preventing Regulatory Capture. Special Interest Influence and How to Limit It*, eds. Daniel Carpenter and David A. Moss. Cambridge: Cambridge University Press. 124-151.

Zubrow, Barry (2010): "Interview with the Financial Crisis Inquiry Commission." FCIC. http://fcic-static.law.stanford.edu/cdn_media/fcic-audio/2010-08-02 FCIC staff audiotape of interview with Barry Zubrow, JPMorgan Chase (Interview 1).mp3 (April 01, 2014).

Zuckerman, Gregory, and Scott Patterson (2012): "J.P. Morgan Struggles to Unwind Huge Bets." The Wall Street Journal online. http://online.wsj.com/article/SB10001424052702303879604577412613778263918.html (September 27, 2013).

Zywicki, Todd (2013): The Consumer Financial Protection Bureau: Savior or Menace? *George Washington Law Review* 81 (3, April 2013): 856-928.

MIX
Papier aus verantwortungsvollen Quellen
Paper from responsible sources
FSC® C105338

If you have any concerns about our products,
you can contact us on
ProductSafety@springernature.com

In case Publisher is established outside the EU,
the EU authorized representative is:
Springer Nature Customer Service Center GmbH
Europaplatz 3, 69115 Heidelberg, Germany

Printed by Libri Plureos GmbH
in Hamburg, Germany